Travel Discount Coupon

This coupon entitles you to special discounts when you book your trip through the

TRAVEL NETWORK ®
RESERVATION SERVICE

Hotels ♦ Airlines ♦ Car Rentals ♦ Cruises
All Your Travel Needs

Here's what you get: *

A discount of $50 on a booking of $1,000** or more for two or more people!

A discount of $25 on a booking of $500** or more for one person!

Free membership for three years, and 1,000 free miles on enrollment in the unique Miles-to-Go™ frequent-traveler program. Earn one mile for every dollar spent through the program. Earn free hotel stays starting at 5,000 miles. Earn free roundtrip airline tickets starting at 25,000 miles.

Personal help in planning your own, customized trip.

Fast, confirmed reservations at any property recommended in this guide, subject to availability.***

Special discounts on bookings in the U.S. and around the world.

Low-cost visa and passport service.

Reduced-rate cruise packages.

Call us toll-free in the U.S. at 1-888-940-5000, or fax us at 201-567-1832. In Canada, call us toll-free at 1-800-883-9959, or fax us at 416-922-6053.

* To qualify for these travel discounts, at least a portion of your trip must include destinations covered in this guide. No more than one coupon discount may be used in any 12-month period, for destinations covered in this guide. Cannot be combined with any other discount or program.
**These are U.S. dollars spent on commissionable bookings.
***A $10 fee, plus fax and/or phone charges, will be added to the cost of bookings at each hotel not linked to the reservation service. Customers must approve these fees in advance.

Valid until December 31, 1997. Terms and conditions of the Miles-to-Go™ program are available on request by calling 201-567-8500, ext 55.

PUE123

W9-CUV-113

Frommer's

3rd Edition

Puerto Rico

by Darwin Porter
& Danforth Prince

Macmillan • USA

ABOUT THE AUTHORS

Ever since the age of 17 when **Darwin Porter** sold his first article on Puerto Rico to a travel magazine, he has been visiting and writing about the island. A bureau chief of *The Miami Herald* at the age of 21, Porter has traveled frequently and extensively throughout Puerto Rico and the rest of the Caribbean. His coauthor is **Danforth Prince,** formerly of the Paris bureau of *The New York Times.* Together they share their secrets and discoveries of travel to Puerto Rico with you.

MACMILLAN TRAVEL

A Simon & Schuster Macmillan Company
1633 Broadway
New York, NY 10019

Find us online at **http://www.mgr.com/travel**
or on America Online at **Keyword: Frommer's.**

ISBN 0-02-860913-1
ISSN 1062-4775

Editor: Bill Goodwin
Production Editor: Lynn Northrup
Design by Michele Laseau
Digital Cartography by Raffaele DeGennaro
Page Creation by Hilary Smith, Troy Barnes, Lissa Auciello, Linda Quigley, Sherri Fugit, Jerry Cole, and Heather Pope
Maps Copyright © by Simon & Schuster, Inc.

SPECIAL SALES

Bulk purchases (10+ copies) of Frommer's travel guides are available to corporations at special discounts. The Special Sales Department can produce custom editions to be used as premiums and/or for sales promotion to suit individual needs. Existing editions can be produced with custom cover imprints such as corporate logos. For more information write to: Special Sales, Simon & Schuster, 1633 Broadway, New York, NY 10019.

Manufactured in the United States of America

Contents

List of Maps

AN INVITATION TO THE READER

In researching this book, we discovered many wonderful places—resorts, inns, restaurants, shops, and more. We're sure you'll find others. Please tell us about them, so we can share the information with your fellow travelers in upcoming editions. If you were disappointed with a recommendation, we'd love to know that, too. Please write to:

Darwin Porter & Danforth Prince
Frommer's Puerto Rico, 3rd Edition
Macmillan Travel
1633 Broadway
New York, NY 10019

AN ADDITIONAL NOTE

Please be advised that travel information is subject to change at any time—and this is especially true of prices. We therefore suggest that you write or call ahead for confirmation when making your travel plans. The authors, editors, and publisher cannot be held responsible for the experiences of readers while traveling. Your safety is important to us, however, so we encourage you to stay alert and be aware of your surroundings. Keep a close eye on cameras, purses, and wallets, all favorite targets of thieves and pickpockets.

WHAT THE SYMBOLS MEAN

✪ Frommer's Favorites

Hotels, restaurants, attractions, and entertainment you should not miss.

⑨ Super-Special Values

Hotels and restaurants that offer great value for your money.

The following abbreviations are used for credit cards:

AE	American Express	EU	Eurocard
CB	Carte Blanche	JCB	Japan Credit Bank
DC	Diners Club	MC	MasterCard
DISC	Discover	V	Visa
ER	enRoute		

The following abbreviations are used in hotel listings:

MAP (Modified American Plan) usually means room, breakfast, and dinner, unless the room rate has been quoted separately, and then it means only breakfast and dinner.

AP (American Plan) includes your room plus three meals.

CP (Continental Plan) includes room and a light breakfast.

EP (European Plan) means room only.

The Best of Puerto Rico

Your aim in flying to Puerto Rico is to relax or have an activity-filled good time—not to waste precious vacation hours searching for the best deals and the best experiences. Take us along and we'll do the work for you. During our years of traveling through the islands that form the Commonwealth of Puerto Rico, we've tested the beaches, reviewed countless restaurants, inspected hotels, sampled the best scuba and adventures, and taken the best hikes. We've even learned where to get away from it all when you want to escape the crowds. Here's what we consider to be the best Puerto Rico has to offer.

1 The Best Beaches

Puerto Rico and its offshore islands are known for their white, sandy beaches, which is what put them on world tourist maps in the first place. This is not true of many other Caribbean islands with only jagged coral outcroppings or black volcanic-sand beaches that get very hot in the noonday sun.

- **Luquillo Beach:** About 30 miles east of San Juan, Luquillo Beach sits in a crescent-shaped bay edged by a vast coconut grove, which makes it not only the best in Puerto Rico, but one of the finest beaches in the entire Caribbean. Coral reefs protecting the crystal-clear lagoon subdue the often-fierce Atlantic waters that can batter this coast. Much photographed because of its white sands, it also has tent sites and other facilities including picnic areas with changing rooms, lockers, and showers. Regrettably, Luquillo Beach isn't as well maintained as it used to be, although it remains the favorite of beach buffs from San Juan. In winter, it's also inhabited by snowbirds (condo owners from up north who live nearby). See chapter 7.

- **Condado Beach:** San Juan's Condado Beach may not be the best, but it is the Caribbean's most famous—which helps explains why it often is overcrowded in winter. Once the stamping ground of the rich, including the Vanderbilts and the Rockefellers, it has long bands of white sand bordering some of the Caribbean's finest resort hotels. When the Condado comes to an end as it stretches toward the airport, the beaches of Isla Verde come into the picture. See chapter 7.

- **Playa Dorado:** West of San Juan, Playa Dorado actually is a term for six white-sand beaches along the northern coast, reached by a series of winding roads. This is the setting for the Hyatt hotel resorts. Although not as famous as Luquillo, the beaches here are better maintained and are a real family favorite. See chapter 9.

- **Palmas del Mar** (Humacao; ☎ 787/852-000 or 800/468-3331 in the U.S.): The huge Palmas del Mar resort near Humacao on the eastern coast of Puerto Rico has been called "the new American Riviera." The architectural dream of this 2,750-acre playground resort built on a former coconut plantation hasn't been realized yet, but the site sports 3 miles of white-sand beaches. Unlike some of the rough-water beaches near Rincón in the west, the sea here is tranquil and calm year-round. There's also a water-sports center and marina. See chapter 9.

- **Playa de Ponce:** The beaches on the southeast coast west of Ponce, the "second city" of Puerto Rico, are far less crowded than those of the Condado, Luquillo, and Dorado. This long strip of white sand opens onto the tranquil waters of the Caribbean. Several very good seafood restaurants are found in the vicinity. See chapter 10.

- **Boquerón Beach:** South of Mayagüez, in the town of the same name, Boquerón Beach has been called "the Cape Cod of Puerto Rico." The town itself stands at the heart of a 3-mile bay, with palm-fringed white sand curving away on both sides. Fishermen and women, sailors, scuba divers, and windsurfers as well as beach devotees are attracted to this beach, where fresh oysters shucked on the spot and doused with Tabasco are sold from shacks. Here the ice cream is made with sweet corn and dusted with paprika (it sounds awful, but tastes good). See chapter 10.

2 The Best Scuba Diving

With the continental shelf surrounding it on three sides, Puerto Rico has an abundance of coral reefs, caves, sea walls, and trenches to be explored by divers of all levels of experience. See "The Active Vacation Planner" in chapter 3 for detailed information.

- **Metropolitan San Juan:** More convenient if not as spectacular as those mentioned below is an easy beach dive off the Condado district in San Juan. Lava reefs sculptured with caverns, tunnels, and overhangs host hiding areas for schools of snapper, grunts, and copper sweepers. The inner and outer reefs here are active breeding spots where divers of all levels can mingle with an impressive array of small tropical fish—French angels, jacks, bluehead wrasse, butterfly fish, and sergeant majors, among them—along with seahorses, arrow crabs, coral shrimp, octopuses, batfish, and flying gunards. Visibility is about 10 to 20 feet. The Condado reef is also ideal for resort courses, certification courses, and night dives. See chapters 3 and 7.

- **Fajardo:** This coastal town in eastern Puerto Rico offers divers the opportunity to explore ringing reefs, small caverns, miniwalls, and channels below a string of palm-tufted islets. The reefs are decked in an array of corals ranging from delicate gorgonians to immense coralheads. Visibility usually exceeds 50 feet. You can hand-feed some of the full assortment of reef fish which inhabit the corals. Sand channels and a unique double barrier reef system surround Palomino Island, where bandtailed puffers and parrot fish harems are frequently sighted. Cayo Diablo farther to the east provides a treasure box of corals and marine animals, from green moray eels and barracudas to octopuses and occasional manatees. See chapters 3 and 9.

- **Humacao Region:** South of Fajardo are some 24 dive sites in a 5-mile radius of the shore. Overhangs, caves, and tunnels perch in 60 feet of water along mile-long

Basslet Reef, where dolphins visit in spring. At "The Cracks," a jigsaw of caves, alleyways, and boulders host an abundance of goby-cleaning stations and shelter a number of lobsters. With visibility often exceeding 100 feet, the Reserve offers a clear look at corals. At the Drift, divers float along with nurse sharks and angelfish into a valley of swim-throughs and ledges. For the experienced diver, Red Hog is the newest site in the area, with a panoramic wall that drops from 80 to 1,160 feet. See chapters 3 and 9.

- **Southern Puerto Rico:** The continental shelf drops off precipitously several miles off the southern coast, producing a dramatic wall 20 miles long and teeming with marine life. Compared favorably to the Cayman Islands' wall, the Puerto Rican wall has become the Caribbean's newest world-class dive destination. Paralleling the coast from the seaside village of La Parguera to the city of Ponce, the wall descends in slopes and sheer drops from 60 to 120 feet before disappearing into 1,500 feet of sea. Scored with valleys and deep trenches, it is cloaked in immense gardens of staghorn and elkhorn coral, deep-water gorgonians, and other exquisite coral formations. Visibility can exceed 100 feet. There are more than 50 dive sites around Parguera alone. See chapters 3 and 10.

- **Mona Island:** Many people consider Mona Island, 40 miles west of the city of Mayagüez in western Puerto Rico, to be the Caribbean version of the Galápagos Islands. Renowned for its pirate tales, cave-pocked cliffs, 3-foot-long iguanas, and other works of nature, its waters are among the cleanest in Puerto Rico, with horizontal visibility at times exceeding 200 feet. More than 270 species of fish have been found in Mona waters, including more than 60 reef-dwelling species. Larger marine animals such as sea turtles, whales, dolphins, and marlins visit the region during migrations. Various types of coral reefs, underwater caverns, drop-offs, and deep vertical walls ring the island. The most accessible reef dives are along the southern and western shores. Getting there is a pain, however. You must brave a 5-hour boat ride across the often rough Mona Passage. See chapters 3 and 10.

3 The Best Golf & Tennis

- **Rio Mar Golf Course** (Palmer; ☎ 787/888-8825): A 45-minute drive from San Juan on the northeast coast, the 6,145-yard Rio Mar Golf Course is shorter than those at both Palmas del Mar and Dorado East. One avid golfer recommended it to "Those whose games and egos have been bruised by the other two courses." Wind is such a factor here that it can seriously influence the outcome of your game. Its greens fees are also a lot less expensive than its two major competitors. See chapter 7.

- **Hyatt Resorts Caribbean** (Dorado; ☎ 787/796-1234 or 800/233-1234 in the U.S.): With 72 holes, Dorado has the highest concentration of golf on the island. Two courses—east and west—belong to the Hyatt Regency Cerromar and the Hyatt Dorado Beach resorts. Dorado East is our favorite. Designed by Robert Trent Jones Sr., it has been the site of the Senior PGA Tournament of Champions all during the 90s.

  And true tennis buffs head here, too. The Dorado courts are the best on the island, and both hotels sponsor tennis weeks and offer special tennis packages. The Hyatt Regency Cerromar has 14 Laykold courts alone, two of them lit for night play. The Hyatt Regency Dorado weighs in with five Laykold courts, two of them lighted. See chapter 9.

- **The Club de Golf at Palmas del Mar** (Humacao; ☎ 787/852-6000, ext. 54): Lying on the southeast coast on the grounds of a former coconut plantation, the Palmas del Mar resort complex sports the second-leading course in Puerto Rico—a par-72, 6,803-yard layout designed by Gary Player. Crack golfers consider holes 11 through 15 the toughest five successive holes in the Caribbean. See chapter 9.

- **El Conquistador Resort & Country Club** (Las Croabas; ☎ 787/863-1000 or 800/468-5228 in the U.S.): This sprawling resort east of San Juan is one of the island's finest tennis retreats, with seven Har-Tru courts and a pro on hand to offer guidance and advice. If you don't have a partner, the hotel will find one for you. Only guests of the hotel are allowed to play here. See chapter 9.
- **Palmas del Mar** (Humacao; ☎ 787/852-0000, ext. 51): On the eastern coastline, this resort complex on the grounds of a former coconut plantation has 20 courts, of which five are Har-Tru and 15 are Tenneflex (a harder surface). Seven of the courts are lighted. The resort offers tennis packages, and an on-site pro conducts private lessons. See chapter 9.

4 The Best Hikes

Bring your boots, for Puerto Rico's mountainous interior offers ample opportunity for hiking and climbing, with many trails presenting spectacular panoramas at the least expected moments. See "The Active Vacation Planner" in chapter 3 for detailed information.

- **El Yunque** (☎ 787/887-2875 for information): Containing the only rain forest on U.S. soil, this Caribbean National Forest east of San Juan offers a number of walking and hiking trails. The rugged El Toro trail passes through four different forest systems enroute to the 3,523-foot Pico El Toro, the highest peak in the forest. El Yunque trail leads to three of the recreation area's most panoramic lookouts, and the Big Tree Trail is an easy walk to La Mina Falls. Just off the main road is La Coca Falls, a sheet of water cascading down mossy cliffs. Nearby, the Sierra Palm Interpretive Service Center offers maps and information and arranges for guided tours of the forest. See chapters 2 and 8.
- **Guánica State Forest** (☎ 787/724-3724 for information): At the opposite extreme of El Yunque's lush and wet rain forest, Guánica State Forest's climate is dry and arid, its Arizonalike landscape riddled with cacti. The area, cut off from the Cordillera Central mountain range, gets little rainfall. Yet it's home to some 50% of all the island's terrestrial bird species, including the rare Puerto Rican nightjar, once thought to be extinct. The forest has 36 miles of trails through four different forest types. We prefer the mile-long Cueva Trail, where hikers look for the endangered bufo lemur toad, another species thought to be extinct but still jumping in this area. See chapter 10.
- **Mona Island:** Off the western coast of Puerto Rico, this fascinating island noted for its scuba diving sites also provides hiking opportunities found nowhere else in the Caribbean. Called the Galápagos of Puerto Rico because of its unique wildlife, Mona is home to giant iguanas and three species of endangered sea turtles. Some 20 endangered animals also have been spotted here. Ecotourists like to hike among Mona's mangrove forests, coral reefs, cliffs, and complex honeycomb of caves, ever on the alert for the diversity of both plant and animal life, including 417 plant and tree species, some of which are unique and 78 of which are rare or endangered. More than 100 bird species have been documented, two of which are unique. Hikers can camp out at Mona for $1 a night. Contact the Puerto Rico Department of Natural Resources (☎ 787/724-3724) for more information. See chapter 10.

5   The Best Natural Wonders

- **El Yunque** (☎ 787/887-2875 for information): Lying 45 minutes by road east of San Juan in the Luquillo Mountains, El Yunque is the greatest natural attraction in Puerto Rico and is protected by the U.S. Forest Service. Some 100 billion gallons of rain fall annually on this home to four forest types containing 240 species of tropical trees. Families can walk one of the dozens of trails that wind past waterfalls, dwarf vegetation, and miniature flowers, while the island's colorful parrots fly overhead. You can hear the sound of Puerto Rico's mascot, the *coquí*, a small frog. See chapters 2 and 8.
- **Río Camuy Cave Park** (☎ 787/898-2770): Some 2½ hours west of San Juan, visitors board a tram to descend into this forest-filled sinkhole at the mouth of the Clara Cave. They walk the footpaths of a 170-foot-high cave to a deeper sinkhole. Once inside, a 45-minute tour helps everyone including kids learn to differentiate stalactites from stalagmites. At the Pueblos sinkhole a platform overlooks the Camuy River, passing through a network of cave tunnels. See chapter 8.
- **Las Cabezas de San Juan Nature Reserve** (☎ 787/722-5834): This 316-acre nature reserve lying only 45 minutes from San Juan encompasses seven different ecological systems, including forest land, mangroves, lagoons, beaches, cliffs, and offshore coral reefs. Visitors may tour the reserve's nature center and 19th-century working lighthouse, El Faro, offering a view of distant Caribbean islands, but call before going, as reservations are required. See chapter 8.

6   The Best Family Resorts

For the family that chooses to play together, Puerto Rico has a bounty of attractions and natural wonders, and an array of resorts welcoming them.

- **Condado Plaza Hotel & Casino** (San Juan; ☎ 787/721-1000 or 800/468-8588 in the U.S.): This resort offers Camp Taíno, a regular program of activities and special events for children ages 4–12. The cost of $25 per child includes lunch. The main pool has a kids' water slide starting in a Spanish-castle turret, plus a toddler pool. For teenagers, the hotel has a video game room, tennis courts, and various organized activities. For the whole family, the resort offers two pools and opens onto a public beach. It also has the best collection of restaurants of any hotel on the Condado. See chapter 5.
- **El San Juan Hotel and Casino** (San Juan; ☎ 787/793-1000 or 800/468-2818 in the U.S.): The grandest hotel in Puerto Rico lies on Isla Verde, the less famous beach strip connecting with El Condado in San Juan. Its Kids Klub features trained counselors and group activities for the 5-to-13 age set. A daily fee of $28 buys lunch and an array of activities. The hotel opens onto a good beachfront and has some of the best restaurants in San Juan. See chapter 5.
- **Hyatt Resorts Caribbean** (Dorado; ☎ 787/796-1234 or 800/233-1234 in the U.S.): Sitting 18 miles west of San Juan, the Hyatt Regency Cerromar Beach Resort & Casino and the Hyatt Dorado Beach Resort & Casino share a Camp Hyatt program available for guests ages 3–12. Certified counselors direct programs of educational, environmental, and cultural activities. In the evening, movies, talent shows, and video games occupy the agenda. All this costs $40 a day per kid. Parents find one of the largest beaches and resort complexes in the Caribbean, including the world's longest freshwater river pool. See chapter 9.
- **El Conquistador Resort & Country Club** (Las Croabas; ☎ 787/863-1000 or 800/468-5228 in the U.S.): Located 31 miles east of San Juan, this resort offers

Camp Coquí on Palomino Island for children 3–12 years of age. The hotel's water taxi takes kids there for a half or full day of water sports, nature hikes, and island crafts, costing $19 for a half day or $38 for a full day. A family package is available for $430 per night, based on two adults and two children occupancy. This resort has some of the best facilities and restaurants in eastern Puerto Rico. See chapter 9.

- **Palmas del Mar Resort** (Humacao; ☎ 787/852-000 or 800/468-3331 in the U.S.): The major rival in the east to El Conquistador, this sprawling resort has an Adventure Club for children ages 3–13. Supervised activities include arts, crafts, and sports, plus horseback riding for those old enough. The cost is $15 per half day or $25 daily, including lunch. Family packages are sold for as low as $63 per person per night, based on four-person occupancy of a room. The resort is one of the most extensive in the Caribbean, with beaches, restaurants, and lots of water sports. See chapter 9.

7   The Best Honeymoon Resorts

- **El San Juan Hotel and Casino** (San Juan; ☎ 787/793-1000 or 800/468-2818 in the U.S.): If you want Vegas-style shows, gambling, nightlife, great restaurants, and the most famous beach in Puerto Rico, the El San Juan is at your disposal. It has the most glamorous lobby in the Caribbean and is set on 12 acres at Isla Verde. Options include a suite in the main tower with a whirlpool or your own private casita with a sunken Roman bath. The best deal is a package, costing from $249 to $399 per night for six nights, with the seventh night free. A lot of freebies are thrown in, including champagne and strawberries, $100 worth of motorized sports, daily tennis, and free admission to the disco and fitness center. See chapter 5.
- **Hyatt Dorado Beach Resort** (Dorado; ☎ 787/796-1234 or 800/233-1234 in the U.S.): This resort offers a more tranquil atmosphere than the nearby Hyatt Regency Cerromar, yet guests here can partake of all the facilities and attractions of its neighbor. You can book one of the elegantly furnished upper-level rooms in the Oceanview Houses and enjoy romantic vistas of two crescent-shaped beaches. There's casino and disco action, plus a spa, health club, jogging trails, and 14 tennis courts. Packages in low season begin at $1,555 for two for the week, including one breakfast, one dinner, and transfers to and from the airport. In high season the tab rises to $3,700 a week per honeymooning couple, but breakfast and dinner are included. See chapter 9.
- **El Conquistador Resort & Country Club** (Las Croabas; ☎ 787/863-1000 or 800/468-5228 in the U.S.): If you'd like lots of good food and plenty of diversions on your honeymoon instead of a romantic tranquil retreat, El Conquistador is the best sprawling bigtime resort on the island. Atop a 300-foot bluff in eastern Puerto Rico, it has virtually everything when you want to play outside, including golf and tennis, but when you want seclusion you can post the PRIVADO sign and the world is yours. It offers a $495 per night honeymoon package (based on 3 nights and 4 days), with many specials such as champagne, a golf clinic, a half-day snorkeling trip, nonmotorized water sports, and even transfers to and from the airport. If you stay a full week, the cost of this package is reduced to $365 per honeymooning night. See chapter 9.
- **Palmas del Mar Resort** (Humacao; ☎ 787/852-000 or 800/468-3331 in the U.S.): This luxury resort complex sits on 2,750 acres of a former coconut planta-tion on Puerto Rico's sheltered southeast coast. It takes only about an hour's drive from San Juan for another world to unfold, with Mediterranean villas, cobblestone

plazas, condos, and Spanish-style fountains. The Palmas Inn suites are best for honeymooners, unless you want to rent a private villa. You get some of the best golf on the island here, along with 14 tennis courts, a spa and health club, and miles of hiking and jogging trails. Honeymoon packages for 7 nights and 8 days begin in the range of $1,142 to $1,588. Of course, you can live more luxuriously here, but included in this package are champagne, a fruit basket, and a free continental breakfast daily, plus one dinner and one lunch. See chapter 9.

- **Horned Dorset Primavera** (Rincón; ☎ 787/823-4030): The most romantic place for a honeymoon on the island unless you stay in a private villa somewhere, this small, tranquil estate lies on the Mona Passage in western Puerto Rico, a pocket of posh where privacy is almost guaranteed. Accommodations are luxurious in the Spanish neocolonial style. The property opens onto a long secluded beach of white sand. There are no phones, TVs, or radios in the rooms to interfere with the soft sounds of pillow talk. This is a retreat for adults only, with no facilities for children. Seven-night packages, including a bottle of champagne, range from $2,000 to $4,000, depending on the season. See chapter 10.
- **Ponce Hilton and Casino** (Ponce; ☎ 787/259-7676 or 800/HILTONS in the U.S.): A first-class act at Puerto Rico's "second city" on the south coast, this sprawling resort is set in an 80-acre garden. There's both a casino and disco, plus lots of amusements including a Jacuzzi, tennis courts, a fitness room, and a beauty salon. Eight suites are ideal for honeymoons. Its three restaurants also serve the best food on the south coast. The first night costs $199, including a bottle of champagne, truffles, chocolates, and fresh strawberries as a gift. Each additional night is only $150. See chapter 10.

8 The Best Big Resort Hotels

- **El San Juan Hotel and Casino** (San Juan; ☎ 787/793-1000 or 800/468-2818 in the U.S.): An opulent circular lobby sets the haute style at the Caribbean's most elegant resort. From its location along Isla Verde Beach, it houses some of the capital's finest restaurants and is the city's major entertainment venue. Guest rooms are tropically designed and maintained in state-of-the-art condition. See chapter 5.
- **Hyatt Dorado Beach Resort** (Dorado; ☎ 787/796-1234 or 800/233-1234 in the U.S.): Lying on the former stamping grounds of the Rockefellers, this resort of lowrise buildings blends into its tropical setting in lush surroundings—all constructed on the site of a grapefruit and coconut plantation. Spacious rooms open onto a long stretch of secluded beach, and grounds include an 18-hole, Robert Trent Jones–designed championship golf course. Tennis, windsurfing, pool swimming, and dozens of water sports are available, as well as the most elegant dining in Dorado. See chapter 9.
- **El Conquistador Resort & Country Club** (Las Croabas; ☎ 787/863-1000 or 800/468-5228 in the U.S.): The finest in Puerto Rico, this is a world-class destination—a sybaritic haven for golfers, honeymooners, families, and anyone else. Three intimate "villages" combine with one grand hotel, draped along 300-foot bluffs overlooking both the Atlantic and the Caribbean at Puerto Rico's northeastern tip. The 500 landscaped acres include tennis courts, an 18-hole Arthur Hills–designed championship golf course, and a marina filled with yachts and charter boats. See chapter 9.
- **Palmas del Mar Resort** (Humacao; ☎ 787/852-000 or 800/468-3331 in the U.S.): Although not as impressive as El Conquistador, this sprawling complex evokes a Mediterranean village, opening onto 3¹/₃ miles of beach on the east coast

of Puerto Rico. Palm trees grow everywhere. The complex boasts the largest tennis center in the Caribbean, plus an 18-hole Gary Player championship golf course, a horseback riding center for beach rides, water sports galore, and an outstanding scuba-diving program along with deep-sea fishing charters. There's even a casino, plus nine restaurants. See chapter 9.

9 The Best Moderately Priced Hotels

- **Galería San Juan** (San Juan; ☎ 787/722-1808): The most whimsically bohemian hotel in the Caribbean sits in the heart of the historic city. Once the home of an aristocratic Spanish family, it is today filled with verdant courtyards adorned with sculpture, silk screens, or original paintings. Staying in one of these comfortable rooms is like living in an art gallery. See chapter 5.
- **Empress Oceanfront Hotel** (San Juan; ☎ 787/791-3083 or 800/678-0757): Far removed from the deluxe megaresorts along the Condado and Isla Verde beaches, this comfortable establishment is run by a local Anglo-Latino family. Its quiet neighborhood is on 2¹/₂ acres of rocky headlands jutting out from the coastline. There's a swimming pool, good spareribs in the hotel restaurant, and a tropical decor. See chapter 5.
- **Hotel Joyuda Beach** (Cabo Rojo; ☎ 787/851-5650): South of Mayagüez in scenic Cabo Rojo, this idyllic little beachfront hotel is far removed from the tourist-trodden districts. It's on one of the island's finest beaches and offers well-furnished and air-conditioned bedrooms. It's a favorite with Puerto Rican honeymooners. See chapter 10.
- **Copamarina Beach Resort** (Caña Gorda; ☎ 787/821-0505 or 800/468-4553 in the U.S.): Near Ponce, this resort was once the private vacation retreat of those local cement barons, the de Castro family. Today it's been converted into one of the best beach hotels along Puerto Rico's southern shore. In fact, its beach is one of the island's best. Set in a palm grove, the resort is handsomely decorated and comfortably furnished, with a swimming pool and two tennis courts. See chapter 10.
- **La Casa del Francés** (Vieques Island; ☎ 787/741-3751): A retired French general built this house in 1905, but it now welcomes the few visitors who show up at this remote island outpost. Bedrooms are high-ceilinged and old fashioned. The hotel is not for everyone, but if you like a funky, laid-back retreat from the world, this is it. See chapter 11.

10 The Best Paradores (Country Inns)

Operated under the auspices and supervision of the Commonwealth Development Company, the *paradores puertorriqueñas* are a chain of privately owned country inns. Although they are mere shanties when compared to the paradores in Spain, each is located in a historic or particularly beautiful spot. All share affordability, hospitable staffs, and high standards of cleanliness. They make fine stops on the island driving tours described in chapter 8.

- **Parador Hacienda Gripiñas** (Jayuya; ☎ 787/828-1717): Situated in a former coffee plantation about 2¹/₂ hours west of San Juan in the Cordillera Central mountain range, this home-turned-inn combines the hacienda era of long ago with modern if modest conveniences. The inn's aromatic brew of coffee in the morning comes from beans harvested on 20 acres of bearing bushes around the parador. The restaurant serves international dishes and good local specialties. See chapter 8.

- **Parador El Guajataca** (Quebradillas; ☎ 787/895-3070): About 70 miles west of San Juan, this establishment enjoys a splendid natural setting facing the Atlantic Ocean. Oceanfront rooms are air-conditioned, with private balconies and baths. All the facilities are named after Taíno Indian words, such as Casabi for the restaurant, which features *criollo* cuisine. There are two swimming pools (one for children) and two tennis courts. It's the most family oriented of the Puerto Rican paradores. See chapter 8.
- **Parador Vistamar** (Quebradillas; ☎ 787/895-2065): Also on the northwest route, this mountaintop paradore is one of the largest in Puerto Rico. It offers such diversions as freshwater fishing in the only green-water river in Puerto Rico. Flocks of rare tropical birds are frequently seen here. The hotel prepares a typical Puerto Rican cuisine, served in a dining room opening onto views of the water. See chapter 8.
- **Parador Hacienda Juanita** (Maricao; ☎ 787/838-2550 or 800/443-0266 in the U.S.): The original building from 1836 was part of a coffee plantation, but the property has been converted into a government parador, 2 miles west of the village of Maricao, within driving distance of Mayagüez. Although the bedrooms are simple, the food is good. It's a family-run place, attracting other families, often islanders themselves. Don't expect a lot of amenities or service, but the welcome is genuine. See chapter 10.

11 The Best Restaurants

- **Chef Marisoll** (San Juan; ☎ 787/725-7454): Puerto Rico's best female chef, Marisoll Hernández, prepares Old Town's finest cuisine in this Spanish colonial building in the heart of the historic district. With a strong background in classic cooking, she has expanded her repertoire to include innovative and memorable dishes, including her curried chicken with fried sweet bananas, homemade mango chutney, and a saffron risotto. Or try her grilled swordfish with calamata olives. See chapter 6.
- **Ramiro's** (San Juan; ☎ 787/721-9049): Chef Jesús Ramiro has the most innovative cookery along the Condado beachfront strip, along with the city's best wine list. Ramiro has made his culinary reputation with such dishes as quail stuffed with lamb in a port sauce or lamb loin in a tamarind coriander sauce, both equally delectable. His dessert menu is two pages long, including the town's best soufflés. His death-by-chocolate mousse on a green grape leaf is equaled only by his caramelized fresh mango Napoleon. See chapter 6.
- **Ajili Mojili** (San Juan; ☎ 787/725-9195): Also on the Condado beachfront, Ajili Mojili provides the most refined interpretation of classic Puerto Rican cookery on the island. Locals find it evocative of the food they enjoyed at their mother's table. Examples include *mofongos*, green plantains stuffed with veal, chicken, shrimp, or pork. The chefs take that cliché dish, *arroz con pollo* (stewed chicken with saffron rice), and raise it to celestial levels. The restaurant takes its name from the lemon-garlic sweet chili salsa that's traditionally served here with fish or meat. See chapter 6.
- **Augusto's** (San Juan; ☎ 787/725-7700): Originally from Austria, much-awarded chef August Schreiner is a five-time winner of *El Nuevo Día's* Five Fork Award, honoring the island's great chefs. Try any of his lobster or game dishes such as venison. His chocolate soufflé Grand Marnier is the island's finest. His mother may not have taught him to make one of the city's best seafood paellas, but somebody did—or else he invented it himself. See chapter 6.

- **La Hacienda/La Cava de la Hacienda** (Ponce; ☎ 787/259-7676): Evoking Puerto Rico's colonial age, these elegant dining rooms in the Ponce Hilton offer the best cuisine on the south coast. The restaurant was designed as a network of rooms in a 19th-century coffee plantation. It offers a changing international menu that is always very good and often achieves perfection. A specialty is a delectable seafood pot pie with shrimps and scallops. See chapter 10.

12   The Best Offbeat Travel Experiences

- **An Excursion to Monkey Island** (off Palmas del Mar Resort, Humacao): Reached from the marina at Palmas del Mar, the 39-acre islet of Cayo Santiago lies off the eastern shore of Puerto Rico. A boat, *Shagrada,* takes snorkelers and the merely curious over to see an island colony of rhesus monkeys whose ancestors were brought here from India in 1938 for study. Many significant breakthroughs in human medicine have been attributed to observing the behavioral patterns of these rambunctious primates. Passengers aren't allowed to actually go on the island, but you can see the monkeys on the shore, swinging through the trees, playing the mating game, nursing their young, or just "going bananas." See chapter 9.
- **Diving off Mona Island** (Mayagüez): Surrounded by some of the most beautiful coral reefs in the Caribbean, Mona Island has the most pristine, extensive, and well-developed reefs in Puerto Rican waters. In fact, they have been nominated as a U.S. National Marine Sanctuary. The tropical marine ecosystem around Mona includes patch reefs, black coral, spore and groove systems, underwater caverns, deep-water sponges, fringing reefs, and algal reefs. The lush environment attracts octopuses, lobster, queen conch, rays, barracuda, snapper, jack, grunt, angelfish, trunkfish, filefish, butterfly fish, dolphin, parrot fish, tuna, flying fish, and more. The crystal waters afford exceptional horizontal vision from 150 to 200 feet as well as good views down to the shipwrecks that mark the site—including some Hispanic galleons. Five different species of whales visit the island's offshore waters. See chapter 10.
- **"Wet and Dry Tour" in Guánica** (near Ponce): Southern Puerto Rico is the site of the world's largest remaining tract of dry coastal forest, and this part of the island allows you to explore miles of mangrove channel systems. Tropix Wellness Tours (☎ 809/268-2173) takes you into a part of the island rarely explored by visitors. Two expeditions combine a dry forest hike with mangrove kayaking at sunset. After traversing waterways by kayaks, you're led to secluded island beaches. It's a 4-day, 3-night adventure, and is fully escorted. See chapters 3 and 10.
- **Nighttime at Mosquito (Phosphorescent) Bay** (Vieques Island): At any time except when there's a full moon, you're taken out in a boat to swim in glowing waters that are lit by dinoflagellates called pyrodiniums (whirling fire). These creatures light up the waters like fireflies, and swimming among them is one of the most unusual things to do in Puerto Rico—truly a magical, almost psychedelic experience. It's estimated that a gallon of bay water might contain about three quarters of a million of these little glowing creatures. See chapter 11.

With 272 miles of Atlantic and Caribbean coastline and a rich culture, lush and verdant Puerto Rico is a formidable tropical destination packed with great beaches, an abundance of outdoor activities, and historical attractions dating back to the Spanish conquistadores 500 years ago. Here you'll find some of the best golf and tennis in the Caribbean, accommodations ranging from posh beach resorts with gambling casinos and Las Vegas–style shows to simple government-sponsored country inns offering a more personal experience. You can sit on a beach here for a week, or spend it hiking into the only tropical rain forest on U.S. soil.

Roughly half the size of New Jersey, this American commonwealth sits strategically some 1,000 miles southeast of Florida at the hub of the Caribbean chain of islands. You'll probably fly in and out of San Juan at least once if you're doing much touring in the region. And with a 2-year, $2.8 million project having restored its waterfront, this oldest capital city under the U.S. flag is also the world's second-largest home port for cruise-ship passengers. Puerto Rico has experienced many political changes since the days of its first Spanish governor, Juan Ponce de León, the conquistador who sailed with Columbus and who tried in vain to find a fountain of youth in Florida. With nearly 500 years reflected in its restored Spanish colonial architecture, Old San Juan is the Caribbean's greatest historic center.

Puerto Rico is the most easterly and the smallest of the four major islands that form the Greater Antilles. The other three are Cuba, Jamaica, and Hispaniola (the latter is home to two nations, Haiti and the Dominican Republic). Surrounded by the Atlantic Ocean to the north and the Caribbean Sea to the south, Puerto Rico is flanked by a trio of smaller islands—Vieques and Culebra to the east and Mona to the west—which are its political and geologic satellites.

1 The Natural Environment: Beaches, Mountains, the Rain Forest & More

The island's terrain ranges from palm-lined beaches on four coastlines to rugged mountain ranges, gently rolling hills, and dry desertlike areas. There are 20 designated forest reserves in Puerto Rico, and six more may be added.

The island has 272 miles of sandy beaches, some long and straight, others broken into coves by headlands. Some stretches near San Juan and the major resorts are incredibly crowded, but it's still possible to find a quiet, remote beach. On the northern coast, the Atlantic waters are often more turbulent than along the more tranquil southern coast. The big resorts have claimed the most ideal beaches, but even so, they are still open to the public. Public bathing beaches in Puerto Rico are called *balnearios.* These are government-run, with lifeguards, parking, and dressing rooms. For more information about Puerto Rico's beaches, refer to the Department of Recreation and Sports (☎ 787-722-1551).

In the northeast of the island are 6 miles of relatively unspoiled beaches, with waters ranging from calm to raging. Visits to El Yunque, the rain forest, are often combined with a stopover at the most popular (and the best) beach in the northeast, **Luquillo Beach,** a balneario. There's a huge stand of majestic coconut palms that shade more than a mile of sand. Dressing facilities, parking, and lockers are found here. It is the major beach used by residents of San Juan and tends to be overcrowded on weekends, especially at places where the most facilities are located.

Some of the best beaches of Puerto Rico are in the east—but offshore—on the two small islands of **Culebra** and **Vieques.** In Culebra, the white-sand beaches, particularly Flamenco Beach, have clear waters and scenic coral reed, including a mile-long formation off Culebrita, where there is also a lighthouse.

The adjoining island, Vieques, contains numerous scalloped beaches along the north and northwest coasts, all of which lie on U.S. Navy land and are open to the public when there are no military maneuvers going on.

On the south coast, the best beaches are centered near the fishing village of **La Parguera,** which becomes busy and bustling on weekends, when locals pour in for fun in the sun. Numerous mangrove cays and islets here form ornate channels in places, attracting boaters. Swimmers and picnickers prefer **Rosada Beach** or **Mata de la Gata Cay,** the best beaches in the area. Snorkelers and scuba divers explore the reefs and the outer shelf walls that lie 7 miles offshore.

On the west coast the best beach is along the bay at **Boquerón,** part of the municipality of Cabo Rojo. The area opens onto a mile of white sand bordered by clear water. Long a balneario, it is frequented mainly by locals. The beach is popular for swimming and picnicking under coconut palms. Nearby is the Boquerón Lagoon, a refuge for ducks and other birds.

In the northwest, rough Atlantic waters deter bathers but attract surfers. Scuba divers and snorkelers also gravitate to a beach here known as **"The Shacks,"** lying near Isabela. They swim among its coral caverns and reefs, while surfers head for **Jobos Beach.**

Other than these beaches, the island's most noteworthy geological feature is the **Cordillera**—the towering mountains that rise high above its central region. Geologists have identified the island's summits as the high parts of a chain of mountains whose mass is mostly submerged beneath the sea. These mountains, probably the oldest of the many land masses of the West Indies, form a dramatic relief in Puerto Rico.

What makes their altitudes even more impressive is the existence, about 75 miles to the island's north, of one of the deepest depressions in the Atlantic, the Puerto Rico Trough. Running more or less parallel to the island's northern shoreline, it plunges to depths of up to 30,000 feet. Although not as obvious as this trench near the northern coastline, the sea floor a few miles from the island's southern coast also drops off, to nearly 17,000 feet below sea level. Geologists have calculated that if the base of this mountain chain were at sea level, it would be one of the highest land masses in the world. Puerto Rico's highest summit—Cerro de Punta at 4,389 feet—would exceed in altitude even Mt. Everest, the world's tallest peak.

Most of Puerto Rico's geology, especially its mountain peaks, resulted from volcanic activity that deposited lava and igneous rock in consecutive layers. To a lesser degree, the island is also composed of quartz, diomites, and, along some of its edges, coral limestone.

The mountains are home to the island's greatest natural attraction, **El Yunque** (☎ 787/887-2875 for information), a 45-minute drive from San Juan. Given national park status by President Theodore Roosevelt, this 28,000-acre preserve is the only tropical rain forest on U.S. soil and is protected by the U.S. Forest Service. On these soaring peaks, the virgin forest remains much like it was in 1493 when Columbus first sighted Puerto Rico.

Today, El Yunque offers its visitors close encounters of the natural kind, from picnics amid rare flora and fauna to hikes along the scenic trails. Encompassing four distinct forest types, it is home to 240 species of tropical trees, flowers including more than 20 kinds of orchids, and other wildlife including millions of tiny tree frogs whose distinctive cry of *coquí* (pronounced *ko-kee*) has given them their name. Tropical birds include the lively, greenish blue- and red-fronted Puerto Rican parrot, once nearly extinct and now making a comeback. Other rare animals include the Puerto Rican boa, which grows to 7 feet, and 26 animal species found nowhere else in the world.

El Yunque also offers a number of walking and hiking trails, including the rugged "El Toro" which passes through four different forest systems en route to the 3,523-foot Pico El Toro, the highest peak in the forest. El Yunque Trail leads to three of the recreation area's most spectacular lookouts, and Big Tree Trail is an easy walk to the panoramic La Mina Falls. Just off the main road is La Coca Falls, a sheet of water cascading down mossy cliffs.

Puerto Rico also has 19 other forest preserves. Directly east of San Juan lies **Piñones Forest,** which contains the island's largest mangrove forest. West of Ponce, **Guánica Forest** borders several white-sand beaches and the historic bay where U.S. troops first landed in 1898 during the Spanish-American War. **Cambalache Forest,** east of Arecibo, contains plantations of eucalyptus, teak, and mahoe trees. The driest vegetation is found in **Maricao Forest,** which also has a new visitors center and expansive views to the west coast. **Toro Negro Forest,** which straddles the peaks of the Cordillera in the center of the island, boasts the island's tallest peak with stunning drops to the Caribbean and the Atlantic. All these forests are open to visitors, and several have picnic areas and campsites.

One of the most interesting areas of Puerto Rico to explore is the **"Karst Country."** For the best way to see this region, refer to Driving Tour 2 in chapter 8, "Island Drives." One of the world's strangest rock formations, karst is formed by the process of water sinking into limestone. As time goes by, larger and larger basins are eroded, forming sinkholes. Mogotes or karstic hillocks are peaks of earth where the land didn't sink into the erosion pits. The Karst Country lies along the island's north coast, directly northeast of Mayagüez in the foothills between Quebradillas and Manatí. The region is filled with an extensive network of caves. One sinkhole contains the 20-acre dish of the world's largest radio/radar telescope at the Arecibo Observatory.

Reached by Route 446, the **Guajataca Forest Reserve** is found here, offering some 25 miles of trails which take you through some of the most rugged part of this country.

Eons ago, one of the world's largest underground rivers carved the **Rio Camuy Caves** in northwest Puerto Rico, which experts today consider to be among the most spectacular on earth. Although relatively new to today's visitors, the Rio Camuy Caves contain evidence of occupation long before the island was discovered by Columbus in 1493. The first professional explorers of the system were led to the site by local boys already familiar with some of the entrances.

Camuy Cave Park opens access to **Tres Pueblos Sinkhole,** measuring 65 feet in diameter with a depth of 400 feet—room enough to fit in all of El Morro Fortress in San Juan. Tres Pueblos, located on the boundaries of the Camuy, Hatillo, and Lares municipalities, is one of two sinkholes in the Rio Camuy Cave system now adapted for visitors. The other, Cueva Clara de Empalme, opened in 1986 and has been the park's featured attraction for the past 7 years.

In Tres Pueblos, visitors can walk along two platforms—one on the Lares side facing the town of Camuy and the other on the Hatillo side overlooking Tres Pueblos Cave and the Rio Camuy.

2 The Regions in Brief

Although the many geological divisions of Puerto Rico might not be immediately apparent to the average visitor, its people take great pride in stressing the island's diversity. Its most important geological and political divisions are as follows:

SAN JUAN

One of the largest and best-preserved complexes of Spanish colonial architecture in the Caribbean, Old San Juan (founded in 1521) is the oldest capital city under the U.S. flag. Once a linchpin of Spanish dominance in the Caribbean, it has three major fortresses, miles of solidly built stone ramparts, a charming collection of antique buildings, and a modern business center. The city's economy is the most stable and solid in all of Latin America.

San Juan is the site of the official home and office of the governor of Puerto Rico (La Fortaleza), the 16th-century residence of Ponce de León's family, and several of the oldest places of Christian worship in the western hemisphere. Its bars, restaurants, shops, and nightclubs attract an animated group of patrons and fans as well. In recent years, the old city has become surrounded by acres of densely populated modern buildings, including an ultramodern airport, which makes San Juan one of the most dynamic cities in the West Indies.

THE NORTHEAST

The capital city dominates Puerto Rico's northeast. Despite the region's congestion, there are still many remote areas, including some of the island's most important nature reserves. Among the region's most popular towns, parks, and attractions are the following:

EL YUNQUE   In the Luquillo Mountains, 35 miles east of San Juan, El Yunque is a favorite escape from the capital. Teeming with plant and animal life, it is a sprawling tropical forest (actually a National Forest) whose ecosystems are strictly protected. Some 100 billion gallons of rainwater fall here each year, allowing about 250 species of trees and flowers to flourish.

LAS CABEZAS DE SAN JUAN NATURE RESERVE   About an hour's drive from San Juan, this is one of the island's newest ecological refuges. It was established in 1991 on 316 acres of forest, mangrove swamp, offshore cays, coral reefs, and freshwater lagoons—a representative sampling of virtually every ecosystem on Puerto Rico.

There is a visitor's center, a 19th-century lighthouse ("El Faro") that still works, and ample opportunity to forget the pressures of urban life.

LOÍZA ALDEA   Located about 12 miles east of San Juan, this coastal town is the center of an area whose population is largely composed of descendants of African, specifically Yoruba, slaves. During the 16th century, African slaves were imported to pan for gold in the nearby watercourse, the Río Grande de Loíza, and to work the sugarcane fields. Later, slaves from other Caribbean islands—either escapees who had been recaptured or spoils of war taken from rival British plantations—were added to the region's cultural mix. The town was founded in 1719, but the foundations of one church were laid about 70 years before that. Loíza Aldea today is one of the three poorest municipalities on Puerto Rico. The region, with about 50,000 inhabitants, is considered the center of African-Hispanic culture on Puerto Rico.

FAJARDO   Small and sleepy, this town was originally established as a supply depot for the many pirates who plied the nearby waters. Today, a host of private yachts bob at anchor in its harbor, and the many offshore cays provide visitors with secluded beaches. From Fajardo, ferryboats make choppy but frequent runs to the offshore islands of Vieques and Culebra.

CAGUAS   Located 20 miles south of San Juan, Caguas is the largest city in the interior and the focal point of the broad and fertile Turabo Valley. Ringed by mountain peaks, the city has a population of around 120,000, many of whom commute to work in San Juan. The city was named after Caguax, the 16th-century Taíno chief who ruled the valley during the Spanish Conquest and whose peacemaking efforts eventually led, according to legend, to his conversion to Christianity. The town's central square, Plaza Palmer, with its 19th-century cathedral, is quite charming.

THE SOUTHEAST

The southeastern quadrant has some of the most heavily developed as well as some of the least developed sections of the island.

HUMACAO   Because of its easy access to San Juan, this small, verdant inland town has increasingly become one of the capital's residential suburbs.

PALMAS DEL MAR   This sprawling vacation and residential resort community is located near Humacao. A splendid golf course covers some of the 2,800-acre grounds, which once housed a sugarcane plantation.

THE RESERVA FORESTAL CARLTE   This 6,000-acre nature reserve is known simply as Guavate. Its relatively cool temperatures (averaging 72°F) and frequent rainfall sustain acres of teak, mahogany, and sierra palm trees. A radio/television tower sits atop the park's highest peak, the 3,000-foot Cerro La Santa.

ARROYO   This village on Puerto Rico's southwestern coast was founded in 1855 and has slumbered ever since in quiet obscurity, a favorite retreat of escapists. It was visited in 1848 by Samuel F. B. Morse, the inventor of the Morse code, who personally installed the local telegraph line. The town's main street, Calle Morse, is named in his honor. Several of the town's most impressive houses were built by New England sea captains who—perhaps piqued by the calm, tropical beauty of the place—decided to settle here.

BARRANQUITAS   Set inland at an altitude of more than 1,800 feet, Barranquitas is one of the most photogenic towns on Puerto Rico. Capped with a dramatically situated Catholic church, the town's houses rise almost on top of one another, in a style similar to that of a fortified village in Spain. Barranquitas's most famous son was the statesman Luís Muñoz Rivera, who is honored by a small museum in the house where

Puerto Rico

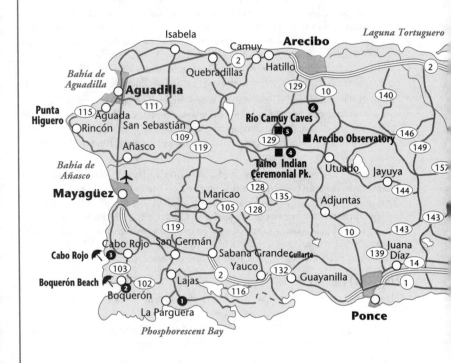

Atlantic Ocean

Isabela
Camuy
Arecibo
Laguna Tortuguero
Quebradillas
Hatillo
Bahía de Aguadilla
Aguadilla
Punta Higuero
Aguada
Rincón
San Sebastián
Río Camuy Caves
Arecibo Observatory
Añasco
Taíno Indian Ceremonial Pk.
Bahía de Añasco
Utuado
Jayuya
Mayagüez
Maricao
Adjuntas
San Germán
Cabo Rojo
Sabana Grande Guilarte
Juana Díaz
Cabo Rojo
Yauco
Guayanilla
Boquerón Beach
Lajas
Boquerón
La Parguera
Ponce
Phosphorescent Bay

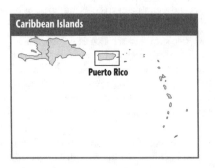

Caribbean Islands

Puerto Rico

Arecibo Observatory ❻
Boqueron Beach ❷
Cabo Rojo ❸
Condado Beach ❾
El Conquistador ⓮
El Faro (The Lighthouse/Las Cabeza de San Juan Nature Reserve) ⓭
El Morro ❽
El Yunque ⓫
Ferries to Vieques & Culebra ⓯

16

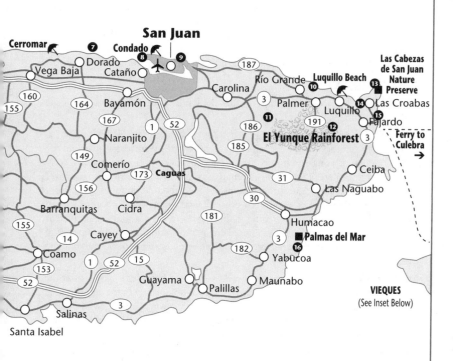

San Juan

Cerromar

Dorado

Vega Baja

Cataño

Condado

Bayamón

Carolina

Río Grande

Las Cabezas
de San Juan
Nature
Preserve

Luquillo Beach

Palmer

Luquillo

Las Croabas

Fajardo

**Ferry to
Culebra**
→

El Yunque Rainforest

Naranjito

Comerío

Caguas

Ceiba

Las Naguabo

Barranquitas

Cidra

Humacao

Cayey

Palmas del Mar

Coamo

Yabucoa

Guayama

Palillas

Maunabo

VIEQUES
(See Inset Below)

Salinas

Santa Isabel

C a r i b b e a n   S e a

Hyatt Resorts ❼
Luquillo Beach ❿
Old San Juan ❽
Palmas del Mar ⑯
Phosphorescent Bay ❶
Río Camuy Cave Park ❺
Sierra Palma
  Visitor Center ⑫
Sun Bay Beach ⑰
Taino Indian Ceremonial Park ❹

Vieques & Culebra

Culebra

Puerto Rico

Fajardo

Vieques

⑰

he was born in 1859. Near Barranquitas is one of Puerto Rico's deepest and most spectacular gorges, the nearly inaccessible canyon of San Cristóbal. There, cliffs nearly 500 feet high overlook the raging waters of the Usabon River.

COAMO   Although today Coamo is a bedroom community for the capital, originally it was the site of two different Taíno communities. Founded in 1579, it now has a main square draped with bougainvillea and one of the best-known Catholic churches on Puerto Rico. Even more famous, however, are the mineral springs whose therapeutic warm waters helped President Franklin D. Roosevelt during his recovery from polio. (Some historians claim that these springs inspired the legend of the Fountain of Youth, which in turn set Ponce de León off on his vain search of Florida.)

THE SOUTHWEST

One of Puerto Rico's most beautiful regions, the southwest is rich in local lore, civic pride, and natural wonders.

PONCE   Puerto Rico's second-largest city, Ponce has always prided itself on its independence from the Spanish-derived laws and taxes that governed San Juan and the rest of the island. Long-ago home of some of the island's shrewdest traders, merchants, and smugglers, it is enjoying a renaissance as citizens and visitors rediscover its unique cultural and architectural charms. Located about 90 minutes by car from the capital on Puerto Rico's southern coast, Ponce contains a handful of superb museums, one of the most charming main squares in the Caribbean, an ancient cathedral, dozens of authentically restored colonial-era buildings, and a number of outlying mansions and villas that, at the time of their construction, were among the most opulent on the island.

MAYAGÜEZ   The third-largest city on Puerto Rico, Mayagüez is named after the *majagua,* the Amerindian word for a tree that grows abundantly in the area. Because of an earthquake that destroyed almost everything in town in 1917, few old buildings remain. The town is known as the commercial and industrial capital of Puerto Rico's western sector. Its botanical garden is among the finest on the island.

SAN GERMÁN   Located on the island's southwestern corner, small, sleepy, and historic San Germán was named after Ferdinand of Spain's second wife, Germaine de Foix, whom he married in 1503. San Germán's central church, Porta Coeli, was built in 1606. At one time much of the populace was engaged in piracy, pillaging the ships that sailed off the nearby coastline. The central area of this village is still sought out for its many reminders of the island's Spanish heritage and colonial charm.

YAUCO   Established relatively late in the island's history (in 1756), Yauco immediately attracted a population of Corsicans and Haitian French, who grew a distinctive brand of coffee known for its low caffeine and mild flavor. By 1900, ravaged by hurricane damage and competition from other coffee-producing countries such as Colombia, the town had declined into obscurity. Today it retains its steeply sloping streets, a handful of old houses, aromatic coffee, and a distinctive air of faded Spanish grandeur.

CABO ROJO   Established in 1772, Cabo Rojo reached the peak of its prosperity during the 19th century, when immigrants from around the Mediterranean, fleeing revolutions in their own countries, arrived to establish sugarcane plantations. Today, cattle graze peacefully on land originally devoted almost exclusively to sugarcane, while the area's many varieties of exotic birds draw bird-watchers from throughout North America. Even the offshore waters are fertile; it's estimated that nearly half of all the fish consumed on Puerto Rico are caught in waters near Cabo Rojo.

BOQUERÓN   Famous for the beauty of its beach and the abundant birds and wildlife in the nearby Boquerón Forest Reserve, this small and sleepy village is now ripe for large-scale tourism-related development. During the early 19th century, the island's most-feared pirate, Roberto Cofresi, terrorized the Puerto Rican coastline from a secret lair in a cave nearby.

LA PARGUERA   Named after a breed of snapper (*pargos*) that abounds in the waters nearby, La Parguera is a quiet coastal town best known for the phosphorescent waters of La Bahía Fosforescente (Phosphorescent Bay). There, sheltered from the waves of the sea, billions of plankton (luminescent dinoflagellates) glow dimly when they are disturbed by movements of the water. The town comes alive on weekends, when crowds of young people from San Juan arrive to party the nights away. Filling modest rooming houses, they temporarily change the texture of the town as bands produce long and loud sessions of salsa music.

THE NORTHWEST

A fertile area with many rivers bringing valuable water for irrigation from the high mountains of the Cordillera, the northwest also offers abundant opportunities for sightseeing. The region's principal districts include the following:

ARECIBO   Located on the northern coastline a 2-hour drive west of San Juan, Arecibo was originally founded in 1556. Although little remains of its original architecture, the town is well known to physicists and astronomers around the world because of the radar/radio-telescope that fills a concave depression between six of the region's hills. Equal in size to 13 football fields and operated jointly by the National Science Foundation and Cornell University, it studies the shape and formation of the galaxies by accumulating and deciphering radio waves from space.

RÍO CAMUY CAVE PARK   Located near Arecibo, this park's greatest attraction is underground, where a network of underground rivers and caves provides some of the most enjoyable spelunking in the world. At its heart lies one of the largest known underground rivers. Covering 300 acres above ground, the park is sought out by cave explorers the world over.

RINCÓN   Named after the 16th-century landowner Don Gonzalo Rincón, who donated its site to the poor of his district, the tiny town of Rincón is famous throughout Puerto Rico for its world-class surfing and beautiful beaches. The lighthouse that warns yachters away from dangerous offshore reefs is one of the most powerful on Puerto Rico.

AGUADILLA   During his second voyage to the New World in 1493, Christopher Columbus landed nearby. Today, the town has a busy airport, fine beaches, and a growing tourism-based infrastructure. It is also the center of Puerto Rico's tiny lace-making industry, a craft imported here many centuries ago by immigrants from Spain, Holland, and Belgium.

UTUADO   Small, sunny, and nestled amid the hills of the interior, Utuado is famous as the center of the *jíbaro* (hillbilly) culture of Puerto Rico. Some of Puerto Rico's finest mountain musicians have come from Utuado and mention the town in many of their ballads. The surrounding landscape is sculpted with caves and lushly covered with a variety of tropical plants and trees.

THE OFFSHORE ISLANDS

Few *norteamericanos* realize that Puerto Rico has at least four well-known islands and a multitude of tiny cays lying offshore. The most famous of these include:

CAYO SANTIAGO   Lying off the southeastern coast is the small island of Cayo Santiago. Home to a group of about two dozen scientists and a community of rhesus monkeys originally imported from India, the island is a medical experimentation center run by the U.S. Public Health Service. Monkeys are studied in a "wild" but controlled environment both for insights into the behavioral sciences and for possible cures for such maladies as diabetes and arthritis. Casual visitors are not permitted on Cayo Santiago, but they can cruise along the shore and watch the monkeys.

CULEBRA & VIEQUES   Located off the eastern coast, these two islands are among the most unsullied and untrammeled areas in the West Indies. Come here for sun, almost no scheduled activities, fresh seafood, clear waters, sandy beaches, and teeming coral reefs. Vieques is especially proud of its phosphorescent bay.

MONA   Remote, uninhabited, and teeming with bird life, this barren island off the western coast is ringed by soaring cliffs and finely textured white beaches. The island has almost no facilities, so visitors seldom stay for more than a day of swimming and picnicking. The currents that surround Mona on all sides are legendary for their dangerous eddies, undertows, and sharks.

3 Puerto Rico Today

Mirroring the U.S. mainland, rising crime, drugs, the AIDS crisis, chronic unemployment, overpopulation, and more plague Puerto Rico. The island has America's third highest AIDS rate and the dubious distinction of being a major gateway into the United States for drugs from Latin America. All the violence and social ills associated with drugs have beset the island. A newspaper headline said it best: "Puerto Rico Reeling Under Scourage of Drugs and Rising Gang Violence." And yet it is possible to visit Puerto Rico for a vacation and be completely unaware that all this criminal activity is going on around you, especially if you're heading to one of the big, self-sufficient resorts.

On a more positive note, the island's 3.56 million people—including a million in the San Juan metropolitan area—have forged ahead economically and made rapid strides. Their annual income is now the highest in Latin America, and their average life expectancy has risen to 73.8 years. And with the island's economy evolving from agriculture to manufacturing and tourism, a demand for an educated workforce has resulted in the average worker having at least 12 years of schooling.

Intensified U.S. interest in developing the island's manufacturing since the end of World War II has made Puerto Rico the Caribbean's most industrially developed island. It has one of the most prosperous economies in all of Latin America and is a major producer and exporter of manufactured goods, pharmaceutical, and high tech equipment. Since the 19th century, Puerto Rico has been a major producer of rum, and today it supplies approximately 83% of the rum sold in the U.S. Despite this relative prosperity, however, personal income still lags behind that in the poorest U.S. state. The commonwealth still relies on direct subsidies from the United States, which amount to 25% of its gross domestic product. Unemployment sometimes runs as high as 20%.

Tourism represents about 6% of the gross national product. Puerto Rico's present governor, Dr. Pedro Rosselló, has challenged both the private and public sectors of the tourism industry to double that contribution to the GNP within the next decade. At once both labor intensive and environmentally friendly, tourism is seen as the island's best alternative to continued heavy industrialization in pursuit of new jobs for its people.

Rosselló isn't just talking. He recently announced the development of a new $173 million tourism project on nearly 600 acres of land located in the municipalities of Rio Grande and Luquillo right outside San Juan. Here will be developed a 600-room hotel, two 18-hole golf courses, 13 tennis courts, a 20,000 square-foot clubhouse, swimming pools, a health club, and sporting facilities for children and teens.

The unspoken fear among developers of megaresorts, however, is the possible impact of Cuba reopening to the American tourism market. Before Fidel Castro took over Cuba in 1959, Americans by the thousands flocked to Havana and Puerto Rico was a mere dot on the tourist map. The island's growth was fueled enormously by the embargo imposed on Castro's Communist government.

As Puerto Rico moves toward the millennium, it faces troubling political questions that have plagued it throughout the 20th century. Statehood, commonwealth, or independence is still an important issue. In a nonbinding plebiscite held in November 1993, 48.4% of Puerto Rican voters indicated their preference for the status quo as a commonwealth, 46.2% preferred statehood, and 4.4% chose independence.

Efforts are being made to solve the commonwealth's most serious problem: drugs. In the mid-90s the government increased the number of police officers, enacted harsher prison sentences for drug dealers, and conducted arms and drug raids—all part of a continuing battle to stop the flow of illegal drugs into the United States.

4 History 101

IN THE BEGINNING

Although the Spanish occupation was the decisive factor defining Puerto Rico's current culture, the island was settled many thousands of years ago by Amerindians. The oldest archaeological remains yet discovered were unearthed in 1948. Found in a limestone cave a few miles east of San Juan, in Loíza Aldea, the artifacts consisted of conch shells, stone implements, and crude hatchets deposited there by tribal peoples during the first century of the Christian Era. These people belonged to an archaic, seminomadic, cave-dwelling culture that had not developed either agriculture or pottery. Some ethnologists suggest that these early inhabitants originated in Florida, immigrated to Cuba, and from there began a steady migration along the West Indian archipelago.

Around A.D. 300, a different group of Amerindians, the Arawaks, migrated to Puerto Rico from the Orinoco Basin in what is now Venezuela. Known by ethnologists as the Saladoids, they were the first of Puerto Rico's inhabitants to make and use pottery, which they decorated with exotic geometric designs in red and white. Subsisting on fish, crabs, and whatever else they could catch, they populated the big island and the offshore island of Vieques as well.

By about A.D. 600, this culture had disappeared, bringing to an end the island's historic era of pottery making. Ethnologists' opinions differ as to whether the tribes were eradicated by new invasions from South America, succumbed to starvation or plague, or simply evolved into the next culture that dominated Puerto Rico—the Ostionoids.

Much less skilled at making pottery than their predecessors but more accomplished at polishing and grinding stones for jewelry and tools, the Ostionoids were the ethnic predecessors of the tribe that became the Taínos. The Taínos inhabited Puerto Rico when it was discovered and invaded by the Spanish beginning in 1493. The Taínos were spread throughout the West Indies but reached their greatest development in Puerto Rico and neighboring Hispaniola (the island shared by Haiti and the Dominican Republic).

Sweet Songs of Love

The Spanish colonialists first recorded some of the Taíno tribespeople's legends, which they had passed down orally from generation to generation. Many of these were ghost tales about demons who roamed the island after dark, pursuing food or people or else protecting gold and loot that pirates long ago stashed away for safekeeping.

But one such tale, dated from about 1511, is the Puerto Rican version of *Romeo and Juliet* or the early Virginian legend of Capt. John Smith and his Native American bride, Pocahontas.

The story is called "Guanina" because it tells of Don Cristóbal de Sotomayor, a young man from Valladolid, Spain, who was enchanted by a graceful Amerindian girl, Guanina. At its end, the two are found dead, Guanina's head resting on his bloody chest.

It was said that a witch doctor buried their bodies under the roots of a towering ceiba tree, and that white lilies and red poppies grew from their graves. Locals claimed to hear sweet songs of love rustling through the leaves of the giant ceiba.

Some people on the island say the lovers still come out on moonlit nights to renew their vows of devotion.

Taíno culture impressed both the colonial Spanish and modern sociologists. Their achievements included construction of ceremonial ball parks whose boundaries were marked by upright stone dolmens, development of a universal language, and creation of a complicated religious cosmology. There was a hierarchy of deities who inhabited the sky. The god Yocahu was the supreme Creator. Another, Jurancán, was perpetually angry and ruled the power of the hurricane. Myths and traditions were perpetuated through ceremonial dances (*areytos*), drumbeats, oral traditions, and a ceremonial ball game played between opposing teams (of 10 to 30 players per team) with a rubber ball; winning this game was thought to bring a good harvest and strong, healthy children.

Skilled at agriculture and hunting, the Taínos were also good sailors, canoe makers, and navigators.

About 100 years before the Spanish invasion, the Taínos were challenged by an invading South American tribe—the Caribs. Fierce, warlike, sadistic, and adept at using poison-tipped arrows, they raided Taíno settlements for slaves (especially female) and bodies for the completion of their rites of cannibalism. Some ethnologists argue that the preeminence of the Taínos, shaken by the attacks of the Caribs, was already jeopardized by the time of the Spanish occupation. In fact, it was the Caribs who fought the most effectively against the Europeans; their behavior led the Europeans to unfairly attribute warlike tendencies to all of the island's tribes. A dynamic tension between the Taínos and the Caribs certainly existed when Christopher Columbus landed on Puerto Rico.

To understand Puerto Rico's prehistoric era, it is important to know that the Taínos, far more than the Caribs, contributed greatly to the everyday life and language that evolved during the Spanish occupation. Taíno place names are still used for such towns as Utuado, Mayagüez, Caguas, and Humacao. Many Taíno implements and techniques were copied directly by the Europeans, including the *bohío* (straw hut) and the *hamaca* (hammock), the musical instrument known as the *maracas,* and the method of making bread from the starchy cassava root. Also, many Taíno superstitions and legends were adopted and adapted by the Spanish and still influence the Puerto Rican imagination.

SPAIN, SYPHILIS & SLAVERY

Christopher Columbus became the first European to land on the shores of Puerto Rico, on November 19, 1493, near what would become the town of Aguadilla, during his second voyage to the New World. Giving the island the name San Juan Bautista, he sailed on in search of shores with more obvious riches for the taking. A European foothold on the island was established in 1508 when Juan Ponce de León, the first governor of Puerto Rico, imported colonists from the nearby island of Hispaniola. They founded the town of Caparra, which lay close to the site of present-day San Juan. The town was almost immediately wracked with internal power struggles among the Spanish settlers, who pressed the native peoples into servitude, evangelized them, and frantically sought for gold, thus quickly changing the face of the island.

Meanwhile, the Amerindians began dying at an alarming rate, victims of imported diseases such as smallpox and whooping cough, against which they had no biologic immunity. The natives also paid the Spanish back, giving them diseases such as syphilis against which they had little immunity. Both communities reeled, disoriented, from their contact with one another. In 1511, the Amerindians rebelled against attempts by the Spanish to enslave them. The rebellion was brutally suppressed by the Spanish forces of Ponce de León, whose muskets and firearms were vastly superior to the hatchets and arrows of the native peoples. In desperation, the remnants of the Taínos joined forces with their traditional enemies, the Caribs, but even that belated union did little to check the inexorable growth of European power.

Because the Indians languished in slavery, sometimes preferring mass suicide to imprisonment, their work in the fields and mines of Puerto Rico was soon taken over by Africans who were imported by Spanish, Danish, Portuguese, British, and American slavers.

By 1521 the island had been renamed Puerto Rico ("Rich Port") and was considered one of the most strategic islands in the Caribbean, which was increasingly viewed as a Spanish sea. Officials of the Spanish Crown dubbed the island "the strongest foothold of Spain in America" and hastened to strengthen the already impressive bulwarks surrounding the city of San Juan.

PIRATES & PILLAGING ENGLISHMEN

Within a century, Puerto Rico's position at the easternmost edge of what would become Spanish America helped it play a major part in the Spanish expansion toward Florida, the South American coast, and Mexico. It was usually the first port of call for Spanish ships arriving in the Americas; recognizing that the island was a strategic keystone, the Spanish decided to strengthen its defenses. By 1540 La Fortaleza, the first of three massive fortresses built in San Juan, was completed. By 1600, San Juan was completely enclosed by some of the most formidable ramparts in the Caribbean whereas, ironically, the remainder of Puerto Rico was almost defenseless. In 1565, the King of Spain ordered the governor of Puerto Rico to provide men and material to strengthen the city of San Agustin (St. Augustine) in Florida.

By this time, the English (and to a lesser extent, the French) were seriously harassing Spanish shipping in the Caribbean and North Atlantic. At least part of the French and English aggression was in retaliation for the 1493 Papal Bull dividing the New World between Portugal and Spain—an arrangement that eliminated all other nations from the spoils and colonization of the New World.

Queen Elizabeth I's most effective weapons against Spanish expansion in the Caribbean were John Hawkins and Sir Francis Drake, whose victories included the destruction of St. Augustine in Florida, Cartagena in Colombia, and Santo Domingo in what is now the Dominican Republic, and the general harassment and pillaging of many Spanish ships and treasure convoys sailing from the New World to Europe with gold and silver from the Aztec and Inca empires. In 1588, Drake's destruction of the Spanish Armada marked the beginning of the rise of the English as a major maritime power and the beginning of an even more aggressive fortification of such islands as Puerto Rico.

In 1595, Drake and Hawkins persuaded an uncertain Queen Elizabeth to embark on a bold and daring plan to invade and conquer Puerto Rico. An English general, the Earl of Cumberland, urged his men to bravery by "assuring your selves you have the maydenhead of Puerto Rico and so possesse the keyes of all the Indies." Confident that the island was "the very key of the West Indies which locketh and shutteth all the gold and silver in the continent of America and Brasilia," he brought into battle an English force of 4,500 soldiers and eventually captured La Fortaleza.

Although the occupation lasted a full 65 days, the English eventually abandoned Puerto Rico when their armies were decimated by tropical diseases and the local population, which began to engage in a kind of guerrilla warfare against the English. After pillaging and destroying much of the Puerto Rican countryside, the English left. Their short but abortive victory compelled the Spanish king, Philip III, to continue construction of the island's defenses. Despite these efforts, Puerto Rico retained a less-than-invincible aspect as Spanish soldiers in the forts often deserted or succumbed to tropical diseases.

A DUTCH TREAT

In 1625, Puerto Rico was covetously eyed by Holland, whose traders and merchants desperately wanted a foothold in the West Indies. Spearheaded by the Dutch West India Company, which had received trading concessions from the Dutch Crown covering most of the West Indies, the Dutch armies besieged El Morro Fortress in San Juan in one of the bloodiest assaults the fortress ever sustained. Frustrated in their siege of the fortress and fearing the arrival of Spanish reinforcements from the western side of the island, the Dutch threatened to burn down every building in San Juan if the Spanish did not surrender. When the commanding officer of El Morro scorned the threat, the Dutch burned San Juan to the ground, including all church and civil archives and the bishop's library, by then the most famous and complete collection of books in America. Fueled by rage and courage, the Spanish rallied their forces and soon threw out the Dutch, who retreated in confusion, never again to assault the communities of Puerto Rico.

In response to the widespread destruction of the strongest link in the chain of Spanish defenses, Spain threw itself wholeheartedly into improving and reinforcing the defenses around San Juan. (Philip IV justified his expenditures by declaring Puerto Rico the "front and vanguard of the Western Indies and, consequently, the most important of them and most coveted by the enemies of Spain.")

Within 150 years, after extravagant expenditures of time and money, the city's walls were considered almost impregnable. Military sophistication was added during the 1760s, when two Irishmen, Tomas O'Daly and Alejandro O'Reilly, surrounded the city with some of Europe's most technically up-to-date defenses. Despite the thick walls, the island's defenses remained precarious because of the frequent tropical epidemics that devastated the ranks of the soldiers; the chronically late pay, which weakened the soldiers' morale; and the belated and often wrong-minded priorities of the Spanish monarchy, which were decided upon thousands of miles away.

AN ARMY OF PRIESTS

From the earliest days of Spanish colonization, an army of priests and missionaries embarked on a vigorous crusade to convert Puerto Rico's Taínos to Roman Catholicism. King Ferdinand himself paid for the construction of a Franciscan monastery and a series of chapels, and required specific support of the church from the aristocrats who had been awarded land grants in the new territories. They were required to build churches, provide Christian burials, and grant religious instruction to both Taíno and African slaves.

Among the church's most important activities were the Franciscan monks' efforts to teach the island's children how to read, write, and count. In 1688, Bishop Francisco Padilla, who is now included among the legends of Puerto Rico, established one of the island's most famous schools. When it became clear that local parents were too poor to provide their children with appropriate clothing, he succeeded in persuading the King of Spain to pay for their clothes.

Puerto Rico was declared by the pope as the first *see*—ecclesiastical headquarters— in the New World. In 1519, it became the general headquarters of the Inquisition in the New World. (About 70 years later, the Inquisition's headquarters was transferred to the important and well-defended city of Cartagena, in Colombia.)

FROM SMUGGLING TO SUGAR

The island's early development was shackled by Spain's insistence on a centrist economy. All goods exported from or imported to Puerto Rico had to pass through Spain itself, usually through Seville. In effect, this policy prohibited any trade (officially, at least) between Puerto Rico and its island neighbors.

In response, a flourishing black market developed. Cities, such as Ponce, became smuggling centers. This black market was especially prevalent after the Spanish colonization of Mexico and Peru, when many Spanish goods, which once would have been sent to Puerto Rico, ended up in those more immediately lucrative colonies instead. Although smugglers were punished, nothing could curb this illegal (and untaxed) trade. Some historians estimate that almost everyone on the island— including priests, citizens, and military and civic authorities—were actively involved.

By the mid-1500s, the several hundred settlers who had immigrated to Puerto Rico from Spain heard (and sometimes believed) rumors of the fortunes to be made in the gold mines of Peru. When the island's population declined because of the ensuing mass exodus, the king enticed 500 families from the Canary Islands to settle on Puerto Rico between 1683 and 1691. Meanwhile, an active trade in slaves—imported as labor for fields that were increasingly used for sugarcane and tobacco production— swelled the island's ranks. This happened despite the Crown's imposition of strict controls on the number of slaves that could be brought in. Sugarcane earned profits for many islanders, but Spanish mismanagement, fraud within the government bureaucracy, and a lack of both labor and ships to transport the finished product to market discouraged the fledgling industry. Later, fortunes were made and lost in the production of ginger, an industry that died as soon as the Spanish government raised taxes on ginger imports to exorbitant levels. Despite the arrival of immigrants to Puerto Rico from many countries, diseases such as spotted fever, yellow fever, malaria, smallpox, and measles wiped out the population almost as fast as it grew.

MORE SMUGGLING

As the philosophical and political movement known as the Enlightenment swept both Europe and North America during the late 1700s and the 1800s, Spain moved to improve Puerto Rico's economy through its local government. The island's defenses were beefed up, roads and bridges were built, and a public education program was launched. The island remained a major Spanish naval stronghold in the New World. Immigration from Europe and other places more than tripled the population. It was during this era that Puerto Rico began to develop a unique identity of its own, a native pride, and a consciousness of its importance within the Caribbean.

The heavily fortified city of San Juan, the island's civic centerpiece, remained under Spain's rigid control. The outlying countryside, without the benefit of encircling ramparts and victim occasionally of raids by both pirates and the forces of England and France, was usually left alone to develop its own local power centers. The city of Ponce, for example, flourished under the Spanish Crown's lax supervision and grew wealthy from the tons of contraband and the high-quality sugar that passed through its port. This trend was also encouraged by the unrealistic law that declared San Juan the island's only legal port. Contemporary sources, in fact, cite the fledgling United States as among the most active of Ponce's early contraband trading partners.

During the 18th century the number of towns on the island grew rapidly. There were five settlements in Puerto Rico in 1700; 100 years later there were almost 40 settlements, and the island's population had grown to more than 150,000.

Meanwhile, the waters of the Caribbean increasingly reflected the diplomatic wars unfolding in Europe. In 1797, the British, after easily capturing Trinidad (which was poorly defended by the Spanish), failed in a spectacular effort to conquer Puerto Rico. The *criollos,* or native Puerto Ricans, played a major role in the island's defense and later retained a growing sense of their own cultural identity.

The islanders were becoming aware that Spain could not enforce the hundreds of laws it had previously imposed to support its centrist trade policies. Thousands of merchants, farmers, and civil authorities traded profitably with privateers from various nations, thereby deepening the tendency to evade or ignore the laws imposed by Spain and its colonial governors. The attacks by privateers on British shipping were especially severe, since pirates based in Puerto Rico ranged as far south as Trinidad, bringing dozens of captured British ships into Puerto Rican harbors. (Several decades earlier, British privateers operating out of Jamaica had endlessly harassed Spanish shipping; the tradition of government-sanctioned piracy was well established.)

It was during this period that coffee—which would later play an essential role in the island's economy—was introduced to the Puerto Rican highlands from the nearby Dominican Republic.

Despite the power of San Juan and its Spanish institutions, 18th-century Puerto Rico was predominantly rural. The report of a special emissary of the Spanish king, Marshal Alejandro O'Reilly, remains a remarkably complete analysis of 18th-century Puerto Rican society. It helped promote a more progressive series of fiscal and administrative policies that reflected the Enlightenment ideals found in many European countries.

Suddenly, Puerto Rico began to be viewed as a potential source of income for the Spanish Empire, rather than a drain on income. One of O'Reilly's most visible legacies was his recommendation that people live in towns rather than be scattered about the countryside. Shortly after this, seven new towns, some in the island's interior, were established.

Meanwhile, as the island prospered and its bourgeoisie became more numerous and affluent, daily life became more refined. New public buildings were erected; concerts were introduced; and the everyday aspects of life—such as furniture and social ritual—grew more ornate. Insights into Puerto Rico's changing life can be seen in the works of its most famous 18th-century painter, José Campeche, whose portraits, religious frescoes, and landscapes are among his era's most distinctive legacies.

THE LAST BASTION

Much of the politics of 19th-century Latin America cannot be understood without reviewing Spain's problems at that time. Up until 1850 there was political and military turmoil in Spain, a combination that eventually led to the collapse of its empire. Since 1796, Spain had been a military satellite of post-revolutionary France, an alliance that brought it into conflict with England. In 1804, Admiral Horatio Lord Nelson's definitive victory for England over French and Spanish ships during the Battle of Trafalgar left England in supreme control of the international sea lanes and interrupted trade and communications between Spain and its colonies in the New World.

These events led to important changes for Spanish-speaking America. The revolutionary fervor of Simón Bolívar and his South American compatriots spilled over to the entire continent, embroiling Spain in a desperate attempt to hold onto the tattered remains of its empire at any cost. Recognizing that Puerto Rico and Cuba were probably the last bastions of Spanish Royalist sympathy in the Americas, Spain liberalized its trade policies, decreeing that goods no longer had to pass through Seville.

The sheer weight and volume of illegal Puerto Rican trade with such countries as Denmark, France, and—most important—the United States, forced Spain's hand in establishing a realistic set of trade reforms. A bloody revolution in Haiti, which had produced more sugarcane than almost any other West Indies island, spurred sugarcane and coffee production in Puerto Rico. Also important was the introduction of a new and more prolific species of sugarcane, the Otahiti, which helped increase production even more.

By the 1820s, the United States was providing ample supplies of such staples as lumber, salt, butter, fish, grain, and foodstuffs, while huge amounts of Puerto Rican sugar, molasses, coffee, and rum were consumed in the United States. Meanwhile, the United States was increasingly viewed as the keeper of the peace in the Caribbean, suppressing the piracy that flourished while Spain's navy was preoccupied with its European wars.

During Venezuela's separation from Spain, Venezuelans loyal to the Spanish Crown fled en masse to the remaining Royalist bastions in the Americas—Puerto Rico and, to a lesser extent, Cuba. Although many arrived penniless, having forfeited their properties in South America in exchange for their lives, their excellent understanding of agriculture and commerce probably catalyzed much of the era's economic development in Puerto Rico. Simultaneously, many historians argue, their unflinching loyalty to the Spanish Crown contributed to one of the most conservative and reactionary social structures anywhere in the Spanish-speaking Caribbean. In any event, dozens of Spanish naval expeditions intended to suppress the revolutions in Venezuela were outfitted in Puerto Rican harbors during this period.

A REVOLT SUPPRESSED & SLAVERY ABOLISHED

During the latter half of the 19th century, political divisions were drawn in Puerto Rico reflecting both the political instability in Spain and the increasing demands of Puerto Ricans for some form of self-rule. As governments and regimes in Spain rose and fell, Spanish policies toward its colonies in the New World changed, too.

In 1865, representatives from Puerto Rico, Cuba, and the Philippines were invited to Madrid to air their grievances as part of a process of liberalizing Spanish colonial policy. Reforms, however, did not follow as promised, and a much-publicized and very visible minirevolt (during which the mountain city of Lares was occupied) was suppressed by the Spanish governors in 1868. Some of the funds and much of the publicity for this revolt came from expatriate Puerto Ricans living in Chile, St. Thomas, and New York.

Slavery was abolished in March 1873, about 40 years after it had been abolished throughout the British Empire. About 32,000 slaves were freed following years of liberal agitation. Abolition was viewed as a major victory for liberal forces throughout Puerto Rico, although cynics claim that slavery was much less entrenched in Puerto Rico than in neighboring Cuba, where the sugar economy was far more dependent on slave labor.

The 1895 revolution in Cuba increased the Puerto Rican demand for greater self-rule; during the ensuing intellectual ferment, many political parties emerged. The Cuban revolution provided part of the spark that led to the Spanish-American War, Cuban independence, and U.S. control of Puerto Rico, the Philippines, and the Pacific island of Guam.

THE YANKS ARE COMING, THE YANKS ARE COMING!

In 1897, faced with intense pressure from sources within Puerto Rico, a weakened Spain granted its colony a measure of autonomy, but it came too late. Other events were taking place between Spain and the United States that would forever change the future of Puerto Rico.

On February 15, 1898, the U.S. battleship *Maine* was blown up in the harbor of Havana, killing 266 men. The so-called "yellow press" in the United States, especially the papers owned by the tycoon William Randolph Hearst, aroused Americans' emotions into a fever pitch for war, with the rallying cry "Remember the *Maine*."

On April 20th of that year, President William McKinley signed a resolution demanding Spanish withdrawal from Cuba. The president ordered a blockade of Cuba's ports, and on April 24th, Spain, in retaliation, declared a state of war with the United States. On April 25th the U.S. Congress declared war on Spain. In Cuba, the naval battle of Santiago was won by American forces, and in another part of the world, the Spanish colony of the Philippines was also captured by U.S. troops.

On July 25, after their victory at Santiago, American troops landed at Guánica, Puerto Rico, and several days later took over Ponce. U.S. Navy Capt. Alfred T. Mahan later wrote that the United States viewed Puerto Rico, Spain's remaining colonial outpost in the Caribbean, as vital to American interests in the area. Puerto Rico could be used as a military base to help the United States maintain control of the isthmus and to keep communications and traffic flowing between the Atlantic and the Pacific.

Spain offered to trade other territory for Puerto Rico, but the United States refused and demanded Spain's ouster from the island. Left with little choice against superior U.S. forces, Spain capitulated. The Spanish-American War ended on August 31, 1898, with the surrender of Spain and the virtual collapse of the once-powerful Spanish Empire. Puerto Rico, in the words of McKinley, was to "become a territory of the United States."

Although the entire war lasted just over 4 months, the invasion of Puerto Rico took only 2 weeks. "It wasn't much of a war," remarked Theodore Roosevelt, who had led the Rough Riders cavalry outfit in their charge up San Juan Hill, "but it was all the war there was." The United States had suffered only four casualties while acquiring Puerto Rico, the Philippines, and the island of Guam. The Treaty of Paris, signed on December 10, 1898, settled the terms of Spain's surrender.

A DUBIOUS PRIZE

Some Americans looked on Puerto Rico as a "dubious prize." One-third of the population consisted of mulattoes and blacks, descended from slaves, who had no money or land. Only about 12% of the population could read or write. About 8% were enrolled in school. It is estimated that a powerful landed gentry—only about 2% of the population—owned more than two-thirds of the land.

Washington set up a military government in Puerto Rico, headed by the War Department. A series of governors-general were appointed to rule the island, with almost the authority of a dictator. Although ruling over a rather unhappy populace, these governors-general brought about much-needed change, including tax and public health reforms. But most Puerto Ricans wanted autonomy, and many leaders, including Luís Muñoz Rivera, tried to persuade Washington to compromise. However, their protests generally fell on deaf ears.

The island's beleaguered economy was further devastated by an 1899 hurricane that caused millions of dollars' worth of property damage and killed 3,000 people. One out of four people was left homeless. Belatedly, Congress allocated the sum of $200,000, but this did little to relieve the suffering.

Tensions mounted between Puerto Ricans and their new American governors. In 1900, U.S. Secretary of War Elihu Root decided that military rule of the island was inadequate; he advocated a program of autonomy that won the endorsement of President McKinley.

Thus began a nearly 50-year colonial protectorate relationship as Puerto Rico was recognized as an unincorporated territory with its governor named by the president of the United States. Only the president had the right to override the veto of the island's governors. The legislative branch was composed of an 11-member executive committee appointed by the president, plus a 35-member chamber of delegates elected by popular vote. A resident commissioner, it was agreed, would represent Puerto Rico in Congress, "with voice but no vote."

As the United States prepared to enter World War I in 1917, Puerto Ricans were granted American citizenship and thus were subject to military service. The people of Puerto Rico were allowed to elect their legislature, which had been reorganized into a Senate and a House of Representatives. The president of the United States continued to appoint the governor of the island and retained the power to veto any of the governor's actions.

FROM HARVARD TO REVOLUTION

Many Puerto Ricans continued, at times rather violently, to agitate for independence. Requests for a plebiscite were constantly turned down. Meanwhile, economic conditions improved, as the island's population began to grow dramatically. Government revenues increased as large corporations from the U.S. mainland found Puerto Rico a profitable place in which to do business. There was much labor unrest, and by 1909, a labor movement demanding better working conditions and higher wages was gaining momentum.

The emerging labor movement showed its strength by organizing a cigar workers' strike in 1914 and a sugarcane workers' strike the following year. The 1930s proved to be disastrous for Puerto Rico, since it suffered greatly from the worldwide depression. To make matters worse, two devastating hurricanes—one in 1928 and another in 1932—destroyed millions of dollars' worth of crops and property. There was also

Impressions

It is a kind of lost love-child, born to the Spanish Empire, and fostered by the United States.

—Nicholas Wollaston, *Red Rumba*, 1962

an outbreak of disease that, along with starvation, demoralized the population. Some relief came in the form of food shipments authorized by Congress.

As tension between Puerto Rico and the United States intensified, there emerged Pedro Albizu Campos, a graduate of Harvard Law School and a former U.S. army officer. Leading a group of militant anti-American revolutionaries, he held that America's claim to Puerto Rico was illegal, since the island had already been granted autonomy by Spain. Terrorist acts by his followers, including assassinations, led to Albizu's imprisonment, but terrorist activities still continued.

In 1935 President Franklin D. Roosevelt launched the Puerto Rican Reconstruction Administration, which provided for agricultural development, public works, and electrification of the island. The following year, Sen. Millard E. Tidings of Maryland introduced a measure to grant independence to the island. His efforts were cheered by a local leader, Luís Muñoz Marín, son of the statesman Luís Muñoz Rivera. The young Muñoz founded the Partida Popular Democratica ("Popular Democratic Party") in 1938, which adopted the slogan "Bread, Land, and Liberty." By 1940 this new party had gained control of more than 50% of the seats of both the upper and the lower houses of government, and the young Muñoz was elected leader of the Senate.

Roosevelt appointed Rexford Guy Tugwell as governor of Puerto Rico; he spoke Spanish and seemed to have a genuine concern for the plight of the islanders. Muñoz met with Tugwell and convinced him that Puerto Rico was capable of electing its own governor. As a step in that direction, Roosevelt appointed Jesús Piñero as the first resident commissioner of the island.

In 1944, the U.S. Congress approved a bill granting Puerto Rico the right to elect its own governor. This was the beginning of the famed Operation Bootstrap, a pump-priming fiscal and economic aid package designed to improve the island's standard of living.

SHOOTING AT HARRY

In 1946, President Harry S. Truman appointed native-born Piñero as governor of Puerto Rico, and the following year the U.S. Congress recognized the right of Puerto Ricans to elect their own governor. In 1948, Luís Muñoz Marín became the first elected governor and immediately recommended that Puerto Rico be transformed into an "associated free state." Endorsement of his plan was delayed by Washington, but President Truman approved the Puerto Rican Commonwealth Bill in 1950, providing for a plebiscite in which voters would decide whether they would remain a colony or become a U.S. commonwealth. In June 1951, Puerto Ricans voted three to one for commonwealth status, and on July 25, 1952, the Commonwealth of Puerto Rico was born.

This event was marred by a group of nationalists who marched on the Governor's Mansion in San Juan, resulting in 27 deaths and hundreds of casualties. A month later, two Puerto Rican nationalists made an unsuccessful attempt on Truman's life in Washington, killing a policeman in the process. And in March 1954, four Puerto Rican nationalists wounded five U.S. congressmen when they fired down into the House of Representatives from the visitors' gallery.

In spite of this violence, during the 1950s Puerto Rico began to take pride in its own culture and traditions. In 1955, the Institute of Puerto Rican Culture was established in San Juan, and 1957 saw the inauguration of the Pablo Casals Festival, which launched a renaissance of classical music and a celebration of the arts, a tradition that continues to this day. In 1959, a wealthy industrialist, Luís A. Ferré, donated his personal art collection toward the establishment of the Museum of Fine Arts in Ponce.

GIVE ME LIBERTY OR GIVE ME STATEHOOD

Luís Muñoz Marín resigned from office in 1964, but his party continued to win subsequent elections. The independent party, which demanded complete autonomy, gradually lost power. An election on July 23, 1967, reconfirmed the desire of most Puerto Ricans to maintain commonwealth status. In 1968, Luís A. Ferré won a close race for governor, spearheading a pro-statehood party, the Partida Progressiva Nueva (New Progressive Party). It staunchly advocated statehood as an alternative to the island's commonwealth status, but in 1972, the Partida Popular Democratica returned to power; by then, the island's economy was based largely on tourism, rum, and industry. Operation Bootstrap had been successful in creating thousands of new jobs, although more than 100,000 Puerto Ricans moved to the U.S. mainland during the 1950s, seeking a better life. The island's economy continued to improve, although perhaps not as quickly as anticipated by Operation Bootstrap.

Puerto Rico grabbed the world's attention in 1979 with the launching of the Pan-American Games. It is vigorously attempting to bring the Summer Olympics there in 2004. The island's culture received a boost in 1981 with the opening of the Center of the Performing Arts in San Juan, which attracted world-famous performers and virtuosos. The international spotlight again focused on Puerto Rico at the time of the first papal visit there in 1986. John Paul II (or Juan Pablo II, as he was called locally) kindled a renewed interest in religion, especially among the Catholic youth of the island.

5 A Portrait of the Puerto Ricans

The people of Puerto Rico represent a mix of races, cultures, languages, and religions. They draw their unique heritage from the original native population, from Spanish royalists who sought refuge here, from African slaves imported to work the sugar plantations, and from other Caribbean islanders who have come here seeking jobs. The Spanish they speak is a mix, too, with many words borrowed from the pre-Columbian Amerindian tongue right up to modern-day English. Even the Catholicism they practice blends some Taíno and African traditions.

THE ISLANDERS

Some 3.56 million people inhabit the island of Puerto Rico, making it one of the most densely populated islands in the world. It has an average of about 1,000 people per square mile, a ratio higher than that within any of the 50 states. It is estimated that if the some 2 million Puerto Ricans who have migrated to the United States were to return home, the island would be so crowded that there would be virtually no room for them to live. Because of this massive migration to the mainland, more Puerto Ricans are said to live in New York City than in San Juan. There has been a reversal of this pattern in recent years, with many Puerto Ricans returning home in large part because of inadequate economic opportunity in the United States.

When the United States acquired the island in 1898, most Puerto Ricans worked in agriculture, but today, most jobs are industrial and are situated in the cities. Today one-third of the commonwealth's population is concentrated in the San Juan/Carolina/Bayamón metropolitan area.

The people of Puerto Rico represent a cultural and racial mix. When the Spanish forced the Taíno peoples into slavery, virtually the entire indigenous population was decimated, except for a few Amerindians who escaped into the remote mountains. Eventually they intermarried with the poor Spanish farmers and became known as *jíbaros*. Because of industrialization and migration to the cities, few jíbaros remain.

Besides the slaves imported from Africa to work on the plantations, other ethnic groups joined the island's racial mix. Fleeing Simón Bolívar's independence movements in South America, Spanish loyalists fled to Puerto Rico—a fiercely conservative Spanish colony during the early 1800s. French families also flocked here from both Louisiana and Haiti, as changing governments or violent revolutions turned their worlds upside down. Meanwhile, as word of the rich sugarcane economy reached economically depressed Scotland and Ireland, many farmers from those countries also journeyed to Puerto Rico in search of a better life.

During the mid-19th century, labor was needed to build roads. Initially Chinese workers were imported for this task, followed by workers from such countries as Italy, France, Germany, and even Lebanon. American expatriates came to the island after 1898. Long after Spain had lost control of Puerto Rico, Spanish immigrants continued to arrive on the island. The most significant new immigrant population arrived in the 1960s, when thousands of Cubans fled from Fidel Castro's Communist state. The latest arrivals in Puerto Rico have come from the economically depressed Dominican Republic.

THEIR LANGUAGES

Spanish, of course, is the language of Puerto Rico, although English is widely spoken, especially in hotels, restaurants, shops, and nightclubs that attract tourists. In the hinterlands, however, Spanish prevails.

If you plan to travel extensively on Puerto Rico but don't speak Spanish, pick up a Spanish-language phrasebook. The most popular is *Berlitz Spanish for Travelers,* published by Collier Macmillan. The University of Chicago's *Pocketbook Dictionary* is equally helpful. If you already have a basic knowledge of Spanish and want to improve both your word usage and your sentence structure while in Puerto Rico, consider purchasing a copy of *Spanish Now,* published by Barron's.

Many Amerindian words from pre-Columbian times have been retained in the language. For example, the Puerto Rican national anthem, entitled "La Borinqueña," refers back to the Arawak name for the island, Borinquen, while Mayagüez, Yauco, Caguas, Guaynabo, and Arecibo are all pre-Columbian place names.

Many Amerindian words were borrowed to describe the phenomena of the New World. The natives slept in *hamacas,* and today Puerto Ricans still lounge in hammocks. The god Juracán was feared by the Arawaks just as much as contemporaries fear autumn hurricanes. African words were also added to the linguistic mix, and Castilian Spanish was significantly modified.

With the American takeover in 1898, English became the first Germanic language to be introduced into Puerto Rico. This linguistic marriage led to what some scholars call Spanglish, a colloquial dialect blending English and Spanish into forms not considered classically correct in either linguistic tradition.

The bilingual confusion was also greatly accelerated by the mass migration to the U.S. mainland of thousands of Puerto Ricans, who quickly altered their speech patterns to conform to the language used in the urban Puerto Rican communities of such cities as New York.

THEIR RELIGIONS

The majority of Puerto Ricans are Roman Catholic, but religious freedom for all faiths is guaranteed by the Commonwealth Constitution. Catholic services are conducted throughout the island in both English and Spanish. There is a Jewish Community Center in Miramar, plus a Jewish Reformed Congregation in Santurce. There are English-speaking Protestant services for Baptists, Episcopalians, Lutherans, Presbyterians, and other interdenominational services.

Although predominantly Catholic, Puerto Rico does not follow Catholic dogma and rituals as assiduously as do the churches of Spain and Italy. Because the church supported slavery, there was a long-lasting resentment against the all-Spanish clergy of colonial days. Island-born men were excluded from the priesthood. When Puerto Ricans eventually took over the Catholic churches on the island, they followed some guidelines from Spain and Italy but modified or ignored others. For example, many Catholic couples in Puerto Rico practice birth control and are married outside the Catholic church.

Following the U.S. acquisition of the island in 1898, Protestantism grew in influence and popularity. There were Protestants on the island before the invasion, but their numbers increased after Puerto Rico became an American colony. Many islanders liked the idea of separation of church and state, as provided for in the U.S. Constitution. In recent years, a Pentecostal fundamentalism has swept across the island. There are perhaps some 1,500 evangelical churches in Puerto Rico today.

As throughout Latin America, the practice of Catholicism in Puerto Rico blends certain native Taíno and African traditions with mainstream tenets of the faith. It has been said that the real religion of Puerto Rico is *espiritismo* (spiritualism), a quasi-magical belief in occult forces. Spanish colonial rulers outlawed spiritualism, but under the U.S. occupation it flourished in dozens of isolated pockets of the island.

Students of religion trace spiritualism to the Taínos, and their belief that *jípia* (the spirits of the dead—somewhat like the legendary vampire) slumbered by day and prowled the island by night. Instead of looking for bodies, the jípia were seeking wild fruit to eat. Thus arose the Puerto Rican tradition of putting out fruit on the kitchen table. Even in modern homes today, you'll often find a bowl of plastic, flamboyantly colored fruit resting atop a refrigerator.

Many islanders still believe in the "evil eye," or *mal de ojo.* To look on a person or a person's possessions covetously, according to believers, can lead to that individual's sickness or perhaps death. Little children are given bead charm bracelets to guard against the evil eye. Spiritualism also extends into healing, folk medicine, and food. Some spiritualists, for example, believe that cold food should never be eaten with hot food. Various island plants, herbs, and oils are believed to have certain healing properties, and spiritualist literature is available throughout the island.

6 Puerto Rican Handcrafts

SANTOS   The most impressive of the island's crafts are the *santos,* carved religious figures that have been produced since the 1500s. Craftspeople who make these are called *santeiros;* using clay, gold, stone, or cedarwood, they carve figurines representing saints, usually from 8 to 20 inches tall. Before the Spanish colonization, small statues called *zemi* stood in native tribal villages and camps as objects of veneration, and Puerto Rico's santos may derive from that pre-Columbian tradition. Every town has its patron saint and every home has its santos to protect the family. For some families, worshipping the santos replaces a traditional mass.

Art historians view the carving of santos as Puerto Rico's greatest contribution to the plastic arts. The earliest figures were richly baroque, indicating a strong Spanish influence, but as the islanders began to assert their own identity, the carved figures often became simpler.

In carving santos, craftspeople often used handmade tools. Sometimes such natural materials as vegetable dyes and even human hair were used. The saints represented by most santos can be identified by their accompanying symbols; for example, Saint Anthony is usually depicted with the infant Jesus and a book. Perhaps the most

Impressions

A machete is the only instrument used in their work. With it, they cut the sticks, vines, and palm leaves to build their houses and also clear the ground and plant and cultivate their crops.

—Fray Inigo Abbad

popular group of santos are the Three Kings. The Trinity and the Nativity also are depicted frequently. Art experts claim that santos-making approached its zenith at the turn of the century, although hundreds of santeiros still practice their craft throughout the island.

Some of the best santos on the island can be seen at the Capilla del Cristo in Old San Juan. Perhaps at some future date a museum devoted entirely to santos will open on Puerto Rico.

OLD LACE   Another Puerto Rican craft has undergone a big revival just as it seemed that it would disappear forever. Originating in Spain, *mundillos* (tatted fabrics) are the product of a type of bobbin lacemaking. This craft, five centuries old, exists today only in Puerto Rico and Spain.

The first lace made in Puerto Rico was called *torchon* ("beggar's lace"). Early examples of beggar's lace were considered of inferior quality, but artisans today have transformed this fabric into a delicate art form, eagerly sought by collectors. Lace bands called *entrados* have two straight borders, whereas the other traditional style, *puntilla*, has both a straight and a scalloped border. The best place to see the craft of the mundillo is the Folk Arts Center at the Dominican Convent in Old San Juan. This center has information on island shops that make and sell mundillos. You can also attend the Puerto Rican Weaving Festival, held annually at the end of April in the town of Isabela.

GROTESQUE MASKS   Perhaps the most popular of all Puerto Rican crafts are the frightening *caret-as—papier-mâché* masks worn at island carnivals. Tangles of menacing horns, fang-toothed leering expressions, and bulging eyes of these half-demon, half-animal creations send children running screaming to their parents. At carnival time, they are worn by costumed revelers called *vejigantes*. Vejigantes often wear bat-winged jumpsuits and roam the streets either individually or in groups.

The origins of these masks and carnivals may go back to medieval Spain and/or tribal Africa. A processional tradition in Spain, dating from the early 17th century, was intended to terrify sinners with marching devils in the hope that they would return to church. Cervantes described it briefly in *Don Quijote*. Puerto Rico blended this Spanish procession with the masked tradition brought by slaves from Africa. Some historians believe that the Taínos also were accomplished mask makers, which would make this a very ancient tradition indeed.

The predominant mask colors, at least traditionally, were black, red, and yellow, all symbols of hellfire and damnation. Today, pastels are more likely to be used. Each vejigante sports at least two or three horns, although some masks may have hundreds of horns in all shapes and sizes. Mask making in Ponce, the major center for this craft, and in Loíza Aldea, a palm-fringed town on the island's northeastern coast, has since led to a renaissance of Puerto Rican folk art.

You can purchase these masks year-round at various places, even in the homes of the mask makers, providing that you have their addresses. Although many masks are extremely elaborate and expensive, they typically range in price from $10 to $75. The premier store selling these masks is Puerto Rican Art and Crafts, at Calle Fortaleza

204, in Old San Juan. Masks can be seen in action at the three big masquerade carnivals on the island: the Ponce Festival in February, the Festival of Loíza Aldea in July, and the Día de las Mascaras at Hatillo in December.

WHERE TO SEE THE BEST ARTS & CRAFTS

Serious students of Puerto Rican art always go to the **Institute of Puerto Rican Culture** in the Dominican Convent in Old San Juan. It's the best source of information on the island about Puerto Rican arts and crafts.

With its dozen or so museums and even more art galleries, Old San Juan is the greatest repository of Puerto Rican arts and crafts. Galleries sell everything from pre-Columbian artifacts to paintings by relatively contemporary artists such as Angel Botello, who died in 1986. The **Galleria Botello,** at Calle del Cristo 208, was his former home. He restored the colonial mansion himself; now his paintings and sculptures are on display there.

Another good place to see Puerto Rican art is the **Museum of the University of Puerto Rico** in Río Piedras. Because of space limitations, the museum's galleries can exhibit only a fifth of their vast collection at one time, but the work is always of top-notch quality. The collection ranges from pre-Columbian artifacts to works by today's major painters.

The greatest art on the island is at the **Museo de Arte de Ponce,** Avenida de las Americas, in Puerto Rico's second-largest city. The collection, donated by former governor Luís A. Ferré, ranges from Jan van Eyck's *Salvatore Mundi* to Rossetti's confrontational *Daughters of King Lear.* The museum building was designed by Edward Durell Stone, who also designed New York's Museum of Modern Art. Works are displayed here in a honeycomb of skylit hexagonal rooms. Puerto Rican artists who are represented include José Campeche and Francisco Oller (see above). In addition to such European masters as Reubens, van Dyck, and Murillo, the museum features works by Latin American artists, including some by the Mexican Diego Rivera.

7 Architecture: In with the Old

The island's architectural heritage is Spanish, of course, as seen in the narrow, winding cobblestone streets and the pastel-colored, tile-roofed buildings with ornate balconies and heavy wooden doors that open onto inner courtyards in the style of Andalusia in southern Spain. The Columbus quincentennial in 1992 sparked a major refurbishing of Puerto Rico's colonial architecture. Current restoration and renewal projects are focused in Old San Juan and in the city of Ponce.

OLD SAN JUAN

It is estimated that there are at least 400 structures of historic value in Old San Juan, including some of the finest examples of Spanish colonial architecture in the New World. Old San Juan was Spain's major center of commerce and military power in the West Indies for nearly four centuries.

Spain ordered that the city be protected by sandstone walls and massive fortresses, since the island was the first port of call for galleons entering the West Indies and the last safe harbor for treasure-laden ships making the return trip to Cádiz or Seville. Because Old San Juan had no space for expansion, new buildings had to be erected to the east of the old town, in what is known today as the modern city of San Juan. Thus, most of the old structures have survived more or less since the 16th century. Among the most notable of these are the **San Juan Cathedral** and the **Dominican Convent. Casa Blanca,** a mansion built for the island's first governor, Ponce de León, still stands.

On a walking tour of Old San Juan (see chapter 7), you will encounter an architectural mélange of buildings that range from the style popular during the Spanish Conquest to the neoclassical style of the 19th century. The most significant of all is **El Morro Fortress,** largest in the Caribbean, which has stood guard over San Juan Bay for more than four centuries. In 1973 it was declared a "World Heritage Site," putting it in the same class as Versailles, the Taj Mahal, and the Egyptian pyramids.

Dating from 1533, **La Fortaleza** is another World Heritage Site. Built to protect Spanish settlers from attack by the cannibalistic Carib tribes, it was at first a small medieval-style fortress with two round towers. In time, it became the residence of the island's governors. Still in use today, it is the official residence of the governor of Puerto Rico and the oldest executive mansion in continuous use in the New World. Built around its 16th-century core is a 19th-century facade with neoclassical motifs and a richly furnished interior.

Other outstanding examples of Spanish colonial military architecture and engineering in San Juan include the **old city walls** and the nearby **San Cristóbal fortress.**

Those who restored La Fortaleza and other landmarks in Old San Juan tried whenever possible to use original materials such as native-grown *ausubo* (ironwood) beams, which had to be salvaged from elsewhere on the island. The Puerto Rican General Archives and the Archives of the Indies in Seville (Spain) were able to provide the original plans of many late 18th- and 19th-century buildings; they were used in the restoration of many of the island's structures. The greatest challenge was to restore 16th-century buildings, for which there were no original plans. One example of this is **San José Church,** the only true Gothic building under the U.S. flag. The walls of this church had to be scraped to uncover the original 16th-century features. Buried under layers of concrete, the restorers found one of the earliest murals painted in the Americas—the work of a friar whose identity will probably never be known.

The facade of **San Juan Cathedral,** added in the early 19th century, is baroque, but it shelters a vaulted tower and four rooms dating from 1540, which are rare examples of medieval architecture in the New World. In 1913, the body of Ponce de León was moved here and is now in a marble tomb near the cathedral's transept.

The **Dominican Convent**—another Old San Juan 16th-century structure—now houses the Institute of Culture. Friars began its construction in 1523. There are tall arcaded galleries set into its two stories, a large interior patio, and a chapel that now serves as a museum.

The waterfront area of San Juan, known as the **paseo de La Princesa,** has been restored to its original 19th-century splendor as a broad esplanade graced with fountains and towering royal palms. The promenade sweeps from the cruise piers to La Princesa, a restored 19th-century prison, now the headquarters of the Puerto Rico Tourism Company. La Princesa sets a good example for future architectural restorations, with its huge mahogany doors, impressive arcades, polished floors, and elegant appointments.

PONCE

At the turn of the century, Ponce rivaled San Juan as an affluent business and cultural center. Many of its central buildings were erected between the late 1890s and the 1930s, when the city was the hub of the island's rum, sugarcane, and shipping industries and was known as La Perla del Sur, the "Pearl of the South." It was home to many artists, politicians, and poets.

The architect Ilia Sánchez Arana, who coordinated many aspects of Ponce's restoration, once said that "The city has a type of architecture found nowhere else in Puerto Rico. For example, the neoclassical style of many of the city's

Impressions

The new cultural pride can be seen increasingly in architectural restoration, environmental preservation, artistic expression, and no less than a culinary revolution.

—Patricia J. Bell, *Gourmet*, 1991

public buildings reflect the local climate and taste, incorporating balconies and facades of the local pink marble. The typical Ponce Créole architecture includes elements such as columns on the balcony, an inside balcony with a wall of small windows to let in light from the patio, and a two- or four-sided roof."

The $440 million restoration project—arguably the most extensive ever undertaken in the West Indies—includes a 66-block downtown area of 1,046 buildings ranging in style from old Spanish colonial to neoclassical, from "Ponce Créole" to art deco. When completed, visitors will be able to stroll along gaslit streets lined with period structures, as old-fashioned horse-drawn carriages clop by. Strollers will enjoy sidewalks edged with pink marble.

With funds provided by the Spanish government, the Institute of Ibero-American Cooperation designated which structures were worthy of preservation. Many of the buildings radiate outward from the stately main square, **Plaza de Las Delicias** (Plaza of Delights). Other streets with buildings of architectural interest include Cristina, Isabel, Luna, Reina, and Pabellones.

The Institute of Puerto Rican Culture restored the neoclassical **Casa Armstrong Poventud,** a mansion with caryatid columns gracing its facade. Today, the restored building houses the Ponce Tourism Information Center, the regional office of the Institute of Puerto Rican Culture, and a museum. Another major 19th-century building, **El Castillo,** originally served as the Ponce Village Infantry Quarter. It later became the Ponce Jail, but is now the Ponce School of Fine Arts.

Yet another notable building, the **Museum of Puerto Rican Music,** was restored in 1990 by the Institute of Culture. It pays tribute to the works of Puerto Rican musicians, including native-born Ruth Fernández. The museum is housed in the old Museum of Art on Cristina Street, built in the 1850s as the home of a wealthy industrialist.

The institute is also responsible for restoring **Casa Serrallés,** the former home of the oldest rum-producing family on the island, the makers of Don Q rum. It also restored **Casa Villaronga,** the former home of Alfredo Wiechers, a famous Ponce architect. Casa Villaronga exemplifies the characteristic elegance and whimsy of Ponce architecture with its trellised roof garden, stucco garlands, colored glass, and Spanish tiles.

Overlooking Ponce from its perch on El Vigía Hill is one more recently restored landmark, the **Castillo Serrallés,** another home of the rum-producing Serrallés family. This is a multilevel Spanish-style hacienda, featuring an elegant open courtyard with fountains and a splendid carved wooden ceiling in the dining room.

Plaza del Mercado, the old marketplace, has been converted to an artisans' market, replete with typical food, fruits, and flowers. Converted from an art-deco movie theater, it probably draws more sightseers and consumers than any other complex in the old town.

At **Plaza de Las Delicias,** Ponce has revived its traditional horse-drawn carriage service. Four carriages offer free rides to visitors. Standing on the square is the boldly painted, century-old **Parque de Bombas** (Firehouse), which reopened as a museum after a $140,000 restoration.

8 Puerto Rico's Exotic Bill of Fare

Although Puerto Rican cooking is somewhat similar to both Spanish and Mexican cuisine, it has a unique style, using such indigenous seasonings and ingredients as coriander, papaya, cacao, nispero, apio, plantains, and yampee.

Cocina Criolla (Créole cooking) can be traced back to the Arawaks and Taínos, the original inhabitants of the island, who thrived on a diet of corn, tropical fruit, and seafood. When Ponce de León arrived with Columbus in 1493, the Spanish added beef, pork, rice, wheat, and olive oil to the island's foodstuffs.

The Spanish soon began planting sugarcane and importing slaves from Africa, who brought with them okra and taro (known in Puerto Rico as *yautia*). The mingling of flavors and ingredients passed from generation to generation among the different ethnic groups that settled on the island, resulting in the exotic blend of today's Puerto Rican cuisine.

APPETIZERS & SOUPS

Lunch and dinner generally begin with sizzling-hot appetizers such as *bacalaítos,* crunchy cod fritters; *surullitos,* sweet plump cornmeal fingers; and *empanadillas,* crescent-shaped turnovers filled with lobster, crab, conch, or beef.

Soups also are a popular beginning for meals on Puerto Rico. There is a debate about whether one of the world's best-known soups, *frijoles negros,* is Cuban or Puerto Rican in origin. Wherever it started, black bean soup makes a savory if filling opening to a meal. Another classic soup is *sopón de pollo con arroz*—chicken soup with rice—which manages to taste somewhat different in every restaurant. One traditional method of preparing this soup calls for large pieces of pumpkin and diced potatoes or yautias (the starchy root of a large-leaved tropical plant whose flesh is usually yellow or creamy white).

The third classic soup is *sopón de pescado* (fish soup), prepared with the head and tail intact. Again, this soup varies from restaurant to restaurant and may depend on the catch of the day. Traditionally, it is made with garlic and spices plus onions and tomatoes, the flavor enhanced by a tiny dash of vinegar and a half cup of sherry. Galician broth (*caldo gallego*) is a dish imported from Spain's northwestern province of Galicia. It is prepared with salt pork, white beans, ham, and *berzas* (collard greens) or *grelos* (turnip greens), and the whole kettle is flavored with spicy chorizos (Spanish sausages).

Garbanzos (chickpeas), are often added to give flavor, body, and texture to Puerto Rican soups. One of the most authentic versions of this is *sopón de garbanzos con patas de cerdo* (chickpea soup with pig's feet). Into this kettle is added a variety of ingredients, including pumpkin, chorizos, salt pork, chile peppers, cabbage, potatoes, tomatoes, and fresh cilantro leaves.

Not really a soup, the most traditional Puerto Rican dish is *asopao,* a hearty gumbo made with either chicken or shellfish. One well-known version, consumed when the food budget runs low, is *asopao de gandules* (pigeon peas). Every Puerto Rican chef has his or her own recipe for asopao. *Asopao de pollo* (chicken asopao) takes a whole chicken, which is then flavored with spices such as oregano, garlic, and paprika, along with salt pork, cured ham, green peppers, chile peppers, onions, cilantro, olives, tomatoes, chorizos, and pimientos. For a final touch, green peas or asparagus might be added.

MAIN COURSES

The aroma that wafts from kitchens throughout Puerto Rico comes from *adobo* and *sofrito*—blends of herbs and spices that give many of the native foods their

Strange Fruit

Reading of Capt. James Cook's explorations of the South Pacific in the late 1700s, West Indian planters were intrigued by his accounts of the breadfruit tree, which grew in abundance on Tahiti. Seeing it as a source of cheap food for their slaves, they beseeched King George III to sponsor an expedition to bring the trees to the Caribbean.

In 1787, the king put Capt. William Bligh in command of H.M.S. *Bounty* and sent him to do just that. One of Bligh's lieutenants was a former shipmate named Fletcher Christian. They became the leading actors in one of the great sea yarns when Christian overpowered Bligh, took over the *Bounty,* threw the breadfruit trees into the South Pacific Ocean, and disappeared into oblivion.

Bligh survived by sailing the ship's open longboat 3,000 miles to the East Indies, where he hitched a ride back to England on a Dutch vessel. Later he was given command of another ship and sent to Tahiti to get more breadfruit. Although he succeeded on this second attempt, the whole operation went for naught when the West Indies slaves refused to eat the strange fruit of the new tree, preferring instead their old, familiar rice.

Descendants of those trees still grow in the Caribbean, and the islanders prepare the head-size fruit in a number of ways. A thick green rind covers its starchy, sweet flesh whose flavor is evocative of a sweet potato. *Tostones*—fried green breadfruit slices—accompany most meat, fish, or poultry dishes served today in Puerto Rico.

distinctive taste and color. Adobo, made by crushing together peppercorns, oregano, garlic, salt, olive oil, and lime juice or vinegar, is rubbed into meats before they are roasted. Sofrito, a potpourri of onions, garlic, and peppers browned in either olive oil or lard and colored with *achiote* (annatto seeds), imparts the bright-yellow color to the island's rice, soups, and stews.

Stews loom large in the Puerto Rican diet. They are usually cooked in a *caldera* (heavy kettle). A popular one is *carne guisada puertorriqueña* (Puerto Rican beef stew). The ingredients that flavor the chunks of beef vary according to the cook's whims or whatever happens to be in the larder. These might include green peppers, sweet chile peppers, onions, garlic, cilantro, potatoes, olives stuffed with pimientos, or capers. Seeded raisins may be added on occasion.

Meat pies (*pastelon de carne*) are the staple of many Puerto Rican dinners. Salt pork and ham are often used for the filling and are cooked in a caldero. This medley of meats and spices is covered with a pastry top and baked.

Other typical main dishes include fried beefsteak with onions (*carne frita con cebolla*), veal (*ternera*) à la parmesana, and roast leg of pork, fresh ham, lamb, or veal, à la criolla. These roasted meats are cooked in the Créole style, flavored with adobo. *Chicharrónes* is very popular especially around Christmastime—fried pork with the crunchy skin left on top for added flavor.

Puerto Ricans also like such dishes as breaded calf's brains (*sesos empanados*), calf's kidney stew (*riñones guisados*), and stuffed beef tongue (*lengua rellena*).

A festive island dish is *lechón asado,* or **barbecued pig,** which is usually cooked for a party of 12 to 15. It is traditional for picnics and alfresco parties; one can sometimes catch the aroma of this dish wafting through the palm trees, a smell that must have been familiar to the Taíno peoples. The pig is basted with *jugo de naranja agria* (sour orange juice) and achiote coloring. Green plantains are peeled and roasted over hot stones, then served with the barbecued pig as a side dish. The traditional dressing served with the pig is *aji-li-mojili,* a sour garlic sauce. The sauce combines garlic, whole black peppercorns, and sweet seeded chile peppers, flavored further with vinegar, lime juice, salt, and olive oil.

Puerto Ricans adore **chicken,** which they flavor with various spices and seasonings. *Arroz con pollo* (chicken with rice) is the most popular chicken dish on the island, and it was brought long ago to the U.S. mainland. Other favorite preparations include chicken in sherry (*pollo al Jerez*), *pollo en agridulce* (sweet-and sour chicken), and *pollitos asados à la parrilla* (broiled chickens).

Most visitors to the island prefer the fresh **fish and shellfish.** A popular dish is fried fish with Puerto Rican sauce (*mojo isleno*). The sauce is made with olives and olive oil, onions, pimientos, capers, tomato sauce, vinegar, and a flavoring of garlic and bay leaves. Fresh fish is often grilled, and perhaps flavored with garlic and an overlay of freshly squeezed lime juice—a very tasty dinner indeed. Caribbean lobster is usually the most expensive item on any menu, followed by shrimp. Puerto Ricans often cook shrimp in beer (*camarones en cerveza*). Another delectable shellfish dish is boiled crab (*jueyes hervidos*).

Many tasty **egg dishes** are served, especially *tortilla española* (Spanish omelet), cooked with finely chopped onions, cubed potatoes, and olive oil.

The rich and fertile fields of Puerto Rico produce a wide variety of **vegetables.** A favorite is the *chayote,* a pear-shaped vegetable called christophine throughout most of the English-speaking Caribbean. Its delicately flavored flesh is often compared to that of summer squash.

Fried *tostones* are made with both **breadfruit** (see box) and **plantains.** In fact, the plantain seems to be the single most popular side dish served on the island. Plantains are a variety of banana that cannot be eaten raw. They are much coarser in texture than ordinary bananas and are harvested while green, then baked, fried, or boiled. When made into tostones, they are usually served as an appetizer with before-dinner drinks. Fried to a deep golden-yellow, plantains may accompany fish, meat, or poultry dishes.

COFFEE, BEER & RUM

Finish your meal with strong, black, aromatic Puerto Rican **coffee,** which has been produced in the island's high-altitude interior for more than 300 years. Originally imported from the nearby Dominican Republic, coffee is still among the island's leading exports and is a suitable ending for any well-presented meal.

Because the island does not produce wine, it is entirely proper to order a **cold beer** before even looking at the menu. Beer, of course, is called *cerveza* throughout the Spanish-speaking world; the most popular brand on Puerto Rico is Medalla.

Rum is the national drink, and you can buy it in almost any shade. Since the island is the world's leading rum producer, it's little wonder that every Puerto Rican bartender worthy of the profession likes to concoct his or her own favorite rum libation. All resorts offer the piña colada, which is made with cream of coconut, white Puerto Rican rum, and canned pineapple juice. The ingredients are thoroughly blended and served frappé-style in a tall cool glass, usually garnished with a maraschino cherry and a small paper parasol. But you may want to be more adventurous and sample some of the island's other cocktails, many of which are made with fresh fruit juices. Planter's punch, served over cracked ice, is the second most popular mixed rum drink for tourists. Often, it combines dark Puerto Rican rum, dark-brown Jamaican rum, citrus juice, and Angostura bitters. Of course, you can substitute rum in many mixed drinks such as rum collins, rum sour, rum screwdriver, and rum and tonic. The classic sangría, which is prepared in Spain with dry red wine, sugar, orange juice, and other ingredients, may be given a thoroughly Puerto Rican twist with a hefty dose of the island's rum.

Today's version of rum bears little resemblance to the raw and grainy beverage consumed by the renegades and pirates of the Spanish Main. Christopher Columbus brought sugarcane, from which rum is distilled, to the Caribbean on his second voyage to the New World, and in virtually no time it became *the* regional drink.

It is believed that Ponce de León introduced rum to Puerto Rico during his governorship, which began in 1508. In time, there emerged large sugarcane plantations. From Puerto Rico and other West Indian islands, rum was shipped to colonial America, where it lent itself to such popular and hair-raising 18th-century drinks as Kill-Divil and Whistle-Belly Vengeance. After America became a nation, rum was largely displaced as the drink of choice by whiskey, distilled from grain grown on the American plains.

It took almost a century before the rum industry regained its former vigor. This occurred during a severe whiskey shortage at the end of World War II. By the 1950s, sales of rum had fallen off again, as more and different kinds of liquor became available on the U.S. market. Rum had been a questionable drink because of inferior distillation methods and quality. Recognizing this problem, the Puerto Rican government drew up rigid standards for producing, blending, and aging rum. Rum factories were outfitted with the most modern and sanitary equipment, and sales figures (encouraged by aggressive marketing campaigns) began to climb.

The color of rum is usually gold, amber, or white. The lightest, driest rum is white. It can easily replace gin or vodka in dozens of mixed drinks that are eminently suited for consumption in the tropics. Many Puerto Ricans make Bloody Marys with rum instead of gin or vodka. The robust flavors of the gold or amber rums make them an effective substitute for whiskey. With white (clear) rum, orange juice and tonic water are the most popular mixers; amber rum is often served on the rocks. Puerto Ricans are fond of mixing it with various cola drinks. Gold rums, aged between 4 and 6 years (sometimes longer) in wooden casks are called *añejos*. They are considered the most flavorful and distinctive of the island rums. They are smooth; drink them straight or on the rocks.

Bacardi is the Puerto Rican rum most widely consumed in the United States. It is followed by other popular brands, including Ronrico, Castillo, and Don Q. The añejos rums carry such labels as Bacardi Gold Reserve, Ron del Barrilito, and Serralles's El Dorado.

Your best introduction to Puerto Rican rum making is to visit the Bacardi distillery in Cataño, just a short ferryboat ride across the San Juan harbor.

9 Salsa & Bomba: Dancing to the Beat

One of Puerto Rico's notable exports is its music, which along with that of Jamaica is the predominant Caribbean music heard in the United States. Few if any American ears haven't been exposed to the vibrant Latin beats of the salsa, the bomba, and the plena.

At least some of these unique sounds come from instruments that originated with the Taíno peoples. Most noteworthy is the *güícharo*, or *güiro*, a notched, hollowed-out gourd, which was adapted from pre-Columbian days. The musical traditions of the Spanish and Africans can also be heard in Puerto Rico's music. At least four different instruments were adapted from the six-string Spanish classical guitar: the *requinto*, the *bordonua*, the *cuatro*, and the *tiple*, each of which produces a unique tone and pitch. The most popular of these, and the one for which the greatest number of adaptations and compositions have been written, is the cuatro, a guitarlike instrument with 10 strings (arranged in five different pairs). Usually carved from solid blocks of laurel wood and known for resonances and pitches different from those produced by its Spanish counterpart, this instrument's graceful baroque body has been revered for decades as the national instrument of Puerto Rico.

Also prevalent on the island are such percussion instruments as *tambours* (hollowed tree trunks covered with stretched-out animal skin), *maracas* (gourds filled with pebbles or dried beans and mounted on handles), and a variety of drums whose original designs were brought from Africa by the island's slaves. All these instruments contribute to the rich variety of folk music with roots in the cultural melting pot of the island's Spanish, African, and Taíno traditions.

PUERTO RICAN FOLK MUSIC

During Puerto Rico's colonial years, a series of musical traditions evolved that were based on the folk songs and romantic ballads of 18th- and 19th-century Spain. Eventually these became fused with music either imported or native to the Hispanic New World. Dealing with life, death, and everyday events of an agrarian society far removed from the royal courts of Europe, this music has been studiously collected and reorchestrated for modern audiences.

One collector of this music was Don Felo, whose 19th-century compositions were based on the melodic traditions of both Spain and the Spanish-speaking Caribbean. In the 20th century, Narciso Figueroa continued the tradition of collecting folk songs and reorchestrating them for chamber orchestras; his recordings have been sponsored by the Institute of Puerto Rican Culture.

Today, the most widely applauded—and, to many, most enjoyable—of the island's folk music are the hillbilly pieces created by the mountain-dwelling *jíbaros*. Using the full array of stringed and percussion instruments described above, they give lyrical performances whose live or recorded versions are popular at everything from island weddings to commencement exercises. Despite the appeal of other island musical forms, such as salsa, it could be argued that the *jíbaro* tradition of cuatro with drums is the island's most notable—and the one most likely to evoke homesickness in the hearts of any expatriate Puerto Rican.

BOMBA & PLENA

Although usually grouped together, *bomba y plena* are actually two entirely different types of music that are coupled with dance. Pure African, **bomba** was brought over by black slaves who worked on the island's sugar plantations. It's a rhythmic music using barrel-shaped drums covered with tightly stretched animal skins and played by hand. This form of music is produced by one large drum plus a smaller drum called a *subidor*. The drums are accompanied by the rhythmical beating of sticks and maracas to create a swelling tide of drumbeats, in which aficionados can hear the drummers bang out a series of responses one to another.

Bomba is described as a dialogue between dancer and drummer. It's as if the drummer were challenging the dancer to a rhythmic duel. The dance can go on just as long as the dancer can continue. Although critics are uncertain about the exact origins of bomba, it is divided into different rhythmic backgrounds and variations, such as the Euba, Cocobale, and Sica. As the dance and the drummer's beat continue, the music grows more spirited and more complex. The best bomba, and the most purely African version of this music and dance, may come from the northeastern coast town of Loíza Aldea.

Whereas bomba is purely African in origin, **plena** blends elements from Puerto Ricans' wide cultural backgrounds, including music that the Taíno tribes may have used during their ceremonies. This type of music first appeared in Ponce, where performing the plena became a hallmark of Spanish tradition and coquetry.

Instruments used in plena include the güiro, a dried-out gourd whose surface is cut with parallel grooves and, when rubbed with a stick, produces a raspy and rhythmical percussive noise. The Taínos may have invented this instrument. From the guitars brought to the New World by the Spanish conquistadores emerged the 10-stringed cuatro. To the güiro and cuatro is added the tambourine, known as *panderos,* originally derived from Africa. Dancing plena became a kind of living newspaper. Singers recited the events of the day and often satirized local politicians or scandals. Sometimes plenas were filled with biting satire; at other times, they commented on major news events of the day, such as a devastating hurricane.

Bomba y plena remain the most popular forms of folk music on the island, and many cultural events highlight this music for entertainment. In a somewhat commercialized form, bomba y plena shows are often presented at resort hotels along San Juan's Condado beachfront strip.

SALSA

The major type of music coming out of Puerto Rico is salsa, *the* rhythm of the islands. Its name literally translates as the "sauce" that makes parties happen. Originally developed within the Puerto Rican community of New York, it draws heavily from the musical roots of the Cuban and the African-Caribbean experience. Highly danceable, its rhythms are hot, urban, rhythmically sophisticated, and compelling. Today, the center of salsa has probably shifted from New York back to Puerto Rico, where local musicians compete fiercely with those from Cuba for the most infectious melodies.

Cuban salsa tends to be less avant-garde than the constantly mutating versions produced in Puerto Rico. Even within the salsa tradition, different groups adhere more or less fervently to the traditions of mainstream jazz, popular Latin song, and African inspirations.

Salsa is not an old form of music at all. Music critics claim that it originated in New York City nightclubs in the years following World War II, an evolution of the era's Big Band tradition. The first great salsa musician was Tito Puente, who, after a stint with the U.S. Navy, studied percussion at New York's Juilliard School of Music. He went on to organize his own band, Puente's Latin Jazz Ensemble, which has been heard by audiences around the world. One critic said that the music is what results when the sounds of Big Band jazz meet African-Caribbean rhythms. Other critics say that salsa is a combination of fast Latin music that embraces the rumba, mambo, cha-cha, guaguancho, and merengue.

Salsa has definitely made Puerto Rico famous in the world of international music. Salsa bands require access to a huge array of percussion instruments, including güiros, the gourds on which the Taíno peoples may have played music. Other instruments include maracas, bongos, timbales, conga drums, and claves—and to add the *jíbaro* (hillbilly) touch, a clanging cowbell. Of course, it also takes a bass, a horn section, a chorus, and a lead vocalist to get the combination right.

No one quite agrees about who is the king of salsa today, but Willie Colón, El Gran Combo de Puerto Rico, and Hector Lovoe are on everyone's list as the "Grand Masters of today's salsa beat." Hundreds of young *salseros* are waiting to take their thrones as the popularity (and income levels) of the emerging salsa stars continues to climb.

3

Planning a Trip to Puerto Rico

This chapter discusses the where, the when, and the how of your trip to Puerto Rico—everything required to plan your trip and get it on the road. Here we've concentrated on what you need to do *before* you go.

In addition to helping you decide when to take your vacation, we've put a wealth of insider information at your fingertips. This chapter also explores different possibilities for getting to Puerto Rico, including not only the most obvious ones but also some that may not have crossed your mind. We also discuss various ways to travel around the island and suggest an itinerary to help you get the most out of a week's vacation. You'll find tips on deciding where to stay, where to eat, and what to buy. Capping off the chapter is a quick-reference list of helpful "Fast Facts" about Puerto Rico.

1 Visitor Information, Entry Requirements & Money

The **LeLoLai VIP Program** gives visitors the opportunity to experience Puerto Rico's unique culture and its Spanish, Amerindian, and African heritage at substantial savings. Included are free performances of song and dance at various San Juan hotels, and discounted sightseeing tours of Old San Juan, Ponce, Rio Camuy Cave Park, El Yunque rain forest, and Luquillo Beach. Savings on folkloric shows and sightseeing tours add up to more than $250, not to mention discounts at shops, restaurants, and sporting activities throughout the island. For information and reservations, call **787/723-3135** or 787/723-3132.

VISITOR INFORMATION

For information before you leave home, contact one of the following **Puerto Rico Tourism Company** offices: 575 Fifth Ave., New York, NY 10017 (☎ **212/599-6262** or 800/223-6530); 200 SE 1st St., Suite 700, Miami, FL 33131 (☎ **305/381-8915**); or 3575 W. Cahuenga Blvd., Suite 560, Los Angeles, CA 90068 (☎ **213/874-5991**).

If you have Internet access, one great travel resource on the Web is **City.Net** (http://www.city.net). City.Net itself does not provide any information on destinations, but it lists links, organized by location and then by subject, to sites that do. Puerto Rico is located under the "USA" heading. Another worthwhile site is **"My Puerto Rico Homepage"** (http://gwis2.circ.gwu.edu/~jacobino/puerto-rico.html). It, too serves as a hotlist to other sites with Puerto Rico content, plus links you to individual homepages that include Puerto Rico in some way.

You may also want to contact the U.S. State Department for background bulletins. Write the Superintendent of Documents, **U.S. Government Printing Office,** Washington, DC 20402 (☎ **202/512-1800**).

A good travel agent can be a source of information. Make sure your agent is a member of the American Society of Travel Agents (ASTA). If you get poor service from an ASTA agent, you can then write to the **ASTA Consumer Affairs Department,** 1101 King St., Alexandria, VA 22314 (☎ **703/739-2782**).

ENTRY REQUIREMENTS

DOCUMENTS   Americans who fly from the mainland to Puerto Rico and return to the mainland don't need passports, as Puerto Rico is a territory of the United States. If they visit no other country from a land base in Puerto Rico, they are asked if they are U.S. citizens upon flying back to the mainland. A simple "yes" will do. In other words, they don't have to prove citizenship or produce documents.

Canadians, however, should carry some form of identification. Acceptable documents include an ongoing or return ticket, plus a current voter registration card or a birth certificate. In addition, you will need some photo ID, which could be a driver's license or an expired passport. Driver's licenses alone are not acceptable as ID. Visitors from the United Kingdom, New Zealand, and most western European nations need only a valid passport so long as they plan to stay in Puerto Rico 90 days or less. Citizens of Australia need both passports and visas to enter Puerto Rico.

Before leaving home, make two copies of your most valuable documents, including your passport, your driver's license, or any other identity document; your airline ticket; and any hotel vouchers. If you're on medication, you should also make copies of prescriptions.

VACCINATIONS   Vaccinations are not required for entry to Puerto Rico if you're coming from the United States or Canada.

Infectious hepatitis has been reported on other Caribbean islands but less frequently on Puerto Rico. Consult your doctor about the advisability of getting a gamma-globulin shot before you leave home.

Typhoid, poliomyelitis, and tetanus are not common diseases on the island, and inoculations against them are recommended mainly to visitors who plan to "rough it" in the wilds. If you're staying in a regular Puerto Rican hotel, such preventive measures are generally not needed, but your doctor can advise you, based on your destination and travel plans.

CUSTOMS   U.S. citizens do not need to clear Puerto Rican Customs upon arrival by plane or ship from the mainland. All non-U.S. citizens must clear Customs and are permitted to bring in items intended for their personal use, including tobacco, cameras, film, and a limited supply of liquor (usually 40 oz.).

On departure, U.S.-bound travelers must have their luggage inspected by the U.S. Agriculture Department, as laws prohibit bringing certain fruits and plants to the U.S. mainland.

MONEY

CURRENCY   The U.S. dollar is the coin of the realm. All major U.S. banks have branches in San Juan, which are open Monday through Friday from 8:30am to

The British Pound & the U.S. Dollar

The U.S. dollar is the only currency accepted on Puerto Rico. If you're a British traveler, your pounds sterling should be converted into dollars. Since the exchange rate will fluctuate during the course of this edition, the following chart (based on £1 = $1.60 U.S.) should be used only as a guideline.

U.S.$	U.K.£	U.S.$	U.K.£
0.25	0.16	15	9.38
0.50	0.31	20	12.50
0.75	0.47	25	15.63
1.00	0.63	50	31.25
2.00	1.25	75	46.88
3.00	1.88	100	62.50
4.00	2.50	150	93.75
5.00	3.13	200	125.00
6.00	3.75	250	156.25
7.00	4.38	300	187.50
8.00	5.00	350	218.75
9.00	5.63	400	250.00
10.00	6.25	500	312.50

2:30pm. Canadian currency is accepted by some big hotels in San Juan, although reluctantly. Foreigners, including visitors from the United Kingdom, should convert their currency into U.S. dollars in their homeland, since changing foreign currency in Puerto Rico is rather difficult.

CURRENCY EXCHANGE   Most banks will provide this service. You can also exchange money at the Luis Muñoz Marín International Airport. In Old San Juan, go to Caribbean Foreign Exchange, Calle Tetuan 201B (☎ **787/722-8222**). Hours are Monday through Friday from 9am to 4:30pm and Saturday noon to 4pm.

TRAVELER'S CHECKS   Although it's now perfectly easy to find ATM machines and get cash as you would at home, some travelers still like the security of carrying traveler's checks so they can get a refund in the event of theft.

Most large banks sell traveler's checks, charging fees that average between 1% and 2% of the value of the checks you buy, although some out-of-the-way banks, in rare instances, have charged as much as 7%. If your bank wants more than a 2% commission, it may pay to call the traveler's check issuers directly for the address of outlets where this commission will be less. The American Automobile Association (AAA) does not charge its members a fee for traveler's checks.

American Express (☎ **800/221-7282** in the U.S. and Canada) is one of the largest and most immediately recognized issuers of traveler's checks. No commission is charged to members of the American Automobile Association or to those who hold certain types of American Express cards. For questions or problems that arise outside the United States and Canada, contact any of the company's many regional representatives.

Other major issuers of traveler's checks include **Citicorp** (☎ **800/645-6556** in the U.S. and Canada, or collect 813/623-1709 from anywhere else in the world);

Thomas Cook (☎ **800/223-7373** in the U.S. or Canada, or collect 609/987-7300 from other parts of the world), which issues MasterCard traveler's checks; and **Interpayment Services** (☎ **800/221-2426** in the U.S. and Canada, or collect 212/858-8500 from other parts of the world), which sells VISA checks sponsored by Barclays Bank and/or Bank of America at selected branches in North America.

ATM NETWORKS   Plus, Cirrus, and other networks connecting automated-teller machines operate in Puerto Rico. For locations of Cirrus abroad, call **800/424-7787**. For Plus locations abroad, call **800/843-7587**.

If your credit card has been programmed with a personal identification number (PIN), it is likely that you can use your card at Puerto Rican ATMs to withdraw money as a cash advance on your credit card. This is possible in such places as San Juan; however, don't count on this service being available in one of the remote villages. There, you must take enough cash or traveler's checks to cover your needs.

Before going, check to see if your PIN must be reprogrammed for usage in Puerto Rico.

MONEYGRAM   Running out of funds while on the road can be one of the worst experiences in the world of travel. Assuming you have friends or relatives who will advance you the money, a burgeoning, fast-growing new service sponsored by American Express might be able to help you out of your jam. **MONEYGRAM,** 6200 S. Quebec St., P.O. Box 5118, Englewood, CO 80155-5118 (☎ **800/926-9400**), can transfer funds from one individual to another in less than 10 minutes between any of thousands of locations throughout the world. An American Express phone representative will give you the names of four or five offices near you;

What Things Cost in Puerto Rico	U.S. $
Taxi from the airport to Condado	13.00
Average taxi fare within San Juan	11.50
Typical bus fare	.25
Local telephone call	.10
Double room at the Caribe Hilton (very expensive)	330.00
Double room at El Canario by the Lagoon (moderate)	100.00
Double room at At Windchimes Inn (inexpensive)	60.00
Lunch for one at Amadeus (moderate)	15.00
Lunch for one at La Bombonera (inexpensive)	10.00
Dinner for one at Ramiro's (very expensive)	45.00
Dinner for one at El Patio de Sam (moderate)	28.00
Dinner for one at Oasis (inexpensive)	18.00
Draft beer in a bar	2.50
Coca-Cola in a cafe	1.75
Glass of wine in a restaurant	2.50
Roll of ASA 100 color film, 36 exposures	7.25
Admission to Castillo San Felipe del Morro	Free
Movie ticket	5.00
Theater ticket	15.00–20.00

locations within the United States are as diverse as a local pharmacy or convenience store in many small communities. The sender fills out a form and pays the designated amount with cash or a credit card. AMEX service charges are $10 for the first $300 sent, with a sliding scale of commissions after that. Sending $5,000 costs about $200 worth of fees. Included in the transfer are a 10-word telex-style message and a 3-minute phone call to the recipient. Naturally, the beneficiary must present photo I.D., and in some cases, a security code established by provider of the funds. This program, although not in effect throughout the Caribbean, operates in Puerto Rico.

CREDIT CARDS　Credit cards are widely used in Puerto Rico. VISA and MasterCard are the major cards, although American Express and to a lesser extent, Diners Club, are also popular. We've noted which cards are accepted at every hotel and restaurant we've reviewed in this book.

2　When to Go

CLIMATE

Puerto Rico has one of the most unvarying climates in the world. Temperatures year-round range from 75°F to 85°F. The island is wettest and hottest in August, averaging 81°F and 7 inches of rain. San Juan and the northern coast seem to be cooler and wetter than Ponce and the southern coast. The coldest weather is in the high altitudes of the Cordillera. Puerto Rico's lowest temperature (39°F) was recorded there.

THE HURRICANE SEASON

The curse of Puerto Rican weather, the hurricane season lasts—officially, at least—from June 1 to November 30. But there's no cause for panic. In general, satellite forecasts give adequate warnings so that precautions can be taken.

If you're heading for Puerto Rico during the hurricane season, you can call your local branch of the National Weather Service (listed in your phone directory under the U.S. Department of Commerce) for a weather forecast.

You can also obtain current weather information by calling WeatherTrak; for the telephone number for your chosen destination, dial 900/370-8725. A taped message will give you the three-digit access code for the place you're interested in. The call costs 75¢ for the first minute and 50¢ for each additional minute.

And don't forget the Weather Channel, if you have it on your local cable TV system.

Average Temperatures on Puerto Rico

	Jan	Feb	Mar	Apr	May	June	July	Aug	Sept	Oct	Nov	Dec
Temp. (°F)	75	75	76	78	79	81	81	81	81	81	79	77

THE "SEASON"

In Puerto Rico the high season runs roughly from mid-December to mid-April. Hotels charge their highest prices during this peak winter period, when visitors fleeing from cold north winds flock to the islands. Winter is generally the driest season but can be a wet period in mountainous areas.

If you plan to travel in the winter, make reservations 2 to 3 months in advance. At certain hotels it's almost impossible to book accommodations for Christmas and the month of February.

SAVING MONEY IN THE OFF-SEASON

Puerto Rico is a year-round destination. The island's "off-season" runs from late spring to late fall, and temperatures in the mid-80s prevail throughout most of the region. Trade winds assure comfortable days and nights, even in accommodations without air-conditioning. Although the noonday sun may raise the temperature to around 90°F, cool breezes usually make the morning, late afternoon, and evening more comfortable than in many parts of the U.S. mainland.

Dollar for dollar, you'll spend less money by renting a summer house or fully equipped unit in Puerto Rico than you would on Cape Cod, Fire Island, Laguna Beach, or the coast of Maine.

The off-season in Puerto Rico—roughly from mid-April to mid-December (rate schedules vary from hotel to hotel)—amounts to a summer sale. In most cases, hotel rates are slashed a startling 20% to 60%. It's a bonanza for cost-conscious travelers, especially families who like to go on vacations together. In the chapters ahead, I'll spell out in dollars the specific amounts hotels charge during the off-season.

OTHER OFF-SEASON ADVANTAGES

Although Puerto Rico may appear inviting in the winter to those who live in northern climates, there are many reasons why your trip may be much more enjoyable if you go in the off-season.

- After the winter hordes have left, a less-hurried way of life prevails. You'll have a better chance to appreciate the food, culture, and local customs.
- Swimming pools and beaches are less crowded—perhaps not crowded at all.
- Year-round resort facilities are offered, often at reduced rates, that may include snorkeling, boating, and scuba diving.
- To survive, resort boutiques often feature summer sales, hoping to clear the merchandise they didn't sell in February to accommodate stock they've ordered for the coming winter.
- You can often appear without a reservation at a top restaurant and get a table for dinner, a table that in winter would have required a reservation far in advance. Also, when waiters are less hurried, you'll get better service.
- The endless waiting game is over in the off-season: no waiting for a rented car (only to be told none is available), no long wait for a golf course tee-time, and quicker access to tennis courts and water sports.
- The atmosphere is more cosmopolitan in the off-season than it is in winter, mainly because of the influx of Europeans. You'll no longer feel as if you're at a Canadian or American outpost. Also, since the Puerto Ricans themselves travel in the off-season, your holiday will become more of a multicultural experience.
- Some package-tour fares are as much as 20% lower, and individual excursion fares are also reduced between 5% and 10%.
- All accommodations and flights are much easier to book.
- Summer is an excellent time for family travel, not usually possible during the winter season.
- Finally, the very best of Puerto Rican attractions remain undiminished in the off-season—sea, sand, and surf, with lots of sunshine.

HOLIDAYS

Puerto Rico has many public holidays when stores, offices, and schools are closed: New Year's Day, January 6 (Three Kings Day), Washington's Birthday, Good Friday, Memorial Day, July 4, Labor Day, Thanksgiving, Veterans' Day, and

Christmas, plus such local holidays as Constitution Day (July 25), and Discovery Day (November 19). Remember, U.S. federal holidays are holidays in Puerto Rico, too.

PUERTO RICO CALENDAR OF EVENTS

January

- **Three Kings Day,** islandwide. On this traditional gift-giving day in Puerto Rico there are festivals with lively music, dancing, parades, puppet shows, caroling troubadours, and traditional feasts. January 6.
- **De Hostos Day,** islandwide. Celebration honoring Eugenio María de Hostos (1839–1903), a Puerto Rican educator, writer, and patriot. January 9.

February

- **San Blas de Illescas Marathon,** Coamo. International and local runners compete in a challenging 13.1-mile half-marathon in the hilly south-central town of Coamo. First week of February. For more information, call Delta Phi Delta Fraternity (☎ **787/825-2775** or 787/825-4077).
- **Cristóbal L. Sánchez Carnival,** Arroyo (southeast coast). Costumes, floats, calypso, and popular music. High points include the naming of a Carnival queen, a parade, and the traditional "burial of the sardine." Daytime and evening activities. February 16–19. For more information, call **787/839-3835.**
- **Coffee Harvest Festival,** Maricao. This festival features folk music, a parade of floats, typical foods, crafts, and demonstrations of coffee preparation. It takes place in Maricao, a 1-hour drive east of Mayagüez in the center of one of the island's coffee-growing districts. February 16–19. For more information, call **787/ 838-2290.**
- **Carnival Ponce.** The island's Carnival celebrations feature float parades, dancing, and street parties. One of the most vibrant festivities is held in Ponce, known for its masqueraders wearing brightly painted horned masks. Live music includes the folk rhythms of the *plena,* which originated in Africa. Festivities include the crowning of a Carnival queen and the closing "burial of the sardine." February 14–20. For more information, call **787/840-4141.**
- **Coffee Harvest Festival,** Yauco. Music, crafts, foods, coffee, and demonstrations of coffee preparation. Events take place in the main square of this southwestern town in the heart of the island's coffee-growing region. For more information, call Aurora Gómez at **787/856-1345.**

March

- **Feria Dulce Sueño,** Guayama. A 2-day competition held in the southern city of Guayama features Puerto Rico's finest Paso Fino steeds, the island's own breed of smooth-gaited horses. March 1–3. For more information, call Juan E. Villanueva (☎ **787/834-1988**).
- **Regional Crafts Fair,** Ponce. The largest artisans' fair on the south coast, this event features folkloric shows, typical Puerto Rican food, and a children's troubadour (folk music) contest. March 22–24. For more information, contact Iris Torres, Institute of Puerto Rican Culture (☎ **787/844-2540** or 787/843-2300).
- **Emancipation Day,** islandwide. Commemoration of the emancipation of Puerto Rico's slaves in 1873, held at various venues. March 22.
- **Good Friday and Easter,** islandwide. Celebrated with colorful ceremonies and processions. Date varies.

April

- **José de Diego Day,** islandwide. Commemoration of the birthday of José de Diego, a patriot, lawyer, writer, orator, and political leader who was the first president of the Puerto Rico House of Representatives under U.S. rule. April 17.
- **Maví Festival,** at the town plaza in Juana Díaz. Traditional carnival in this southern coastal town honors *maví* (pronounced mah-*vee*), a fermented drink made from the bark of the ironwood tree (*Colubrina reclinata*). Daytime and evening festivities, parade, floats, costumes, live music, typical food, plenty of *maví,* and a carnival queen contest. For more information, contact Elenia Acosta (☎ 787/ 837-2185, ext. 2201).
- **Sugar Harvest Festival,** in the western town of San Germán. Festival marks the end of the island's sugar harvest, with live music, crafts, and typical foods, as well as exhibitions of sugarcane plants and past and present harvesting techniques. For more information, contact Luís Cruz (☎ 787/892-5574). Late April.

May

- **Virgin del Pozo Marathon,** in the southwestern town of Sabana Grande. The annual 13.1-mile half-marathon starts in front of the sanctuary of the Virgin del Rosario. Mid-May. For more information, contact José Valentín (☎ 787/ 873-2093).
- **Danza Week,** Ponce. A week of historical and cultural events commemorating the *danza,* the popular turn-of-the-century ballroom dance. Developed in Ponce, it is slightly similar to the waltz. Conferences, *danza* concerts by string quartets, a parade, a *danza* competition, and demonstrations by senior couples who danced *danza* in their youth in period dress. The main event is a concert by the Ponce Municipal Band on the last day at La Perla Theater. May 13–17. For more information, call **787/284-4141.**

June

- **San Juan Bautista Day.** Puerto Rico's capital and other cities celebrate the island's patron saint with week-long festivities. At midnight, Sanjuaneros walk backward into the sea (or nearest body of water) three times to renew good luck for the coming year. June 21.
- **Aibonito Flower Festival,** at Road 722 next to the City Hall Coliseum, in the central mountain town of Aibonito. This annual flower competition festival features acres of lilies, anthuriums, carnations, roses, gardenias, and begonias. June 28– July 7. For more information, call **787/735-3871.**

July

- **Barranquitas Artisans' Fair.** The island's oldest crafts fair marks its 32nd year in 1996 with craft exhibitions by more than 130 artisans from around Puerto Rico; also features traditional music and food. For more information, call Orlando Torres at **787/857-0520.**
- **Luis Muñoz Rivera's Birthday,** islandwide. A birthday celebration commemorating Luis Muñoz Rivera (1829–1916), statesman, journalist, poet, and resident commissioner in Washington, D.C. July 17.
- **Vieques Patron Saint Festival,** on the eastern coast island of Vieques. The festival is a favorite of residents on the Puerto Rican "mainland," who often stay at inns and beach houses, or camp out that weekend in Vieques, an island with a population of 8,000. July 15–25. For more information, call **787/741-5000.**
- **Loíza Carnival.** An annual folk and religious ceremony honoring St. James the Apostle. Colorful processions take place, with costumes, masks, and bomba

dancers. A jubilant celebration reflecting the African and Spanish heritage of the northeastern town of Loíza. July 24–August 4.

September

- **Fishing Tournament,** at Boca de Cangrejos Marina, between Isla Verde and Piñones in the northeast coastal city of Carolina. Early August. For more information about this deep-sea fishing event, contact Humberto Donato (☎ 787/ 781-8105).

September

- **International Light Tackle Tournament,** a blue marlin fishing competition off the southwestern coastal town of Cabo Rojo. It's sponsored by the three west coast deep-sea fishing clubs: Club Náutico de Boquerón, Club Náutico de Rincón, and Club Deportivo del Oeste. Late September to early October. For more information, contact Marta T. Guzmán (☎ 787/851-8880).

October

- **La Raza Day (Columbus Day),** islandwide. Commemoration of Columbus's landing in the New World. October 12.
- ✪ **National Plantain Festival,** in the northern town of Corozal. Annual festivity with crafts, paintings, agricultural products, exhibition, and sale of plantain dishes; *nueva trova* music and folk ballet are performed. Late October.

November

- **Puerto Rican Day of Bomba and Plena**, in Ponce. Festivities celebrate two local rhythms and dances, the bomba and plena, which are still popular today. Groups from all over the island present their repertoires. A colorful parade, handcraft exhibits, and typical food. Dates vary. For more information, call **787/284-4141,** ext. 430.
- **Puerto Rico Discovery Day.** This commemorates the "discovery" by Columbus of the already inhabited island of Puerto Rico in 1493. He is thought to have come ashore at the northwestern municipality of Aguadilla, although the exact location is unknown. November 19.
- **Jayuya Indian Festival,** at Jayuya. This fiesta features the culture and tradition of the island's original inhabitants, the Taíno Indians and their music, food, and games. More than 100 artisans exhibit and sell their works. There is also a Miss Taíno Indian Pageant, where contestants are judged by their features and garments which are designed to evoke—both in style and materials—the typical dress of a Taíno woman. November 21–23. For more information, call **787/828-5010.**

December

- **Las Mañanitas,** Ponce. A religious procession starts out from Lolita Tizol Street toward the city's Catholic church, led by *mariachis* singing songs to honor Our Lady of Guadeloupe, the city's patron saint. The lead song is the traditional Mexican birthday song, *Las Mañanitas.* There's a 6am mass. December 12. For more information, contact the Ponce City Hall (☎ 787/284-4141).
- **Hatillo Masks Festival,** at this northwestern coastal town of Hatillo. A tradition celebrated since 1823 represents the Biblical story of King Herod's ordering the death of all infant boys in an attempt to kill the baby Jesus. Men with colorful masks and costumes represent the soldiers, who run or ride through the town from early morning looking for the children. Food, music, and crafts exhibits in the town square. December 28. For more information, call **787/898-3835.**

SAN JUAN CALENDAR OF EVENTS

January

- **San Sebastián Street Festival,** Calle San Sebastián in Old San Juan. Nightly cel-ebrations with music, processions, crafts, and typical foods, as well as graphic arts and handcraft exhibitions. January 19–21. For more information, call **787/724-7171.**

February

- **Opera: Gala Concert "An Evening of Zarzuela."** Arias, duets, and choruses offered by Spanish *zarzuela* singers, sponsored by the Fundación de la Opereta y Zarzuela, at the Luis A. Ferré Performing Arts Centre in San Juan. For more information, call **787/724-4747.**

May

- **Artisan Mothers' Day.** Fifty or more artisans from all over the island participate with their children, showing and selling their crafts at the Plaza de la Dársena and Paseo de la Princesa in Old San Juan. May 5. For more information, call Raquel Tirado or Carmen Vargas (☎ **787/721-2891** or 787/723-0692).

June

- ✪ **Casals Festival.** Sanjuaneros and visitors alike eagerly look forward to the annual Casals Festival, the Caribbean's most celebrated cultural event. The bill at San Juan's Performing Arts Center includes a glittering array of international guest conductors, orchestras, and soloists. They come to honor the memory of Pablo Casals, the renowned cellist who was born in Spain to a Puerto Rican mother. When Casals died in Puerto Rico in 1973 at the age of 97, the Casals Festival was 16 years old and attracting the same class of performers who appeared at the Pablo Casals Festival he founded in France after World War II. When he moved to Puerto Rico in 1957 with his wife, Marta Casals Istomin (past artistic director of the John F. Kennedy Center for the Performing Arts), he founded not only this festival but also the Puerto Rico Symphony Orchestra to foster musical develop-ment on the island.

    Where: Performing Arts Center in San Juan. **When:** Usually the second and third weeks in June (the dates vary). **How:** Ticket prices for the Casals Festival range from $20 to $40. A 50% discount is offered to students, senior citizens, and the disabled. Tickets are available through the Performing Arts Center in San Juan (☎ **787/721-7727**). Information is also available from the Puerto Rico Tourism Company, 575 Fifth Ave., New York, NY 10017 (☎ **212/599-6262** or 800/223-6530).

August

- **International Billfish Tournament,** at Club Náutico. This is one of the premier game-fishing tournaments and the longest consecutively held billfish tournament in the world. Fishers from many countries angle for blue marlin that can weigh up to 900 pounds. Late August to early September.

September

- **Inter-American Festival of the Arts,** at the Performing Arts Center. A 3-week series of musical art performances that includes classical, popular, and folk music; ballet and modern dance productions; and musical theater. September 20–October 10. Call **787/721-7727** for more information.

November

- **Start of Baseball Season,** in Hiram Bithorn Park in San Juan and throughout the island. Six Puerto Rican professional clubs compete. Professionals from North America also play here through February. Usually November 2, lasting until February.
- **Festival of Puerto Rican Music.** Annual classical and folk music festival. One of its highlights is a cuatro-playing contest. Early November. For more information, call **787/721-7727.**

December

- **Puerto Rico International Offshore Cup,** in San Juan Bay. First of its kind on the island, this competition matches local speedboat racing teams with some of the best offshore teams from the United States and the Caribbean. Early December. For more information, call Pepe Llama, the Puerto Rico offshore Association (☎ **787/753-7715**).
- **Bacardi Artisans' Fair.** The best and largest artisans' fair on the island is held the first two Sundays in December, when more than 100 artisans turn out to exhibit and sell their wares. The fair includes shows for both adults and children, a Puerto Rican troubadour contest, rides, typical food and drink—all sold by nonprofit organizations. On the grounds of the world's largest rum-manufacturing plant, in early Cataño. For more information, call **787/788-1500.**
- **Old San Juan's White Christmas Festival,** Old San Juan. Special musical and artistic presentations take place in stores, with window displays. December 1–January 12.
- **Lighting of the Town of Bethlehem,** between San Cristóbal Fort and Plaza San Juan Bautista in Old San Juan. During the Christmas season.

YEAR-ROUND FESTIVALS

In addition to the individual events described above, Puerto Rico has two year-long series of special events.

Many of Puerto Rico's most popular events are during the **Patron Saint Festivals** (*fiestas patronales*) in honor of the patron saint of each municipality. The festivities, held in each town's central plaza, include religious and costumed processions, games, local food, music, and dance.

At **Festival La Casita** prominent Puerto Rican musicians, dance troupes, and orchestras perform; puppet shows are staged; and painters and sculptors display their works. It's on every Saturday at Puerto Rico Tourism's "La Casita" Tourism Information Center, Plaza Darsenas, across from Pier 1, Old San Juan.

For more information about all these events, contact the **Puerto Rico Tourism Company,** 575 Fifth Ave., New York, NY 10017 (☎ **212/599-6262** or 800/223-6530).

3 The Active Vacation Planner

Puerto Rico offers a wide variety of participant and spectator sports, including golf, tennis, horseback riding, and all kinds of water sports—from scuba diving to deep-sea fishing.

Many resorts offer a large choice of sports activities, and a variety of all-inclusive sports-vacation packages are available from hotels and airlines serving Puerto Rico.

Dorado Beach, Cerromar Beach, and Palmas del Mar are the chief centers for golf, tennis, and beach life. San Juan's hotels on the Condado/Isla Verde coast also generally offer a complete array of water sports.

Beisbol

Whereas the United States may claim baseball as its national pastime, the sport also has a long, illustrious history in Puerto Rico. Imported around the turn of the century by plantation owners as a leisure activity for workers, *beisbol* quickly caught fire, and local leagues have produced such major-league stars as Roberto Alomar, Carlos Balarga, and the late great Roberto Clemente.

A top-notch league of six teams—featuring many rising professionals honing their skills during the winter months—begins its season in October and plays in ballparks throughout the island. Many baseball fans from the U.S. mainland come down specifically to see these teams play. For a chance to see good baseball in a more intimate setting than is afforded in the major leagues, call **Professional Baseball of Puerto Rico** (☎ 787/765-6285) for information about professional games and, if available, a schedule.

BEACHES

With some 300 miles of Atlantic and Caribbean coastline, Puerto Rico obviously has plenty of beaches. The **Condado** and **Isla Verde** beaches in San Juan are the most frequented. Good snorkeling is possible, and rental equipment is available for water sports at both. These and other beaches such as the excellent **Luquillo,** 30 miles east of San Juan (see chapter 8), are overcrowded, especially on Saturday and Sunday. On the other hand, others are practically deserted. The public beaches on the north shore of San Juan at **Ocean Park** and **Park Barbosa** are good and can be reached by bus.

The best surfing beaches in the Caribbean are on the west coast north of Mayagüez, including the beach at **Punta Higuero,** on Route 413 near the town of Rincón, which is said to be one of the finest surfing spots in the world (see chapter 10).

Puerto Rico's public beaches are open to the public, and some of them are practically deserted. You will be charged for parking and for use of *balneario* facilities, such as lockers and showers, at the public beaches. They are closed on Monday (if Monday is a holiday, they are open then but closed on Tuesday). In winter, public beach hours are 9am to 5pm; in summer, from 9am to 6pm. For more information about the island's many beaches, call the **Department of Sports and Recreation** (☎ 787/722-1551).

The following public beaches have *balnearios:*

Punta Salinas (Rte. 868, Cataño)
Escambron (Puerta de Tierra, San Juan)
Isla Verde (Rte. 187, Isla Verde)
Luquillo (Hwy. 3, Luquillo)
Seven Seas (Rte. 987, Fajardo)
Sun Bay (Rte. 997, Vieques)
Punta Santiago (Hwy. 3, Humacao)
Punta Guilarte (Hwy. 3, Humacao)
Punta Guilarte (Hwy. 3, Arroyo)
Cana Gora (Rte. 333, Guánica)
Boquerón (Rte. 101, Boquerón)
Añasco (Rte. 410, Añasco)
Cerro Gordo (Rte. 690, Vega Baja)
Sardinera (Rte. 698, Dorado)

Warning: Don't go walking along the beaches at night. Even if you find that secluded, hidden beach of your dreams, proceed with caution. On unguarded beaches you will have no way to protect yourself or your valuables should you be approached by a robber or mugger, which has been known to happen.

BOATING & SAILING

The waters off Puerto Rico provide excellent boating in all seasons. For sailors, winds average 10 to 15 knots virtually year-round. Marinas provide facilities and services on a par with any in the Caribbean, and many have powerboats or sailboats for rent, crewed or bareboat charter.

Marinas include the **San Juan Bay Marina** (☎ 787/721-8062); **Isleta Marina,** Puerto Chico (☎ 787/863-0834); **Marina del Mar** and **Palmas del Mar** in Humacao (☎ 787/852-6000); and **Marina de Salinas** (☎ 787/752-8484) in Salinas. The Caribbean's largest and most modern marina, **Puerto del Rey** (☎ 787/ 860-1000), is located on the island's east coast in Fajardo.

Annual sailing regattas include the Copa Velasco Regatta for ocean racing, at Palmas del Mar Resort in Humacao (see chapter 9).

CAMPING

The island abounds in sandy beaches and forested hillsides suitable (if permission is given by the landowner) for erecting a tent. More protected and much safer are sites throughout the island where simple cabins, sometimes with fireplaces, are maintained by the **Recreational Development Company of Puerto Rico.** Although accommodations are bare-boned minimalist, the costs are often less than those charged by hotels. For more information and an application to rent one of the units, call **787/722-1551** or 787/722-1771.

Additional information about camping may be available from the **Parks and Recreation Association of Puerto Rico** (☎ 787/721-2800).

DEEP-SEA FISHING

It's top-notch! Allison tuna, white and blue marlin, sailfish, wahoo, dolphin, mackerel, and tarpon are some of the fish that can be caught in Puerto Rican waters, where 30 world records have been broken.

Charter arrangements can be made through most major hotels and resorts. In San Juan, **Capt. Mike Benitez** is said to set the standard by which to judge other captains (see chapter 7). In Palmas del Mar, which has some of the best year-round fishing in the Caribbean, you'll find **Capt. Bill Burleson** (see chapter 9).

GOLF

Home to 13 golf courses, including 8 championship links, Puerto Rico justifiably is known as the "Scotland of the Caribbean." In fact, the 72 holes at the Hyatt resorts at Dorado offer the greatest concentration of golf in the Caribbean.

The courses at the **Hyatt Dorado Beach Hotel** and the **Hyatt Regency Cerromar** are among the 25 best created by Robert Trent Jones. Jack Nicklaus rates the challenging 13th hole at the Hyatt Dorado Beach as one of the top ten in the world. On the southeast coast, crack golfers consider holes 11 through 15 at **The Golf Club at Palmas del Mar** to be the toughest five successive holes in the Caribbean. At **El Conquistador Resort and Country Club,** the spectacular $250 million resort at Las Croabas east of San Juan, the course's 200-foot changes in elevation provide panoramic vistas. At Palmer on the northeast coast, inexperienced golfers prefer the **Rio Mar Golf Course** to the more challenging courses at Dorado.

With the exception of the El Conquistador Resort and Country Club, these courses are open to the public. See chapter 9 for details.

HIKING

The mountainous interior of Puerto Rico provides ample opportunities for hill climbing and nature treks. These are especially appealing because panoramas open at the least expected moments, often revealing spectacular views of the faraway sea.

The most popular trekking spots include **El Yunque,** the sprawling jungle maintained by the U.S. Forest Service, as well as the dozens of forest reserves scattered throughout the island. These range from coastal mangrove swamps teeming with bird life to densely forested palm groves in the high-altitude interior.

Equally suitable for hiking are the protected lands (especially the **Río Camuy caves**) whose topography is characterized as "karst"—that is, limestone riddled with caves, underground rivers, and natural crevasses and fissures. Although these regions pose additional risks and technical problems for trekkers, some people prefer the opportunities they provide for exploring the territory both above and below its surface. See chapter 8 for details about El Yunque and the Río Camuy caves.

A word of warning: When you hike in the tropics, you can quickly become dehydrated and also sustain more serious insect bites and sunburn than you would while hiking in more temperate climes. Drink water frequently, wear a sun hat, and consider the advisability of long-sleeved shirts and sunscreen to protect yourself from heat exhaustion and sunstroke.

HORSEBACK RIDING

The **Equestrian Center at Palmas del Mar** has 42 horses, including English hunters for jumping, plus a variety of trail rides and instruction for all levels of ability. See chapter 9.

SCUBA DIVING & SNORKELING

The continental shelf, which surrounds Puerto Rico on three sides, is responsible for an abundance of coral reefs, caves, sea walls, and trenches for scuba diving and snorkeling.

Open-water reefs off the southeastern coast near Humacao are visited by migrating whales and manatees. Many caves are located near Isabela on the west coast. The Great Trench, off the island's south coast, is ideal for experienced open-water divers. Caves and the sea wall at La Parguera are also favorites. Vieques and Culebra islands, off the east coast, have coral formations. Mona Island, off the west coast, offers unspoiled reefs at depths averaging 80 feet; seals are one of the attractions. Uninhabited islands, such as Icacos, off the northeastern coast near Fajardo, are also popular with snorkelers and divers.

These sites are now within reach since many of Puerto Rico's dive operators and resorts offer packages that may include daily or twice-daily dives, scuba equipment, instruction, and excursions to the island's popular attractions.

In San Juan, the **Caribbean School of Aquatics** offers an array of sailing, scuba, and snorkeling trips, as well as boat charters and fishing. **Karen Vega's Carib Aquatic Adventures,** in the lobby of the Radisson Normandie Hotel, teaches PADI and NAUI diving certification courses (see chapter 7). At the Palmas del Palms resort, **Coral Head Divers & Water Sports Center** offers daily two-tank open-water dives for certified divers, plus snorkeling trips to Monkey Island and Vieques (see chapter 9).

Elsewhere on the island, several other companies offer scuba and snorkeling instruction. We'll provide details in each section.

For reservations or more information about Puerto Rico diving packages, contact Kathy Rothschild at **Rothschild Travel Consultants** (☎ **212/662-4858** in New York City, or 800/359-0747).

NATURE TOURS

Lectures on wildlife and the environment of Puerto Rico are offered by the Commonwealth of Puerto Rico Department of Natural Resources, especially for scientists and students. Also, tours of the nature reserves and forests on the island can be arranged in advance. You need to specify the name of the reserve or forest you'd like to visit. Contact the **Department of Natural Resources,** Forest, Reserves and Refuge Area, P.O. Box 5887, San Juan, PR 00906 (☎ **787/721-5495** for the reserve and refuge, 787/723-1717 for the forest).

Tropix Wellness Tours (☎ **787/268-2173;** fax 787/268-1722) offers four tours to some of the island's varied natural treasures. This company's "Happy Turtle Tour" on Culebra includes a half-day kayaking/snorkeling expedition and a visit to sea turtles' nesting sites during the spring and summer (see chapter 11). Its "Phosphorescent Bay Tour" goes to Vieques and includes an expedition to Isla Nena, home of one of Puerto Rico's most spectacular reefs, bird sanctuaries, and deserted sandy beaches (see chapter 11). The "Camuy Caveman Tour" includes an expedition through the Camuy Caves, one of the largest underground cave river systems in the world (see chapter 8). The "Wet and Dry Tour" in Guánica on the relatively arid southwestern coast includes a dry forest hike and mangrove kayaking at sunset (see chapter 10).

SURFING

Puerto Rico's northwest beaches attract surfers from around the world. Called the Hawaii of the East, the island has hosted a number of international competitions. October through February are considered the best surfing months, but the sport is enjoyed in Puerto Rico from August through April. The most popular areas are from Isabela around Punta Borinquén to Rincón—with beaches such as Wilderness, Surfers, Crashboat, Los Turbos in Vega Jaja, Pine Grove in Isla Verde, and La Pared in Luquillo. Surfboards are available at many water-sports shops.

International competitions held in Puerto Rico have included the 1968 and the 1988 World Amateur Surfing Championships, the annual Caribbean Cup Surfing Championship, and the 1989 and 1990 Budweiser Puerto Rico Surfing Challenge events, stops on the professional tour.

TENNIS

There are approximately 100 tennis courts in Puerto Rico. Many are located at hotels and resorts, whereas others can be found in public parks throughout the island. Several paradores also have courts. A number of courts are lighted for nighttime play.

In San Juan, the **Caribe Hilton,** the **Condado Plaza Hotel & Casino,** the **Carib Inn,** and the **Condado Beach Trio** all have tennis courts. Also in the area is a **public court** at the old navy base, Isla Grande, in Miramar. The entrance is from Avenida Fernández Juncos at bus stop 11. See chapter 7.

The twin **Hyatt Resorts Caribbean** at Dorado and Cerromar maintain a total of 21 courts between them. The **Tennis Center** at Palmas del Mar in Humacao, the largest in Puerto Rico, features 20 courts. See chapter 9.

WINDSURFING

Windsurfing is another popular water sport on Puerto Rico, with the sheltered waters of the Condado Lagoon in San Juan a favorite spot. Other sites include

Ocean Park, Ensenada, Boquerón, Honda Beach, and Culebra. Puerto Rico hosted its first major windsurfing tournament, the Ray Ban Windsurfing World Cup, in June 1989.

Throughout the island, many companies offering snorkeling and scuba also provide windsurfing equipment and instruction, and dozens of hotels have facilities on their own premises.

One of the best places to arrange for windsurfing in San Juan is at **Karen Vega's Carib Aquatic Adventures,** whose main office is in the lobby of the Radisson Normandie Hotel (see chapter 7). Along the north shore, windsurfing is excellent at the beachfront of the Hyatt Dorado Beach Hotel, where the **Lisa Penfield Windsurfing School** offers lessons and rentals (see chapter 9).

4 Health & Insurance

STAYING HEALTHY

Traveling to Puerto Rico should not adversely affect your health. Finding a good doctor in Puerto Rico presents no real problem, and most doctors speak English. See "Fast Facts: Puerto Rico," below, for the locations of hospitals.

POTENTIAL PROBLEMS   Although tap water is generally considered safe, it's better to drink mineral water. Avoid iced drinks. Stick to beer, hot tea, or soft drinks. Many visitors experience diarrhea, even if they follow the usual precautions. It usually passes quickly without medication if you eat simply prepared food and drink only mineral water until you recover. If symptoms persist, consult a doctor.

The sun can be brutal, especially if you're coming from a winter climate and haven't been exposed to it in some time. Experts advise that you limit your time on the beach the first day. If you do overexpose yourself, stay out of the sun until you recover. If your exposure is followed by fever or chills, a headache, or a feeling of nausea or dizziness, see a doctor.

Sandflies (or "no-see-ums") are one of the biggest insect menaces in Puerto Rico. They appear mainly in the early evening, and even if you can't see these tiny bugs, you sure can "feel-um," as any native Puerto Rican will attest. Screens can't keep them out, so you'll need to use your favorite insect repellent.

Although mosquitoes are a nuisance, they do not carry malaria in Puerto Rico. On the other hand, dengue fever is widespread. This severe, flulike disease is borne by the *Aëdes aegypti* mosquito, which lives indoors and bites only during daylight hours. To date, no cure has been developed, and treatment is only for the symptoms until the disease subsides, usually within 2 weeks. Do not take aspirin or aspirin-based pain killers if you're infected, since dengue attacks the blood and you don't want to thin yours any more than it already is. Dengue is seldom fatal in adults, but take extra precautions to keep children from being bitten by mosquitoes.

Hookworm and other intestinal parasites are relatively common in the Caribbean, though you are less likely to be affected on Puerto Rico. Hookworm can be contracted by just walking barefoot on an infected beach. Schistosomiasis (also called bilharzia), caused by a parasitic fluke, can be contracted by submerging your feet in rivers and lakes infested with a certain species of snail.

And don't forget that Puerto Rico has been especially hard hit by AIDS. Exercise *at least* the same caution in choosing your sexual partners, and in practicing safe sex, as you would at home.

If you have a chronic medical condition, speak to your doctor before leaving home. For conditions such as epilepsy, a heart condition, diabetes, or allergy, consider wearing a **Medic Alert Identification Tag.** For a lifetime membership, the cost is $35 for a steel tag, $45 if silver plated, and $60 if gold plated. In addition, there is a $15 annual fee. Contact the Medic Alert Foundation, P.O. Box 1009, Turlock, CA 95381-1009 (☎ **800/432-5378**). Medic Alert's 24-hour hotline enables a foreign doctor to obtain your medical records.

Take along an adequate supply of any prescription drugs that you need and a written prescription specifying the generic name of the drug—not the brand name. However, U.S. brand names are commonly available at most pharmacies. You may also want to take such over-the-counter items as first-aid cream, insect repellent, aspirin, and Band-Aids.

INSURANCE

Before purchasing insurance, check your current homeowner's, automobile, and medical insurance policies, as well as the membership contracts of automobile and travel clubs and credit/charge cards, for any coverage extended to you while you travel.

Many credit- and charge-card companies insure their users in case of a travel accident when the travel cost was paid with their card. Sometimes fraternal organizations have policies that protect members in case of sickness or accidents abroad.

Many homeowners' insurance policies cover theft of luggage during foreign travel and loss of such documents as your passport and your airline ticket. Coverage is usually limited to about $500. Remember that to submit a claim on your insurance, you'll need police reports or a statement from a local medical authority that you did suffer the loss or experience an illness. Some policies provide advances in cash or arrange for immediate transferals of funds.

If you feel you need additional insurance, check with the following companies:

Access America, 6600 W. Broad St., Richmond, VA 23230 (☎ **804/285-3300** or 800/284-8300), offers a comprehensive travel insurance and assistance package, including medical expenses, on-the-spot hospital payments, medical transportation, baggage insurance, trip-cancellation/interruption insurance, and collision damage insurance for a car rental. Their 24-hour hotline connects you to multilingual coordinators who can offer advice and help with medical, legal, and travel problems. Varying coverage levels are available.

Mutual of Omaha, Mutual of Omaha Plaza, Omaha, NE 68175 (☎ **800/228-9792**), offers insurance packages priced from $113 for a 3-week trip. Included in the packages are travel-assistance services, and financial protection against trip cancellation, trip interruption, flight and baggage delays, accident-related medical costs, accidental death and dismemberment, and medical evacuation coverage. Application for insurance can be taken over the phone for holders of major credit and charge cards.

Travel Guard International, 1145 Clark St., Stevens Point, WI 54481 (☎ **800/826-1300** outside Wisconsin, 715/345-0505 in Wisconsin), offers a comprehensive 7-day policy that covers lost luggage, emergency assistance, accidental death, trip cancellation, and medical coverage abroad. The cost of the package is $62, but there are restrictions that you should understand before you accept the coverage.

5 Tips for Travelers with Special Needs

FOR TRAVELERS WITH DISABILITIES

Hotels rarely give much publicity to the facilities, if any, they offer the disabled, so it's always wise to contact the hotel directly, in advance. Tourist offices usually have little data about such matters.

You can obtain a free copy of *Air Transportation of Handicapped Persons,* published by the U.S. Department of Transportation. Write for Free Advisory Circular No. AC120032, Distribution Unit, U.S. Department of Transportation, Publications Division, 3341Q 75 Ave., Landover, MD 20785 (☎ **301/322-4961;** fax 301/386-5394). Only written requests are accepted.

You may want to consider joining a tour specifically for disabled visitors. For names and addresses of such tour operators, contact the **Society for the Advancement of Travel for the Handicapped,** 347 Fifth Ave., Suite 610, New York, NY (☎ **212/447-7284;** fax 212/725-8235). Yearly membership costs $45 for adults, $25 for senior citizens and students. Send along a self-addressed, stamped envelope. SATH will also provide you with hotel/resort accessibility for Caribbean destinations including Puerto Rico.

The **Information Center for Individuals with Disabilities,** 29 Stanhope St., 4th Floor, Boston, MA 02116 (☎ **617/450-9888** or 800/462-5015 in Mass.) is another good source. It has lists of travel agents who specialize in tours for the disabled, and provides travel-tip fact sheets for Caribbean destinations.

For the blind or visually impaired, the best source is the **American Foundation for the Blind,** 11 Penn Plaza, Suite 300, New York, NY 10001 (☎ **212/502-7600** or 800/232-5463 to order information kits and supplies). It acts as a referral source for travelers and can offer advice on various requirements for the transport and border formalities for seeing-eye dogs.

One of the best organizations serving the needs of the disabled (wheelchairs and walkers) is **Flying Wheels Travel,** 143 W. Bridge St. (P.O. Box 382), Owatoona, MN 55060 (☎ **507/451-5005** or 800/535-6790). It offers customized, all-inclusive vacation packages in the Caribbean.

For a $25 annual fee, consider joining **Mobility International USA,** P.O. Box 10767, Eugene, OR 97440 (☎ **503/343-1284** (TDD), or fax 503/343-6812). It answers questions on various destinations and also offers discounts on its programs, videos, and publications. Their quarterly newsletter, "Over the Rainbow," provides information on Puerto Rican hotel chains, accessibility, and transportation.

Finally, a bimonthly publication, **Handicapped Travel Newsletter,** keeps you current on worldwide, accessible sights for the disabled. To order an annual subscription for $10, call **903/677-1260.**

FOR GAY & LESBIAN TRAVELERS

Puerto Rico is the most gay-friendly destination in the Caribbean, with lots of accommodations, restaurants, clubs, and bars that actively cater to a gay clientele.

Men can order *Spartacus,* the international gay guide ($29.95), or *Odysseus 1996, The International Gay Travel Planner,* a guide to international gay accommodations ($25). Both lesbians and gay men might want to pick up a copy of *Ferrari Travel Planner* ($16), which specializes in general information, as well as listings of bars, hotels, restaurants, and places of interest for gay travelers throughout the world. These books and others are available from **Giovanni's Room,** 1145 Pine St., Philadelphia, PA 19107 (☎ **215/923-2960**).

Our World, 1104 North Nova Rd., Suite 251, Daytona Beach, FL 32117 (☎ 904/441-5367), is a magazine devoted to options and bargains for gay and lesbian travel worldwide. It costs $35 for 10 issues. *Out and About,* 8 W. 19th St., Suite 401, New York, NY 10011 (☎ **800/929-2268**), has been hailed for its "straight" reporting about gay travel. It profiles the best gay or gay-friendly hotels, gyms, clubs, and other places, with coverage of destinations throughout the world. It costs $49 a year for 10 information-packed issues. It aims for the more upscale gay male traveler, and has been praised by everybody from *Travel & Leisure* to *The New York Times.*

The **International Gay Travel Association (IGTA),** P.O. Box 4974, Key West, FL 33041 (☎ **305/292-0217** or voice mailbox 800/448-8550), encourages gay and lesbian travel worldwide. With around 1,200 member agencies, it specializes in networking, providing the information travelers would need for an individual traveler to link up with the appropriate gay-friendly service organization or tour specialist. It offers quarterly newsletters, marketing mailings, and a membership directory that is updated four times a year. Travel agents who are IGTA members will be tied into this organization's information resources.

FOR SENIORS

For information before you go, obtain a free copy of **"101 Tips for the Mature Traveler"** available from Grand Circle Travel, 347 Congress St., Suite 3A, Boston, MA 02210 (☎ **617/350-7500** or 800/221-2610). This tour operator offers extended vacations, escorted programs, and cruises that feature unique learning experiences for seniors at competitive prices.

SAGA International Holidays, 222 Berkeley St., Boston, MA 02115 (☎ **800/ 343-0273**), is known for its all-inclusive tours and cruises for seniors, preferably those 50 years of age or older. Both medical and trip-cancellation insurance are included in the net price of any of its tours, except cruises.

Information is also available from the **National Council of Senior Citizens,** 1331 F St. NW, Washington, DC 20004 (☎ **202/347-8800**). A nonprofit organization, the council charges $12 per person/couple, for which you receive a regular magazine, part of which is devoted to travel tips. Benefits of membership include discounts on hotel and auto rentals and also supplemental medical insurance for members.

Mature Outlook, P.O. Box 10448, Des Moines, IA 50306 (☎ **800/336-6330**), is a membership program for people over 50 years of age. Members are offered discounts at ITC-member hotels and receive a bimonthly magazine. The annual membership fee of $14.95 entitles its members to free coupons for discounts from Sears Roebuck Co. Savings are also offered on selected auto rentals and restaurants.

Golden Companions has been successful in helping travelers 45-plus find compatible companions since 1987. It is the only travel companion network to offer personal voicebox mail service enabling members to connect instantly 24 hours a day. Membership services also include free mail exchange, the bimonthly newsletter *Golden Gateways,* get-togethers, and tours. Annual membership is $85, and newsletter-only subscriptions are $17.95 for 12 months or $26.95 for 24 months. For a free brochure, write Golden Companions, P.O. Box 5249, Reno, NV 89513 (☎ **702/324-2227**). A sample newsletter costs $2.

FOR FAMILIES

Puerto Rico is a terrific family destination. The smallest toddlers can spend blissful hours on sandy beaches and in the shallow seawater or pools specifically constructed for them. There's no end to the fascinating pursuits available for older children, ranging from boat rides to shell collecting to horseback riding and hiking. Perhaps your children are old enough to learn to snorkel and explore the wonderland of underwater Puerto Rico. Skills such as swimming and windsurfing are taught here, and there are a variety of activities unique to the islands. Most resort hotels will advise you of what there is in the way of fun for the young, and many have play directors and supervised activities for various age groups. Look for the "Family-Friendly Hotels" and "Family-Friendly Restaurants" boxes we've included throughout the book, pointing you to places that cater to kids.

Family Travel Times, published four times a year by TWYCH (Travel With Your Children), includes a weekly call-in service for subscribers. Subscriptions cost $40 a year and can be ordered by writing to **TWYCH,** 40 Fifth Ave., New York, NY 10011 (☎ **212/477-5524**). TWYCH also publishes two nitty-gritty information guides, *Skiing with Children* and *Cruising with Children,* which sell for $29 and $22, respectively, and are discounted for newsletter subscribers. An information packet describing TWYCH's publications, including a recent sample issue, is available by sending $3.50 to the above address.

6 Flying to Puerto Rico

Based on the number of flights from North America, Puerto Rico is by far the most accessible of all the Caribbean islands. It is, in fact, the airline capital of the West Indies. Even if you're not planning a holiday in Puerto Rico, chances are you'll pass through here if you do any extensive touring through the Caribbean Basin.

THE AIRLINES

American Airlines (☎ **800/433-7300**) has spent millions of dollars to make San Juan its most prominent Latin American hub. American offers nonstop daily flights to San Juan from New York (JFK), Newark, Boston, Miami, Dallas–Fort Worth, Washington (Dulles), Orlando, Tampa, Chicago, Baltimore, Hartford, and Philadelphia, as well as flights (with one intermediate stop in Chicago or Miami) to San Juan from both Montréal and Toronto. There are also at least two daily flights from Los Angeles to San Juan that touch down in Dallas. In all, the carrier now provides more than 42 daily nonstop flights to Puerto Rico, far more than any of its competitors.

American, through its subsidiary, **American Eagle,** is also the undisputed leader among the short-haul commuter flights of the Caribbean. It specializes in these services, using propeller planes that carry 19 to 64 passengers. American Eagle links Puerto Rico with almost 100 daily incoming flights from nearly 40 destinations throughout the Caribbean.

Delta Airlines (☎ **800/221-1212**) has four daily nonstop flights from Atlanta Monday through Friday, nine nonstop on Saturday, and seven nonstop on Sunday. It also offers one daily nonstop flight to San Juan from Orlando. Flights into Atlanta from around the world are frequent, with excellent connections from points throughout Delta's network in the South and Southwest.

United Airlines (☎ **800/241-6522**) offers daily service between Chicago and San Juan, with convenient connections through its widespread network.

Carnival Air Lines (☎ **800/824-7386**), a Florida-based carrier wholly owned by the Carnival Group (of cruise-line fame), flies once daily nonstop to both Ponce (Puerto Rico's second-largest city) and Aguadilla (on the northwestern coast) from the New York area. Connections are also made through Newark (New Jersey) and Miami to both Aguadilla and Ponce. Schedules are constantly changing; call for the latest flight information.

A handful of European carriers also flies to Puerto Rico, carrying winter-weary Europeans toward Caribbean sunshine. These include **British Airways** (☎ **800/ 247-9297** in the U.S.), which goes to San Juan from London weekly on Sunday. **Lufthansa** (☎ **800/645-3880** in the U.S.) flies in from Frankfurt on Saturday (one weekly flight) via Condor, a subsidiary operating the flight. **Iberia** (☎ **800/772-4642** in the U.S.) has one or two weekly flights from Madrid to San Juan, operating on Saturday, Thursday, or both, depending on the month.

HOW LONG WILL IT TAKE?

You won't be in the air long to reach the sun and sands of Puerto Rico, since the commonwealth is no more than $3^{1}/_{2}$ hours flying time from most eastern U.S. cities, less than $4^{1}/_{2}$ hours from the Midwest. Following are the approximate nonstop flying times to San Juan from some major cities:

Atlanta: 3 hrs. 15 min.	Miami: 2 hrs. 20 min.
Baltimore: 3 hrs. 45 min.	New Orleans: 3 hrs. 25 min.
Boston: 3 hrs. 45 min.	New York: 3 hrs. 30 min.
Chicago: 4 hrs. 20 min.	Philadelphia: 3 hrs. 25 min.
Los Angeles: 6 hrs. 25 min.	Washington: 3 hrs. 45 min.

In recent years, the traditional expectation that winter fares to the Caribbean were higher than those in summer has changed. On their island routes, most airlines now divide their year into peak season and basic season, eliminating what used to be known as shoulder season. **Peak season** for fares between North America and Puerto Rico now generally means midwinter and midsummer, while the less expensive **basic season** covers spring and fall.

Also noteworthy is the fact that most airlines are eliminating business class on their routes from North America to Puerto Rico. Instead, they are offering only economy class and first class. (On most American Eagle flights, first class has been eliminated entirely in favor of single-service flights; since most intra-Caribbean American Eagle flights rarely exceed 90 minutes, no one seems to mind.)

OTHER WAYS TO SAVE

Proceed with caution through the next grab bag of suggestions. What constitutes good value keeps changing in the airline industry. It's hard to keep up, even if you're a travel agent. Fares, especially to Puerto Rico, change all the time—what was the lowest possible fare one day can change the very next day when a new promotional fare is offered.

CHARTER FLIGHTS These flights allow you to travel at rates lower than those of regularly scheduled flights. Many of the major carriers offer charter flights at rates that can cost 30% or more less than the regular airfare.

There are some drawbacks to charter flights that you need to consider. Advance booking, for example, of up to 45 days or more may be required, and there are hefty cancellation penalties, although you can take out insurance against emergency cancellation. Also, you must depart and return on your scheduled dates or else you'll lose your money. If you don't have proper insurance, it will do you no good to call the airline and tell them you've had a ski accident in Aspen. If you're not on the plane, you can kiss your money good-bye.

Since charter flights are so complicated, it's best to go to a good travel agent and ask him or her to explain the problems and advantages. Sometimes charters require ground arrangements, such as prebooking hotel rooms.

One company that arranges charters is the **Council Travel,** 205 E. 42nd St., New York, NY 10017 (☎ **212/661-1414** or 800/226-8624 in the U.S.).

One of the biggest New York charter operators is **Travac,** 989 Sixth Ave., New York, NY 10018 (☎ **212/563-3303** or 800/TRAV-800). Other Travac offices include 2601 East Jefferson St., Orlando, FL 32803 (☎ 407/896-0014).

BUCKET SHOPS (CONSOLIDATORS) In its purest sense, a bucket shop acts as a clearinghouse for blocks of tickets that airlines discount and consign during normally slow periods of air travel (for Puerto Rico, that usually means from mid-April to mid-December). Charter operators and bucket shops used to perform separate functions, but their offerings have often become blurred in recent years. Many outfits perform both functions.

Tickets are sometimes—but not always—discounted as much as 20% to 35%. Terms of payment can vary, from perhaps 45 days prior to departure to the last minute. Some consolidators require you to buy their discounted tickets through a regular travel agent, who usually marks up the ticket 8% to 10%, maybe more, thereby greatly reducing your discount. If you go through an agent, ask him or her to comparison shop for you, since prices can vary from consolidator to consolidator.

A survey conducted of flyers who use consolidator tickets found only one major complaint: Such a ticket doesn't qualify you for an advance seat assignment, so you are likely to be assigned a poor seat on the plane at the last minute.

Another possible hitch: Many people who booked consolidator tickets reported no savings at all, since the airlines will sometimes match the price of the consolidator ticket by announcing a promotional fare. Because the situation is a bit tricky, you need to investigate carefully just how much you can expect to save.

One more bit of advice: Inquire as to any and all restrictions, and always pay by credit card.

Although bucket shops abound from coast to coast (look for their usually small ads in your local newspaper's Sunday travel section), there are few who specialize in the highly competitive Caribbean market. One of these is **TFI Tours International,** 34 W. 32nd St., 12th Floor, New York, NY 10001 (☎ **212/736-1140** in New York state or 800/745-8000 elsewhere in the U.S.).

REBATORS   To make matters even more confusing, rebators have also begun to compete in the low-airfare market. Rebators are organizations that pass along to the passenger part of their commission, although many of them assess a fee for their services. And although rebators are not the same as travel agents, they sometimes offer roughly similar services. Sometimes a rebator will sell you a discounted travel ticket and also offer discounted land arrangements, including hotels and car rentals. Most rebators offer discounts averaging anywhere from 10% to 25% (but this varies from place to place), plus a $25 handling charge.

Rebators include **Travel Avenue,** 10 S. Riverside Plaza, Suite 1404, Chicago, IL 60606 (☎ **312/876-1116** or 800/333-3335); and **The Smart Traveller,** 3111 SW 27th Ave. (P.O. Box 330106), Miami, FL 33133 (☎ **305/448-3338** or 800/448-3338 in the U.S.). This agency also discounts hotel or condo packages and cruises. The Smart Traveller also rebates 6% on package tours.

7 Package Tours

If you want everything done for you and want to save money as well, consider taking a package tour. Besides general tours, many have specific themes—tennis packages, golf packages, scuba and snorkeling packages, and honeymooners' specials. Puerto Rico is prominently featured in most of these offerings.

Economy and convenience are the chief advantages of a package tour—the costs of transportation (usually by plane), a hotel room, food (sometimes), and sightseeing (sometimes) are combined and neatly tied up with a single price tag. There are extras, of course, but in general you'll know in advance roughly what the cost of your vacation will be and you can budget accordingly. The disadvantage is that you may find yourself, for example, in a hotel you dislike but cannot leave because you've already paid for it.

Choosing the right package can be a bit of a problem. It's best to go to a travel agent, tell him or her what island (or islands) you'd like to visit, and see what's currently offered.

Packages are available because tour operators can mass-book hotels and make volume purchases. You generally have to pay the cost of the total package in advance. Transfers between your hotel and the airport are often included (this may be more of a break than it sounds at first since some airports are situated a $40-or-more taxi ride from a resort). Many packages carry several options, including the possibility of low-cost car rentals. Nearly all tour packages are based on double occupancy.

To save time comparing the price and value of all the package tours out there, consider calling **TourScan Inc.,** P.O. Box 2367, Darien, CT 06820 (☎ **203/655-8091** or 800/962-2080). Every season, the company gathers and computerizes the contents of about 200 brochures containing 10,000 different vacations in the Caribbean, The Bahamas, and Bermuda. TourScan selects the best value at each hotel and condo. Two catalogs are printed each year. Each lists a broad-based choice of hotels on most of the islands of the Caribbean, in all price ranges. Write to TourScan for their catalogs costing $4 each, the price of which is credited to any TourScan vacation.

Some of the leading tour operators to the Caribbean include the following:

Caribbean Concepts Corp., 575 Underhill Bend, Syosset, NY 11791 (☎ **516/ 496-9800** or 800/423-4433; fax 516/496-9880), offers air and land packages to the islands, including apartments, hotels, resorts, or condo rentals. Car rentals and local sightseeing also can be arranged.

You might also want to consider one of the many tours offered by **American Airlines** (☎ **800/433-7300**) or **American Express** (☎ **212/687-3700** in New York City or 800/YES-AMEX in the U.S. and Canada).

Finally, advertising more packages to the Caribbean, including Puerto Rico, than any other agency is **Liberty Travel** (☎ **800/216-9776**), with offices in many states.

PACKAGES FOR BRITISH TRAVELERS

British travelers can contact **Caribbean Connection,** Concorde House, Forest Street, Chester, England CH1 1QR (☎ **01244/341131**), which offers all-inclusive packages (airfare and hotel) to the Caribbean and customizes tours for independent travel. It publishes two catalogs of Caribbean offerings, one featuring more than 160 properties on all the major islands, and a 50-page catalog of luxury all-inclusive properties.

Other Caribbean specialists operating out of England include **Kuoni Travel,** Kuoni House, Dorking, Surrey RH5 4AZ (☎ **01306/740-888**). **Caribtours,** 161 Fulham Rd., London SW3 6SN (☎ **0171/581-3517**), a small, very knowledgeable organization, also specializes in Caribbean travel and will tailor itineraries.

8 Cruises

If you'd like to sail the Caribbean in a hotel with an ocean view, a cruise ship might be for you. Cruises are slow and easy and are no longer enjoyed only by the idle rich who have months to spend away from home. Most cruises today appeal to the middle-income traveler who probably has no more than 1 or 2 weeks to spend cruising the Caribbean. Miami is the cruise capital of the world, but San Juan is second.

Most cruise-ship operators emphasize the concept of a total vacation. Some are mostly activity-centered; others offer the chance to do nothing but relax. Cruise ships are self-contained resorts, offering a large variety of services and activities on board and sightseeing once you arrive in a port of call.

For those who don't want to spend all their time at sea, some lines offer a fly-and-cruise vacation. You spend a week cruising the Caribbean and another week staying at an interesting hotel at reduced prices. These total packages should cost less than the cruise and air portions purchased separately.

Another version of fly-and-cruise is to fly to and from the cruise. Most plans offer a package deal from the principal airport closest to your residence to the major airport nearest to the cruise-departure point. It's possible to purchase your air ticket on your own and book your cruise ticket separately, but you'll save money by combining the fares in a package deal.

Most cruise ships travel at night, arriving the next morning at the day's port of call. In port, passengers can go ashore for sightseeing, shopping, and a local meal. Cruise prices vary widely. Sometimes the same route with the same ports of call carries different fares, depending on the ship's luxury (as well as your accommodations on board). Consult a good travel agent for the latest offerings.

Vacations to Go, 1502 Augusta Dr., Suite 415, Houston, TX 77057 (☎ **800/ 338-4962** in the U.S.), provides catalogs and information on discount cruises through the Atlantic, the Caribbean, and the Mediterranean. Annual membership costs $5.95 per family.

Here's only a brief rundown of some of the major cruise lines serving San Juan and the Caribbean. For far more detailed information, pick up a copy of our companion guide in this series, *Frommer's Caribbean Cruises.*

- **Carnival Cruise Lines** (☎ **305/599-2600** or 800/327-7373). Chances are if you're sailing the Caribbean it will be on a Carnival ship. Operating not only from San Juan but from such ports as Miami, St. Thomas, and Grand Cayman, this enormous company dominates the industry. Cruises range from 3 to 7 nights and tend to feature lots of partying. In the main, Carnival ships are for those who want a wide array of Las Vegas–style entertainment and recreational possibilities. They are known for offering good value, and you get the widest array of fellow passengers, from all walks of life and from widely different income levels. The average age is 42, although ages range from 3 to 95 (and in one case, 105). The food is pretty standard, though plentiful, and there's little chance to escape from the hordes at sea. Many single passengers with a gleam in their eye opt for a Carnival cruise, and some actually get lucky.

- **Celebrity Cruises** (☎ **305/262-6677** or 800/437-5111). It maintains three newly built, medium-size ships, each offering cruises of between 5 and 11 nights. San Juan is a usual port of call, along with Key West, Grand Cayman, Ocho Rios, St. Thomas, Antigua, and St. Barts. Accommodations are roomy and well-equipped, and many passengers compare their vessels to well-equipped all-inclusive resorts. Celebrity ships are stylish and sleek, a kind of moderate level first-class passage. The ships are strong on cuisine but lack wraparound promenade decks. In winter, most passengers—typical age about 48 to 50—are in the upper middle-class income bracket. The ships emphasize recreation and entertainment, but their shore excursions can be on the dull side.

- **Commodore Cruise Line** (☎ **305/529-3000** or 800/237-5361). Although Commodore's *The Enchanted Isle* might be a bit old-fashioned and worn, many clients like this company because of its reasonable prices. Cruises range from 7 to 14 days, and ports include the largest ports of Puerto Rico, St. Croix, Antigua, Martinique, Grand Cayman, and ports along the Mexican coast. There's a share of families with children on board, as well as lots of couples who don't care about the ships' relative lack of state-of-the-art facilities.

- **Costa Cruise Lines** (☎ 305/358-7325 or 800/327-2537). Its ships are relatively large and hold around 1,300 passengers each. In addition to San Juan, ports of call include Nassau, St. Thomas, St. Martin, and Key West. Cruises range from 7 to 11 nights at sea. There's an Italian atmosphere here, with entertainment like Carnival in Venice. The itineraries and the food are generally first-rate, except for some lackluster buffets. You get Italian flair and service. There may be as many Europeans as Americans on board.
- **Cunard** (☎ 212/880-7500 or 800/221-4770). Some visitors remember Cunard fondly from transatlantic journeys they've taken in the past on the line's very British flagship, the *QE2*. The company is one of the premier cruise lines in the world, with an undeniable flair that extends even to its less expensive vessels. There are drawbacks, however. With an aging fleet and wide-ranging prices and destinations, the line's offerings are uneven and sometimes confusing. Depending on the ship, Cunard can offer lavish style and appointments, suitable enough for the queen herself, Elizabeth II—or small discounted cabins that can be quite bleak. Because of this diversity and price structures, Cunard's ships carry the widest range of passengers of any vessels afloat. Ports of call include San Juan, St. Thomas, St. Kitts, Barbados, and in some cases, isolated ports in the southern Caribbean.
- **Dolphin Cruise Line** (☎ 305/358-2111 or 800/992-4299). Its pair of ships are among the oldest in the industry. Each has been refurbished, and today they ply the waters between the ports of southern Florida, Nassau, and San Juan. Less frequently, they travel to other ports farther south that include Dominica, Martinique, and Curaçao. Nothing is particularly fancy, but no one seems to mind in view of the good values. Bargain-hunters and retirees often make up the passenger list.
- **Holland America Line** (☎ 206/281-3535 or 800/426-0327). Its vessels represent the Netherlands, one of the great maritime nations of Europe, and the crew and staff are as cosmopolitan as any you're likely to find on the high seas. The company was founded in 1873, and many really wonderful pieces of cruising memorabilia grace the public areas of its ships. Tours range from 7 to 17 days, and the vessels cruise to such places as San Juan, Nassau, Key West, the coast of Mexico, Grand Cayman, Dominica, and St. John. Passengers tend to be somewhat older than those on other lines. In lieu of the often lackluster entertainment, late-night revelers and serious partyers might want to book other cruises such as Carnival.
- **Princess Cruises** (☎ 310/553-1770 or 800/568-3262), with its large fleet, is a frequent visitor to San Juan. The company is one of the very few in the world offering luxury accommodations and upscale service on its megaships. These usually carry a smaller complement of passengers than similarly sized vessels at less elegant lines. Cruises last 7 to 10 days each and incorporate both major and minor islands, as well as off-the-beaten-track places. The clientele is upscale, with an average passenger age of 55 or over. Much of the staff is British. Cuisine is often uneven, and the entertainment can be lackluster.
- **Royal Caribbean Cruise Line** (☎ 305/539-6000 or 800/659-7225). This company led the industry in the development of megaships, and three of its six vessels are among the largest anywhere, including *Sovereign of the Seas*. RCCL remains one of the most popular and best-run cruise lines, its ships appearing frequently at the Port of San Juan. A house-party theme tends to permeate the on-board ambience of these ships, some of which are aging and in need of refurbishment. There are enough on-board activities to suit most tastes and age levels, but the cabins are notoriously small.

9 Getting Around

BY PLANE

American Eagle (☎ 787/749-1747) flies from Luis Muñoz Marín International Airport to Mayagüez, which can be your gateway to western Puerto Rico. Most one-way fares are $59, or $85 to $95 round-trip. For information about air connections to the offshore islands of Vieques and Culebra, see chapter 11.

BY RENTAL CAR

Rental cars are readily available, but many of your fellow readers have offered this advice: *Drive on Puerto Rico only if necessary.* They point out that local drivers are often dangerous, as evidenced by the number of fenders with bashed-in sides. The older coastal highways provide the most scenic routes but are often congested. Some of the roads, especially in the mountainous interior, are just too narrow for automobiles. Proceed with caution along these poorly paved and maintained roads, which most often follow circuitous routes. Cliffslides or landslides are not uncommon.

If you do rent a vehicle, some local agencies may tempt you with special reduced prices. But if you're planning to tour the island by car, you won't find any local branches to help you if you experience trouble. And some of the agencies widely advertising low-cost deals won't take credit cards and want cash in advance. Also, watch out for "hidden" extra costs and the difficulties connected with regulating insurance claims, which sometimes proliferate among the smaller and not very well-known firms.

If you're planning to do much touring on the island, it's best to stick with the old reliables: **Avis** (☎ 787/791-2500 or 800/331-2112), **Budget** (☎ 787/791-3685 or 800/527-0700), and **Hertz** (☎ 787/791-0840 or 800/654-3001).

Budget offers many reasonable rates from a fleet of well-maintained cars. A small but peppy Nissan Sentra with air-conditioning and automatic transmission rents for $193.28 plus tax per week, with unlimited mileage. A more substantial mid-sized car, a Ford Tempo (also with automatic transmission and air-conditioning), rents for about $225 per week, also with unlimited mileage. These prices, as well as those offered by the competition, will undoubtedly change during the lifetime of this edition, although discounts are sometimes offered to members of organizations such as the AAA, depending on the policies of the rental companies.

Avis usually requires customers to be at least 21 years old; Budget and Avis prefer drivers to be 25 or older, although Budget will accept those who are 21 to 25 if they pay a small supplemental charge. In all cases, a valid credit or charge card must be presented at the time of rental; otherwise, a substantial cash deposit must be paid. Cash is not accepted at Budget—they require a valid credit card.

Each of the "big three" companies offers minivan transport to their airport offices and car depots. Added security is achieved with double-locking antitheft mechanisms installed in most rental cars available on Puerto Rico. Car theft is high on the island, so use caution when choosing a parking spot. Always lock your vehicle when you park it, and don't leave valuables in plain view on the seats.

Distances are often posted in kilometers rather than miles (1km = 0.62 mi.), but speed limits are reckoned in miles per hour.

INSURANCE   Each company offers an optional collision damage waiver priced at around $12 to $14 a day. Purchasing the waiver eliminates most or all of the financial responsibility you would face in case of an accident. With it, you can simply go

Highway Signs

Road signs using international symbols are commonplace in the San Juan metropolitan area and other urban centers, but they are written in Spanish. The following translations will also help you figure out what they mean:

Spanish	English
Autopista	Expressway
Balneario	Public beach
Calle sin salida	Dead end
Carretera cerrada	Road closed to traffic
Carretera dividida	Divided highway
Carretera estrecha	Narrow road
Cruce	Crossroad
Cruce de peatones	Pedestrian crossing
Cuesta	Hill
Desprendimiento	Landslide
Desvío	Detour
Estación de peaje	Toll station
Manténgase a la derecha	Keep right
No entre	Do not enter
No estacione	Do not park
Parada de guaguas	Bus stop
Peligro	Danger
Puente estrecho	Narrow bridge
Velocidad máxima	Speed limit
Zona escolar	School zone

home, leaving the rental company to sort it all out. Without it, you would be liable for up to the full value of the car in case it was damaged. Paying for the rental with certain credit or charge cards sometimes eliminates the need to buy this extra insurance. Also, your own automobile insurance policy may cover some or all of the damages. You should check with both your own insurer and your credit card issuers before leaving home.

GASOLINE   There is usually an abundant supply of gasoline in Puerto Rico, especially on the outskirts of San Juan, where you'll see all the familiar signs, such as Mobil. Gasoline stations are also plentiful along the main arteries traversing the island. However, if you're going to remote areas of the island, especially on Sunday, it's advisable to start out with a full tank. *Note:* In Puerto Rico, gasoline is sold by the liter, not by the gallon.

DRIVING RULES   Driving rules can be a source of some confusion. Speed limits are often not posted on the island, but when they are, they're given in miles per hour. For example, the limit on the San Juan–Ponce *autopista* (superhighway) is 70 m.p.h. Speed limits elsewhere, notably in heavily populated residential areas, are much lower. Since you're not likely to know what the actual speed limit is in some of these areas, it's better to confine your speed to no more than 30 m.p.h. The highway department places *lomas* (speed-bumps) at strategic points to deter speeders. Sometimes these are called "sleeping policemen."

Puerto Ricans drive, as do U.S. and Canadian motorists, on the right-hand side of the road.

ROAD MAPS ~~The best map both for touring the Puerto Rican countryside and~~ for exploring some of its major cities is the *H. M. Gousha Roadmap of Puerto Rico* (about $2.50). Printed in an array of easy-to-decipher colors, it's available in bookstores throughout the island. In addition to showing the major and minor roads of the island, it contains blowups of Greater San Juan, Ponce, Arecibo, Aguadilla, Mayagüez, Carolina, and Caguas.

BREAKDOWNS AND ASSISTANCE All the major towns and cities have garages that will come to your assistance and tow your vehicle in for repairs if necessary. There's no national emergency number to call in the event of a mechanical breakdown. If you have a rental car, call the rental company first. Usually, someone there will bring motor assistance to you. If your car requires extensive repairs because of a mechanical failure, a new one will be sent to replace it.

BY PUBLIC TRANSPORTATION

Cars and minibuses known as *públicos* provide low-cost transportation around the island. Their license plates have the letters "P" or "PD" following the numbers. They serve all the main towns of Puerto Rico. Passengers are let off and picked up along the way. Rates are set by the Public Service Commission. Públicos usually operate during daylight hours, departing from the main plaza (central square) of a town.

Information about público routes between San Juan and Mayagüez is available at **Lineas Sultana,** Calle Esteban González 898, Urbanización Santa Rita, Río Piedras (☎ 787/765-9377). Information about público routes between San Juan and Ponce is available from **Choferes Unidos de Ponce** (☎ 787/764-0540).

Fares vary according to whether or not the público will make a detour to pick up or drop off a passenger at a specific locale. (If you want to deviate from the predetermined routes, you'll pay more than if you wait for a público beside the main highway.) Fares from San Juan to Mayagüez range from $10 to $25; from San Juan to Ponce, from $7 to $20. Be warned that although prices of públicos are admittedly low, the routes are slow, with frequent stops, often erratic routing, and lots of inconvenience.

FAST FACTS: Puerto Rico

American Express See "Fast Facts: San Juan," in chapter 4.

Area Code The telephone area code for Puerto Rico is **787.** For calls on the island, the area code is not used.

Banks All major U.S. banks have branches on Puerto Rico; their hours are 8am to 2:30pm Monday through Friday and 9:45am to noon on Saturday.

Business Hours Regular business hours are Monday through Friday from 8am to 5pm. Shopping hours vary considerably. Regular shopping hours are Monday through Thursday and Saturday from 9am to 6pm. On Friday, stores have a long day: 9am to 9pm. Many stores also open on Sunday from 11am to 5pm.

Camera and Film Nearly all well-known brands of film are sold on Puerto Rico. Rolls of film cost about what they do on the U.S. mainland. It's relatively easy to get film processed on the island, especially in San Juan. It's important to protect your camera not only from theft but also from saltwater and sand; furthermore, the camera can become overheated and ruin any film it contains if left in the sun or locked in the trunk of a car. For the best commercial camera stores in Puerto Rico, see "Fast Facts: San Juan," in chapter 4.

Car Rentals   See "Getting Around," earlier in this chapter.

Climate   See "When to Go," earlier in this chapter.

Currency   The U.S. dollar is the coin of the realm. Canadian currency is accepted by some big hotels in San Juan, although reluctantly.

Customs   See "Visitor Information, Entry Requirements & Money," earlier in this chapter.

Dentists and Doctors   Dental emergencies can be taken care of at the **San Juan Health Center,** 200 De Diego Ave., Santurce (☎ 787/725-0202). This center also handles medical emergencies within the Greater San Juan area.

Documents   See "Visitor Information, Entry Requirements & Money," earlier in this chapter.

Driving Rules   See "Getting Around," earlier in this chapter.

Drugs   A branch of the Federal Narcotics Strike Force is permanently stationed on Puerto Rico, where illegal drugs and narcotics are a problem. Convictions for possession of marijuana can bring severe penalties, ranging from 2 to 10 years in prison. Possession of hard drugs, such as cocaine or heroin, can lead to 15 years in prison.

Drugstores   Carry all prescription medications with you, enough for the duration of your stay. If you need any additional medications, you'll find many drugstores in San Juan and other leading cities. If you're going into the hinterlands, it's advisable to take along the medicines you'll need. One of the most centrally located pharmacies in Old San Juan is the **Puerto Rican Drug Co.,** Calle San Francisco 157 (☎ 787/725-2202); it's open Monday through Saturday from 7:30am to 9:30pm and on Sunday from 8am to 7:30pm.

Electricity   The electricity is 110 volts A.C., as it is in the continental United States and Canada.

Embassies and Consulates   Since Puerto Rico is part of the United States, there is no U.S. embassy or consulate. Instead, there are branches of all the principal U.S. federal agencies. Canada has no embassy or consulate either. In case of a problem, citizens of the United Kingdom can call **787/721-5193** to receive recorded directions to leave a message including their name, address, telephone number, and a brief description of their problem. A staff member will eventually return the call.

Emergencies   In an emergency, dial 911. Or call the local **police** (☎ 787/ 343-2020), **fire department** (☎ 787/343-2330), **ambulance** (☎ 787/343-2550), or **medical assistance** (☎ 787/754-3535).

Health Care   Medical-care facilities on the island are on par with those in the United States, with excellent hospitals and clinics. Hotels can arrange for a doctor in case of an emergency. Most major U.S. health insurance plans are recognized, but it's advisable to check with your carrier or insurance agent in advance of your trip, since medical attention is very expensive. See "Health & Insurance" earlier in this chapter.

Holidays   See "When to Go," earlier in this chapter.

Hospitals   In a medical emergency, call 911. The following facilities maintain 24-hour emergency rooms: **Ashford Memorial Community Hospital,** 1451 Ashford Ave. (☎ 787/721-2160), and the **San Juan Health Center,** Avenida De Diego 200 (☎ 787/725-0202).

Information   See "Visitor Information," earlier in this chapter.

Language   English is understood at the big resorts and in most of San Juan. Out in the island, Spanish is still *numero uno.* See the Appendix for basic English and Spanish words.

Liquor Laws   You must be 21 years of age to purchase liquor in stores or buy drinks in hotels, bars, and restaurants. If you are 21 or over but look younger, bring a photo identification such as a driver's license which gives your date of birth.

Maps   See "Getting Around," earlier in this chapter.

Marriages   There are no residency requirements for getting married in Puerto Rico. You'll need parental consent if either of you is under 18. Blood tests are required, although a test conducted within 10 days of the ceremony on the U.S. mainland will suffice. A doctor must sign the license after an examination of the bride and groom. For complete details, contact the **Commonwealth of Puerto Rico Health Department,** Demographic Register, 26 Fernandez Juncos (P.O. Box 9342), San Juan, PR 00908 (☎ 787/728-7980).

Newspapers/Magazines   *The San Juan Star,* a daily English-language newspaper, has been called the *"International Herald Tribune* of the Caribbean." It concentrates extensively on news from the United States. You can also pick up copies of *USA Today* at most news kiosks. If you read Spanish, you might enjoy *El Nuevo Dia,* the most popular local tabloid. Few significant magazines are published on Puerto Rico, but *Time* and *Newsweek* are available at most newsstands.

Passports   See "Visitor Information," earlier in this chapter.

Pets   To bring your pet in, you must produce a health certificate from a mainland veterinarian and show proof of vaccination against rabies. Very few hotels allow animals, so check in advance. Many veterinarians are listed in the yellow pages of the local telephone book.

Postal Services   Since the U.S. Postal Service is responsible for handling mail on the island, the regulations and tariffs are the same as on the mainland. Stamps may be purchased at any post office, each of which is open Monday through Friday from 8am to 5pm. Saturday hours are 8am to noon (closed Sunday). As on the mainland, one can purchase stamps at vending machines in airports, stores, and hotels. First class letters to addresses within Puerto Rico, the United States, and its territories cost 32¢; postcards, 20¢. Letters and postcards to Canada both cost 46¢ for the first half-ounce. Letters and postcards to other countries cost 60¢ for the first half-ounce.

Safety   Crime exists here as it does everywhere. Use common sense and take precautions. Muggings are commonplace on the Condado and Isla Verde beaches, so you might want to confine your moonlit beach nights to the fenced-in and guarded areas around some of the major hotels. The countryside of Puerto Rico is safer than San Juan, but caution is always the rule. Avoid small and narrow country roads and isolated beaches, either night or day.

Taxes   In addition to the government tax of 7% in regular hotels or 10% in hotels with casinos, some hotels add a 10% service charge to your bill. If they don't, you're expected to tip for services rendered. There is no airport departure tax.

Telephone, Telex, and Fax   Coin-operated phones are found throughout the island, with a particularly dense concentration in San Juan. After depositing your coins, you can dial a seven-digit number at the sound of the dial tone. If you're calling long distance, to either a distant corner of Puerto Rico or anywhere off-island, add a "1" before the numbers. When you're placing a call to the U.S. mainland or to anywhere else overseas, preface the number with 011. An operator (or a recorded voice) will tell you how much money to deposit, although you'll probably find it more practical to read him or her the digits of a calling card issued by such long-distance carriers as Sprint, AT&T, or MCI. Public phones that allow credit cards such as American Express, Visa, or MasterCard to be inserted or "swiped" through a magnetic slot are rare on the island. Most of these are located at the San Juan airport. Most phone booths contain printed instructions for dialing. Local calls are 10¢.

Most hotels will send a telex or fax for you and bill the costs to your room, and in some cases, they'll even send a fax for a nonresident if you agree to pay a surcharge. Barring that, several agencies in San Juan will send a fax anywhere you want for a fee. Many are associated with print shops/photocopy stands. A worthy candidate is **Insti-Print,** 1229 F.D. Roosevelt Blvd., Puerto Nuevo, San Juan, PR 00920 (☎ 787/782-7830), which charges $2.50 per page for faxes sent to New York City.

Time   Puerto Rico is on Atlantic Standard Time year-round, which is 1 hour later than Eastern Standard Time. Puerto Rico does not go on Daylight Saving Time, however, so the time here is the same year-round.

Tipping   Tip as you would on the U.S. mainland. That usually means 15% in restaurants, except for fast-food places; 10% in bars; and 10% to 15% for taxi drivers, hairdressers, and other services, depending on the quality of the service rendered. Tip a porter, either at the airport or at your hotel, between 75¢ and $1 per bag. Europeans and others may not like this method of compensation, but the U.S. government imposes income tax on wait staff and other service industry workers whose income is tip-based according to the gross receipts of their employers; therefore, those workers could end up paying tax on a tip you didn't give them.

Visitor Information   See "Visitor Information, Entry Requirements & Money" earlier in this chapter.

Weights and Measures   There's a mixed bag of measurements in Puerto Rico. Due to its Spanish tradition, most weights (meat and poultry) and measures (gasoline and road distances) are metric. But because of the American presence, speed limits appear in miles per hour, and liquids such as beer are sold by the ounce.

10 Tips on Choosing Your Accommodations

HOTELS & RESORTS

There is no rigid classification of Puerto Rican hotels. The word "deluxe" is often used—or misused—when "first class" might have been a more appropriate term. First class itself often isn't. For that and other reasons, we've presented fairly detailed descriptions of the properties, so that you'll get an idea of what to expect once you're there.

Even in the deluxe and first-class properties, however, don't expect top-rate service and efficiency. The slow tropical pace is what folks mean when they talk about

---

What the Symbols Mean

First-time travelers to Puerto Rico may at first be confused by classifications on hotel-room rate sheets. We've used these same classifications in this guide. One of the most common rates is **MAP,** meaning Modified American Plan. Simply put, that means room, breakfast, and dinner, unless the room rate is quoted separately in a listing, and then it means only breakfast and dinner. **CP** means Continental Plan—that is, room and a light breakfast. **EP** is European Plan—room only. **AP** (American Plan) is the most expensive rate because it includes your room and three meals a day.

"island time." Also, "things" often don't work as well in the tropics as they do in some of the fancy resorts of California or Europe. When you go to turn on the shower, sometimes you get water and sometimes you don't. You may even experience power failures.

SPAS

The Penthouse spa at the **El San Juan Hotel & Casino** has full amenities for men and women, including fitness evaluations, supervised weight-loss programs, aerobics classes, sauna, steam room, and massage. It's open 7 days a week, year-round. A daily fee for individual services is assessed. See chapter 5.

The Plaza Spa at the **Condado Plaza Hotel & Casino** features Universal weight-training machines, video exercycles, sauna, whirlpool, facials, and massages. See chapter 5.

The fitness center at the **Palmas del Mar Resort** in Humacao features hydra-fitness exercise equipment, exercise programs, free-weight training, and computerized fitness evaluations. It's open 7 days a week. See chapter 9.

The Spa Caribe at the **Hyatt Regency Cerromar Beach** offers shape-up programs, including aerobics and "talking" Powercise machines, health evaluations, plus skin- and body-care treatments, such as massage facials. See chapter 9.

At the **Parador Baños de Coamo** in Coamo there are therapeutic thermal springs—one hot, one cool. There are also two swimming pools (one for children) and a tennis court. It's open daily. See chapter 8.

THE PUERTO RICAN GUESTHOUSE

An entirely different type of accommodation is the guesthouse, where Puerto Ricans themselves usually stay when they travel. Ranging in size from 7 to 25 rooms, they offer a familial atmosphere. Many are on or near the beach, some have pools or sundecks, and a number serve meals.

In Puerto Rico, however, the term "guesthouse" can mean anything. Sometimes they are like simple motels built around swimming pools. Others have small individual cottages with their own kitchenettes, constructed around a main building in which you'll often find a bar and a restaurant serving local food. Some are surprisingly comfortable, often with private baths and swimming pools. You may or may not have air-conditioning. The rooms are sometimes cooled by ceiling fans or the trade winds, blowing through open windows at night.

For value, the guesthouse can't be topped. Staying at a guesthouse, you can journey over to a big beach resort, using its seaside facilities for only a small charge, perhaps no more than $3. Although bereft of frills, the guesthouses we've recommended are clean and safe for families or single women. However, the cheapest ones are not places where you'd want to spend a lot of time because of their modest furnishings.

For further information, contact the **Puerto Rico Tourism Company,** 575 Fifth Ave., New York, NY 10017 (☎ **212/599-6262** or 800/223-6530).

PARADORES

In an effort to lure travelers beyond the hotels and casinos of San Juan's historic district to the tranquil natural beauty of the island's countryside, the Puerto Rico Tourism Company offers *paradores puertorriqueños*—charming country inns—which are comfortable bases for exploring the island's varied attractions. Vacationers seeking a peaceful idyll can also choose from several privately owned and operated guesthouses.

Using Spain's parador system as a model, the Puerto Rico Tourism Company established the paradores in 1973 to encourage tourism across the island. Each of the paradores is situated in a historic place or site of unusual scenic beauty and must meet high standards of service and cleanliness.

Some of the paradores are located in the mountains and others by the sea. Most have swimming pools, and all offer excellent Puerto Rican cuisine. Many are within easy driving distance of San Juan (see chapter 8). To make a reservation at one of the paradores, call **800/443-0266** in the United States (8am to noon and 1 to 4:30pm Atlantic time).

VILLAS & VACATION HOMES

Throughout the Caribbean, including Puerto Rico, you can often secure good deals by renting privately owned villas and vacation homes.

Many villas have a staff, or at least a maid who comes in a few days a week, and they also provide the essentials of home life, including bed linen and cooking paraphernalia. Condos usually come with a reception desk and are often comparable to life in a suite at a big resort hotel. Nearly all condo complexes have swimming pools (some have more than one).

Private apartments are rented either with or without maid service. This is more of a no-frills option than the villas and condos. The apartments may not be in buildings with swimming pools, and they may not have a front desk to help you. Cottages offer the most free-wheeling way to live among the major categories of vacation homes. Most cottages are fairly simple, many opening in an ideal fashion onto a beach, whereas others may be clustered around a communal swimming pool. Many contain no more than a simple bedroom together with a small kitchen and bath. For the peak winter season, reservations should be made at least 5 or 6 months in advance.

Dozens of agents throughout the United States and Canada offer these types of rentals (see "Rental Agencies," below, for some recommendations). You can also write to local tourist offices, which can advise you on vacation home rentals.

Travel experts agree that savings, especially for a family of three to six people, or two or three couples, can range from 50% to 60% of what a hotel would cost. If there are only two in your party, these savings probably don't apply.

RENTAL AGENCIES

Agencies specializing in renting properties in Puerto Rico and the other Caribbean islands include:

Villas of Distinction, P.O. Box 55, Armonk, NY 10504 (☎ **914/273-3331** or 800/289-0900), is one of the best offering "complete vacations," including airfare,

The Paradores of Puerto Rico

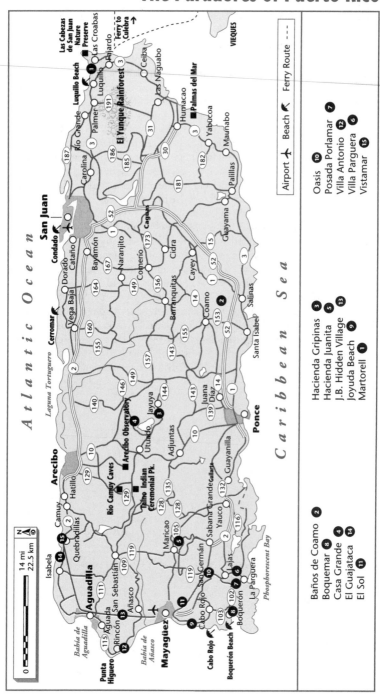

Airport ✈ Beach ⌖ Ferry Route - - -

Baños de Coamo ❷
Boquemar ❽
Casa Grande ❹
El Guajataca ⓮
El Sol ⓫

Hacienda Gripinas ❸
Hacienda Juanita ❺
J.B. Hidden Village ⓭
Joyuda Beach ❾
Martorell ❶

Oasis ❿
Posada Porlamar ❼
Villa Antonio ⓬
Villa Parguera ❻
Vistamar ⓯

rental car, and domestic help. Some private villas have two to five bedrooms, and almost every villa has a swimming pool.

Caribbean Connections Plus, P.O. Box 261, Trumbull, CT 06611 (☎ 203/261-8603; fax 203/261-8295), offers many apartments, cottages, and villas in the Caribbean. Caribbean Connections specializes in island hopping with JetAir, and it offers especially attractive deals for U.S. West Coast travelers. This is one of the few reservations services whose staff has actually been on the islands, so members can talk to people from experience and not from a computer screen.

VHR, Worldwide, 235 Kensington Ave., Norwood, NJ 07648 (☎ 201/767-9393 or 800/633-3284 in the U.S. and Canada), offers the most comprehensive portfolio of luxury villas, condominiums, resort suites, and apartments for rent in the Caribbean, including complete packages for airfare and car rentals. The company's more than 4,000 homes and suite resorts are handpicked by the staff, and accommodations are generally less expensive than comparable hotel rooms.

Hideaways International, 767 Islington St., Portsmouth, NH 03801 (☎ 603/430-4433 or 800/843-4433; fax 603/430-4444), provides a 144-page guide with illustrations of its accommodations in the Caribbean so you'll get some idea of what you're renting. Most of its villas, which can accommodate up to three couples or a large family of about 10, come with maid service. You can also ask this travel club about discounts on plane fares and car rentals as well.

Rent-a-Home International, 7200 34th Ave. NW, Seattle, WA 98117 (☎ 206/789-9377; fax 206/789-9379), maintains an inventory of several thousand properties, specializing in condos and villas with weekly rates ranging from $700 to $30,000. It arranges weekly or longer bookings. For their color catalog including prices, descriptions, and pictures, send $15, which will be applied to your next rental.

Sometimes local tourist offices will also advise you on vacation-home rentals if you write or call them directly.

Getting to Know San Juan

San Juan, the capital city, will introduce you to the commonwealth. All but a handful of visitors arrive here. This is the political base, economic powerhouse, and cultural center of the island, and home to about one-third of all Puerto Ricans.

The second-oldest city in the Americas (behind Santo Domingo in the Dominican Republic), this metropolis presents two completely different faces to the world. On one hand, the charming historic district, Old San Juan, is strongly reminiscent of the Spanish Empire. On the other, modern expressways cut through its urban sprawl to link towering concrete buildings and beachfront hotels resembling those of Miami Beach.

Old San Juan is a seven-square-block area that was once completely enclosed by a wall erected by the Spanish with slave labor. This most powerful fortress in the Caribbean repeatedly was able to hold off would-be attackers. By the 19th century, however, the old city had become one of the most charming residential and commercial areas of the Caribbean. Today it's a setting for restaurants and shops. Most of the major resort hotels are located nearby along the Condado beachfront and at Isla Verde (see chapter 5).

1 Orientation

ARRIVING

BY PLANE

Visitors from overseas arrive at **Luis Muñoz Marín International Airport** (☎ 787/791-1014), the major transportation center of the Caribbean. Both American Airlines and its subsidiary, American Eagle, use it as their Caribbean hub. The international and domestic flights of other airlines also land here. The airport is situated on the easternmost side of the city, rather inconvenient to nearly all hotels unless you're staying at one of the resorts or small inns at Isla Verde.

The airport offers an array of services including a tourist information center, fast-food restaurants, barbershops and hairdressers, coin lockers to store luggage (particularly useful if you're visiting one of the smaller islands on a shuttle plane), bookstores, banks, money-exchange kiosks, and even a bar (open daily from noon to 4pm) offering a sampling of the best Puerto Rican rums in all their many hues and flavors.

Getting from the Airport into the City

BY TAXI   Dozens of taxis line up outside the airport to meet arriving flights, so you rarely have to wait. Fares can vary widely, depending on traffic conditions. If you're staying at one of the beachfront hotels along the Condado, the average fare from the airport will be about $13.

Although technically cab drivers should turn on their meters, more often than not they'll quote a flat rate before starting out.

BY MINIVAN OR LIMOUSINE   Be aware that a wide variety of vehicles at the San Juan airport call themselves *limosinas* (their Spanish name). One outfit whose sign-up desk is in the arrivals hall of the international airport, near American Airlines, is the **Airport Limousine Service** (☎ 787/791-4745). They offer minivan service from the airport to various San Juan neighborhoods for prices that are lower than what a taxi would charge. If eight passengers can be rounded up to share a minivan, the fare per person for transportation, with luggage, to any hotel in Isla Verde is $3.50 to $4.50; to the Condado district, $4 to $5; and to Old San Juan, $4.50 to $5.70. Or you can rent the entire van or limousine from the airport for yourself for $30 to Isla Verde, $35 to the Condado, or $40 to Old San Juan.

For conventional limousine service, **Bracero Limousine** (☎ 787/740-0444) offers upholstered cars with drivers to meet you and your entourage at the arrivals terminal of the airport for luxurious and strictly private transportation to your hotel. The charge within San Juan ranges from $105 to $145, depending on your destination; arrangements should be made before your arrival.

BY CAR   Details on car rentals can be found in the "Getting Around" section of chapter 3, "Planning a Trip to Puerto Rico."

It's best to reserve a car before you leave home. However, it's also possible to reserve a car once you arrive at the San Juan airport, where all the major car-rental companies have kiosks.

To drive into the city, head west along Route 26, which becomes Route 25 as it enters Old San Juan. If you stay on Route 25 (also called Avenida Muñoz Rivera), you'll have the best view of the ocean and the monumental city walls.

Just before reaching the Capitol building, turn left between the Natural Resources Department and the modern House of Representatives office building. Go two blocks until you reach the intersection of Paseo de Covadonga, then take a right past the Treasury Building and park your car in the Covadonga Parking Garage on the left. This garage is open 24 hours. A free shuttle bus service loops the old town from here on two different routes.

BY BUS   Those with little luggage can take the T1 bus, which runs to the center of the city.

BY CRUISE SHIP

The Port of San Juan is the busiest ocean terminal in the West Indies. It's estimated that half the trade in the Caribbean passes through here. The harbor where both commercial cargo and cruise ships arrive lies outside San Juan Bay, a body of water that's about 3 miles long and 1 mile wide—and almost completely landlocked. The long bay protects vessels from any roughness in the Atlantic Ocean.

The major cruise ships of the Caribbean, such as the *Sovereign of the Seas,* anchor alongside the various piers. There are about 710 cruise-ship arrivals every year, bringing nearly 851,000 passengers.

From the docks, a spacious walkway connects the piers to the cobblestone streets of Old San Juan. Most cruise-ship passengers head for this district to shop. One can also take a waiting taxi and head for the beaches of Condado. For advice and maps, contact the **Tourist Information Center** at La Casita, near Pier 1 in Old San Juan (☎ 787/721-2400). The dock area, now restored, is an attractive place for strolling, with its plazas, fountains, promenades, and beaches.

VISITOR INFORMATION

Tourist information is available at the **Luis Muñoz Marín Airport** (☎ 787/791-1014), daily from 9am to 5:30pm. Another office is at **La Casita,** Pier 1, Old San Juan (☎ 787/722-1709).

CITY LAYOUT

Metropolitan San Juan includes the old walled city on San Juan Island; the city center on San Juan Island, containing the Capitol building; Santurce, on a larger peninsula, which is reached by causeway bridges from San Juan Island (the lagoonfront section here is called Miramar); Condado, the narrow peninsula that stretches from San Juan Island to Santurce; Hato Rey, the business center; Río Piedras, site of the University of Puerto Rico; and Bayamón, an industrial and residential quarter.

The Condado strip of beachfront hotels, restaurants, casinos, and nightclubs is separated from Miramar by a lagoon. Isla Verde, another resort area, is near the airport, which is separated from the rest of San Juan by an isthmus.

FINDING AN ADDRESS   Finding an address in San Juan isn't always easy. You'll have to contend not only with missing street signs and numbers but also with street addresses that appear sometimes in English and at other times in Spanish. The most common Spanish terms for thoroughfares are *calle* (street) and *avenida* (avenue). When they are used, the street number will follow them; for example, the Gran Hotel El Convento is located at Calle del Cristo 100, in Old San Juan. Locating a building in Old San Juan is relatively easy, with the odd numbers on one side of the street and the even numbers on the other. The area is only seven square blocks, so by walking around it's possible to locate most addresses.

STREET MAPS   *Qué Pasa?,* the monthly tourist magazine distributed free by the tourist office, contains accurate, easy-to-read maps of San Juan and the Condado, pinpointing the major attractions.

NEIGHBORHOODS IN BRIEF

Old San Juan   This seven-square-block area is probably the most historic in the West Indies. Filled with Spanish colonial architecture and under constant restoration, it lies on the western end of an islet. It's encircled by water; on the north is the Atlantic Ocean and on the south and west is the tranquil San Juan Bay. Ponte San Antonio bridge connects the old town with "mainland" Puerto Rico. Ramparts and old Spanish fortresses form its outer walls.

Puerto de Tierra   Translated as "gateway to the land" or "gateway to the island," Puerto de Tierra lies just east of the old city walls of San Juan. This section of metropolitan San Juan is split by Avenida Ponce de León and interconnects the historic peninsula of Old San Juan with the Puerto Rican "mainland." The settlement, founded by freed black slaves, today functions as the island's administrative center and is the site of many military and government buildings, including the Capitol building and various U.S. naval reserves.

Miramar   This is an upscale residential neighborhood, across the bridge from Puerto de Tierra. Many yachts anchor in its waters on the bay side of Ponte Isla Grande, and some of the finest homes on Puerto Rico are found here. It's also the

San Juan Orientation

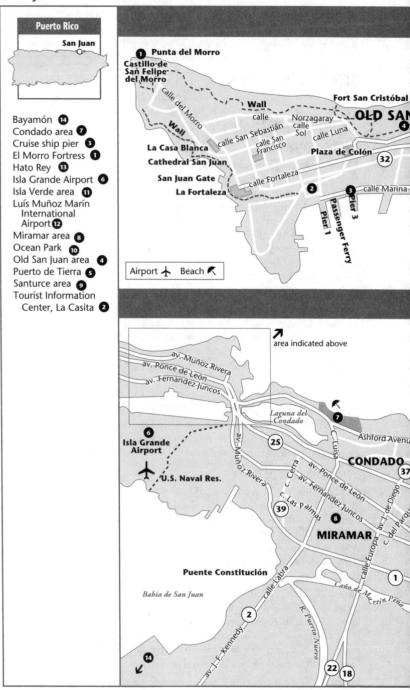

Puerto Rico

San Juan

1 Punta del Morro

Castillo de
San Felipe
del Morro

Fort San Cristóbal

Wall

calle

calle del Morro

Norzagaray
calle
Sol

OLD SAN

4

Wall

calle San Sebastián

calle San
Francisco

calle Luna

La Casa Blanca

Cathedral San Juan

Plaza de Colón **32**

San Juan Gate

calle Fortaleza

La Fortaleza

2

3 Pier 3

calle Marina

Passenger Ferry

Pier 1

Airport ✈ Beach ⌐

↗
area indicated above

av. Muñoz Rivera
av. Ponce de León
av. Fernandez Juncos

Laguna del
Condado

⌐
7

Ashford Avenu

6
Isla Grande
Airport
✈

25

C. Luisa

CONDADO

37

U.S. Naval Res.

av. Muñoz Rivera

c. Cerra

av. Ponce de León

av. Fernandez Juncos

av. J. de Diego

39

c. Las Palmas

8

MIRAMAR

calle Europa

c. del Parqu

1

Puente Constitución

calle Labra

Caño de Martín Peña

Bahía de San Juan

2

R. Puerto Nuevo

14 ↙

av. J. F. Kennedy

22 **18**

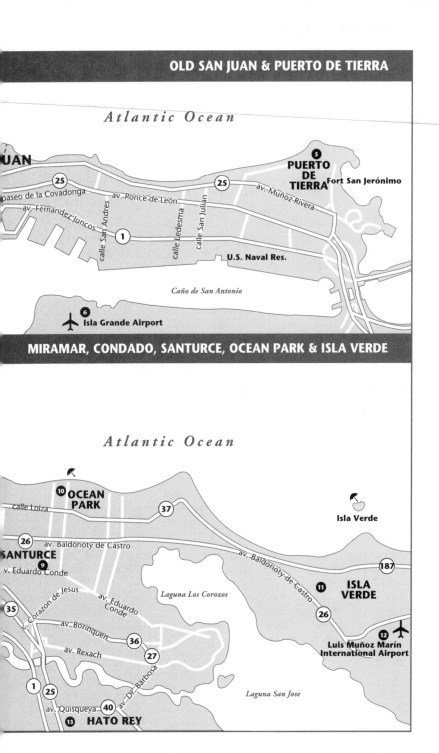

Atlantic Ocean

JUAN

5
PUERTO DE TIERRA
Fort San Jerónimo

25
25
av. Muñoz Rivera

paseo de la Covadonga
av.-Ponce-de-León
calle San Andrés
calle Ledesma
calle San Julián

av. Fernandez Juncos

1

U.S. Naval Res.

Caño de San Antonio

6
Isla Grande Airport

Atlantic Ocean

10 OCEAN PARK
calle Loiza
37

Isla Verde

26
av. Baldorioty de Castro
SANTURCE
av. Baldorioty de Castro
187

v. Eduardo Conde
9

11 ISLA VERDE

c. Corazon de Jesus
av. Eduardo Conde
Laguna Los Corozos

35
26

av. Borinquen
36
12
Luis Muñoz Marín International Airport

av. Rexach
27

1
25

av. Quisqueya
40
av. Dr. Barbosa
Laguna San Jose

13 HATO REY

site of Isla Grande Airport, where you can board flights to the offshore islands of Vieques and Culebra.

Condado/Santurce   The Condado is the glittering beachfront strip of San Juan—site of most of the major hotels. It's linked to Puerto de Tierra and Old San Juan by a bridge built in 1910. The greater neighborhood of Santurce, adjoining the Condado, was once the most exclusive in San Juan. However, now it's in sad decline.

Hato Rey   Santurce's loss was Hato Rey's gain. Situated to the south of the Martín Peña canal, this area today is the Wall Street of the West Indies, filled with many high-rises, a large federal complex, and many business and banking offices. Actually, it was once a marsh until landfill and concrete changed it forever.

Río Piedras   South of both Hato Rey and Santurce, this is the site of the University of Puerto Rico and its student population. It's dominated by the landmark Roosevelt Bell Tower, named for Theodore Roosevelt, who donated the money for its construction. The main thoroughfare is Paseo de Diego, site of a popular local market where produce is sold. The Agricultural Experimental Station of Puerto Rico maintains a Botanical Garden; there are many tropical plants here, including 125 species of palms.

Bayamón   The San Juan sprawl has reached this once-distant southwestern suburb, which had been farmland before industry moved in and took over. Some 200,000 people and nearly 200 factories are now located in this geographically large district. Bus no. 46 from the center of San Juan runs out here. At Route 2, km 6.4, in Guayanobo are the ruins of Caparra, the first colonial settlement on the island.

2 Getting Around

BY TAXI   Taxis—operated by the Public Service Commission (PSC)—are metered in San Juan, or are supposed to be. Make sure when you get in that the meter is turned off and that it registers zero. You don't want to end up paying the previous passenger's fares as well as your own. The initial charge is $1, plus 10¢ for each one-tenth of a mile and 50¢ for every suitcase. The minimum fare is $3.

Various taxi companies are listed in the yellow pages of the phone book under "Taxis," or you can call the PSC at **787/756-1919** to request information or report any irregularities.

BY BUS   The Metropolitan Bus Authority operates buses in the greater San Juan area. Bus stops are marked by upright metal signs or yellow posts reading PARADA. There's one bus terminal in the dock area and another at the Plaza de Colón. A typical fare is 25¢ to 50¢.

You can take an air-conditioned bus from the Condado or Isla Verde hotels to Old San Juan. You'll be deposited at the main bus terminal across the street from the Cataño ferry pier and the Plaza de Colón. This section of San Juan is the starting point for many metropolitan bus routes.

For example, bus no. 2 goes from the Plaza de Colón along the Condado, eventually reaching the commercial section of San Juan, Hato Rey. Bus no. A7 also passes from Old San Juan to the Condado and goes on to Avenida Isla Verde, and no. T1 heads for Avenida De Diego in the Condado district, then makes a long run to Isla Verde and the airport.

For more information about bus routes in San Juan, call **787/767-7979.**

BY TROLLEY   When you tire of walking around Old San Juan, you can board one of the free trolleys that run through the historic area. Departure points are the

Marina and La Puntilla, but you can get on anyplace along the route. Relax and enjoy the sights as the trolleys rumble through the old and narrow streets.

ON FOOT   This is the only way to explore Old San Juan. All the major attractions can easily be covered in a day. However, if you're going from Old San Juan to Isla Verde, you'll need to rely on public transportation.

Walking can, of course, be risky. Muggings are sometimes reported during the daylight hours, although nighttime is certainly more dangerous. Take extreme caution if walking in Old San Juan at night. Never walk along the Condado beaches at night; the muggers there are just waiting for you.

BY RENTAL CAR   See chapter 3, "Planning a Trip to Puerto Rico," for details—including some reasons why you *shouldn't* plan to drive on Puerto Rico.

BY FERRY   The *Agua Express* connects Old San Juan with the industrial and residential communities of Hato Rey and Cataño, across the bay. Ferries depart daily every 30 minutes from 6am to 9pm. The one-way fare to Hato Rey is 75¢, and the one-way fare to Cataño is 50¢. Departures are from the San Juan Terminal at the pier in Old San Juan. However, it's best to avoid rush hours since hundreds of locals who work in town use this ferry. Each ride lasts about 20 minutes. For more information, call **787/751-7055.**

FAST FACTS: San Juan

American Express   The agency is represented in San Juan by **Travel Network,** 1035 Ashford Ave., Condado (☎ **787/725-0950**). The office is open Monday through Friday from 9am to 1pm and 2 to 5pm, on Saturday from 9am to noon.

Bookstores   The **Book Store,** at Calle San José 255 (☎ **787/724-1815**), in Old San Juan, has one of Puerto Rico's best selections of English-language titles. Hours are Monday through Saturday from 9am to 7pm.

Camera and Film   Both **Cinefoto** (☎ **787/753-7238**) and **Rabola** (☎ **787/753-8778**), located in the Plaza Las Americas Shopping Mall in Hato Rey, offer a wide variety of photographic supplies. Cinefoto is open Monday through Saturday from 9am to 10pm. Rabola is open Monday through Saturday from 9am to 9pm, Sunday 11am to 5pm.

Car Rentals   See "Getting Around," in chapter 3. If you want to reserve after you've arrived in Puerto Rico, call **787/791-2500** to reserve a car at **Avis, 787/791-3685** to reserve a car at **Budget,** or **787/791-0840** to reserve a car at **Hertz.**

Currency Exchange   The unit of currency is the U.S. dollar, so American travelers will not need this service. But for British and Canadian travelers, most banks will provide this service. You can also exchange money at the **Luis Muñoz Marín International Airport.** Otherwise, in Old San Juan, go to **Caribbean Foreign Exchange,** Calle Tetuan 201B (☎ **787/722-8222**). Hours are Monday through Friday from 9am to 4:30pm and Saturday noon to 4pm. Also see "Visitor Information, Entry Requirements & Money" in chapter 3.

Drugstores   One of the most centrally located pharmacies is the **Puerto Rican Drug Co.,** Calle San Francisco 157 (☎ **787/725-2202**), in Old San Juan. It's open Monday through Saturday from 7:30am to 9:30pm and on Sunday from 8am to 7:30pm. **Walgreen's,** 1130 Ashford Ave., Condado (☎ **787/725-1510**), is open 24 hours a day.

Emergencies   In an emergency, dial 911. Or call the local **police** (☎ **787/343-2020**), **fire department** (☎ **787/343-2330**), **ambulance** (☎ **787/343-2550**), or **medical assistance** (☎ 787/754-3535). Dental emergencies are handled at the **San Juan Health Center** at Avenida De Diego 200 in Santurce (☎ 787/725-0202).

Eyeglasses Go to **Pearle Vision Express,** Plaza Las Americas Shopping Mall (☎ 787/753-1033). Hours are Monday through Saturday from 9am to 10pm and Sunday 11am to 7pm.

Hospitals **Ashford Memorial Community Hospital,** 1451 Ashford Ave. (☎ 787/721-2160), and the **San Juan Health Center,** Avenida De Diego 200 (☎ 787/725-0202), both maintain 24-hour emergency rooms.

Information See "Visitor Information," earlier in this chapter.

Post Office In San Juan, the General Post Office is at 585 Roosevelt Ave. (☎ 787/767-3604). If you don't know your address in San Juan, you can ask that your mail be sent here "c/o General Delivery." This main branch is open Monday through Friday from 7:30am to 4:30pm. A letter from Puerto Rico to the U.S. mainland will arrive in about 4 days. See "Fast Facts: Puerto Rico," in chapter 3, for more information.

Safety Stay away from the back streets of San Juan and don't venture onto the unguarded public stretches of the Condado and Isla Verde beaches at night. See "Getting Around," above, for more information about walking in Old San Juan.

Telephone, Telex, and Fax Many public telephones are available at **World Service Telephone (AT&T),** Pier 1, Old San Juan (☎ 787/721-2520). To send a fax or telex, go to **Fax & Telex Service,** Pereira Diversified Communications, 1020 Ashford Ave., Santurce (☎ 787/723-8233). For more information, see also "Fast Facts: Puerto Rico," chapter 3.

Tourist Offices See "Visitor Information," earlier in this chapter.

Transit Information For information about bus routes in San Juan, call **787/ 767-7979.**

Where to Stay in San Juan 5

Whatever your preferences in accommodations—a beachfront resort or a place in the midst of historic Old San Juan, sumptuous luxury or an austere, inexpensive base from which to see the sights—you can find a perfect fit in San Juan.

In addition to checking the recommendations listed here, you may want to confer with a travel agent; there are package deals galore that can save you money and match you with an establishment that meets your requirements. See "Package Tours" in chapter 3.

In general, hotels charging more than $250 a night for a double room are considered **very expensive;** those asking $180 to $250 for a double are **expensive;** and those costing $100 to $180 are **moderate.** Anything under $100 is **inexpensive.** All rooms have private baths unless otherwise noted.

TAXES & SERVICE CHARGES

All hotel rooms in Puerto Rico are subject to a 7% to 9% tax, which is *not* included in the rates given here. Most hotels also add a 10% service charge. When booking a room, it's always best to inquire about these added charges.

RESERVATIONS

You may make your reservations by telephone, mail, or fax. If you're booking into a chain hotel, such as a Hilton, you can call toll free in many countries and easily make your reservations by phone. Whenever this service is available, the North American toll-free numbers are given in the listings below.

You can usually cancel a room reservation 1 week ahead of time and get a full refund. A few hotelkeepers will return your money on cancellations up to 3 days before the reservation date; others won't return any of your deposit, even if you cancel far in advance. It's best to clarify this issue in advance. It's a good idea to include a stamped, self-addressed envelope with your payment so the hotel can easily send you a receipt and confirmation.

If you arrive without a reservation, begin your search for a room as early in the day as possible. If you arrive late at night and without a reservation, you may have to take what you can get, often in a price range much higher than you'd like to pay.

San Juan Accommodations

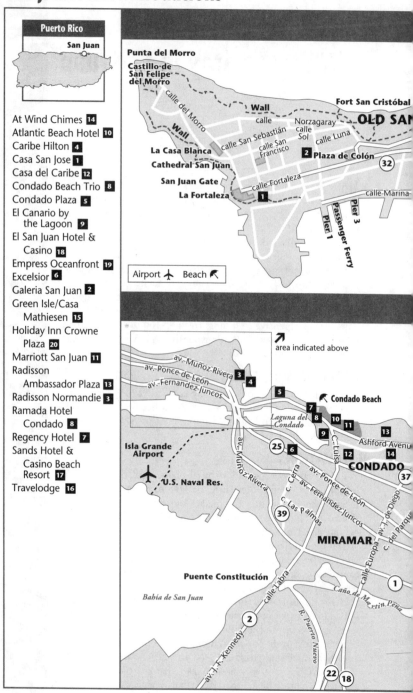

Puerto Rico

San Juan

At Wind Chimes **14**
Atlantic Beach Hotel **10**
Caribe Hilton **4**
Casa San Jose **1**
Casa del Caribe **12**
Condado Beach Trio **8**
Condado Plaza **5**
El Canario by
  the Lagoon **9**
El San Juan Hotel &
  Casino **18**
Empress Oceanfront **19**
Excelsior **6**
Galeria San Juan **2**
Green Isle/Casa
  Mathiesen **15**
Holiday Inn Crowne
  Plaza **20**
Marriott San Juan **11**
Radisson
  Ambassador Plaza **13**
Radisson Normandie **3**
Ramada Hotel
  Condado **8**
Regency Hotel **7**
Sands Hotel &
  Casino Beach
  Resort **17**
Travelodge **16**

Punta del Morro
Castillo de San Felipe del Morro
Fort San Cristóbal
Wall
calle del Morro
Wall
calle Norzagaray
OLD SAN
calle San Sebastián
calle Sol
calle Luna
La Casa Blanca
calle San Francisco
Plaza de Colón **2**
32
Cathedral San Juan
San Juan Gate
calle Fortaleza
La Fortaleza **1**
calle Marina
Pier 3
Passenger Ferry
Pier 1

Airport ✈   Beach 🏖

area indicated above
av.-Muñoz-Rivera **3**
av.-Ponce-de-León **4**
av.-Fernandez-Juncos **5**
Condado Beach
7
Laguna del Condado **8** **10** **11**
9 **13**
Isla Grande Airport
25 **6**
Ashford Avenu
C. Luisa **12** **14**
✈ U.S. Naval Res.
av.-Muñoz-Rivera
c. Cerra
av.-Ponce-de-León
CONDADO
37
c. Las palmas
av.-Fernandez-Juncos
av.-J.-de-Diego
39
MIRAMAR
calle-Europa
c. del Parque
Puente Constitución
1
Caño de Martin Peña
Bahía de San Juan
calle-Labra
R. Puerto Nuevo
2
av.-J.-F.-Kennedy
22 **18**

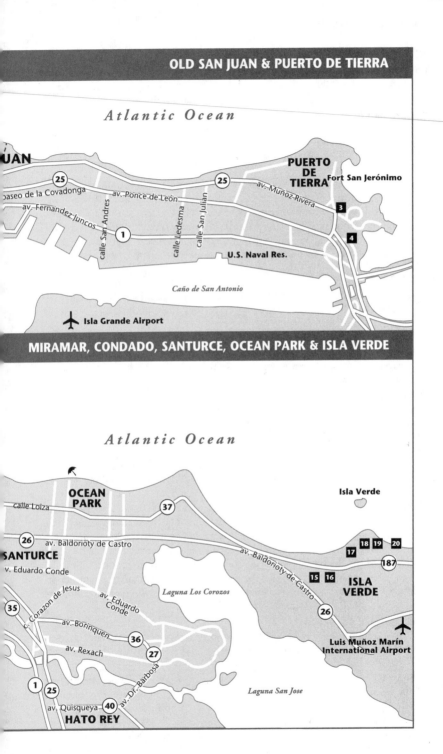

Atlantic Ocean

JUAN

PUERTO DE TIERRA

Fort San Jerónimo

(25) paseo de la Covadonga

av. Ponce de León

(25)

av. Muñoz Rivera

3

av. Fernandez Juncos

calle San Andres

calle Lledesma

calle San Julián

(1)

4

U.S. Naval Res.

Caño de San Antonio

✈ **Isla Grande Airport**

MIRAMAR, CONDADO, SANTURCE, OCEAN PARK & ISLA VERDE

Atlantic Ocean

OCEAN PARK

calle Loiza

Isla Verde

(37)

(26) av. Baldorioty de Castro

SANTURCE

v. Eduardo Conde

av. Baldorioty de Castro

18 **19** **20**

17

(187)

15 **16**

ISLA VERDE

(35)

c. Corazon de Jesus

av. Eduardo Conde

Laguna Los Corozos

(26)

av. Borinquen

✈

(36)

av. Rexach

(27)

Luis Muñoz Marín International Airport

(1) (25)

av. Dr. Barbosa

av. Quisqueya (40)

Laguna San Jose

HATO REY

1 Old San Juan

Choose a hotel in Old San Juan if you're more interested in shopping and attractions than you are in water sports (it's a long way from the beach).

✪ Casa San Juan

Calle San José 159, San Juan, PR 00901. ☎ **787/723-1212** or 800/443-0266 in the U.S. and Canada. Fax 787/723-7620. 4 rms, 5 suites. A/C TEL. Winter, $225–$245 double; $345–$600 suite. Off-season, $180–$200 double; $270–$500 suite. Rates include continental breakfast and evening cocktails. AE, DC, MC, V. Free parking. Bus: A7, T1, or 2.

By anyone's estimate, this is the most stylish hotel in the historic heart of San Juan. Set midway between Calle San Francisco and Calle Luna, near Plaza de Armas, it was originally designed as a private house more than 300 years ago. Shortly before a $1.5 million restoration in 1991 by members of the Mehta family, it suffered the indignity of functioning as a run-down pension, a supermarket, and a variety store. Since the restoration, it has been hailed as one of the best renovations in Puerto Rico.

Today the three-story facade opens to reveal an interior with beamed ceilings, exposed brick, gray-and-white marble floors, and an eclectic collection of European antiques. Accommodations are furnished comfortably with antiques for the most part. An interior patio filled with flowering plants brings light into the establishment's remote corners. Children under 12 are not welcomed.

Dining/Entertainment: Other than breakfast, no meals are served. Drinks are served in the second-floor Salón Grande (free 5 to 7pm, a charge after that).

Services: 24-hour room service (for drinks and light snacks), a staff that can arrange almost anything.

✪ Galería San Juan

Calle Norzagaray 204-206, San Juan, PR 00901. ☎ **787/722-1808.** Fax 787/724-7360. 10 rms (8 with bath), 4 suites. TEL. $85 double without bath, $95 double with bath; $150–$175 suite. Rates include continental breakfast. AE, MC, V. Three free parking spaces (other parking available on street). Bus: A7, T1, or 21.

Set on a hilltop in Old San Juan, across the street from a sweeping view of the sea, this unusual hotel contains a maze of verdant courtyards. During the 1700s, the premises were built to serve as headquarters for an aristocratic Spanish family. Today, the Galería is one of the most whimsically bohemian hotels in the Caribbean, with trompe l'oeil paintings and a labyrinthine layout that has been compared to a large and intriguing piece of sculpture. The guesthouse is run by its Connecticut-born owner, Jan D'Esopo, a noted painter, sculptor, and silk-screen artist. She is assisted by her husband, Manuco Gandía. All courtyards and rooms are adorned with sculptures, silk-screens, or original paintings, usually for sale. The Library Room and the Study Room share a bath and have no air-conditioning; all other units do have air-conditioning. Breakfast is the only meal served.

Gran Hotel El Convento

100 Calle Cristo, Old San Juan, PR 00902. ☎ **787/723-9020** or 1/200/CONVENT. Fax 787/721-2877. 51 rms, 4 suites. A/C MINIBAR TV TEL. Winter, $285–$380 double, off-season, $195–$320 double. Suites $500–$1,200 year round. AE, MC, V. Bus: A7, T1, or 21.

Although it lacks all the glitter and many of the amenities you'd expect from newer and glossier hotels along the Condado or in Isla Verde, this is the most memorable hotel in Puerto Rico. It was built in the 1600s as a Carmelite convent, and despite the modern plumbing and electricity that exist today, it retains many of the solid Spanish colonial features of its original construction. Although it recently closed for a much-needed renovation, the grand opening in the autumn of 1996 marks the

350th anniversary celebration of this historic landmark, whose construction was authorized by King Philip IV of Spain in 1636. The hotel is located 25 minutes from the airport and a mere 5 minutes from the port. It lies just a stroll away from Old San Juan's premier shops, galleries, museums, and monuments.

Since renovation, the first two floors of the hotel house a variety of shops and restaurants. Guest rooms are located on the third through fifth floors. Each unit is equipped with a refrigerator, hairdryer, fax machine, multi-line phone, and VCR. Guests have exclusive use of the pool, fitness center, bar, and dining room for breakfast and lunch. The hotel also boasts an intimate casino for those who enjoy the thrill of gambling but wish to avoid the crowds.

2 Puerto de Tierra

Stay in Puerto de Tierra only if you have a desire to stay at either the Caribe Hilton or the Radisson Normandie (both of which are excellent choices), because when you stay there, you're sandwiched halfway between Old San Juan and the Condado, but you're not getting the advantages of staying right in the heart of either.

Caribe Hilton

Calle Los Rosales, San Juan, PR 00903. ☎ **787/721-0303** or 800/HILTONS in the U.S. or Canada. Fax 787/724-6992. 616 rms, 52 suites. A/C MINIBAR TV TEL. Winter, $330–$449 double; off-season, $239–$349 double. Year-round $660–$1,200 suite. Children stay free in parents' room. AE, DC, MC, V. Self-parking $5 per day, valet parking $14 per day. Bus: A7.

The Hilton stands near the old Fort San Jerónimo, which has been incorporated into its complex. With Old San Juan at its doorstep and San Juan Bay as its backyard, it can be called the gateway to the walled city. Built in 1949 in a 17-acre tropical park, the hotel underwent a major $40-million renovation in the early 1990s. The bedrooms have been given a fresh, modern styling and pastel-colored shades, with color-coordinated carpets, fabrics, and draperies. You can walk to the 16th-century fort or spend the day on a tour of Old San Juan, then come back and enjoy the beach and swimming cove.

Dining/Entertainment: The Caribe Terrace restaurant complex features cuisines from all over the world, with different menus each night. Its venues include El Batey del Pescador, a fish restaurant; La Rôtisserie, devoted to northern Italian cuisine; the Peacock Paradise Chinese restaurant; and the Carib Terrace Bar, with deep and comfortable chairs and huge windows. The 12,400-square-foot casino, adjacent to the lobby atrium area, is open daily from noon to 4am, featuring blackjack, craps, baccarat, roulette, and slot machines.

Services: Room service (6am to 1am), laundry/valet, baby-sitting.

Facilities: Two freshwater swimming pools, health club, aerobics, beach activities, children's playground and playroom, six lighted tennis courts, business center.

Radisson Normandie

Avenida Muñoz Rivera (at the corner of Calle Los Rosales), San Juan, PR 00902. ☎ **787/729-2929** or 800/333-3333. Fax 787/729-3083. 177 rms, 3 suites. A/C MINIBAR TV TEL. Winter, $175–$240 double; $490 suite. Off-season, $165–$195 double; $450 suite. Rates include full American breakfast. AE, DC, MC, V. Parking $3. Bus: A7.

Geared to the upscale business traveler but also a haven for vacationers, the seven-story Normandie first opened in 1942, then reopened in 1988 after a $20-million renovation and reconstruction. Designed in the shape of the famous French ocean liner, the *Normandie,* the hotel is a monument to art deco. Adorned with columns, cornices, and countless decorations, it was built originally for a Parisian cancan dancer who had married a construction tycoon (see box below). The Caribe Hilton next door

A Skinny Dipping Scandal

Much San Juan legend and lore—and at least one scandal—has taken place at what is today the Radisson Normandie hotel. Designed to resemble the famous French ocean liner *Normandie,* it was built by prominent construction tycoon Benitez Rexach to honor his French-born wife, Moineau, a former cancan dancer.

Moineau was a liberated woman well before her time. She wore pants, smoked cigarettes and drank in public, and was always surrounded by men. It is said that "she did everything a lady was not supposed to do at that time" in conservative Old San Juan.

On the night of the hotel's inaugural party in 1942, Moineau and some French friends dived stark naked into the swimming pool. Word of their scandalous skinny dip quickly spread across San Juan, and some conservatives claim it led to the eventual downfall of the hotel (it has since been restored to its former luster). At any rate, many local society matrons boycotted social events at the hotel because of Moineau Rexach.

Benitez Rexach must not have been too upset with Moineau, for he gave her the largest yacht in the world—one equipped with a bed made of pure gold.

has more facilities, but the Radisson Normandie has its own charms and history. Its beachside setting adjoins the Sixto Escobar Stadium.

The elegant and elaborate rooms are well furnished, each with a private bath and all the amenities. The more expensive units are executive rooms.

Dining/Entertainment: The Atrium Lounge is set in a swirl of greenery. A continental menu with tableside cookery is served in the elegant Normandie Restaurant.

Services: Room service (to 11pm), laundry, concierge desk, baby-sitting.

Facilities: Freshwater swimming pool, bar, hair salon, water sports nearby.

3 Condado

This is where you'll find the city's best beaches. Once the Condado area was filled with the residences of the very wealthy, but all that changed with the construction of the Puerto Rico Convention Center. Private villas gave way to high-rise hotel blocks, restaurants, and nightclubs. The Condado shopping area, along Ashford and Magdalena avenues, attracted an extraordinary number of boutiques. There are good bus connections into Old San Juan, or you can take a taxi.

VERY EXPENSIVE

✪ Condado Plaza Hotel & Casino

999 Ashford Ave., San Juan, PR 00902. ☎ **787/721-1000** or 800/468-8588. Fax 787/253-0178. 540 rms, 15 suites. A/C MINIBAR TV TEL. Winter, $220–$380 double; $390–$1,160 suite. Off-season, $220–$320 double; $305–$750 suite. AE, DC, MC, V. Parking $8. Bus: A7.

In this two-in-one hotel complex, the original oceanfront structure is linked by an elevated passageway across Ashford Avenue to its Laguna section. The Hilton is its major rival, but we prefer the style and flair here. In the Laguna wing, which has its own lobby with direct access from the street, every room has a private terrace and a king-size or double bed. The deluxe part of the hotel, the Plaza Club, has 75 units with five bilevel suites. This section has a VIP lounge reserved for the use of its guests, and accommodations have cable TVs and private check-in/check-out service.

The least expensive rooms offered by the hotel are labeled "Ashford," whereas the higher-priced units are called either "Laguna View" or "Oceanfront."

The hotel is linked to El San Juan Hotel (use of the facilities of one can be charged to a room at the other).

Dining/Entertainment: The Lotus Flower is one of the island's premier restaurants. Ristorante Capriccio has seafood prepared northern Italian style as well as a variety of other classic Italian dishes. There are also Las Palmas and Tony Roma's. La Posada, open 24 hours, is known for its prime beef and seafood. For nighttime entertainment, La Fiesta offers live Latin music.

Services: Room service, laundry, chaise longues, and towels provided free at beach and pool.

Facilities: Five swimming pools, water sports, fitness center in the Laguna wing, two lighted Laykold tennis courts.

Radisson Ambassador Plaza Hotel & Casino

1369 Ashford Ave., San Juan, PR 00907. ☎ **787/721-7300** or 800/468-8512. Fax 787/723-6151. 146 rms, 87 suites. A/C TV TEL. Winter, $225–$255 double; from $315 suite. Off-season, $210–$240 double; from $240 suite. AE, DC, DISC, MC, V. Self-parking $5, valet parking $10. Bus: A7.

Although it had always enjoyed an enviable reputation, the Radisson Ambassador Plaza emerged as a star-studded hotel after New York entrepreneur Eugene Romano poured more than $40 million into its restoration in 1990. The hotel offers theatrical drama and big-time pizzazz, with its Czech and Murano chandeliers; hand-blown wall sconces; Turkish, Greek, and Italian marble; and yards of exotic hardwoods. Considering the rates charged here, it would be nice to have the sports facilities offered by the Hilton and the Condado Plaza for approximately the same price.

The accommodations are located in a pair of high-rise towers, one of which is devoted exclusively to suites. Each suite is decorated in a style inspired by 18th-century Versailles, 19th-century London, Imperial China, or art deco California. Each unit has pay-per-view movies and a balcony with outdoor furniture.

Dining/Entertainment: La Scala's northern Italian restaurant is the hotel's culinary highlight. For casual dining there is Café Ventana. The Jade Beach Chinese restaurant offers Szechuan and Cantonese cuisine. The casino (open noon–4am) has a higher percentage of slot machines than any casino on the Condado and a resident singer/pianist who performs in a quiet corner bar. There are also two bar/lounges.

Services: 24-hour concierge, VIP floors with extra amenities and enhanced services, a social director who offers a changing array of daily activities, room service (daily 6:30am to midnight), baby-sitting, laundry.

Facilities: Penthouse-level fitness and health club, beauty salon, rooftop swimming pool, business center (staffed with typists, translators, guides, and stenographers).

San Juan Marriott Resort

1309 Ashford Ave., San Juan, PR 00907. ☎ **787/722-7000** or 800/228-9290. Fax 787/289-6006. 512 rms, 13 suites. A/C MINIBAR TV TEL. Winter, $265–$380 double; from $525 suite. Off-season, $153–$330 double; from $425 suite. AE, DC, DISC, MC, V. Parking $8 per day.

After a tragic fire gutted it in 1989, Marriott spent staggering sums renovating and enlarging this 21-story landmark, the tallest building on the Condado. Radically different from its former incarnation, the new entity packs lots of postmodern style. Furnishings within the soaring lobby were inspired by the Chippendale salon of a high-style hotel in Europe. Manicured gardens are the site of occasional filmings of a popular soap opera. And the staff has been prodded and motivated into making this a smoothly functioning whole. If there's a flaw here, it's that a pastel color theme makes the otherwise comfortable rooms look washed out when compared to the rich mahoganies and jewel tones at other properties such as the Condado Plaza, but that's nit-picking. Nevertheless, the units here boast one of the most advanced telephone networks on the island, carefully maintained security and fire-prevention systems, safes, and in-room VCRs. About half of them occupy a nine-story, pink-and-turquoise new wing that Marriott added during the hotel's reconfiguration and rebuilding.

Dining/Entertainment: There's live music in the lobby every day from 6 to 9pm, and two merengue bands that perform there Thursday through Saturday from 9pm to 3am. Dining options include Tuscany (see separate recommendation in chapter 6); La Vista, whose buffet lunches and dinners are worth detouring for; and a poolside grill that serves tropical drinks, sandwiches, and salads.

Services: 24-hour room service, concierge, beauty salon, shopping kiosks, tour desk, car-rental facilities.

Facilities: The Stellaris Casino, which has a noteworthy absence of the glitter and neon that marks some of its competitors, clangs and jingles from a position adjacent to the hotel's main lobby. There's one of the best beaches on the Condado right outside the hotel; two swimming pools (whose mosaic bottoms glow luminously when viewed from a perch on the hotel's observatory-style 21st floor); a health club with massage and many spa treatments available.

EXPENSIVE

The Condado Beach Trio

1061 Ashford Ave., Condado, San Juan, PR 00907. ☎ **787/721-6090** or 800/468-2775 in the U.S. Fax 787/468-2822. Condado Beach Hotel: 241 rms, 18 jr. suites, 4 suites. A/C TV TEL. Winter, $195–$231 double; $235–$262 triple; $252–$457 suite. Off-season, $155–$175 double; $185–$205 triple; $215–$340 suite. AE, DC, MC, V. La Concha Hotel: 234 rms, 22 jr. suites, 12 suites. A/C TV TEL. Winter, $173–$205 double; $198–$230 triple; $294–$788 suite. Off-season, $145–$165 double; $170–$190 triple; $455–$600 suite. AE, DC, MC, V. Parking $5 at both. Bus: T1.

In 1991, Carnival Cruise Lines and other investors bought a sprawling trio of Condado properties and (after renovation) incorporated them into a coherent whole. The original hostelries were El Centro (built in the 1970s and still used as a convention center), La Concha, and the Condado Beach Hotel & Casino. Parts of the new trio have distinct identities that can still be recognized from the former properties.

The Condado Beach Hotel was built in 1919 by the Vanderbilts as the first hotel along what is now the heavily congested Condado. Although its once-elaborate gardens were long ago swallowed up by the surrounding neighborhood, it still has its dignified colonial facade, which some visitors feel resembles an archbishop's palace in Spain. This part of the new entity retains some of its dignified grandeur as well as a legendary double staircase in the lobby. Most of the hotel's accommodations are in a rambling modern wing (invisible from the street) whose red-tile roof mimics the detailing of the original core.

The La Concha part looks and smells like the 1959-vintage hotel it is. It's only redeeming feature is that the beach here is wider than that in front of the Condado Beach. If you book at the Trio, insist on a room in the Condado Beach section, not in the shop-worn La Concha.

Dining/Entertainment: Both hotels share the small but elegant casino on the lobby level of the Condado Beach Hotel. Restaurants on the premises include Vivas and the Café del Arte (in the Condado Beach Hotel). Cabaret shows—some of the best on the island—are often presented at El Teatro, in the Convention Center.

Also recommended separately is La Concha's Ibiza, the most architecturally interesting nightclub on the island (see chapter 7).

Services: Room service (7am to 11pm), same-day laundry, baby-sitting, a sports and activities desk. Bordering on indifferent in our opinion, service at La Concha leaves much to be desired.

Facilities: Guests at both hotels have free use of all facilities in the complex. Both hotels have their own freshwater pools with bars and sundecks, two beaches, an array of water-sports options, two tennis courts.

MODERATE

⊕ El Canario by the Lagoon Hotel

Calle Clemenceau 4, San Juan, PR 00907. ☎ **787/722-5058** or 800/533-2649. Fax 787/723-8590. 40 rms. A/C TV TEL. Winter, $100–$110 double; off-season, $80–$90 double. Rates include continental breakfast and morning newspaper. AE, DC, MC, V. Free parking. Bus: A7 or 2.

A relaxing, informal atmosphere prevails at this European-style bed-and-breakfast hotel operated by Keith and Jude Olson. El Canario is situated in a quiet residential neighborhood just a block from Condado Beach. The attractive rooms all have their own balconies, and the hotel has a guest laundry and an in-house tour desk.

Ramada Hotel Condado

1045 Ashford Ave., San Juan, PR 00907. ☎ **787/723-8000** or 800/468-2040. Fax 787/722-8230. 96 rms, 2 suites. A/C MINIBAR TV TEL. Winter, $170 double; from $300 suite; off-season, $140 double; from $200 suite. AE, DC, DISC, MC, V. Parking $5. Bus: A7 or 10.

Catering to both vacationers and business travelers, this modest hotel is right on the oceanfront in the heart of the Condado section. It lacks the style or facilities of some of its very expensive neighbors, but you can bask in the sun by the pool, have lunch or drinks on the sundeck, and dance the night away in the Polo Lounge to live music that alternates between Latin rhythms and soft romantic melodies. The Ocean View Restaurant serves only breakfast. Shopping, sights, and island nightlife are within walking distance or just a short ride away. The rooms are classified as standard, superior, or deluxe. The price seems rather high for what you get here, but then again, you must pay dearly for a prime beachfront Condado location. Laundry service is available. Guests sometimes swim in salt water from a point within the hotel's garden. However, it's advisable to avoid the rocky shoreline adjacent to the hotel and head instead for the sandy beach at the Condado Plaza, a 5-minute walk away.

Regency Hotel

1005 Ashford Ave., San Juan, PR 00907. ☎ **787/721-0505** or 800/468-2823 in the U.S. Fax 787/722-2909. 109 rms, 18 suites. A/C TV TEL. Winter, $150–$180 double; $240 suite. Off-season, $125–$150 double; $200 suite. Third occupant in any room $20 per day extra. Rates include continental breakfast. AE, DC, MC, V. Parking $5. Bus: A7.

This hotel is a very modest choice but it occupies prime Condado real estate and has generally spacious rooms. Many of them are equipped with kitchenettes, and all of the suites contain fully equipped kitchens. Although the rooms have balconies, not all open onto the seascape. Most of the accommodations are fairly comfortable, but not style-setters by any means. Most are decent, clean, and considered good value for the tab-happy Condado district. Whether you like this hotel or not may depend on your room assignment, however, since some units have drawn dragon fire from your fellow readers. If possible, see the room before checking in. The beach here is approached through an underground parking garage. On the premises are a bar and the St. Moritz restaurant, a dining enclave with conservatively classic food. Although the hotel has its own small-scale freshwater pool, some guests prefer to do their swimming, gambling, dining, and drinking at the Condado Plaza next door.

A GAY HOTEL

Atlantic Beach Hotel

1 Vendig St., Condado, San Juan, PR 00907. ☎ **787/721-6900.** Fax 787/721-6917. 37 rms. A/C TV TEL. Winter, $107–$124 double; off-season, $90.95–$101.65 double. Rates include continental breakfast. AE, DC, MC, V. Bus: A7, M7, or T1.

This is the best-known gay hotel in Puerto Rico. It's set in a five-story building with styling that's vaguely art deco and has appealed to a loyal clientele since it originally opened in the 1960s. Since taking over in 1977, owner William Cislak has offered a friendly refuge, mostly for men, but with an occasional smattering of women. Bedrooms are outfitted with tropical fabrics and accessories and rattan furnishings. The hotel's location directly beside the sands of Condado Beach, near the San Juan Marriott, adds to its appeal. There's a simple snack-style bar and restaurant on the premises. A Sunday afternoon tea and dance attracts many of the city's gay men.

INEXPENSIVE

⑤ At Wind Chimes Inn

Calle Taft 53, Condado, San Juan, PR 00911. ☎ **787/727-4153** or 800/946-3244. Fax 787/728-0671. 12 rms, 2 suites. A/C TV TEL. Winter, $60–$85 double; $85–$140 suite. Off-season, $50–$70 double; $70–$120 suite. Rates include continental breakfast. AE, DC, MC, V. Bus: T1, A7, or 2.

This restored and renovated Spanish manor is one of the best Puerto Rican guesthouses on the Condado; it's one block from the beach and $3^1/2$ miles from the airport. Upon entering a tropical patio, you'll find tile tables surrounded by palm trees and bougainvillea. There's plenty of space on the deck and a covered lounge for breakfast, sunbathing, and socializing. Dozens of decorative wind chimes add melody to the daily breezes. The variety of rooms available offers a choice of size, beds, and kitchens, although all of them contain both ceiling fans and air-conditioning.

Casa del Caribe

Calle Caribe 57, San Juan, PR 900907. ☎ **787/722-7139.** Fax 787/728-0671. 9 rms. A/C. Winter, $65–$80 double; off-season, $50–$65 double. Rates include continental breakfast. AE, DC, MC, V. Bus: T1, A7, or 2.

Formerly known as Casablanca, this renovated guesthouse with garden lies in the heart of Condado on a shady side street just off Ashford Avenue. Built in the 1940s, it was later expanded, then totally refurbished with a tropical decor in 1995. A very Puerto Rican ambience has been created, with a stress on Latin hospitality and comfort. The cozy guest rooms have ceiling fans and air conditioners, and most of them feature original Puerto Rican art. The wraparound veranda provides a social center for guests. Don't expect the Ritz, but this is a bargain on the Condado.

4 Miramar

Miramar, a residential neighborhood, is very much a part of metropolitan San Juan, and a long brisk walk will take you where the action is. Regrettably, the beach is at least half a mile away.

Hotel Excelsior

Avenida Ponce de León 801, San Juan PR 00907. ☎ **787/721-7400** or 800/298-4274. Fax 787/723-0068. 130 rms, 10 suites. A/C TV TEL. Winter, $137–$165 double; $179 suite. Off-season, $110–$141 double; $147 suite. Children under 10 stay free in parents' room; cribs free. AE, MC, V. Free parking. Bus: T1 or 2.

Handsome accommodations and good service are offered at this family-owned and -operated hotel. The bedrooms have been completely refurbished; many have fully equipped kitchenettes, and all have hairdryers, two phones (one in the bathroom), and marble vanities. Included in the rates are use of the swimming pool, daily coffee, a newspaper, shoeshines, and transportation to the nearby beach, as well as parking in the underground garage or the adjacent parking lot. This hotel is known for its excellent maintenance and meticulous housekeeping.

The award-winning Augusto's Restaurant is open for lunch Tuesday through Friday and for dinner Monday through Saturday; Café Miramar serves breakfast, lunch, and dinner, open 7am to 10pm. A cocktail lounge, an exercise room, and a beauty shop complete the hotel's facilities. Services include laundry and baby-sitting, plus limited room service.

5 Isla Verde

Beach-bordered Isla Verde is closer to the airport than the other sections of San Juan. The hotels here are farther from Old San Juan than those in Miramar, Condado, and Ocean Park. It's a good choice if you don't mind the isolation and want to be near fairly good beaches.

VERY EXPENSIVE

✪ El San Juan Hotel and Casino

Isla Verde Ave. (Rte. 37; P.O. Box 2872), San Juan, PR 00902. ☎ **787/793-1000** or 800/ 468-2818. Fax 787/253-2003. 372 rms, 20 suites. A/C MINIBAR TV TEL. Winter, $320–$410 double; from $960 suite. Off-season, $250–$395 double; from $760 suite. AE, DC, MC, V. Parking $10. Bus: A7, M7, or T1.

This is considered the best hotel in Puerto Rico and possibly the entire Caribbean basin. Built in the 1950s, it has been restored with an infusion of $45 million. Totally sheathed in russet-colored marble and hand-carved mahogany paneling, the public rooms stretch on almost endlessly. Its lobby is the most opulent and memorable in the Caribbean.

The hotel is surrounded by 350 palms, century-old banyans, and gardens; with its almond trees, the beach is the finest in the San Juan area. At the hotel's river pool, currents and cascades evoke a freshwater jungle stream with lagoons.

The accommodations have intriguing high-tech touches. Each makes maximum use of irregular spaces to include such amenities as dressing rooms, three phones, and VCRs. A few feature Jacuzzis. Each benefits from a harmonious color scheme of restful but stimulating Caribbean colors. About 150 of the accommodations are in the outer reaches of the garden; each of these is designed as a rustic but comfortable bungalow known as a *casita*. They include Roman tubs, atrium showers, and access to the fern-lined paths of a tropical jungle a few steps away.

Dining/Entertainment: La Veranda Restaurant, near the sands, is open 24 hours. Dar Tiffany is a steak-and-seafood restaurant and the best at the hotel. Good Italian food is served for lunch and dinner at La Piccola Fontane. Or you can promenade down a re-creation of a Hong Kong waterfront street to a Chinese restaurant called Back Street Hong Kong. The in-house casino is open daily from noon to 4am.

Services: 24-hour room service, dry cleaning, baby-sitting, massage.

Facilities: Rooftop health club, water sports, steam room, sauna, spa, two swimming pools, tennis court, ping pong.

Sands Hotel & Casino Beach Resort

187 Isla Verde Ave., Isla Verde, PR 00913. ☎ **787/791-6100** or 800/443-2009. Fax 787/ 791-8525. 397 rms, 17 suites. A/C TV TEL. Winter, $325–$435 double; from $800 suite.

Off-season, $210–$255 double; from $340 suite. AE, DC, MC, V. Self-parking $5, valet parking $10. Bus: A7, M7, or T1.

Originally built in the 1960s, this hotel received a new lease on life in 1987 when it was overhauled and became a Caribbean version of the Sands Hotel in Atlantic City (the Hotel El San Juan next door is far swankier). Today, amid tropical gardens, it enjoys a high occupancy rate and attracts tour groups. The bedrooms are comfortable, with balconies and terraces. The most desirable rooms are in the Plaza Club, a minihotel within the hotel that offers a private entrance, concierge service, complimentary food and beverage buffets, and spa and beach facilities.

Dining/Entertainment: The hotel's most upscale restaurant is Giuseppe's, which serves northern Italian cuisine. Equally appealing is Ruth's Chris Steak House (a chain that nevertheless offers some of the best steaks in San Juan), and Tucano's (a 24-hour tropical theme restaurant serving seafood and Caribbean cuisine). Simple beachfront dining is offered at the Boardwalk Grill. The nightclub offers revue-style spoofs of Hollywood legends and glittery Vegas-inspired revues, depending on bookings. The in-house casino is also popular.

Services: Room service from 6am to 2pm and 5pm to 2am, baby-sitting, laundry, limousine, massage.

Facilities: The Caribbean's largest free-form swimming pool, complete with waterfalls, rockscapes, and a swim-up bar; business center; scuba-diving facilities.

EXPENSIVE

Holiday Inn Crowne Plaza Hotel & Casino

Rte. 187 km 1.5, San Juan, PR 00979. ☎ **787/253-2929** or 800/2-CROWNE. Fax 787/253-0079. 254 rms, 22 suites. A/C TV TEL. Winter, $209–$249 double; $229–$299 suite. Off-season, $171–$211 double; from $229 suite. AE, DC, MC, V. Valet parking $10, self-parking $6. Bus: T1.

Set on a landscaped plot of seafront close to the airport, this is the easternmost of the grand modern hotels of San Juan and the leading Caribbean showcase of the Holiday Inn chain. Rising 12 stories above a beach, the resort has attracted a loyal clientele from North America and the Caribbean since it opened in 1991.

Each bedroom offers an ocean view and is decorated in pastel shades of peach or mint green. Bathrooms, constructed in both marble and tile, are equipped with hairdryers and a phone. Each accommodation is double insulated against noise from the nearby airport.

⊕ Family-Friendly Hotels

El San Juan Hotel and Casino *(see p. 97)*　This hotel, although expensive, offers more programs for children than any other hotel on Puerto Rico. Its supervised Kids Klub provides daily activities—ranging from face painting to swimming lessons—for children 5 to 12 years of age.

Empress Oceanfront Hotel *(see p. 99)*　Although this moderately priced hotel doesn't provide specific activities for children, all its units have two double beds. Thus, two children under 12 can stay here free.

Caribe Hilton *(see p. 91)*　Children under 16 stay free in their parents' room at this deluxe hotel, which has two swimming pools and is situated in a 17-acre tropical park.

Dining/Entertainment: The premier dining spot is Windows on the Sea, an oceanfront emporium serving international and Puerto Rican food. El Tropical Lounge offers drinking and dancing every evening. El Tropical also is the name of the hotel's large casino.

Services: Laundry, room service (daily 6:30am–midnight), baby-sitting. A concierge staff provides free continental breakfast and complimentary early-evening hors d'oeuvres on those floors offering enhanced facilities and services.

Facilities: Large, free-form swimming pool with swim-up bar; sandy beachfront studded with palm trees and sea grapes; car-rental facilities; tour desk; children's game room and pool; fitness center; gift shop; sports club and beach club both offering land and water sports.

MODERATE

Empress Oceanfront Hotel

Calle Amapola 2, Isla Verde, PR 00913. ☎ 787/791-3083 or 800/678-0757. Fax 787/791-1423. 30 rms. A/C TV TEL. Winter, $148–$168 double; off-season, $88–$128 double. AE, DC, MC, V. Free parking for hotel guests. Bus: T1.

Set on $2^1/_2$ acres of rocky headlands jutting out from the coastline of a quiet neighborhood in Isla Verde, this four-story pink-sided hotel is efficiently run by a local Anglo-Latino family. From its enclosed swimming pool terrace, you'll enjoy one of the most sweeping views anywhere of the high-rise hotels and valuable real estate nearby.

On the premises is a popular bar, the Blue Dolphin, and a likeable restaurant, Sonny's Oceanfront Place for Ribs (see chapter 6). There's a Jacuzzi near the pool; the pleasantly airy decor is inspired by the tropics.

Travelodge

Avenida Isla Verde (P.O. Box 6007, Loiza Station), Santurce, PR 00914. ☎ 787/728-1300 or 800/468-2028. Fax 787/727-7150. 88 rms, 2 suites. A/C TV TEL. Winter, $137 double; $175 suite. Off-season, $91 double; $150 suite. AE, MC, V. Bus: T1.

Rising eight stories above the busy traffic of Isla Verde, this member of a national hotel chain offers comfortable bedrooms outfitted with unremarkable modern furniture. There's only one restaurant (the Country Kitchen), one swimming pool, and one bar (the Escort Lounge), so many guests carry a tote bag to the beach across the street, then patronize the bars, restaurants, and swimming facilities of the nearby expensive hotels. Don't expect very personalized service.

INEXPENSIVE

Green Isle/Casa Mathiesen

36 Calle Uno, Villamar, Isla Verde, PR 00979. ☎ 787/726-4330 or 800/677-8860 in the U.S. Fax 787/268-2415. 45 rms. A/C TV TEL. Winter, $69 double; off-season, $60 double. AE, MC, V. Bus: A7, M7, or T1.

Small, unassuming, and subject to the roar of the nearby traffic, this hotel stands across the busy avenue from the beach used by the larger and much more expensive Sands Hotel. Each of the simple, low-slung accommodations contains its own kitchenette and simple, summery furniture. There's a small swimming pool on the premises, although most residents prefer to swim in the sea. Dozens of cheap hamburger joints are nearby.

6 | Where to Dine in San Juan

San Juan has the widest array of restaurants in the Caribbean. You can enjoy fine continental, American, Italian, Chinese, Mexican, and Japanese cuisines, to name a few. In recent years, many restaurants have shown a greater appreciation for traditional Puerto Rican cooking, and local specialties now appear on the menus of leading restaurants. Whenever possible, many chefs make use of local ingredients, which enhances all their dishes.

Before searching for a local restaurant, you should review "Puerto Rico's Exotic Bill of Fare" in chapter 2 and "Tips on Dining Out" in chapter 3.

Many of San Juan's best restaurants are in the resort hotels along the Condado and at Isla Verde. There has been a restaurant explosion in San Juan in the past few years. Many of the newer ones are off-the-beaten tourist path. However, some of these newer places have not yet achieved the fine quality found at many of the older and more traditional restaurants.

In Puerto Rico, a **very expensive** restaurant is one charging more than $50 per person for a meal, excluding drinks and service. In restaurants classified as **expensive** or **moderate,** meals range from $25 to $50, and from $15 to $25, respectively. Any meal under $15 is definitely **inexpensive.**

1 Old San Juan

EXPENSIVE

✪ Chef Marisoll

202 Calle del Cristo. ☎ **787/725-7454.** Reservations required. Lunch main courses $14–$24; dinner main courses $19–$26. AE, MC, V. Tues–Sat noon–2:30pm; Tues–Sun 7–10:30pm. CONTEMPORARY.

Marisoll Hernández is the finest female chef in San Juan. Trained in the Hilton properties, including one in London, she broke away to become an independent restaurateur in Old San Juan. In a Spanish colonial building, with a courtyard patio for dining, her eight-table restaurant is warm and intimate. Service is low-key and slightly formal.

You could have a sandwich for lunch, but few would want to settle for that when they can sample one of the chef's imaginative dishes.

Two of her soups are worthy of having their recipes appear in *Gourmet* magazine, including a cream of exotic wild mushrooms with an essence of black truffles. Her butternut squash soup with crisp ginger is also delectable. There's usually a catch of the day, perhaps swordfish, or else you can try her stuffed breast of pheasant with pistachios and truffles in a cognac sauce, perhaps her medallions of venison with a black currant and port wine sauce, or else curried chicken with papaya and cilantro.

Il Perugino

Calle del Cristo 105. ☎ **787/722-5481.** Reservations recommended. Main courses $18–$27. MC, V. Thurs–Sat noon–3pm, Tues–Sat 7–10:30pm. TUSCAN/UMBRIAN.

Except for those within some of the island's major hotels, this is the most elegant and best Italian restaurant in Old San Juan. In 1994, it moved from nearby premises into this 200-year-old town house, a short walk uphill from the town's cathedral. Its courtyard was covered over for additional dining room space, its antique well converted into an annex for the wine cellar, and the entire setting painted in shades of ochre and umber reminiscent of Perugia, the homeland of its owner/chef, Franco Seccarelli.

Assisted by his Puerto Rican wife, Luzalma, he serves a well-prepared menu that is a bit biased in favor of clichés of the Umbrian culinary repertoire. Examples include *polenta con gamberetti* (baked cornmeal with baby shrimp); *carpaccio;* macaroni with eggplant and porcini mushroom sauce; spaghetti with clam sauce; and piccata of veal with raisins, nuts, balsamic vinegar, and sugar. Daily specials sometimes add variety to the menu.

✪ La Chaumière

Calle Tetuan 367. ☎ **787/722-3330.** Reservations recommended. Main courses $20.50–$39.50. AE, DC, MC, V. Mon–Sat 6pm–midnight. Closed July–Aug. Bus: A7, T1, or 2. FRENCH.

Behind the famous Tapía Theater, this restaurant enjoys a local following drawn to its classic French cuisine. It serves the kind of dishes that you might find in a roadside tavern somewhere deep in France, and does so with considerable flair. The setting is appropriate, with heavy ceiling beams, black-and-white checkerboard floors, and large rows of wine racks.

You might begin with a rather heartily flavored country pâté, then follow with a rack of baby lamb in the style of Provence. A tender chateaubriand is served only for two. Veal Oscar and oysters Rockefeller are regular features of the menu, and you can also look for daily specials such as fish soup.

Yukiyu

Calle Recinto Sur 311. ☎ **787/721-0653.** Reservations recommended. Main courses $14–$19; fixed-price dinners $19–$36; sushi $2.50–$2.75 apiece. AE, MC, V. Mon–Sat noon–2:20pm, Mon–Fri 5–11pm, Sat 7–11pm. Bus: A7, T1, or 2. JAPANESE.

Traditional Japanese and Oriental cooking techniques are combined in this restaurant. Its extensive sushi bar is acclaimed as the best in the Caribbean (be careful: tabs can mount quickly). Sushi is available at both lunch and dinner, although the teppanyaki grill at the front, where your own personal chef will attend to you, is open only for dinner.

The dining room itself is postmodern, all monochromatic gray. Against this backdrop, the various chefs tempt you with hibachi chicken or chicken with scallops and sesame seeds. You might begin with miso soup or steamed pork dumplings, then go on to a shrimp-and-vegetable tempura, or perhaps filet of sole with capers. Fresh yellowfin tuna with teriyaki is a favorite, as is the chicken teriyaki.

San Juan Dining

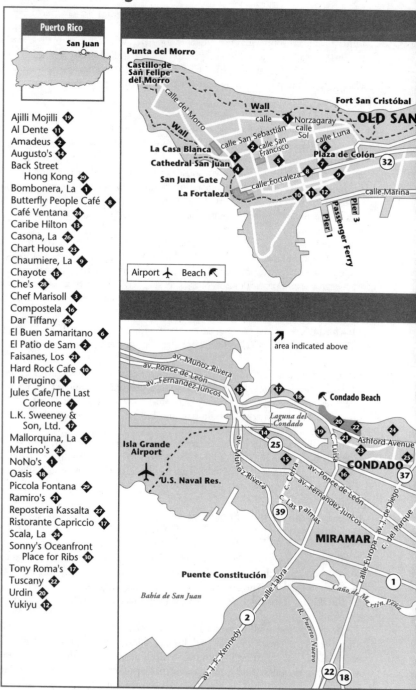

Puerto Rico
San Juan

Ajilli Mojilli 19
Al Dente 11
Amadeus 2
Augusto's 14
Back Street
  Hong Kong 29
Bombonera, La 1
Butterfly People Café 8
Café Ventana 24
Caribe Hilton 13
Casona, La 26
Chart House 23
Chaumiere, La 9
Chayote 15
Che's 28
Chef Marisoll 3
Compostela 16
Dar Tiffany 29
El Buen Samaritano 6
El Patio de Sam 2
Faisanes, Los 21
Hard Rock Cafe 10
Il Perugino 4
Jules Cafe/The Last
  Corleone 7
L.K. Sweeney &
  Son, Ltd. 17
Mallorquina, La 5
Martino's 25
NoNo's 1
Oasis 18
Piccola Fontana 29
Ramiro's 21
Reposteria Kassalta 27
Ristorante Capriccio 17
Scala, La 24
Sonny's Oceanfront
  Place for Ribs 30
Tony Roma's 17
Tuscany 22
Urdin 20
Yukiyu 12

OLD SAN JUAN area

Punta del Morro
Castillo de San Felipe del Morro
Fort San Cristóbal
Wall
calle del Morro
calle Norzagaray
calle Sol
calle San Sebastián
calle Luna
La Casa Blanca
calle San Francisco
Plaza de Colón
Cathedral-San Juan
San Juan Gate
calle Fortaleza
La Fortaleza
calle Marina
Pier 3
Passenger Ferry
Pier 1

Airport ✈   Beach ☂

Condado / Miramar area

area indicated above
av. Muñoz Rivera
av. Ponce de León
av. Fernández-Juncos
Condado Beach
Laguna del Condado
Ashford Avenue
CONDADO
Isla Grande Airport
U.S. Naval Res.
C. Luisa
C. Cerra
av. Muñoz Rivera
av. Ponce de León
av. Fernández-Juncos
c. Las Palmas
MIRAMAR
Puente Constitución
Bahía de San Juan
Caño de Martín Peña
calle Labra
R. Puerto Nuevo
av. J. F. Kennedy
calle Europa
av. Parque
calle del Parque

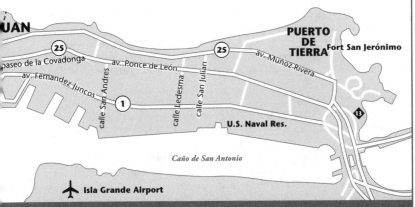

Atlantic Ocean

JUAN

PUERTO DE TIERRA

Fort San Jerónimo

paseo de la Covadonga

25

av. Ponce de León

25

av. Muñoz Rivera

av. Fernandez Juncos

calle San Andres

calle Ledesma

calle San Julian

1

U.S. Naval Res.

13

Caño de San Antonio

✈ **Isla Grande Airport**

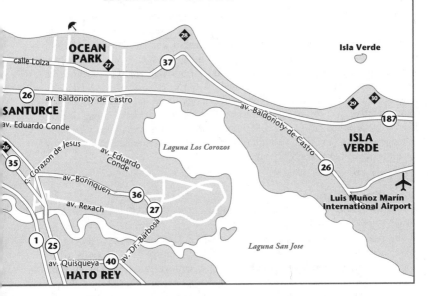

Atlantic Ocean

OCEAN PARK

calle Loiza

28

27

37

Isla Verde

26

av. Baldorioty de Castro

29

30

SANTURCE

av. Eduardo Conde

av. Baldorioty de Castro

187

26

35

c. Corazon de Jesus

av. Eduardo Conde

Laguna Los Corozos

ISLA VERDE

av. Borinquen

36

26

av. Rexach

27

✈

Luis Muñoz Marín International Airport

1

25

av. Dr. Barbosa

Laguna San Jose

av. Quisqueya

40

HATO REY

MODERATE

Al Dente

Calle Recinto Sur 309. ☎ **787/723-7303.** Reservations recommended. Main courses $9–$13.95. AE, MC, V. Mon–Sat 11:30am–10:30pm. Bus: A7, T1, or 2. SICILIAN.

Located in the heart of Old San Juan, this unpretentious restaurant has a decor that might remind you of the trattoria you enjoyed in Palermo, and the food is faithful to the recipes that placed Sicily on the gastronomic map of Europe. Both the dress code and the ambience are relaxing and casual. Nearly all dishes are genuinely satisfying and reasonably priced. You might begin with a selection of seafood antipasti, followed by gnocchi with pesto, fettuccine maestro, ravioli, or well-seasoned calamari. Brochettes of fresh tuna laced with pepper and Mediterranean herbs is an excellent choice.

Amadeus

Calle San Sebastián 106. ☎ **787/722-8635.** Reservations recommended. Main courses $13.50–$19.50. AE, MC, V. Tues–Sun noon–2am (kitchen closes at 12:30am). Bus: M2, M3, or T1. CARIBBEAN.

In the heart of the old city, opposite the side of the Church of San José, this brick-and-stone building was constructed in the 18th century by a wealthy merchant. In this setting, Amadeus offers Caribbean food with a nouvelle twist. While receiving a cordial welcome, you can enjoy dishes *de la tierra* (from the land) or *del mar* (from the sea), including a fresh catch of the day. Appetizers alone are worth the trip here, especially chayote and king crab salad with black olives, or an eggplant tart filled with spinach, mozzarella, and tomato sauce. The chef will even prepare a smoked salmon and caviar pizza. One zesty specialty is pork tenderloin stuffed with fruits and Italian sausage and smothered in red wine sauce.

El Patio de Sam

Calle San Sebastián 102. ☎ **787/723-1149.** Main courses $6.95–$32.95. AE, DC, MC, V. Sun–Thurs 11am–midnight, Fri–Sat 11am–1:30am. Bus: A7, T1, or 2. AMERICAN/PUERTO RICAN.

Located opposite the Church of San José, the oldest building on the island, this restaurant faces the statue of Ponce de León, the island's first governor. A popular old town gathering spot for American expatriates, journalists, and shopkeepers, it's known for having the best burgers in San Juan. Many other items on the menu, however, have not met with favor from many of your fellow readers. A typical comment: "The food is overpriced, and the service confused." Nevertheless, it remains Old Town's most popular dining room. Even though the dining room is not outdoors, it has the look and feel of a patio. The illusion is so credible you'll swear you're dining alfresco: Every table is placed near a cluster of potted outdoor plants, and canvas panels and awnings cover the skylight. For a filling lunch, try the black-bean soup, followed by the burger platter and then a key lime tart.

INEXPENSIVE

Butterfly People Café

Calle Fortaleza 152. ☎ **787/723-2432.** Main courses $8.50–$10. AE, DC, MC, V. Mon–Sat 11am–5pm. Bus: A7, T1, or 2. CONTINENTAL/AMERICAN.

On the second floor of a restored mansion in Old San Juan, next to the world's largest gallery devoted to butterflies, this 15-table café opens onto a patio. It specializes in lunches of tropical and light European fare prepared with fresh ingredients. You might begin with gazpacho or vichyssoise, follow with quiche or one of the daily specials, and top it all off with chocolate mousse or the tantalizing raspberry chiffon pie with fresh raspberry sauce. A full bar offers tropical specialties featuring piña coladas, fresh-squeezed Puerto Rican orange juice, and Fantasias—a frappé of seven fresh fruits. Wherever you look, framed butterflies will delight you.

El Buen Samaritano

Calle Luna 255. ☎ **787/721-6184.** Reservations not accepted. Platters and main courses $4–$7. No credit cards. Daily 7am–7pm. PUERTO RICAN.

Only the most experimental foreign tourists would venture in here, despite the fact that its format provides lots of insights into the subculture of this thriving inner-city neighborhood. Set adjacent to the back door of city hall, near the corner of San Justo Street, on one of our favorite "backwater" streets of the historic old town, it contains no more than four well-scrubbed tables in a setting Hemingway would have praised. Almost no English is spoken here: It's as Créole and ethnic as anything on the island. The menu, which depends largely on whatever was available in the marketplace that morning, will be recited lethargically by a member of the family who owns this tiny hole-in-the-wall. Except during the midday crush, no one will mind if you opt just for a cup of thick Puerto Rican coffee, a beer, or a soda, which you'll consume beneath the high rafters of a building from the Old Town's dimly remembered colonial past.

Don't expect gourmet fare here; we have included this authentic little eatery to answer the question, "Where do the locals dine?" Everything is predictably filling and starchy, including roast pork with yellow rice and beans, or a filet of red snapper in pungent tomato sauce.

Hard Rock Cafe

Calle Recinto Sur 253. ☎ **787/724-7625.** Main courses $7.95–$16.95. AE, MC, V. Daily 11am–midnight; bar: daily 11am–2am. Bus: A7, T1, or 2. AMERICAN.

Filled with rock 'n' roll memorabilia, this member of the famous and ubiquitous American chain lies in a historic section of Old San Juan. Serving a "classic" American cuisine against a backdrop of loud rock music, it is here to stay. Between drinks and burgers, diners look at the café's collection of artifacts from the Rock 'n' Roll Hall of Fame, ranging from a wig worn by Elton John to a jacket worn by John Lennon. There's also a Pink Floyd guitar and Phil Collins's drumsticks. Well-stuffed sandwiches and juicy burgers are served throughout the day, although many prefer to come here at dinner to fill up on fajitas, barbecued chicken, pork ribs, or even the catch of the day. The chili will set you ablaze. There's even a selection of salads. This is the most frequented dining spot in the old town, and of course it comes complete with a gift shop selling T-shirts and other merchandise.

Jules Café/The Last Corleone

Plaza Fortaleza, #206 Calle Fortaleza. ☎ **787/725-4309.** Reservations not necessary. Sandwiches and pastas $4.50–$12.50; main courses $8.50–$17.95. Mon–Sat 10am–midnight, Sun 11am–4pm. AE, MC, V. SICILIAN/PUERTO RICAN.

Set into an inner courtyard at the edge of Calle Fortaleza, in the heart of the Old Town's shopping district, this restaurant/café is likely to be blaring recorded opera arias beneath its twin rows of "Carnival in Venice" awnings. Its owner is Jules Hemet, whose Dutch and Italian parents and long-term residency in Portugal make him one of the island's most cosmopolitan restaurateurs. Don't expect a full-blown gourmet meal, as the venue is better-suited to midday platters, sandwiches, exotic coffees, and drinks. Menu items are "mostly Sicilian" with a scattering of Puerto Rican staples— such as black-bean soup—added "for luck." Examples include a salad of anchovies and pimientos which is quite good, veal marsala or piccata-style, a rather ordinary lasagne, a zesty chicken à l'orange, six kinds of coffee, and frothy piña coladas. Movie posters of the Hollywood version of Mafia adventures decorate the walls.

⑨ La Bombonera

Calle San Francisco 259. ☎ **787/722-0658.** Reservations recommended. Main courses $5.75–$15.90. AE, MC, V. Daily 7:30am–8:30pm. Bus: M2, M3, or T1. PUERTO RICAN.

This longtime local favorite was established in 1902 and has been offering homemade pastries and endless cups of coffee (the best in Old San Juan) in a traditional colonial decor ever since. For decades it was a rendezvous for the island's literati and for old San Juan families, but now it has been discovered by foreign visitors. The food is authentic and inexpensive. La Bombonera serves sandwiches, but most patrons prefer one of the main regional dishes, perhaps rice with squid, roast leg of pork, or seafood asopao. For dessert, you might choose an apple, pineapple, or prune pie, or one of many types of flan. Service is polite, if a bit rushed. The place fills up quickly at lunch.

⑨ La Mallorquina

Calle San Justo 207. ☎ **787/722-3261.** Reservations not accepted at lunch, recommended at dinner. Main courses $8.95–$26.95 at lunch, $13.95–$29.95 at dinner. AE, DC, MC, V. Mon–Sat 11:30am–10pm. Bus: A7, T1, or 2. PUERTO RICAN.

San Juan's oldest restaurant was founded in 1848. There's a bit of Old Spain transplanted to the New World here. The restaurant is in a three-story, glassed-in courtyard with arches and antique wall clocks. Even if you aren't hungry, you might want to visit just to perch at the old-fashioned wooden bar running the length of the left wall as you enter. The chef specializes in the most typical Puerto Rican rice dish—*asopao*, which some readers have found to be "too salty." You can have it with chicken, shrimp, or lobster and shrimp. Arroz con pollo is almost as popular. We suggest that you begin with garlic soup or gazpacho. Other recommended main dishes are red snapper in a tomato-onion sauce and lobster rice with fried plantains, beef tenderloin Puerto Rican style, and assorted seafood stewed in wine. Lunch is busy, but dinners are sometimes quiet. Don't come looking for innovative cookery; come for the old-fashioned setting and food that seems little changed over the decades.

2 Puerto de Tierra

Caribe Hilton

Calle Los Rosales. ☎ **787/721-0303.** Reservations recommended. All-you-can-eat buffet brunch $38.50 for adults, $18.50 for children under 10. AE, DC, MC, V. Sun only, 12:30–4:30pm. Bus: A7. INTERNATIONAL.

Every Sunday this brunch—served in the first hotel along the beachfront strip—captivates the imagination of island residents with its combination of food, glamour, and entertainment. There's a clown to keep the children amused, as well as live music on the bandstand for anyone who cares to dance. Champagne is included in the price. Food is arranged at several different stations: Puerto Rican food, seafood, paella, ribs, cold cuts, steaks, pastas, and salads. Afterward, you might like to stroll amid the boutiques and seafront facilities of this famous hotel.

3 Condado

VERY EXPENSIVE

La Scala

In the Radisson Ambassador Plaza Hotel & Casino, 1369 Ashford Ave. ☎ **787/721-7300.** Reservations recommended. Main courses $16–$35. AE, MC, V. Mon–Fri noon–3pm; daily 5pm–midnight. Bus: A7. NORTHERN ITALIAN.

One of the most sophisticated Italian restaurants in San Juan caters to discerning diners who appreciate the nuances of fine cuisine and service. The decor includes neutral colors, stucco arches, and murals. The menu lists just about the entire repertoire of northern Italian cuisine. You'll find a specialty version of Caesar salad, fresh mushrooms in garlic sauce, a succulent half-melted version of fresh mozzarella in carozza, and many different preparations of seafood, veal, chicken, and beef. The fresh seafood is flown in from New York and Boston. Most meals here are memor-able, and the cookery, for the most part, is creative and delicate. Service is attentive.

✪ Los Faisanes
Avenida Magdalena 1108, Condado. ☎ **787/725-2801.** Reservations recommended. Main courses $19.95–$39.95. AE, DC, MC, V. Sun–Fri noon–3pm, Mon–Thurs 6:30–11pm; Fri & Sat 6:30–11:30pm; Sun 6–10pm. Bus: A7, T1, or 2. INTERNATIONAL.

Located in a masonry-sided Iberian-inspired house on a corner of the Condado, this is one of the finest and most discreetly elegant restaurants in San Juan. The restrained decor is what you might find in a comfortable but sedate private home. There's a sophisticated array of wines and a selection of dishes inspired by the cuisines of France, Italy, and the Hispanic world. Several pheasant preparations are usually available (including one with sherry and mango sauce), as well as a changing variety of chicken, beef, veal, and seafood dishes, several of which will be prepared at your table. One specialty is the Hemingway-style fresh filet of tuna, cooked with onions, chardonnay, lemon juice, and olive oil. A winner is the roast duck, flavored with cinnamon and guava. There's a fresh, assertive taste to the food, backed up by a good wine cellar.

✪ Ramiro's
Avenida Magdalena 1106. ☎ **787/721-9049.** Reservations recommended. Main courses $23–$35; fixed-price five-course meal $56.95. AE, DC, MC, V. Lunch Mon–Fri noon–3pm, Sun noon–3pm; dinner Mon–Thurs 6:30–10:30pm, Fri–Sat 6:30–11pm, Sun 6–10pm. Bus: A7, T1, or 2. SPANISH/INTERNATIONAL.

Here you'll find a refined cuisine, the city's best wine list, and a touch of Old Spain. One of the most distinguished dining places on Puerto Rico, this elegantly decorated restaurant prepares what it terms a *cocina imaginativa,* sometimes called "New Créole" cooking—a style pioneered by its owner and chef, Jesús Ramiro. The menu is the most imaginative on the Condado. You might begin with breadfruit *mille feuille* with local crabmeat and avocado. For your main course, you can request any fresh fish or meat charcoal-grilled. Rack of lamb is one of the house specialties; you can also enjoy fresh filet of grouper with tamarind sauce and caper sauces. Among the many homemade desserts are caramelized mango on puff pastry with strawberry-and-guava sauce, and "four seasons" chocolate.

Ristorante Capriccio
On the mezzanine level of the Condado Plaza Resort, 999 Ashford Ave. ☎ **787/721-1000.** Reservations recommended. Main courses $16.50–$35. AE, DC, DISC, MC, V. Daily noon–11pm. ITALIAN.

Despite superb service from a team of French, Italian, and Puerto Rican staff members, this likable restaurant manages to remain surprisingly unpretentious. Much of this is because of the tact and charm of its Provence-born director, Roger Duperray, whose Italian cuisine is among the best in Puerto Rico. Climb to the mezzanine level of a hotel known for its ability to pull together big business deals and big casino stakes. Tables overlook an ocean view that seems to stretch all the way to Spain and are enhanced at night with soft lighting, stiff drinks, and well-chosen wines.

Food is Italian, with hints of Iberia and frequent references to the sea. There are at least 14 kinds of pastas, including versions with vodka, and a specialty version (*linguine Roger*) made with fresh spinach, mushrooms, onions, and smoked salmon that's particularly delectable. There's also an ultra-fresh seafood of the day prepared in any of three ways: *lobster fra diavola*; grilled salmon with hollandaise sauce; and a succulent version of *cioppino Genovese*. Veal, chicken, and beef dishes range from the standardized (*saltimboca Romana*) to the idiosyncratic (medallions of filet steak Atilla, prepared with anchovy-flavored garlic, cognac, and cream sauce).

EXPENSIVE

Chart House
214 Ashford Ave. ☎ **787/724-0110.** Reservations required on weekends, recommended otherwise. Main courses $16.50–$40. AE, DC, MC, V. Mon–Thurs 6–11:15pm, Fri–Sat 6pm–12:15am, Sun 6–10:15pm; bar: Mon–Thurs 5pm–1am, Fri–Sat 5pm–midnight, Sun 5–10pm. Bus: A7, T1, or 2. STEAK/SEAFOOD.

This restaurant, one of the best on the island, attracts literally hundreds of locals on any night. It's housed in a lattice-trimmed villa built in 1910. Today the heavy ceiling beams have been exposed, track lighting has been installed, and paintings have been hung to create a warm ambience. The food is well prepared, with prime rib a specialty. You also can order New England clam chowder, top sirloin, shrimp teriyaki, live Maine lobster, Alaskan king crab, and a copious salad. The special dessert is "mud pie." The Chart House belongs to a chain of restaurants based in California.

✪ Chayote
In the Olimpo Hotel, Avenida Miramar 603. ☎ **787/722-9385.** Reservations recommended. Main courses $15.95–$19.95. AE, MC, V. Mon–Fri noon–2:30pm and 7–10pm; Sat 7–10:30pm. SEAFOOD/PUERTO RICAN.

Its cuisine is considered among the most innovative in San Juan, so Chayote enjoys the patronage of many local business leaders, government officials (including the governor and his wife), and such temporary visitors as "Rambo" (Sylvester Stallone) and Melanie Griffith. The setting is a modern, basement-level, peach-colored enclave within a surprisingly obscure hotel (the Olimpo). Some aspects of the place might remind you of an artsy bistro in Washington, D.C. or New York City. At least half of the menu is devoted to appetizers (veal cubes with spicy mango sauce, stuffed cabbage with locally made sausages, crab cakes with gazpacho-flavored passion fruit), tempting some diners to concentrate on them exclusively.

Other dishes range from fresh filet of codfish with sweet and spicy mojo sauce to cornmeal tamales stuffed with shrimp in coconut sauce to an array of local fish with a medley of Asian-style stir-fried vegetables specially composed for each dish. Many of the flavors are enhanced with tropical tubers (yams, cassava, sweet potatoes, and celery root) and herbal infusions (such as leaves, flowers, and herbs steeped in hot water). Some dishes taste wonderful when accompanied by the signature house starch: french-fried cassava with aioli sauce.

✪ Compostela
Avenida Condado 106. ☎ **787/724-6088.** Reservations recommended. Main courses $16–$30. AE, DC, MC, V. Mon–Fri noon–3pm; Mon–Fri 6:30–10:30pm, Sat 6–11pm. Bus: 2. SPANISH/PUERTO RICAN.

With a comfortably unpretentious pine-trimmed decor, this restaurant achieves formality through its battalion of formally dressed waiters whose manners evoke Old Spain. Established by a Galician-born family, who named it after the most famous religious shrine in northern Spain (Santiago de Compostela), the restaurant has achieved a reputation as one of the best in the capital. The chef made his reputation on his roast peppers stuffed with salmon mousse. Equally delectable is brochettes of filet studded with truffles. Of course, any shellfish grilled in a brandy sauce is a sure winner. Nouvelle touches include the duck with kiwi sauce. The chef also makes two different versions of savory paella. The tried and true classics of yesterday also appear on the menu: rack of lamb and lobster au gratin. The wine cellar of some 10,000 bottles is one of the most impressive in San Juan.

Martino's

In the Dutch Inn Hotel & Casino, 55 Condado Ave. ☎ **787/722-5256.** Reservations recommended. Main courses $14.55–$34.50. AE, DC, MC, V. Daily 5:30pm–midnight. Bus: A7. NORTHERN ITALIAN.

Under a steel-and-glass canopy on the 13th (top) floor of this well-known but run-down hotel and casino, Martino's offers not only some of the finest service on the Condado, but also a classic Italian cuisine. A critically acclaimed restaurant, it is the domain of its chef and owner, Martin Acosta. His picture windows offer stunning views of the Atlantic and the night lights of the Condado. Clams on the half shell are a fine beginning, or even better a fresh-tasting hot seafood antipasti, the best along the Condado. Our osso buco Milanese was so perfectly cooked the tender pieces of veal fell off the bone. Veal appears again in a delectable parmigiana style, or else you may prefer the seafood suprême, always a delight, as Puerto Rico has some of the best fish in the Caribbean. Many pasta dishes make a meal unto themselves, especially the savory, rich manicotti Tuscan style. Fried calamari will satisfy anyone who believes that a day without calamari is a day in hell. Don't ignore the vegetables, especially the perfectly done fried zucchini, the sautéed fresh spinach, and the broccoli in garlic and olive oil.

Tuscany

In the San Juan Marriott Resort, 1309 Ashford Ave. ☎ **787/722-7000.** Reservations and jackets for men recommended. Main courses $18.50–$26. AE, DC, DISC, MC, V. Daily 6–11pm. NORTHERN ITALIAN.

Richly appointed with mahogany and granite, and decorated in tones of umber and sienna, this is the showcase restaurant of one of Puerto Rico's most elaborate hotel reconstructions. In 1995, its team of chefs swept away most of the first prizes from the annual Culinary Exposition, a contest held by the Puerto Rico Tourism Association. You'll be fêted by a wide assortment of culinary options here, including a range of gourmet pizzas prepared in a wood-burning oven tucked into one corner.

🅜 Family-Friendly Restaurants

Caribe Hilton *(see p. 106)*   The Sunday brunch here—which is half price for children—is an all-you-can-eat buffet. There's even a clown on hand to keep the kids entertained.

Hard Rock Cafe *(see p. 105)*   The local branch of this international chain is a sure-fire hit with kids (and despite the hype, the burgers are pretty good).

Butterfly People Café *(see p. 104)*   Children love eating lunch in this fantasy world of mounted butterflies. A favorite drink is Fantasia—a frappé made from seven fresh fruits.

The chef doesn't skimp on ingredients and prepares such elegant selections as a veal chop with a Brunnelo Tuscan red wine sauce, and seafood casserole with shrimps, scallops, and prawns with tomato sauce. There are several appealing pastas, such as pappardelle tossed with rabbit sauce, and a trio of risottos which can be ordered as an appetizer or main course. T-bone steak Florentine style arrives perfectly cooked, as does a roast rack of lamb with *jus* and rosemary potatoes.

MODERATE

✪ Ajili Mojili

Calle Joffre 6 (at the corner of Calle Clemenceau). ☎ **787/725-9195.** Reservations recommended. Main courses $12–$22. AE, MC, V. Mon–Thurs 6–10pm, Fri–Sat 6–11pm. PUERTO RICAN/CRÉOLE.

This is the only restaurant in San Juan's tourist zone devoted exclusively to *la cocina criolla*, the starchy, sometimes greasy cuisine whose multicultural recipes and tropical tenets were developed on the island at least a century ago. It lies within an annex of the Condado near the Convention Center. Look for a decor of dark wood and deliberately spartan, almost monastic-looking white walls.

A member of the staff will willingly describe the menu items in colloquial English. Locals find it evocative of the food they enjoyed at their mother's table, and a meal here might afford insights into the bedrock of the island's culture. Examples include *mofongos* (green plantains stuffed with veal, chicken, shrimp, or pork); *arroz con pollo* (stewed chicken with saffron rice); *medallones de cerdo encebollado* (pork loin sautéed with onions); *lechon asado con maposteado* (roast pork with rice and beans); and *carne mechada* (beef ribeye stuffed with ham). The preferred accompaniment for this hearty island fare is a cold bottle of local beer such as Medalla. The restaurant was named, incidentally, after a lemon-garlic sweet chili salsa (*ajila mojili*) that's traditionally served with fish or meat.

Urdin

1105 Ave. Magdalena. ☎ **787/724-0420.** Reservations recommended. Main courses $11.95–$24.95. AE, MC, V. Daily noon–11pm. PUERTO RICAN/INTERNATIONAL.

Urdin is proud of the position it's built up among the bright new restaurants of the island's capital. It occupies a low-slung, stucco-covered house set within a cluster of competing restaurants adjacent to the Condado. Inside, a fanciful decor of postmodern, Caribbean-inspired accents (cutout metal sculpture, references to stars and palm trees in an otherwise Puerto Rican setting) bring a touch of Latino New York to an otherwise Puerto Rican setting.

Food is innovative and flavorful, but the staff can diminish the dining experience if they're sulky, or enhance if they choose to be welcoming. The food is strong, opinionated, and earthy, filled with authentic Spanish flavor not necessarily geared to the palates of timid diners. They include baby eels Bilbaina style or a Castilian lentil soup. Preferred main dishes include roast duck with a blueberry sauce, loin of venison, and roast veal chop in its own juice with eggplant, spinach, and cheese. Opinion was divided at our table over the shrimp with mango and ginger sauce. One always pleasing dish is piquillo peppers stuffed with a seafood mousse and black olive sauce. Savvy locals finish their meals with a slice of sweet potato cheese cake.

INEXPENSIVE

⊛ Oasis

1043 Ashford Ave. ☎ **787/724-2005.** Main courses $6.50-$32. AE, DC, MC, V. Daily 11:30am–11pm. Bus: A7, T1, or 2. CUBAN/INTERNATIONAL.

This budget eatery manages to hold its own along the Condado beachfront, where prices in the better-known establishments are sometimes astronomical. The Oasis really is a family-style dining room with a large variety of "Cuban Créole" dishes, as well as international and Puerto Rican regional specialties. Caldo gallego, that rich flavored soup of beans and greens, with meat and sausage, is a hearty opener, followed by any number of main courses, such as stuffed Cornish hen, oxtails in a Créole sauce, breaded red snapper filet, or lobster *asopao*. Paella is another specialty, although at least two diners must order this dish. Good value, plenty of good food, and an informal, relaxed atmosphere keep this place going year after year. The tables in back, with views of the ocean, are usually taken first.

4 Santurce

✪ La Casona

Calle San Jorge 609 (at the corner of Avenida Fernández Juncos). ☎ **787/727-2717.** Reservations required. Main courses $17–$35. AE, DC, MC, V. Mon–Fri noon–11pm, Sat 6–11pm. Bus: 1. SPANISH/INTERNATIONAL.

One of the finest dining rooms on Puerto Rico offers the kind of experience usually found in Madrid, complete with a strolling guitarist. Since 1972 the chefs here have dispensed their special blend of Spanish and international dishes in a turn-of-the-century mansion surrounded by gardens. Guests pass by sweet-scented plants and trailing bougainvillea to enter a much-renovated but still charming and sophisticated dining room that draws some of the most fashionable diners in Puerto Rico. Paella marinara, prepared for two or more diners, is a specialty, as is a *zarzuela de mariscos*, or seafood medley. Or you might select filet of grouper in Basque sauce, octopus vinaigrette, rabbit stew, or a rack of lamb. The cuisine has flair and flavor. Much effort and expense go into serving a classic type of cuisine.

5 Miramar

✪ Augusto's

In the Hotel Excelsior, Avenida Ponce de León 801. ☎ **787/725-7700.** Reservations required. Main courses $23–$26. AE, MC, V. Tues–Fri noon–3pm; Tues–Sat 7–9:30pm. Closed July 7–Aug 1. Bus: A7, T1, or 2. INTERNATIONAL.

One of Puerto Rico's most successful chefs, Austrian-born August Schreiner first came to prominence on the island during his long stay at the Caribe Hilton, where he won many awards for outstanding international cuisine. His restaurant has a sophisticated decor with light-gray walls and masses of fresh flowers. The menu changes frequently. The restaurant is a serious rival of the previously recommended Compostela. It is also a five-time winner of the "Gold Fork Award," given by the local newspaper, *El Nuevo Día*. One devoted fan and rather savvy foodie told us, "Augusto's is the only serious dining choice in San Juan." That's a gross exaggeration, but Augusto's is good.

Begin with his sautéed fresh foie gras with glazed apples and a cider sauce, something you'd normally get at a three-star restaurant in Europe. Such Austrian exotica served is veal brains *au beurre noir* with capers, or else you might try the innovative guinea hen terrine with spicy mustard fruits. The lobster risotto with basil oil is one of the best we've ever had, and the masterpiece is a venison tournedos in a wild huckleberry sauce with a Moroccan couscous. Grilled Long Island duck breast with its sautéed salsify and Calvados sauce is better than what you are likely to get, say, on Long Island itself.

6 Isla Verde

VERY EXPENSIVE

✪ Dar Tiffany

In the Hotel El San Juan, Isla Verde Ave. ☎ **787/791-7272.** Reservations required. Main courses $18.95–$50. AE, DC, MC, V. Daily 6–11pm. Bus: M4 or T1. SEAFOOD/STEAK/AMERICAN.

The best choice in San Juan for a taste of the good life, Dar Tiffany is usually jammed, especially on weekends, with visiting celebrities like Joan Rivers and Eddie Murphy. On the ground floor of Puerto Rico's most glamorous hotel, it provides considerate service and an elegant etched-glass decor in a multilevel room, with lots of plants and tropical furniture.

The wine list is actually more extensive than the food menu, which offers the best steaks in town. They weigh 22 ounces and are U.S. prime dry-aged with a choice of porterhouse, T-bone, or shell steak. They are aged on the premises. Although generally ignored in favor of the steaks, the 18-ounce veal loin chop and the two double loin lamb chops are worth the trip out here. Live Maine lobsters weighing from 2¹/₂ to 5 pounds are also served as you like, but at "market price," which you won't.

EXPENSIVE

Back Street Hong Kong

In the Hotel El San Juan, Isla Verde Ave. ☎ **787/791-1224.** Reservations recommended. Main courses $12.95–$32.95. AE, MC, V. Mon–Sat 6pm–midnight, Sun 1pm–midnight. Bus: M4 or T1. MANDARIN/SZECHUAN/HUNAN.

To reach this, the best Asian restaurant in San Juan, you head down a re-creation of a waterfront street in Hong Kong. Disassembled from its original home at the 1964–65 New York World's Fair, it was rebuilt with the exposed electrical meters and lopsided facades of its original design intact. A few steps later you enter this dramatic enclave, serving Mandarin, Szechuan, and Hunan dishes. Beneath a soaring redwood ceiling, surrounded by teakwood lattices and iron filigree, and served by formally dressed employees, you can enjoy pineapple fried rice served in a real pineapple, a superb version of scallops with orange sauce, Szechuan beef with chicken, or a succulent Dragon and Phoenix (lobster mixed with shrimp).

✪ La Piccola Fontana

In El San Juan Hotel and Casino, Isla Verde Ave. ☎ **787/791-1000,** ext. 1271. Reservations required. Main courses $19.95–$36. AE, DC, MC, V. Daily 6pm–midnight. Bus: T1. NORTHERN ITALIAN.

Right off the luxurious Palm Court in this grand hotel, La Piccola Fontana serves some of the finest classic northern Italian cuisine on Puerto Rico. With white linen and classically formal service, it enjoys a worldwide reputation. Small and intimate, it's like a jewel box, an octagonal Neo-Palladian room with lattices and crystal chandeliers.

To begin, there are such temptations as hot seafood antipasti and a Caesar salad. Then look for the daily specials, such as fish of the day, or try one of the eight classic veal dishes. From the sea come such main courses as hot seafood suprême and a delectable calamari marinara. However, many diners prefer one of the pasta dishes as their main course, perhaps the succulent homemade manicotti or baked ziti. The chocolate cheesecake, a chef's specialty, is a smooth finish.

INEXPENSIVE

Café Ventana

In the Radisson Ambassador Plaza Hotel & Casino, 1369 Ashford Ave. ☎ **787/721-7300.** Reservations not required. Main courses $5–$19; full American breakfast $6–$12. AE, DC, MC, V. Daily 6:30–midnight. INTERNATIONAL.

On the lobby level of one of the best hotels of the Condado is this comfortable and cozy eatery which for many years was the most famous Howard Johnson's in the Caribbean. It attracts some of the most prestigious politicians and financiers on Puerto Rico to its booths and tables (many luminaries live nearby and consider it their neighborhood diner). Depending on the time of day, you can be served pancakes, omelets, muffins, hash-brown potatoes, and sausages; or you can order lunch and dinner foods such as fish fries, teriyaki steaks, clam platters, and an array of sandwiches and burgers as well as typical Puerto Rican dishes. Don't overlook the many varieties of ice cream.

7 Ocean Park

Reposteria Kassalta

Calle McLeary 1966. ☎ **787/727-7340.** Reservations not accepted. Full American breakfast $3.50; soups $4; sandwiches $3.35–$4.35; pastries from 75¢ each. AE, MC, V. Daily 6am–10pm. Bus: T1. SPANISH/PUERTO RICAN.

This is the most famous of the cafeteria/bakery/delicatessens of San Juan because of its reasonable prices and eat-in and take-out foods. It's in Ocean Park, a commercial neighborhood four miles east of Old San Juan. When you get there, you'll enter a cavernous room flanked with modern sun-flooded windows and endless ranks of glass-fronted display cases. Depending on the season, these will be filled with meats, sausages, and pastries appropriate to Christmas, Easter, Thanksgiving, or whatever the forthcoming holiday.

At one end of the room, patrons line up to place their order at a cash register, then carry their selections, cafeteria style, to one of the establishment's many tables. A knowledge of Spanish is helpful but not essential. Among the selections offered are steaming bowls of the best caldo gallego in Puerto Rico. Laden with collard greens, potatoes, and sausage slices, accompanied by hunks of bread, and served in thick earthenware bowls, this soup makes a meal in itself. Also popular are Cuban sandwiches (sliced pork, cheese, and fried bread), steak sandwiches, a savory octopus salad, and an assortment of perfectly cooked omelets.

8 Punta Las Marias

Che's

Calle Caoba 35. ☎ **787/726-7202.** Reservations recommended for lunch, required for dinner. Main courses $10–$22. AE, DC, MC, V. Sun–Thurs noon–midnight, Fri–Sat noon–1am. Bus: T1. ARGENTINE/ITALIAN.

Named after the colorful Latino revolutionary Che Guevara, this place re-creates some of the color and drama of the Argentine pampas. It's about two miles east of the Condado's resorts. Many of the specialties are grilled in the style preferred by cowherding gauchos. If you're not in the mood for highly seasoned flank steak or any of the grilled meats, you can choose a variety of pastas and veal dishes. Meats are very tender here and well flavored.

7

What to See & Do
in San Juan

Around 1521 the Spanish began to settle in the area now known as Old San Juan. At the outset, the city was called Puerto Rico ("Rich Port"), and the whole island was known as San Juan.

The streets are narrow and teeming with traffic, but a walk through Old San Juan—in Spanish, *El Viejo San Juan*—is like a stroll through 5 centuries of history. You can do it in less than a day (see "Walking Tour: Old San Juan," below). In this historic seven-square-block area of the western side of the city, you can see many of Puerto Rico's chief sightseeing attractions and do some shopping along the way.

Many of the museums in Old San Juan close for lunch between 11:45am and 2pm, so schedule your activities accordingly if you intend to museum-hop.

On the other hand, you may want to just plop yourself down on the sand with a tropical drink, or get outside and play. See Section 3 of this chapter for details on all the beaches and active sports in the San Juan area.

SUGGESTED ITINERARIES

In case you would like to drag yourself away from the beach, here are some suggestions about how to see San Juan.

If You Have 1 Day

To make the most of a short stay, head immediately for Old San Juan for an afternoon of sightseeing and shopping. You should definitely schedule a visit inside El Morro Fortress. Try to spend 2 hours at Condado beach. Enjoy a Puerto Rican dinner at a local restaurant, listen to some salsa music, and enjoy a rum punch before retiring for the night.

If You Have 2 Days

The first day, spend the morning shopping and sightseeing in Old San Juan. Schedule interior visits to El Morro Fortress and San Juan Cathedral, then relax on Condado beach for the rest of the day. Enjoy a Puerto Rican dinner and some local music before retiring.

On your second day, spend the morning exploring El Yunque rain forest, a lush 28,000-acre site east of San Juan (see chapter 8). Schedule 2 or 3 hours at nearby Luquillo Beach, the finest on Puerto Rico.

Buy lunch from one of the open-air kiosks. Return to San Juan for the evening, attending either a folk-culture show (if available) or a Las Vegas–style revue. Visit the casinos for some action before retiring.

1 Seeing the Sights

Although we have outlined a walking tour of Old San Juan later in this chapter, here is an introduction to some of the sights mentioned there, as well as others you may wish to seek out yourself.

FORTS

✪ Castillo San Felipe del Morro

At the end of Calle Norzagaray. ☎ **787/729-6960.** Free admission. Daily 9am–5pm. Bus: T1, M3.

Called "El Morro," this fort stands on a rocky promontory dominating the entrance to San Juan Bay. Ordered built in 1540, the original fort was a round tower which can still be seen deep inside the lower levels of the castle. Additional walls and cannon-firing positions were constructed, and by 1787 the fortification had attained the complex design we see today. This fortress was attacked repeatedly by both the English and the Dutch. The U.S. National Park Service oversees the fortifications of Old San Juan, which have been declared a World Heritage Site by the United Nations. Offering some of the most dramatic views in the Caribbean, El Morro is an intriguing labyrinth of dungeons, barracks, vaults, lookouts, and ramps. A video is presented in English and Spanish. Free tours, in English and Spanish, are given daily from 10am to 4pm.

The closest parking to the historic fort is the underground facility beneath the Quincentennial Plaza at the Ballajá Barracks on Calle Norzagaray.

Fort San Cristóbal

Calle Norzagaray, uphill from Plaza de Colón. ☎ **787/729-6960.** Free admission. Daily 9am–5pm. Bus: T1, M3—then free trolley.

This fort in the northeast corner of Old San Juan, begun in 1634 and redesigned 200 years ago, is one of the largest defenses ever built in the Americas. Its walls rise more than 100 feet above the sea, a marvel of military engineering. Protecting San Juan against attackers coming by land, San Cristóbal is connected to El Morro by half a mile of massive walls filled with cannon-firing positions. Tunnels and dry moats connect the center of San Cristóbal to its "outworks" (trenches, traps, bunkers, and bastions arranged defensively, layer upon layer, over a 27-acre site). You'll get the idea of the defenses if you look at a scale model that's on display. Like El Morro, this fort is administered by the National Park Service. Museum exhibits depict what a soldier's life was like in the late 18th century, and a video is shown in English and Spanish. Free tours, in English or Spanish, are given daily from 10am to 4pm.

Because of the steep hillside and enormous 18th-century walls, there are only a small number of parking spaces available.

Fort San Jerónimo

East of the Caribe Hilton, at the entrance to Condado Bay. ☎ **787/724-1844.** Free admission. Wed–Sat 9am–4:30pm. Bus: T1.

Completed in 1788, this fort was badly damaged during the English assault of 1797. Reconstructed in the closing year of the 18th century, it has now been taken over by the Institute of Puerto Rican Culture. At present the fort can only be viewed from the outside.

CHURCHES

Capilla de Cristo

Calle del Cristo (directly west of Paseo de la Princesa). Free admission. Tues 10am–2pm. Bus: T1.

The Cristo Chapel was built to commemorate a legendary miracle. Horse racing down Calle del Cristo was the highlight of the fiestas on St. John's Day, which honored the patron saint of the city. In 1753 a young rider lost control of his horse and plunged over the precipice. Moved by the accident, a spectator, the secretary of the city, Don Mateo Pratts, invoked Christ and the youth was saved. To express his thanks, the young man had the chapel built later that same year. Today, it is a landmark in the old city and one of the best-known historical monuments. The chapel's Campeche paintings and gold-and-silver altar can be seen through its glass doors.

Since the chapel is open only 1 day a week, most visitors have to settle for a view of its exterior.

Catedral de San Juan

Calle del Cristo 151 (at the corner of Caleta San Juan), Old San Juan,. ☎ **787/722-0861.** Free admission. Daily 8:30am–4pm. Bus: T1.

The San Juan Cathedral was begun in 1540 and has been subjected to some rough treatment through the years. It hardly resembles the thatch-roofed building that stood here until 1529, when it was wiped out by a hurricane. Hampered by lack of funds, church officials slowly added a circular staircase and two adjoining vaulted Gothic chambers to the cathedral. But along came the Earl of Cumberland to loot it in 1598, and a hurricane to blow off its roof in 1615. In 1908 the body of Juan Ponce de León was brought here. (After he died in 1521 from a poisoned-arrow wound in Florida, his body was first taken to the Iglesia de San José.) Extensively renovated in recent years, the cathedral faces the Plaza de las Monjas (Nuns' Square), a tree-shaded old-town spot where you can rest and cool off.

Iglesia de San José

Calle del Cristo. ☎ **787/725-7501.** Free admission. Church and Chapel of Belém Mon–Wed and Fri 7am–2:30pm, Sat 8am–noon. Bus: T1.

The Church of San José is centered in Plaza de San José, right next to the Dominican monastery. Initial plans for the church were drawn in 1523 and construction, supervised by Dominican friars, began in 1532. Before going into the church, look for the statue of Ponce de León on the adjoining plaza. It was made from British cannons captured during Sir Ralph Abercromby's unsuccessful 1797 attack on San Juan.

Both the church and its monastery were closed by decree in 1838, the property confiscated by the royal treasury. Later, the Crown turned the convent into a military barracks. The Jesuits restored the badly damaged church. The church had been the place of worship for Ponce de León's descendants, who are buried here under the family's coat-of-arms. The conquistador was interred here until his body was removed to the cathedral in 1908.

Although looted several times over the years, the church still has some treasures, including *Christ of the Ponces,* a carved crucifix presented to Ponce de León. Packed in a crate, the image survived a terrible shipwreck outside San Juan Harbor. The church has four oil paintings by José Campeche and two large works by Francisco Oller. Many miracles have been attributed to a painting in the Chapel of Belém, a 15th-century Flemish work called *The Virgin of Bethlehem.*

MUSEUMS

Museo de las Americas

Cuartel de Ballajá. ☎ **787/724-5052.** Free admission. Tues–Fri 10am–4pm, Sat–Sun 11am–5pm.

One of the major new museums of San Juan, the Museo de las Americas showcases the artisanal skill of North, South, and Central America, featuring everything from carved figureheads from New England whaling ships to dugout canoes carved by Carib Indians in Dominica. Also featured is a changing collection of paintings by artists from throughout the Spanish-speaking world, some of which are for sale.

Museo de Arte y Historia de San Juan

Calle Norzagaray (at the corner of Calle MacArthur). ☎ **787/724-7171.** Free admission. Mon–Sat 8am–noon and 1–4pm. Bus: T1 to Old San Juan Terminal, then a trolley car from the terminal to the museum.

This is a contemporary cultural center today, but in the mid-19th century it was a marketplace. Local art is displayed in the east and west galleries, and audiovisual materials reveal the history of the often-beleaguered city. Sometimes major cultural events are staged in the museum's large courtyard. English-language audiovisual shows are presented Monday through Friday every hour on the hour from 9am to 4pm.

Museo del Indio

Calle Luna (at the corner of Calle San José). ☎ **787/724-5477.** Free admission. Tues–Sat 9am–4pm. Bus: T1.

This museum is housed in a 250-year-old colonial building, with green trim. Its cramped and airless rooms open onto a colonial courtyard. Exhibits include a modest collection of petroglyphs, maps celebrating the geography and diversity of the Americas, and a not particularly exciting collection of glassed-in exhibits. This is not a major museum, but a possible detour if you're shopping in the neighborhood.

Museo de Pablo Casals

Calle San Sebastián 101 (at the corner of Plaza de San José). ☎ **787/723-9185.** Admission $1 adults, 50¢ children. Tues–Sat 9:30am–5:15pm. Bus: T1.

Adjacent to the Iglesia de San José, this museum houses the memorabilia left by the famed musician to the people of Puerto Rico. The maestro's cello is here, along with a library of videotapes (played on request) of some of his festival concerts. This small 18th-century house also contains Casals's manuscripts and photographs. Born in 1876, he achieved fame as a cellist as well as a conductor and composer.

The **Casals Festival** draws worldwide interest and attracts some of the greatest performing artists to Puerto Rico. The festival is held the first 2 weeks of June every year.

Museum of the University of Puerto Rico

Avenida Ponce de León, Recinto de Río Piedras. ☎ **787/764-0000,** ext. 2452. Free admission. Mon–Fri 9am–4:30pm, Sat–Sun 9am–4pm. Closed holidays. Bus: Take the bus marked RIO PIEDRAS from Plaza de Colón in Old San Juan to stop 36.

Here you'll find good collections of paintings by Puerto Rican artists, including Francisco Oller (late 19th and early 20th century) and José Campeche (18th century). There is also a large collection of pre-Columbian Puerto Rican Amerindian artifacts from the Ingeri, sub-Taíno, and Taíno civilizations.

HISTORIC SIGHTS

In addition to the forts and churches listed above, you may want to see the following.

San Juan Gate, calles San Francisco and Recinto Oeste, built in 1639 just north of La Fortaleza, was the main gate and entry point into San Juan—that is, if you arrived by ship in the 18th century. The gate is the only one remaining of the several entries to the old walled city. Take bus T1.

Plazuela de la Rogativa, Caleta de las Monjas, basks in legend. In 1797 the British held the old town under siege from their position across San Juan Bay at Santurce. However, that same year they mysteriously sailed away. Later, the commander claimed he feared that the enemy was well prepared behind those walls—he apparently saw many lights and believed them to be reinforcements. Some people believe that the lights were torches carried by women in a *rogativa,* or religious procession, as they followed their bishop. A handsome statue of a bishop trailed by a trio of torch-bearing women was donated to the city on its 450th anniversary. Take bus T1.

The **City Walls,** Calle Norzagaray, around San Juan were built in 1630 to protect the town against both European invaders and Caribbean pirates. The thickness of the walls averages 20 feet at the base and 12 feet at the top, with an average height of 40 feet. Between Fort San Cristóbal and El Morro, bastions were erected at frequent intervals. You can start to see the walls as you approach from Fort San Cristóbal on your way to El Morro. Take bus T1.

The **San Juan Cemetery,** Calle Norzagaray, officially opened in 1814 and has since been the final resting place for many prominent Puerto Rican families. The circular chapel, dedicated to Saint Magdalene of Pazzis, was built in the 1860s. Aficionados of old graveyards can wander among marble monuments, mausoleums, and statues, marvelous examples of Victorian funereal statuary. However, since there are no trees or any form of shade here, it would be best not to go exploring in the noonday sun. In any case, be careful here—the cemetery is often a venue for illegal drug deals and can be dangerous. Take bus T1.

Alcaldía (San Juan City Hall)

Calle San Francisco. ☎ **787/724-7171,** ext. 3070. Free admission. Tours by appointment, Mon–Sat (except holidays) 8:30am–noon and 1–2:30pm. Bus: T1.

The City Hall, with its double arcade flanked by two towers resembling Madrid's City Hall, was constructed in stages from 1604 to 1789. Still in use, this building is more than a historical site—it's a unique place full of monuments and legends.

Casa Blanca

Calle San Sebastián 1. ☎ **787/724-4102.** Admission $1. Tues–Sat 9am–noon and 1–4:30pm. Bus: T1.

Juan Ponce de León never lived here, although construction of the house (in 1521) is sometimes attributed to him. The house was erected 2 years after the explorer's death, as ordered by his son-in-law, Juan García Troche. The parcel of land was given to Ponce de León as a reward for services rendered to the Crown. His descendants lived here for about 2½ centuries until the Spanish government took it over in 1779 to use as a residence for military commanders. The U.S. government later used it as a home for army commanders.

On the first floor, the Juan Ponce de León Museum is furnished with antiques, paintings, and artifacts from the 16th through the 18th centuries, illustrating the various uses of the house.

Casa de los Contrafuertes (House of the Buttresses)

Calle San Sebastián 101. ☎ **787/724-5477.** Free admission. Tues–Sat 9am–4:30pm. Bus: T1.

Adjacent to the Museo de Pablo Casals, this building with thick buttresses is believed to be the oldest residence remaining in Old San Juan. The complex also contains a Pharmacy Museum, which in the 19th century was a working business located in the town of Cayey. If you go upstairs, you'll find a Graphic Arts Museum, displaying an exhibit of prints and paintings by local artists.

El Arsenal

La Puntilla. ☎ **787/724-5949.** Free admission. Tues–Sun 8:30am–4:30pm. Bus: T1.

The Spaniards used a shallow craft to patrol lagoons and mangroves in and around San Juan. Needing a base for these vessels, they constructed El Arsenal around 1800. It was at this base that they staged their last stand on Puerto Rico, flying the Spanish colors until the final Spaniard was removed in 1898, at the end of the Spanish-American War. There are exhibits in the building's three galleries.

La Casa de Libro

Calle del Cristo 255. ☎ **787/723-0354.** Free admission. Tues–Sat 11am–4:30pm. Bus: T1.

This restored 19th-century building houses a library devoted to the arts of printing and bookmaking, with examples of fine printing dating back 8 centuries, as well as some medieval illuminated manuscripts.

La Fortaleza and Mansion Ejecutiva

Calle Fortaleza, overlooking San Juan Harbor. ☎ **787/721-7000,** ext. 2211. Free admission. Mon–Fri 9am–4pm. Bus: T1.

The office and residence of the governor of Puerto Rico is the oldest executive mansion in continuous use in the western hemisphere, having served as the island's seat of government for more than 3 centuries. It dates back even further, to 1553, when construction began on a fortress to protect San Juan's Spanish settlers during raids by Carib tribesmen and pirates. The original medieval towers remain, but as the edifice was subsequently enlarged into a palace, other modes of architecture and ornamentation were incorporated, including baroque, Gothic, neoclassical, and Arabian. La Fortaleza has been designated a national historic site by the U.S. government. Informal but proper attire is required. Tours of the gardens, conducted in both Spanish and English, are given every half hour. Tour duration is 30 minutes.

PARKS & GARDENS

Administered by the University of Puerto Rico, the **Botanical Garden,** Barrio Venezuela at the intersection of routes 1 and 847 in Río Piedras (☎ **787/766-0740**), is a lush tropical garden with some 200 species of vegetation. You can pack a picnic lunch and bring it here if you choose. The orchid garden is exceptional, and the palm garden is said to contain some 125 species. Footpaths blaze a trail through heavy forests opening onto a lotus lagoon. Admission is free. It's open Tuesday through Sunday from 9am to 4:30pm (if Monday is a holiday the park is open, but it's closed the next day, Tuesday). Take bus 19 to reach it.

Muñoz Rivera Park, Avenida Ponce de León (☎ **787/724-4430**), is affiliated with Luis Marín Park (see below), with which it is frequently confused. This green space is administered by the Park Trust of Puerto Rico (☎ **787/763-0613**). More closely linked to central San Juan than to the suburbs, it's a rectangular, seaward-facing park that was built about 50 years ago to honor Luis Muñoz Rivera, the Puerto Rican statesman, journalist, and poet. It's filled with picnic areas, wide walks, shady trees, landscaped grounds, and recreational areas. Its centerpiece (The Peace Pavilion) is sometimes used for cultural events and expositions of handcrafts. Admission is free, and the park is open 24 hours. Take the Los Américas Expressway to Avenida Piñero, then head west until you reach the entrance.

Luis Muñoz Marín Park, Avenida Piñero, at Alto Rey (☎ **787/763-0787**), also is administered by the Park Trust of Puerto Rico and is the best known, most frequently visited children's playground in Puerto Rico. Conceived as a verdant oasis in an otherwise crowded urban neighborhood, it's a fenced-in repository of swings, jungle gyms, and slides set amid several small lakes. A small-scale cable car carries children and their parents aloft at 10-minute intervals for views of the surrounding landscape ($1.25 per person). Entrance for pedestrians is free, although parking costs $4 per vehicle. Open Wednesday through Sunday from 8:30am to 5pm.

San Juan Central Park, Calle Cerra (☎ **787/722-1646**), was inaugurated in 1979 for the Pan-American Games. This mangrove-bordered park covers 35 acres and lies southwest of Miramar. Joggers appreciate its labyrinth of trails, tennis players come to use the courts, and all kinds of city dwellers stroll to relieve the pressures of urban life. Admission for pedestrians is free, although parking costs 75¢. Open Monday from 2 to 10pm, Tuesday through Thursday from 6:30 to 10pm, Friday from 1 to 9pm, and Saturday and Sunday from 6am to 6pm.

HORSE RACING

Great thoroughbreds and outstanding jockeys compete all year at **El Comandante,** Avenida 65 de Infanteria, Route 3, km 15.3, at Canóvanas (☎ **787/724-6060**), Puerto Rico's only race track. Post time varies from 2:15pm to 2:45pm on Monday, Wednesday, Friday, and Sunday. Clubhouse admission is $3; entrance to the grandstand is free. An air-conditioned terrace dining room opens at 12:30pm each race day. Telephone for luncheon reservations. Most credit cards are accepted.

ORGANIZED TOURS

Castillo Watersports & Tours, Calle Don Tella 27, Punta La Marias, Santurce (☎ **787/791-6195** or 787/726-5752), maintains offices at some of the capital's best-known hotels, including the San Juan Hilton, the El San Juan, and the Holiday Inn (Santurce). Using either its own vehicle (a 29-passenger van) or that of a subcontractor, it operates bus tours that pick up passengers at their hotel as an added convenience.

One of the most popular half-day tours departs most days of the week between 8:30 and 9am, lasts between 4 and 5 hours, and costs $35 per person. Departing from San Juan, it travels along the northeastern part of the island to El Yunque rain forest, later making a brief stop at Luquillo Beach.

The company also offers a city tour of San Juan that departs daily at 1 or 1:30pm. The 4-hour trip costs $25 per person and includes a stopover at Bacardi's rum factory, where you're treated to a complimentary rum drink.

ESPECIALLY FOR KIDS

In addition to the places listed below, children should love **El Morro Fortress** (see "Forts," above), since it looks just like the castles they have seen on TV and at the movies. On a rocky promontory, El Morro is filled with dungeons and dank places and also has lofty lookout points for viewing San Juan Harbor.

Luis Muñoz Marín Park (see "Parks and Gardens," above) is one of the best places to take your children for a picnic. It has the most popular children's playground in Puerto Rico. It's filled with landscaped grounds and recreational areas— lots of room for fun in the sun.

Plaza Acuatica

Las Américas Expressway, opposite Plaza de las Américas, Hato Rey. ☎ **787/754-9595.** Free admission (activities are extra). Daily 9:30am–10pm.

This water park is an outdoor amusement area that the whole family enjoys. Activities range from water slides and "rapids" to miniature golf. There's also a video arcade as well as dining facilities.

Time Out Family Amusement Center

Plaza de las Américas, Las Américas Expressway at Roosevelt Ave., Hato Rey. ☎ **787/753-0606.** Free admission (activities are extra). Sun–Thurs 9:30am–10pm, Fri–Sat 9:30am–11pm.

This is the most popular venue for family outings on Puerto Rico. On weekends, seemingly half the families in the city show up. It has a large variety of games for children, but adults also join in the fun.

WALKING TOUR
Old San Juan

Start: Plaza de la Marina.
Finish: Fort San Cristóbal.
Time: 2 hours (not counting stops).
Best times: Any sunny day between 7am and 6pm.
Worst times: When several cruise ships are in port simultaneously.

No other city in the Caribbean cries out to be explored on foot as much as Old San Juan. Beneficiary of millions of dollars' worth of restoration since the early 1970s, it's one of the world's most potent reminders of the power and grandeur of the Spanish Empire.

Begin your walking tour near the post office, amid the taxis, buses, and urban congestion of:

1. **Plaza de la Marina,** a sloping, many-angled plaza situated at the eastern edge of one of San Juan's showcase promenades—Paseo de la Princesa. This 19th-century paseo was an esplanade where the Spanish colonial gentry once strolled while enjoying the balmy Caribbean air. The paseo sweeps from the cruise piers past La Princesa (see below), around the old city walls beneath the Casa Blanca, the ancestral home of the Ponce de León family, and continues to the entrance of 16th-century El Morro fortress.

Towering royal palms shade the broad esplanade which was repaved with new brick. On the paseo's west side overlooking the sea, a large bronze fountain sculpted by the Spanish artist Luís Sanguino and titled *Raices* (Roots) depicts the Amerindian, African, and Spanish origins of Puerto Rico as human figures with dolphins cavorting at their feet. Viewed from afar, the entire ensemble looks like a caravel being steered out to sea by dolphins, setting its course for the 21st century. On the paseo's east side stand five allegorical pieces on the island's heritage by José Buscaglia.

Special amenities provided for the Paseo de la Princesa include a gazebo serving light seafood dishes, salads, and the island's famed rich coffee. Outdoor tables with umbrellas allow parents to keep an eye on their children who may be enjoying the playground nearby. More than 20 trees were planted to shade the tables. "Criollo" dishes are also available from specially designed food carts with colored awnings.

Walk westward along Paseo de la Princesa, past heroic statues and manicured trees until you reach:

2. La Princesa, the gray-and-white building on your right, which for centuries served as one of the most-feared prisons in the Caribbean. Today it houses a museum and the offices of the Puerto Rico Tourism Company. In front of La Princesa stands a sculpture of one of the island's most beloved leaders, Doña Felisa Gautier, mayor of San Juan from 1946 to 1968.

Continue walking westward to the base of the heroic fountain near the edge of the sea. Turn to your right and follow the seaside promenade as it parallels the edge of the:

3. City Walls, once part of one of the most impregnable fortresses in the New World and even today considered an engineering marvel. At their top, notice the balconied buildings that have served for centuries as hospitals and residences of the island's governors.

Continue walking between the sea and the base of the city walls until the walkway goes through the walls at the:

4. San Juan Gate, at Calle San Francisco and Recinto del Oeste, which actually is more of a tunnel than a gate. It was built in 1639 as the main point of access from the wharves to the colony's interior.

Now that you're inside the once-dreaded fortifications, turn immediately right and walk uphill along Calle Recinto del Oeste. The wrought-iron gates at the street's end, which will probably be guarded by a pair of attendants, lead to:

5. La Fortaleza and Mansion Ejecutiva, the centuries-old residence of the Puerto Rican governor, located on Calle La Fortaleza.

Now retrace your steps along Calle Recinto del Oeste, walking first downhill and then uphill for about a block until you reach Caleta de las Monjas. Fork left until you see a panoramic view and a contemporary statue marking the center of:

6. Plazuela de la Rogativa, the small plaza of the religious procession. The statue on the square commemorates a time in 1797 when British soldiers mistook a religious procession for the arrival of Spanish reinforcements and fled.

Now, continue your promenade westward, passing between a pair of urn-capped gateposts. You'll be walking parallel to the crenellations of the 17th-century city walls. The cool, tree-shaded boulevard will fork (take the right-hand fork) and pass just above the pink walls of:

7. La Casa Rosada, a graceful villa built in 1812 for leaders of the Spanish army. Although it was empty at press time, plans are in effect to eventually open it as an artisans' center. Continue climbing the steeply inclined cobble-covered ramp to its top, where a sweeping view over a grassy, treeless meadow will appear. Walk westward across the field toward the neoclassical gateway of a fortress believed impregnable for centuries, the:

8. Castillo de San Felipe del Morro ("El Morro"), whose treasury and strategic position were the envy of both Europe and the Caribbean. Here, Spanish Puerto Rico struggled to defend itself against the navies of Great Britain, France, and Holland, as well as the hundreds of pirate ships that wreaked havoc throughout the colonial Caribbean. The fortress walls were designed as part of a network of defenses that made San Juan *La Ciudad Murada* (the Walled City).

The fortifications were financed by the Treasury of Mexico on orders from the King of Spain, beginning in 1539. Its design inspired by the French military strategist Vauban, El Morro repulsed attackers such as English privateer Sir Francis Drake, who bombarded it in 1595, and a much larger English armada in 1797. The American navy finally took El Morro during the Spanish-American War of 1898.

Walking Tour—Old San Juan

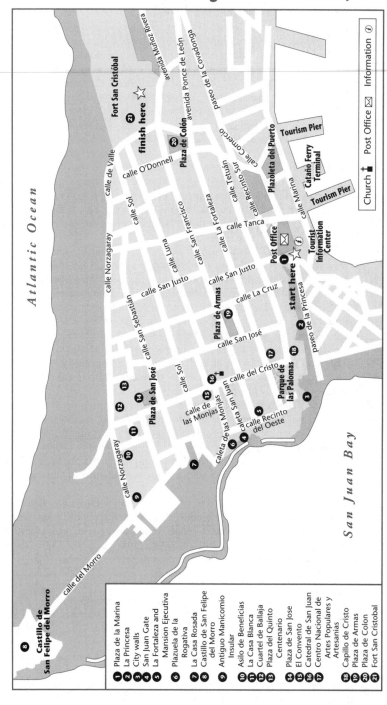

Atlantic Ocean

San Juan Bay

Fort San Cristóbal

avenida Muñoz Rivera
avenida Ponce de León
paseo de la Covadonga
finish here
Plaza de Colón
calle de Valle
calle O'Donnell
calle Sol
calle Norzagaray
calle Comercio
Tourism Pier
Plazoleta del Puerto
Cataño Ferry Terminal
Tourism Pier
calle Tetuán
calle La Fortaleza
calle San Francisco
calle Luna
calle San Justo
calle San Justo
calle La Cruz
calle Tanca
calle Recinto Sur
calle Marina
Post Office
Tourist Information Center
start here
Plaza de Armas
calle San José
calle del Cristo
calle San Juan
calle de las Monjas
caleta de las Monjas
caleta San Juan
calle Recinto del Oeste
Parque de las Palomas
Plaza de San José
calle Sol
calle San Sebastián
calle Norzagaray
paseo de la Princesa
calle del Morro

Castillo de San Felipe del Morro 8

1 Plaza de la Marina
2 La Princesa
3 City walls
4 San Juan Gate
5 La Fortaleza and Mansion Ejecutiva
6 Plazuela de la Rogativa
7 La Casa Rosada
8 Castillo de San Felipe del Morro
9 Antiguo Manicomio Insular
10 Asilo de Beneficias
11 La Casa Blanca
12 Cuartel de Ballaja
13 Plaza del Quinto Centenario
14 Plaza de San Jose
15 El Convento
16 Catedral de San Juan
17 Centro Nacional de Artes Populares y Artesanías
18 Capillo de Cristo
19 Plaza de Armas
20 Plaza de Colon
21 Fort San Cristobal

Church ✝ Post Office ⊠ Information ⓘ

After your visit, with El Morro behind you, retrace your steps through the sunlit, treeless field to the point you stood at when you first sighted it. The bulky neo-classical building at the side of the above-mentioned cobble-covered ramp is the:

9. **Antiguo Manicomio Insular,** whose construction was decreed by the Spanish King in 1854 as an insane asylum. Converted to a U.S. army barracks after the Spanish-American War, it has functioned since 1965 as the Puerto Rican Academy of Fine Arts. Notice the iron fences that protect a pair of courtyards centered around splashing fountains. Walk parallel to the facade of this former asylum, turning right at an unmarked street which passersby might tell you is the Calle de Beneficias. Notice the stately neoclassical building (painted buff with fern-green trim) on your right. It's the:

10. **Asilo de Beneficias** ("Home for the Poor") which dates from the 1840s. It has two attractive interior patios, an austere dignity, and usually an echoing silence. To-day, it houses the administrative offices of the Institute of Puerto Rican Culture. Continue walking uphill to the small, formal, and sloping plaza at the street's top. On the right-hand side, within a trio of buildings which comprise the only all-white buildings in sight, is:

11. **La Casa Blanca,** whose gardens and fountains in back offer an intimate and ver-dant respite from the monumental buildings you've just visited. It was built by the son-in-law of Juan Ponce de León as the great conquistador's island home (he never actually lived here). This "White House" today accommodates a small museum (see above) and served as the home of the American governor of Puerto Rico for many years. Begun in 1521, it was reputed to be the oldest continuously inhabited house in the New World before it was converted from a private home into a museum.

After your visit, exit by the compound's front entrance and walk downhill, re-tracing your steps for a half-block, heading toward the massive and monumental tangerine-colored building on your right, the:

12. **Cuartel de Ballajá,** the military barracks of Ballajá, which once housed troops from Spain along with their wives and children, in a setting evocative of the most austere and massive monasteries of Old Spain. On the building's second floor is the **Museo de las Americas** (see above).

After your visit, exit through the barrack's surprisingly narrow back (eastern) door, where you'll immediately spot one of the most dramatic modern plazas in Puerto Rico, the:

13. **Plaza del Quinto Centenario,** a terraced tribute to the European colonization of the new world, and one of the most elaborate and symbolic formal piazzas in Puerto Rico. From its lowest elevation, on a distant rim of land adjacent to the sea, notice the Old San Juan Cemetery, sun-bleached burial site of many of the island's first colonists. From the plaza's uppermost elevation, the inlaid pavements ringing a totemic ceramic cylinder represent the eight points of the compass.

Now, walk a short block eastward to reach the ancient borders of the:

14. **Plaza de San José,** whose center is dominated by a heroic statue of Juan Ponce de León, which was cast from an English cannon captured during a naval battle in 1797. Around the periphery of the square, notice three important sites: the Museo de Pablo Casals, whose exhibits honor the life and work of the Spanish-born cellist who adopted Puerto Rico as his final home; the Casa de los Contrafuertes (House of the Buttresses), previously described under "Historic Sights," above, which is adjacent to the Museo de Pablo Casals; and the Iglesia de San José, where the conquistador's coat-of-arms hangs above the altar. Established

by the Dominicans in 1523, this church is one of the oldest places of Christian worship in the New World.

Tucked away into one corner of the square is the *Libreria* (Bookstore) of the Institute of Puerto Rican culture, an academic enclave of books that showcases the complexity of the island's culture and colonial roots. (For more information, see "Shopping," below.)

☕ **TAKE A BREAK**   Plaza de San José is home to at least three prominent bars and restaurants, any of which would be pleased to serve beer, coffee, or a simple meal to passersby participating in a local walking tour. They include El Patio de Sam and a supremely informal tavern, NoNo's, where local night owls occupy virtually every nook and barstool, especially after sundown. Both are separately recommended in chapter 6. Also appealing is El Boquerón, operating out of a narrow storefront midway between the two above-mentioned eateries.

Now exit from the plaza's southwestern corner and walk downhill along one of the capital's oldest and best-known streets, Calle del Cristo (also known as Calle Cristo). Two blocks later, at the corner of Caleta de las Monjas, you'll find the venerable walls of:

15. El Convento, which originally was conceived as a convent in the 17th century but functioned for many decades as one of the few hotels within the old city. At press time, it was undergoing another in an endless series of renovations and was scheduled to reopen in 1997. Across the street from El Convento lies the island's most famous church and spiritual centerpiece, the:

16. Catedral de San Juan, a distinguished landmark which in recent years has been restored to its original Spanish beauty. In front of the cathedral, a gnarled tree was planted in soil contributed by dozens of North and South American nations as a gesture of international friendship.

Now walk at least two more blocks southward along Calle del Cristo, through one of the most attractive shopping districts in the Caribbean. After passing Calle Fortaleza, look on your left-hand side for the:

17. Centro Nacional de Artes Populares y Artesanias, a popular arts and crafts center that belongs to the Institute of Puerto Rican Culture. A selection of handcrafts is available for sale inside; the store is open Tuesday through Saturday from 9:30am to 5:30pm.

After your visit, continue to the southernmost tip of Calle del Cristo (just a few steps away) to the wrought-iron gates that surround a chapel no bigger than an oversized newspaper kiosk, the:

18. Capilla de Cristo, its silver altar dedicated to the "Christ of Miracles."

Now retrace your steps about a block along the Calle del Cristo, walking north. Turn right along Calle Fortaleza. One block later, turn left onto Calle de San José, which leads to the site of the capital's most symmetrical and beautiful square:

19. Plaza de Armas, a broad and open plaza designed along Iberian lines during the 19th century. Two important buildings flanking this square are the neoclassic Intendencia (which houses certain offices of the U.S. State Department) and San Juan's City Hall (Alcaldía). Relax on one of the benches, if you choose, before leaving the square via the continuation of Calle San Francisco.

☕ **TAKE A BREAK**   **La Bomoneria Puig & Abraham,** Calle San Francisco 259 (☎ 787/722-0658), offers take-away baked goods as well as sandwiches, spicy platters of Puerto Rican food, and endless cups of richly scented coffee. No one will mind if you just order something to drink, but if you want lunch, the portions are copious and inexpensive. It's rather informal; the place bustles, but no one goes away hungry.

After your pick-me-up, continue your promenade eastward along the length of Calle San Francisco. It will eventually deposit you beside the traffic, parked cars, and open-air conviviality of the very large:

20. Plaza de Colón, with its stone column topped with a statue of Christopher Columbus. Erected in 1893 to commemorate the 400th anniversary of the discovery of Puerto Rico, it is considered by some residents the most famous statue on the island. To the side of the square is the Tapía Theater, which has been restored to its original 19th-century elegance.

Continue to the end of Calle San Francisco to the intersection with Calle Norzagaray and follow the signs to:

21. Fort San Cristóbal, built along Calle Norzagaray as an adjunct to El Morro fortress. Today, like its twin, it is maintained by the National Park Service and can be visited throughout the day.

2 Nearby Attractions

The outskirts of metropolitan San Juan have some interesting attractions; all you'll need to see them is a car and about a half day for touring. Here's how to see them.

From the Santurce area, take Route 2 southwest to km 6.4. To the right you'll see a small park containing the ruins of the **house erected in 1509 by Ponce de León** in Caparra, the first Spanish settlement in Puerto Rico.

Continue west on Route 2 until you reach **Bayamón.** Facing the town plaza is an old church built in 1877, an excellent example of period architecture.

From here, turn right onto Route 167 north, heading toward Cataño, and take a left at km 5.2. Within a short distance you'll find yourself in the **Barrilito Rum Distillery.** To the left is a 200-year-old mansion with grand outdoor staircases leading to the second-floor galleries. This is the original mansion of the former 2,400-acre Santa Ana plantation and is still occupied by members of the family, the owners of the distillery. There's an office on the right, near a tower that was originally a windmill from which the entire valley and bay could be seen.

Nearby is the **Bacardi Rum Plant,** at Route 888 (km. 2.6 at Cataño; ☎ 787/788-1500), which produces 100,000 gallons of rum daily. Guided tours lasting 45 minutes are conducted every 20 minutes Monday through Saturday from 9:30 to 10:30am and from noon to 4pm. This is not only a distillery but a bottling plant and a small museum devoted to rum. A gift shop is on site, and you are invited to sample the product. Admission is free.

Follow Route 167 until you reach the shore and Route 165. Turn right, then turn left onto Route 870 and drive until you reach Isla de Cabras. From this point, you can see the entire San Juan Bay. At the end of the road in Isla de Cabras you'll come upon **Fort Cañuelo,** erected in 1610 and reconstructed in 1625 after the Dutch attack on Puerto Rico. Built on what was then a tiny islet, the fort seemed to be emerging from the water. Today, however, because of modern landfill techniques, it's connected to Isla de Cabras. Picnic facilities are available. Here, the sea breezes will cool you while you take in the view of San Juan Bay and El Morro Fortress.

On the way back, head toward **Cataño,** where you can take a short car-ferry ride to Old San Juan. Boats leave every half hour from 6am to 10pm. The fare is 50¢ round-trip. For more information, call **787/788-1155.**

From Cataño, continue on Route 24 until you reach the Caparra intersection with Route 20, then take Route 20 to Guaynabo until you come to Route 21. You'll pass the psychiatric hospital, the medical center, and the state penitentiary before getting to the Río Piedras intersection, at which point turn left toward Carolina by way of Avenida 65 de Infantera (Route 3). You'll see **El Yunque** from this road (see chapters 2 and 8 for more information).

When you reach km 18.3, turn onto the bridge and stay to the left to reach **Loíza Aldea.** If you're in Puerto Rico between July 19 and July 29, the trip to Loíza Aldea will be quite an experience, for that's when the whole town comes out to celebrate the feast day of its patron saint (Santiago Apostol). The festivities are an unusual mixture of African-Caribbean and Christian elements.

The **Iglesia de San Patricio** in Loíza Aldea, dating from 1645, is in front of the road that leads you to the barge for crossing the Río Grande de Loíza. It's a bit of a thrill to cross this river with your car on a barge propelled by a man pulling on ropes. After the crossing, drive for half an hour on the sandy but firm road, lined with coconut palms and shady trees, until you reach the Nautical Club, then go on to Santurce and the center of Old San Juan.

3 Diving, Fishing, Tennis & Other Outdoor Pursuits

Active vacationers will have a wide choice of things to do in San Juan, from beaching to windsurfing. The beachside hotels, of course, offer lots of water-sports activities (see chapter 5).

THE BEACHES

With their big resorts, the **Condado** and **Isla Verde** beaches are the most frequented in town. Good snorkeling is possible, and both have rental equipment for water sports. However, don't go walking along these beaches at night.

The public beaches on the north shore of San Juan at **Ocean Park** and **Park Barbosa** are good and can be reached by bus from San Juan. See the accompanying box for a tour of nearby beaches.

BOATING

San Juan area marinas with boats to rent include the **San Juan Bay Marina** (☎ 787/ 721-8062); **Isleta Marina,** Puerto Chico (☎ 787/863-0834); and **Marina de Salinas** (☎ 787/752-8484) in Salinas.

DEEP-SEA FISHING

It is said in deep-sea-fishing circles that **Capt. Mike Benitez,** who has chartered out of San Juan for more than 40 years, sets the standard by which to judge other captains. (In 1993, the Sport Fishing Tournament Guide listed him as one of the 15 most qualified sport-fishing captains in the world. Past clients have included, among others, ex-President Jimmy Carter.) His Atlanta-born wife, Erin, handles the company's reservations and can be contacted directly at ☎ **787/723-2292,** daily until 9pm. The captain offers a 45-foot air-conditioned deluxe Hatteras, the *Sea Born.* Fishing tours, for up to six participants, cost $390 for a half-day excursion and $690 for a full day, with beverages and all equipment included.

GOLF

A 45-minute drive from San Juan on the northeast coast, there's the 6,145-yard **Rio Mar Golf Course** (☎ 787/888-8825) at Palmer. Inexperienced golfers prefer this course to the more challenging and more famous courses at Dorado, even though trade winds can influence your game along the holes bordering the water, and occasional fairway flooding can present some unwanted obstacles. Greens fees are a lot less expensive than at its two major competitors. A gallery of 100 iguanas also adds spice to your game at Rio Mar.

SCUBA DIVING & SNORKELING

The **Caribbean School of Aquatics,** 1 Taft St., Suite 10F, San Juan (☎ 787/ **728-6606** or 787/383-5700), offers an array of sailing, scuba, and snorkeling trips, as well as boat charters and fishing. Trips last a full day from 8am to 5:30pm daily. Scuba divers pay $124 for the entire trip, including lunch and a two-tank dive. Snorkelers go along on the trip for $79 per person. A bus transports divers and snorkelers to a site, where they board *Innovation,* which has sun- and shade-decks, along with a toilet and fresh water shower. A complimentary picnic lunch is provided.

The Grand Beach Tour

If you tire of the beaches in town, you can make the following scenic trip to the sands between San Juan and Arecibo. Allow about 5 1/2 hours, not counting beach time, for this interesting drive, for the ever-changing colors of the Atlantic make it a memorable experience.

Start at Route 2 to the Caparra intersection, where you turn onto Route 24 to Cataño; then continue west on Route 165. El Morro and Old San Juan can be seen across the bay.

After passing a dense coconut grove, you'll reach Levittown City—a housing development, as its name implies. The sea turns a blue-green shade at this spot. Continue up to the river and the town of **Dorado** (see chapter 9) by way of Route 690 north. Within a short distance you'll reach **Cerro Gordo Beach.** Watch your time, for you might be mesmerized by the natural beauty of this beach and stay longer than planned.

If you can break away from Cerro Gordo, take Route 688 back to Route 2, heading toward **Vega Baja,** founded in 1776. The residents of Vega Baja are nicknamed *melao-melao* ("molasses-molasses") because of the large amount of molasses produced here.

Route 676 north takes you to a panoramic beach in the west where the water turns jade green with touches of purple and lots of white foam. East of this beach the water is less turbulent, held back by a giant rocky barrier where the waves crash thunderously. This beach is dotted with cabins and cabañas belonging to the local residents. Continue on Route 686 until you reach Route 648, which will take you to **Mar Chiquita,** where the high rocks enclose an oval lagoon perfect for swimming.

Return by way of Route 648 to Route 685, which will lead you to Route 2. Head north on Route 2 to Route 140 until you get to Barceloneta; then take Route 681 up to the Plazuela sugar mill and go through cane fields edged with almond trees.

Continue toward the beach and look for a sign that reads LA CUEVA DEL INDIO (the Indian Cave). Many Amerindian symbols can be seen on the cave walls.

Leave the area by following Route 681 up to Route 2 in Arecibo. Route 2 east will take you back to San Juan through cane fields and perfumed pineapple plantations.

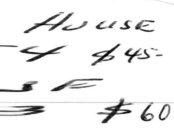

ommended opportunity for underwater diving is
quatic Adventures, P.O. Box 2470, San Juan Sta-
7/729-2929, ext. 240). Its dive shop is in the lobby
tel. The company offers a choice of full-day diving
d wrecks surrounding the island. PADI and NAUI
cost $355. A resort course for first-time divers is $97.

ts rentals available along the Condado and Isla Verde
b Aquatic Adventures (☎ 787/729-2929, ext. 240)
indsurfers for $40 per hour.

87/721-0303), the Condado Plaza Hotel & Casino
Caribe Inn, 58 Isla Verde (☎ 787/728-8400), and the
787/721-6990) have tennis courts (see chapter 5). Also
urt at the old navy base, Isla Grande, in Miramar. The
Fernández Juncos at bus stop 11.

Shopping

Puerto Rico has the same tariff barriers as the U.S. mainland. That's why you don't
pay duty on purchases brought back to the United States—but that means you don't
walk away with great bargains either. Nevertheless, there are many boutiques and
specialized stores—especially in Old San Juan—that may tempt you to do some
shopping.

Native handcrafts can be good buys. Look for *santos,* hand-carved wooden religious
figures, needlework (women are no longer paid 3¢ an hour for it!), straw work,
ceramics, hammocks, guayabera shirts for men, papier-mâché fruit and vegetables,
and paintings and sculptures by island artists. For more information, see "Puerto
Rican Arts & Crafts" in chapter 2.

Many stores are open from 9am until 6pm, and certain shops also open on Sunday, especially when large cruise ships are in port. The streets of the old town, such
as Calle San Francisco and Calle del Cristo, are the major venues for shopping.

The biggest and most up-to-date shopping plaza in the Caribbean Basin is **Plaza
Las Américas,** which is situated in the financial district of Hato Rey, right off Las
Américas Expressway. The complex, with its fountains and modern architecture, has
more than 200 shops, most of them upscale. The plaza is open Monday through
Thursday and Saturday from 9:30am to 6pm, and on Friday from 9:30am to
9:30pm.

ANTIQUES

José E. Alegria & Associates
Calle del Cristo 152-154. ☎ 787/721-8091.

Opposite El Convento Hotel, this shop is housed in an impressive, old Spanish building dating from 1523 with rooms opening onto patios and courtyards. It displays
antique furniture and paintings, and the collection is considered the finest in San
Juan. The specialty here is 18th-century furniture and paintings, and there is also a
collection of French furnishings and Spanish exhibits from the 16th through the 19th
century. Intermingled are the paintings of contemporary artists from Puerto Rico and
elsewhere. Prices are not low, but the quality is very high. There is also a wine boutique in the old cellars. Open Tuesday through Saturday from 8am to 5pm.

ART

Galería Botélo
Calle del Cristo 208. ☎ 787/723-2879.

A contemporary Latin American art gallery, Galería Botélo is a living tribute to the success story of the late Angel Botélo, one of Puerto Rico's outstanding artists, who died in 1986. Born in a small village in Galicia, Spain, he fled after the Spanish Civil War to the Caribbean and spent 12 years in the art-conscious country of Haiti. His paintings and bronze sculptures, evocative of his colorful background, are done in a style uniquely his own. This *galería* is his former home, a colonial mansion that he restored himself. Today a setting to display his paintings and sculptures, it also offers a large collection of Puerto Rican antique santos—small, carved wooden figures of saints. The gallery not only sells works by Botélo, but they showcase many outstanding local artists as well. Open Monday through Saturday from 10am to 6pm.

Galeria Palomas
207 Calle de Cristo. ☎ 787/724-8904.

This and Galleria Botélo (see above) are the two leading art galleries of Puerto Rico. This one was established in 1978 by a New York-born, long-term resident of San Juan, Sharon Moya. Works of art range in price from $70 to $35,000, include some of the leading painters of the Latin American world, and are rotated every 2 to 3 weeks to keep the inventory fresh. The setting is a 17th-century colonial house whose name derived from the hundreds of *palomas* (pigeons) that inundated the gallery with their soil when the site was first renovated by the Moya family after years of disuse. Of special note are works by such local artists as Homer, Moya, and Alicea. Open Tuesday through Saturday from 10:30am to 6pm.

Haitian Souvenirs
Calle San Francisco 206. ☎ 787/723-0959.

This is our favorite of the three stores in San Juan specializing in Haitian art and artifacts. Its walls are covered, edge to edge, with framed versions of primitive Haitian landscapes, portraits, crowd scenes, and whimsical visions of jungles where lions, tigers, parrots, and herons take on quasi-human personalities and forms. Paintings range from $80 to $500 each, although prices can usually be bargained downward a bit. Look for the brightly painted wall hangings crafted from sheets of metal (priced at around $120 each). Open daily from 9am to 6pm.

BOOKS

The Book Store
Calle San José 255. ☎ 787/724-1815.

This is the leading bookstore in the Old Town, with the largest selection of titles. It sells a number of books on Puerto Rican culture and also good touring maps of the island. It will ship purchases back to the States. Open daily from 9am to 7pm.

BUTTERFLIES

Butterfly People
Calle Fortaleza 152. ☎ 787/723-2432.

Butterfly People is a gallery and café (see chapter 6) in a handsomely restored building in Old San Juan. It has the largest privately owned collection of mounted butterflies in the world, second only to the collection at the Smithsonian Institution. The store doesn't use endangered species, although its butterflies come from virtually every tropical region of the world—the most beautiful are from the densest jungles of Borneo and Malaysia. Sold here in artfully arranged boxes, they cost from $20 for a single butterfly to as much as $70,000 for a swarm. The butterfly wings are preserved by a secret formula so that the color lasts forever. The dimensional artwork is sold in limited editions, and the gallery ships worldwide. Open Monday through Saturday from 10am to 6pm.

FASHION

Jolie Boutique
1015 Ashford Ave. ☎ 787/723-5575.

One of the best-known specialty shops on the island, it offers a large and exclusive selection of imported bathing suits, maillots, bikinis, and *pareos* (colorful sarongs) as well as high-fashion loungewear and beachwear. It's near the Condado Plaza Hotel and the Regency Hotel, and there is free parking. Open Monday through Saturday from 9am to 6pm.

Lindissima Shop
Calle Fortaleza 300. ☎ 787/721-0550.

This is the finest, most tasteful, and most elegant women's shop in Old San Juan, one of only three or four which cater to supremely well-dressed social icons. (One of the clients happens to be the wife of the island's governor; other patrons tend to live in discreet isolation behind the gardens and walls of upscale private homes.) If you feel underdressed, or lack an outfit for a special formal night aboard ship, this shop would have what you need. Garments range from $99 to $700 each, are scattered over two well-accessorized floors, and always—regardless of the manufacturer—come with the Lindissima label sewn inside. Some of the most dazzling items are beaded *bolero* blazers, which go well with clingy skirts and halter tops crafted from black crêpe chiffon. Open Monday through Saturday from 9:30am to 5:30pm.

London Fog
Calle del Cristo 156. ☎ 787/722-4334.

One of the last things you might be looking for in steamy San Juan is a winter overcoat or parka, but the prices at this factory outlet of London Fog are usually so low that a purchase of cold-weather protection is often well worth the trouble of hauling it home. Prices are between 30% and 35% less than equivalent garments on the U.S. mainland. Very few (if any) of the garments are made in Puerto Rico, but are imported from Mexico, Hong Kong, and Sri Lanka. Men's, women's, and children's garments are abundantly inventoried within a warren of small rooms on two floors of an antique colonial house. Open Monday through Saturday from 10am to 6pm, Sunday from noon to 5pm.

NoNo Maldonado
1051 Ashford Ave. ☎ 787/721-0456.

Named after its owner, a Puerto Rico–born designer who worked for many years as the New York–based fashion editor of *Esquire* magazine, this is one of the most fashionable and upscale haberdashers in the Caribbean. Selling both men's and women's clothing, the shop has everything from socks to dinner jackets, as well as ready-to-wear versions of Maldonado's twice-a-year collections. Both ready-to-wear and couture are available here. Although this is the main store for the designer (midway between the Condado Plaza and the Condado Beach Trio), the establishment also maintains a boutique in El San Juan Hotel in Isla Verde. Open Monday through Saturday from 10am to 6pm and on Sunday from noon to 5pm.

Polo/Ralph Lauren Factory Store
Calle del Cristo 201. ☎ **787/722-2136.**

It's as stylish and carefully orchestrated as anything you'd expect from one of North America's leading clothiers. Even better, its prices are from 35% to 40% less than equivalent garments sold retail on the U.S. mainland. Look for displays that feature irregular or slightly damaged garments, where discounts can—according to whatever temporary promotion is in effect at the time—be even greater. If you're a first-time visitor, it pays to wander around a bit. The store occupies two floors of a pair of interconnected colonial buildings, with one upstairs room devoted to the designer's home furnishings collection. Beware if you've been overeating at those groaning shipboard buffet tables, for men's garments are almost never stocked in sizes larger than a 42 waist. If you're large, tall, or generously proportioned, you're unlikely to find anything to fit you. Open Monday through Saturday from 10am to 6pm, Sunday from noon to 5pm.

South of Home (SoHo)
258 Calle Fortaleza. ☎ **787/722-4602.**

It's little more than a cubbyhole set into an antique house on Fortaleza Street, but its fame is growing almost weekly. Established by a pair of English-speaking fashion hounds (Maria Frias and Mirtha Roges), it specializes in a line of cotton-knit garments (short and long skirts, blouses, T-shirts, and short and long pants) for women that adapt remarkably well to either formal or informal occasions. Each garment is lavishly decorated with linear blobs of brightly colored acrylics, applied by artists with a device that resembles a squeeze-bottle for ketchup. Designs are accented with glitter, derived from Spanish baroque and/or Bauhaus designs, are highly individualized, and are cheap enough (from $20 to $50 per garment) to anchor them firmly in the "fun to wear" category of resort-wear clothing. Garments for children are also inventoried. Open Monday through Saturday from 10am to 6pm.

W. H. Smith
On the lobby level of the Condado Plaza Hotel, 999 Ashford Ave. ☎ **787/721-1000,** ext. 2094.

This outlet sells mostly women's clothing—everything from bathing suits and beach attire to jogging suits and a collection of semiformal evening wear. For men, there are shorts, bathing suits, and jogging suits. There's also a good selection of books and maps. Open daily from 7am to 11pm.

GIFTS & HANDCRAFTS

Anaiboa
Calle San Francisco 100. ☎ **787/724-0444.**

This shop occupies a tuckaway cubbyhole that opens onto a pedestrian-only stretch of cobblestones adjacent to the Calle de Cristo. Run by the married artist team of Edgard Rodriguez and Marianne Ramirez, it sells one-of-a-kind artifacts which are as utilitarian as they are charming. Inventory includes ceramic boxes, hat racks, mirrors, serving trays, and small-scale furniture accented with whimsical drawings of faces, plants, and animals. Everything that's for sale is decorated by the store's owners, creating one of the most personalized emporiums in San Juan. Many objects sell for as little as $15. Open Monday through Saturday from 10am to 6pm.

Bared and Sons
Calle Fortaleza at Calle San Justo. ☎ **787/724-4811.**

The main outlet of a chain of at least 20 upper-bracket jewelry stores scattered across Puerto Rico, this shop carries a worthy inventory of gemstones, gold, diamonds, and wristwatches on its street level (it does a thriving business whenever cruise ships pull into port). But the real value of this store lies upstairs, where a monumental collection of porcelain and crystal is displayed in claustrophobic proximity. More socially conscious families register their daughter's tastes in wedding gifts here than at any other jeweler on the island. It's especially valuable as a source of hard-to-get and discontinued patterns (priced at around 20% less than at equivalent outlets stateside) from Christofle, Royal Doulton, Wedgwood, Limoges, Royal Copenhagen, Lalique, Baccarat, and Daum. Because of their large inventories, they can often provide on-the-spot replacements for broken place settings that would otherwise require months of delay if ordered from smaller outlets on the U.S. mainland. Also available is a wide selection of porcelain sculpture from such Spanish manufacturers as Lladró. Ask about patterns that are microwave- and dishwasher-safe. Open Monday through Saturday from 9am to 6pm.

El Artesano
Calle Fortaleza 314. ☎ **787/721-6483.**

The arts and crafts of South America are among the most intriguing in the world, and San Juan is an outlet for many of them. If your budget doesn't allow for an excursion to the Andes, head for this shop, which serves as the local outlet for a well-established company in Caracas, Venezuela. You'll find Mexican and Peruvian icons of the Virgin Mary similar (but less dour) than what you might have found in old Russia; charming depictions of fish and South American birds in terra-cotta and brass; all kinds of woven goods; painted cupboards, chests, and boxes; and supremely comfortable mortise-and-tenon leather-covered chairs from Ecuador which last for many generations of hard family use. Ask a member of the staff how they can be dismantled and broken down for easy shipment in a suitcase. Open Monday through Saturday from 10am to 6pm.

Galeria Bóveda
209 Calle del Cristo. ☎ **787/725-0263.**

Few other shops in San Juan show the eclectic skill of this boutique, where every item has been selected with unusually good taste by owner Linda Williams. Established in the mid-1980s, it's a long narrow space crammed with exotic jewelry, clothing, wall hangings, and elaborately detailed masks from Thailand, Sri Lanka, Ghana, and India. Most of the clothing is designed for women, but the artwork is of universal appeal. Open daily from 10am to 6pm.

Olé
Calle Fortaleza 105. ☎ **787/724-2445.**

Even if you don't buy anything, you can still learn a lot about the crafts shown here, where practically everything that wasn't made in Puerto Rico comes from South America. Every object is artistically displayed in a high-ceilinged room decorated clear to the top. If you want a straw hat from Ecuador, hand-beaten Chilean silver, Christmas ornaments, or Puerto Rican santos, this is the place to buy them. Open Monday through Saturday from 9:30am to 6pm, Sunday from 10am to 5pm.

Puerto Rican Arts & Crafts
Calle Fortaleza 204. ☎ **787/725-5596.**

Set within a 200-year-old colonial building, whose soaring ceiling exposes a view of antique rafters, this unique store is one of the premier outlets on the island for authentic artifacts from Puerto Rico. Of particular interest are papier-mâché carnival masks (from $20 to $250) from the south-coast town of Ponce. The masks' grotesque and colorful features were originally conceived to chase away evil spirits.

Taíno designs inspired by ancient petroglyphs are incorporated into most of the sterling-silver jewelry (from $12 to $60) sold here. When faced with the riches at the front of the store, it's easy to overlook browsing through the art gallery in back, where silk-screened serigraphs by local artists cover virtually every available wall space. Open Monday through Saturday from 9am to 6pm and Sunday from noon to 5pm.

JEWELRY

Barrachina's

Calle Fortaleza 104 (between Calle del Cristo and Calle San José). ☎ **787/725-7912.**

Revered as the acknowledged birthplace of the piña colada in 1963, the store consists of a series of departments sprawling over a single floor. A favorite of visiting cruise-ship passengers, it offers one of the largest selections of jewelry, perfume, and gifts in San Juan. There's a patio—a calm oasis amid the commercial hubbub—where you can order a piña colada. You will also find a Bacardi rum outlet, a costume-jewelry department, a gift shop, and a section for authentic jewelry. Watches by Raymond Weil, Movado, Bulova, and Rado are available. Open Monday through Saturday from 9am to 6pm.

The Gold Ounce

Plaza los Muchachos, 201 Calle Fortaleza. ☎ **787/724-3102.**

This is the direct factory outlet for the oldest jewelry factory in Puerto Rico, the Kury Company. Most of the output is shipped stateside to mass-market jewelry chains such as Friedman's in the Southeast. Don't expect a top-notch (or socially prestigious) jeweler here. Many of the pieces are replicated in endless repetition and are exactly similar to hundreds of others. Even its owner admits that the company's output should be considered "the pop music of the jewelry biz" and has absolutely no pretentions about its exclusivity. But don't overlook the place as a source of cost-conscious 14-karat gold ornaments. Some (but not all) of the designs are charming, and prices are about 20% less than at retail stores on the North American mainland. Regardless of the design, everything here is sold by its weight, based on a factor which represents the current market value of gold augmented by the workmanship involved. Open Monday through Saturday from 10am to 6pm and Sunday from noon to 5pm.

Joyería Riviera

205 Calle de la Cruz. ☎ **787/725-4000.**

Some local residents consider this the Puerto Rican equivalent of Tiffany's, a high-quality emporium of 18-karat gold and diamonds whose reputation is impeccable. Its owner, Julio Abislaiman, travels to such diamond centers as Antwerp, Tel Aviv, and New York for a store his forebears established in 1961 in a showroom (paneled in exotic purpleheart wood) adjacent to the Plaza de Armas. This is the major distributor of Rolex watches in Puerto Rico, although other brands (including Patek Philippe) are also sold. The store does not appraise stones and does not sell costume jewelry of any kind. Prices range from $250 to $5,000. Open Monday through Saturday from 9:30am to 5pm.

200 Fortaleza

Calle Fortaleza 200 (at the corner of Calle Cruz). ☎ **787/723-1989.**

Known as a leading cost-conscious place to buy fine jewelry in Old San Juan, this shop has 14-karat Italian gold chains and bracelets, which are measured, fitted, and sold by weight—and priced according to the latest figures from the gold market. The center also carries the latest styles in Seiko and Citizen watches. You can purchase beautiful gems in modern settings in both 14 karat or 18 karat gold. Open Monday through Saturday 9am to 5pm.

Vergina Gallery
202 Calle del Cristo. ☎ **787/721-0592.**

It's known as the most exotic emporium of jewelry in San Juan, and the only outlet in the Caribbean showcasing the neo-Byzantine and ancient Greek designs of Zolotos, one of Greece's most spectacular jewelers. Most of the pieces are made of hammered 18 karat and 22 karat gold, inset with glittering gemstones colorful enough to have impressed even the ancient rulers of Constantinople. There's also an inventory of streamlined platinum jewelry from Germany, and worthy reproductions of medieval Greek and Russian icons, priced from $10 to $1,500. The gallery is named after the burial site of both Alexander the Great and Philip of Macedonia, a site revered by Greeks throughout the world. Open Monday through Saturday from 10am to 6pm.

Yas Mar
Calle Fortaleza 205. ☎ **787/724-1377.**

This shop sells convincingly glittering fake diamonds for those unable or unwilling to wear the real thing. It also stocks real diamond chips, emeralds, sapphires, and rubies. Open Monday through Saturday from 9:30am to 5:30pm.

LEATHER

Leather & Pearls
Calle Tanca 252 (at the corner of Calle Tetuan). ☎ **787/724-8185.**

Majorca pearls and fine leather garments, bags, shoes, and accessories (including Gucci, Mark Cross, Fendi, and Paloma Picasso) are sold here. There is also a collection of Lladró leather bags. The shop is located one block from the parking building and post office. Open Monday through Saturday from 9am to 6pm.

LINEN

The Linen House
Calle Fortaleza 250. ☎ **787/721-4219.**

It isn't flashy, and the staff is indifferent, but there's first-class merchandise in this unpretentious store specializing in napery, bed linens, and lace. Inventories include cunningly embroidered shower curtain liners selling for around $35 each, and lace doilies, bun warmers, place mats, and tablecloths that teams of Irish and Asian seamstresses took weeks to complete. Some astonishingly beautiful items are available for around $30 each, including an all-time best-seller, an embroidered wrapper designed to conceal the edges of a standard-size box of Kleenex. One corner of this emporium is devoted to aluminum-pewter serving dishes, crafted in Mexico, which are dishwasher-proof, never tarnish, and are strikingly beautiful because of their bold, Spanish-colonial designs. Prices here are probably only 40% of those charged at upscale gift shops on the North American mainland. Open Monday through Saturday from 9:30am to 6pm and Sunday 11am to 5pm.

5 San Juan After Dark

San Juan nightlife comes in all varieties. From the vibrant performing-arts scene to street-level salsa or the casinos, discos, and bars, there's plenty of entertainment available almost any evening.

VEGAS IN THE TROPICS: SPLASHY SHOWS & REVUES

El Teatro

In San Juan's Convention Center, in El Centro, the Condado Beach Trio, Ashford Ave. ☎ **787/ 721-6090**. Tickets average $28 but vary depending on the show and the event. Bus: A7.

Part of the previously recommended hotel complex, this venue is known for staging the most spectacular show revues in San Juan. Usually these are in the *Olé Latino* style, with colorful costumes, Latin music, and dancing. A "taste of the tropics" is promised and ultimately delivered. However, since this room is also used for special events, call to find out what's scheduled at the time of your visit. Show time is either 9 or 10:30pm (sometimes both), daily except Thursday and Sunday.

Copa

In the Sands Hotel & Casino, Avenida Isla Verde, Isla Verde. ☎ **787/791-6100**. Cover (including two drinks) $28, but the price can vary. Bus: A7, T1, or 2.

This is one of the major showrooms for revues along the San Juan beachfront strip. Although we can't predict what show may be featured at the time of your visit, previous revues have included *Hollywood Legends*, with impersonators appearing as Liza, Cher, or Tina Turner. There might also be a major Las Vegas–type headliner from the mainland such as Whitney Houston or Diana Ross. Shows are Monday through Wednesday and Friday through Sunday at 10pm.

El Tropicoro

In El San Juan Hotel, Avenida Isla Verde, Isla Verde. ☎ **787/791-1000**. Cover $28 for nonresidents (including two drinks), $21 for hotel guests (including 1 drink). Bus: A7, T1, or 2.

The format and nature of the shows presented here change frequently, although visitors can usually be assured of lots of glittering lights and plenty of theatricality. Currently, most of the shows include a bit of flamenco, as well as a bit of fashionably revealing décolletage from a bevy of feathered-and-beaded beauties. The hotel usually presents two shows a night, each of which lasts an hour and usually begins at 9 or 11pm. Call ahead to find out about the show and to make reservations.

WHERE TO DANCE THE NIGHT AWAY

Amadeus Disco

In El San Juan Hotel & Casino, Avenida Isla Verde, Isla Verde. ☎ **787/791-1000**. No cover Tues, Wed, and Sun; Thurs $8; Fri–Sat $10. Cover includes one drink. Bus: A7, T1, or 2.

A conservative art deco interior here welcomes a widely divergent collection of the rich and beautiful, the merely rich, and a gaggle of onlookers pretending to be both. The Amadeus Disco is in the most exciting hotel in San Juan (see chapter 5), and a visit here offers a chance to explore the adjacent casino and the best-decorated lobby in Puerto Rico. The duplex area has one of the best sound systems in the Caribbean. The club is open Tuesday through Sunday from 9:30pm to 4am.

El Chico Bar

In El San Juan Hotel, Avenida Isla Verde, Isla Verde. ☎ **787/791-1000**. No cover. Bus: A7, T1, or 2.

Located just off the expansive and richly paneled lobby of the most glamorous hotel in San Juan, this bar provides live music that permeates most of the hotel's bustling lobby. Decorated in shades of scarlet, with risqué paintings evocative of a brothel in turn-of-the-century San Francisco, it is avidly appreciated by local residents, who court, flirt, converse, celebrate anniversaries, and dance on the sometimes-crowded dance floor. It's open Tuesday through Saturday from 9pm to 1:30am. Drinks start at $3.50.

Ibiza

In the Condado Beach Trio, Ashford Ave. ☎ **787/721-6090.** Cover $7–$8. Bus: A7.

Animated and fun, and accustomed to packing in as many as 400 dancers on a Saturday night, this disco is situated in one of the most unusual concrete structures on Puerto Rico. Designed like the upper half of a clam shell and surrounded by raised patios that offer a view of the sea, La Concha (seashell) was the name of the original hotel before it became part of the Condado Beach Trio. Once you're past the doorman, you can sit at one of the many tables, dance beneath the shell, or make conversation at the elongated bar area. It's open Thursday through Saturday from 9pm to 4am.

Peggy Sue

1 Roberto H. Todd Ave. ☎ **787/725-4664.** Cover (including one or two drinks) $5–$10, depending on the night of the week and the time you arrive. Bus: T1.

This is one of the busiest nightclubs for young, upwardly mobile singles. There's a dance floor well worn by years of boogeying feet, although many visitors come only for drinks at the long and very accommodating bar. The decor was inspired by 1950s retro-chic, the music embraces most of the major musical movements since the 1960s, and people can usually meet and mingle easily.

There's live music every Friday night. The club is on two floors: normally one devoted to disco, the other to Latin music. Jeans are not allowed. Its transformation from a bar into a crowded disco usually occurs around 9pm. Open Thursday through Saturday from 5pm to 6am.

GAY DISCOS

Abbey/Laser

Calle del Cruz 251. ☎ **787/725-7581.** Cover $5 or free upon presentation of any of the coupons distributed at such gay hotels as the Atlantic Beach.

Every Monday, Tuesday, Friday, and Saturday, this disco in Old San Juan is known as Laser and attracts a mixed crowd of straights and gays into the three floors of its historic premises. Every Sunday and Thursday, however, the place changes its name to Abbey, and rocks and rolls in an almost exclusively gay genre. Thursday nights feature all modern releases of every imaginable musical style; Sundays are nostalgia nights, with music from the great disco years of the 70s and 80s. The most interesting nights, regardless of your sexual orientation, are Mondays and Thursdays, when the many cruise ships that dock in San Juan disgorge their staffs, crew members, and passengers into Old San Juan. Many of them head directly to Abbey/Laser, causing the place to be absolutely packed beginning at 9:30pm. Take a breather on the panoramic terrace overlooking the bay. Beer costs from $2 to $4, depending on what time of the night you consume it. It's open Thursday through Tuesday from 8pm until dawn.

Crush

1257 Ponce de León, Santurce. ☎ **787/722-1131.** No cover 8–10pm, $10 after 10pm, or free upon presentation of any of the coupons distributed at such gay hotels as the Atlantic Beach.

One of the two most popular gay discos in Puerto Rico, Crush combines music you'd expect in New York with lots of Latin sounds and stiff rum-based drinks. Open nightly from 8pm to 4am, with most of the flirting, dancing, and dialogues beginning after 10:30pm.

THE BAR SCENE

Fiesta Bar
In the Condado Plaza Hotel & Casino, 999 Ashford Ave. ☎ **787/721-1000.** Bus: T1.

This bar succeeds at attracting a nice mixture of local residents who mingle happily with hotel guests. The margaritas are appropriately salty, the rhythms are hot and typically Latin, and the free admission may help you forget any losses you may have suffered at the nearby casinos. It's open Monday from 5pm to midnight, Tuesday and Wednesday from 5pm to 1am, Thursday from 5pm to 2am, Friday from 5pm to 3am, and Saturday and Sunday from noon to 3am. Happy hour is from 5 to 7pm, when drinks are half price.

María's
Calle del Cristo 204. Bus: T1.

Perched on a stool here, you'll be served some of the coolest and most refreshingly original drinks in the capital—a banana, pineapple, or chocolate frost; an orange, papaya, or lime freeze; or a mixed-fruit frappé. The students, TV personalities, writers, and models who gather here also enjoy the Mexican dishes, such as chili with cheese, tacos, or enchiladas. If that sounds too heavy on a hot day, then we suggest the fruit salad. Open daily from 11am to 2am.

Palm Court
In El San Juan Hotel, Avenida Isla Verde, Isla Verde. ☎ **787/791-1000.**

This is the most beautiful bar on the island—perhaps in the entire Caribbean. Set amid the russet-colored marble and burnished mahogany of the hotel, and designed as an oval that wraps around a sunken bar area, the Palm Court is graced with one of the world's largest chandeliers and an undeniable sense of style. After 9pm Monday through Saturday, live music emanates from an adjoining room (El Chico Bar). Otherwise, patrons can relax while watching one of the most animated lobbies on the island. It's open Sunday to Thursday from 11am to 2am, Friday and Saturday from 11am to 4am.

Shannon's Irish Pub
Calle Bori 496, Rio Piedras. ☎ **787/281-8466.**

Ireland and its ales become "tropicalized" at this pub with a Latin accent and seven TV monitors. Dedicated sports fans come here to watch their favorite teams play back home. It's the regular watering hole for many of the island's university students, a constant supplier of high-energy rock 'n' roll, and the after-hours hangout of the staff from many of the city's restaurants. Happy hour is from 4 to 9pm, when drinks are half price. There are pool tables and a simple café that serves inexpensive lunches daily from 11:30am to 11pm. Beer costs $2.75, except during happy hour, when you get two for $3.50. Open daily from 12:30pm to 1:30am.

Tiffany's Pub
Calle del Cristo 213. ☎ **787/725-1167.** Bus: T1.

Many young guests have wandered into this popular spot expecting a quick piña colada or daiquiri, only to stay all evening. Tropical drinks and frappés are also popular. The establishment is on one of the main streets of Old San Juan. Hard drinks start at $3. Open 24 hours daily.

Violeta's
Calle Fortaleza 56. ☎ **787/723-6804.**

Stylish, comfortable, and urbanized, Violeta's occupies the ground floor of a 200-year-old beamed house two blocks from the landmark Gran Hotel El Convento.

Sometimes a pianist performs at the oversized grand piano. An open courtyard in back provides additional seating. Margaritas are the drink of choice. Open daily from noon to 2am, except Thursday, when it's 4pm to 2am.

CASINOS

Casinos are one of the island's biggest draws. Many visitors come here on package deals and stay at one of the posh hotels at Condado or Isla Verde with just one intention—to gamble at games ranging from blackjack to baccarat.

You can try your luck at the **Caribe Hilton** (☎ 787/721-0303), one of the better ones; the **Condado Beach Trio** (☎ 787/721-6090), **El San Juan Hotel and Casino** (☎ 787/791-1000) at Isla Verde, and the **Condado Plaza Hotel & Casino** (☎ 787/721-1000). There are no passports to flash, admissions to pay, or whatever, as is often the case in European gambling casinos. The **Radisson Ambassador Plaza Hotel and Casino** (☎ 787/721-7300) is another deluxe hotel noted for its casino action. There's yet another casino at the **Dutch Inn Hotel & Casino,** 55 Condado Ave. (☎ 787/721-0810). One of the latest casinos to open on the island is at the **Holiday Inn Crowne Plaza Hotel and Casino** (☎ 787/253-2929) on Route 187. But the very newest is the Stellaris Casino at the **San Juan Marriott Resort** (☎ 787/722-7000).

One of the largest casinos on the island is the **Sands Casino** at the Sands Hotel & Casino at Isla Verde (☎ 787/791-6100), on Isla Verde Road. Open from noon to 4am daily, this 10,000-square-foot gaming facility is an elegant rendezvous. One of its Murano crystal chandeliers is longer than a bowling alley. The casino offers 207 slot machines, 16 blackjack tables, three dice tables, four roulette wheels, and one minibaccarat table. Puerto Rican law provides that a percentage of gaming revenues be set aside for education funding.

The best casinos "out on the island" are those at the **Hyatt Regency Cerromar Beach** and **Hyatt Dorado Beach** (☎ 787/796-1234). In fact, you can drive to either of these from San Juan to enjoy their nighttime diversions.

Most casinos are open daily from noon to 4pm and again from 8pm to 4am. Jackets for men are sometimes requested, since the commonwealth wants to maintain a "dignified, refined atmosphere."

THE LELOLAI VIP PROGRAM

For $10, the cost of membership in Puerto Rico's LeLoLai VIP (Value in Puerto Rico), visitors to the island can enjoy the equivalent of up to $200 in travel benefits. Admission to folkloric shows and discounts on guided tours of historic sites and natural attractions, as well as on lodgings, meals, shopping, sports activities, and more, add up to significant savings.

In addition to special discounts and offers, the card entitles you to free admission to folkoric musical shows, including "My Island Sings for You," at the **Condado Plaza Hotel & Casino** on Monday at 9pm and Puerto Rico *Jolgorio* at the **Caribe Terrace of the Caribe Hilton** on Wednesday at 8:30pm. For more information about this card, call **787/723-3135.**

THE PERFORMING ARTS

Qué Pasa, the official visitors' guide to Puerto Rico, lists cultural events, including music, dance, theater, film, and art exhibits. It's distributed free by the tourist office.

Major cultural venues include **Centro de Bellas Artes,** Avenida Ponce de Léon 22 (☎ 787/724-4747 or 787/725-7334), where tickets for most performances range from $12 to $40, depending on the show and the seat. Seniors should ask about discounts. Built in 1981 in the heart of Santurce, the Performing Arts Center is a

6-minute taxi jaunt from most of the hotels on Condado Beach. Costing $18 million (relatively modest for such a complex), the center has 1,883 seats in the Festival Hall, 760 in the Drama Hall, and 210 in the Experimental Theater. Some of the events here will be of interest only to those who speak Spanish, whereas others attract an international audience. Take bus 1.

Another major cultural venue is **Teatro Tapía,** Avenida Ponce de León (☎ 787/ 722-0407). Standing across from the Plaza de Colón, it's one of the oldest theaters in the western hemisphere, built about 1832. In 1976 a restoration returned the theater to its original appearance. Much of Puerto Rican theater history is connected with the Tapía, named after the island's first prominent playwright, Alejandro Tapía y Rivera (1826–82). Various productions—some musical—are staged here throughout the year, representing a repertoire of drama, dance, and cultural events. You'll have to call the box office (open Monday through Friday from 9am to 4pm). Sunday matinees, when performed at all, always begin at 3:30pm, and evening performances, when featured, always begin at 8:30pm. Prices here are determined by the producers of the various shows, but most tickets range from $10 to $30. Take bus T1.

MOVIES

Movie theaters in San Juan showing films in English include the **UA Paramount,** Avenida Ponce de León 1313, Santurce (☎ 787/725-1101); **Metro 1, 2, 3,** Avenida Ponce de León 1255, Santurce (☎ 787/722-0465); and **Fine Arts Cinema,** Avenida Ponce de León 654, Miramar, Santurce (☎ 787/721-4288).

Exploring Puerto Rico off the Beaten Track: Island Drives & Paradores

8

Although San Juan has traditionally been the focus of tourism in Puerto Rico, the rest of the island has an appeal of its own. A rental car (see chapter 3) will allow visitors to add new dimensions to their experience, such as seeing some of the towns of the inland, each of which has a unique charm and flavor.

This relatively small island, barely 100 miles long and about 35 miles wide, has a panoramic countryside loaded with a wide variety of natural scenery. From your car, you can see terrain ranging from the rain forests and lush mountains of El Yunque in the east to arid stretches where cacti grow along the south shore. You will pass centuries-old coffee plantations and sugar estates, an almost lunar subterranean landscape of caves, and enormous boulders with mysterious petroglyphs carved by the ancient but vanished Taíno peoples.

Seasonal changes transform the landscape here. In November the sugarcane fields are in bloom, and in January and February red and orange blossoms cover the flowering trees along the roads. Springtime brings delicate pink flowers to the Puerto Rican oak and deep-red blossoms to the African tulip tree. Summer is a flamboyant time when the roadsides seem to be on fire with blooming flowers.

Puerto Rico has colorful but often narrow and steep roads. While driving on mountain roads, blow your horn before every turn; this will help you avoid an accident. Commercial road signs are forbidden, so make sure you take along a map and this guide to keep you abreast of restaurants, hotels, and possible points of interest. There are white roadside markers noting distances in kilometers (1km is equivalent to 0.62 mi.) in black lettering. Remember that speed limits are given in miles per hour.

Following are two driving tours of the Puerto Rican countryside. The first will take you to the lush tropical forests and sandy beaches of eastern Puerto Rico, the second to the subterranean sights of Karst Country and on to the west and south coasts. They are both extended tours—the first takes approximately 2 days to complete and the second approximately 6 days—but Puerto Rico's small size and many roads will give you many places to pick up or leave the tour.

In fact, there are several points in the tours where we give you the opportunity to cut your tour short and head back to San Juan.

INNS & RESTAURANTS

Two programs that have helped the Puerto Rico Tourism Company successfully promote the commonwealth as "The Complete Island"—the *paradores puertorriqueños* and the *mesones gastronómicos*—will help make your travels even more enjoyable.

The paradores puertorriqueños are a chain of privately owned and operated country inns under the auspices and supervision of the Commonwealth Development Company. These hostelries are easily identified by the Taíno grass hut that appears in the signs and logos of each one. The Puerto Rico Tourism Company started the program in 1973, modeling it after Spain's parador system, although many of those here are mere shanties when compared to some of the deluxe hostelries of Spain. Each parador is situated in a historic or particularly beautiful spot. They vary in size, but all share the virtues of affordability, hospitable staffs, and high standards of cleanliness.

The paradores are also known for Puerto Rican cuisine of excellent quality, with meals starting at $18. There are now paradores at locations throughout the island, many within an easy drive of San Juan. For reservations or further information, contact the **Paradores Puertorriqueños Reservation Office,** Old San Juan Station, San Juan, PR 00905 (☎ **787/721-2884** or 800/443-0266 in the U.S.).

As you tour the island, you'll find few well-known restaurants, except for those in major hotels. However, there are plenty of roadside places and simple taverns. For authentic island cuisine, you can rely on the *mesones gastronómicos* ("gastronomic inns"). This established dining "network," sanctioned by the Puerto Rico Tourism Company, highlights restaurants recognized for excellence in preparing and serving Puerto Rican specialties at modest prices.

Mesón gastronómico status is limited to restaurants outside the San Juan area that are close to major island attractions. Membership in the program requires that restaurants have attractive surroundings and comply with strict standards of good service. Members must specialize in native foods, but if you ask for any fresh fish dish, the chances are you'll be pleased.

DRIVING TOUR 1
Eastern Puerto Rico

Start: San Juan.
Finish: San Juan.
Time: Allow approximately 2 days, although you may wish to stay longer at places along the way.
Best Times: Any sunny days Monday through Friday.
Worst Times: Weekends, when the roads are often impossibly crowded.

This tour will take you through some of Puerto Rico's most stunning natural scenery, including El Yunque forest and Luquillo Beach. You will travel through the small towns of Trujillo Alto, Gurabo, Fajardo, Naguabo, Humacao, Yabucoa, San Lorenzo, and Caguas before returning to San Juan.

From downtown San Juan, go to Río Piedras and take Route 3 (Avenida 65 de Infantera, named after the Puerto Rican regiment that fought in World War II and the Korean War). Turn south onto Route 181 toward Trujillo Alto, then take Route 851 up to Route 941. At the end of the valley you can spot the:

1. **Lake of Loíza.** Houses can be seen nestled on the surrounding hills. You may even see local farmers (*jíbaros*) riding horses laden with produce going to or from the marketplace. The lake is surrounded by mountains. Your next stop is the town of:

2. **Gurabo.** This is tobacco country, and you'll know that you're nearing the town from the sweet aroma enveloping it (tobacco smells sweet before it's harvested). Part of the town of Gurabo is set on the side of a mountain, and the streets consist of steps.

   Leave the town by heading east on Route 30. Near Juncos, turn left onto Route 185 north, follow it up through Lomas, and then get on Route 186 south. This road offers views of the ocean beyond the mountains and valleys. At this point you'll be driving on the lower section of the Caribbean National Forest; the vegetation is dense, and you'll be surrounded by giant ferns. The brooks descending from the mountains become small waterfalls on both sides of the road. At about 25 miles east of San Juan is:

3. ✪ **El Yunque.** Consisting of about 28,000 acres, this rare natural treasure is the only tropical rain forest in the U.S. National Forest system. Its Spanish name derives from its distinctive anvil shape. It lies in the Luquillo Mountains, a name that harks back to the benign Indian god *Yuquiyú*, who, according to ancient legend, ruled from the forest's mighty peaks and protected the Taíno Indians, the island's original inhabitants. Today, El Yunque offers its visitors close encounters of the natural kind, from picnics amid rare flora and fauna to hikes along the panoramic trails. If the outdoors appeals, give yourself at least a day to explore this natural wonderland. See "The Natural Environment" in chapter 2 and Section 3 on Ceiba and El Yunque in chapter 9 for details.

   Continue driving on Route 186 through Benitez and El Verde until you reach Route 986. Turn south and drive until you reach Route 191, which will take you to the:

4. **Sierra Palma Visitor Center.** Located at km 11.6 on Route 191, the center is open daily from 7:30am to 2pm and 5 to 9:30pm. Guides here give lectures and show slides; groups, if they make arrangements in advance, can go on guided hikes. Since the center has no working telephone, call the Administrative Headquarters of the El Yunque Ranger District (☎ **787/887-2875**) for information about the area.

   To make your way back, backtrack on Route 191 until you reach Route 3. Five miles east from the intersection is:

5. ✪ **Luquillo Beach.** Edged by a vast coconut grove, this crescent-shaped beach is not only the best on Puerto Rico but also one of the finest in the Caribbean. You pay $1 to enter with your car, and you can rent a locker, take a shower, and use the changing rooms. Luquillo Beach becomes rather crowded on weekends, so if possible go on a weekday when you'll have more sand to yourself. Picnic tables are available as well.

   The beach is open Tuesday through Sunday from 9am to 5pm; it's closed Monday (if Monday is a holiday, the beach will be open Monday and closed Tuesday). Before entering the beach, you may want to stop at one of the roadside thatched huts that sell Puerto Rican snacks and pick up the makings for a picnic.

   Not far from the beach is the **Parador Martorell,** where you can spend a restful night at the seaside (see "Where to Stay Along the Way in Luquillo," at the end of this tour).

   From Luquillo, return to Route 3 east until the first exit to Fajardo, where you make a left onto Route 194. At the traffic light at the corner of the Monte Brisas Shopping Center, turn left; stay on this road until the next traffic light, turn right, and continue to the intersection with Route 987. Turn left onto Route 987 and continue until you reach the entrance to:

6. Las Cabezas de San Juan Nature Reserve, better known as *El Faro,* or "The Lighthouse." In the northeast corner of Puerto Rico, north of Fajardo, this is one of the most beautiful and important areas of the island—unique because of the number of different ecological communities that flourish here.

Surrounded on three sides by the Atlantic Ocean, the 316-acre site encompasses forest land, mangroves, lagoons, beaches, cliffs, offshore cays, and coral reefs. El Faro serves as a research center for the scientific community. Home to a vast array of flora and fauna (such as sea turtles and other endangered species), including abundant and varied underwater life, it is an important spawning ground for fish and crustaceans, and for shore and migratory birds.

The nature reserve is open Wednesday through Sunday. Reservations are required, so call **787/722-5834** before going. Admission is $5 for adults, $2 for children under 12 (parking included). Guided tours, lasting 2 to 2^1/$_2$ hours, are scheduled four times daily: at 9:30am, 10am, 10:30am, and 2pm.

After visiting the reserve, you can take the same road back to Route 3 and then follow the highway signs into:

7. Fajardo. This fishing port was hotly contested during the Spanish-American War. Puerto Ricans are fond of giving nicknames to people and places—for many years, the residents of Fajardo have been called *cariduros* ("the hard-faced ones"). Don't let the label mislead you; the people here are very friendly.

Sailors and fishers are attracted to the shores of Fajardo and nearby Las Croabos, which has a lot of seafood restaurants. If you have time, you can take a very satisfying trip by ferry from Fajardo to either Vieques or Culebra, small islands off the Puerto Rican coast that make urban troubles seem far, far away (see chapter 11).

Continue south on Route 3, following the Caribbean coastline. At Cayo Lobos, just off the Fajardo port, the Atlantic meets the Caribbean. Here, the vivid colors of the Caribbean seem subdued compared to those of the deep blue ocean. Go through the town of Ceiba, near the Roosevelt Navy Base, until you reach:

8. Naguabo Beach. Here you can have coffee and *pastelillos de chapin,* pastry turnovers that were actually used as tax payments during Spanish colonial days. At km 70.9 of Route 3, take a brief detour to the town of Naguabo and enjoy the town plaza's scented, shady laurel trees, imported from India.

Continue south along Route 3, going through Humacao and its sugarcane fields. When the cane blooms during November and December, the tops of the fields change colors according to the time of day. Humacao itself isn't of much interest, but it has a *balneario*-equipped beach with changing facilities, lockers, and showers. From here you can detour to the sprawling resort of:

9. Palmas del Mar. See chapter 9 for a full discussion of the offerings of this sun-and-sports paradise.

After this stopover, you can continue along Route 3 through Yabucoa, nestled amid some hills. The view along the road opens up at Cerro La Pandura, a mountain from which there's a panoramic outlook over giant boulders onto the Caribbean.

At the town of Maunabo, leave Route 3 for Route 181, which passes through the mountains to San Lorenzo. There, Route 183 will lead you to Caguas, where you may choose between the scenic tour (Route 1) or the speedy highway (Route 52) back into San Juan.

Driving Tour—Eastern Puerto Rico

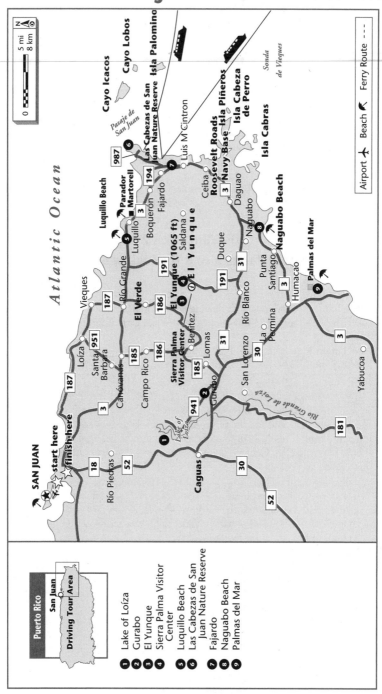

145

WHERE TO STAY ALONG THE WAY IN LUQUILLO

Parador Martorell

6A Ocean Dr., Luquillo, PR 00773. ☎ **787/889-2710.** Fax 787/889-4520. 10 rms (4 with bath). TV. $64.20 double without bath; $74.90 double with bath. Rates include breakfast. MC, V. At km 36.2 along Route 3, turn toward the shore, then turn left and drive four short blocks.

Back in 1800 the Martorell family came to Puerto Rico from Spain and fell in love with the island. Today their descendants own and operate this Luquillo parador near the island's most impressive beach. When you arrive at the parador, you'll enter an open courtyard. Breakfast always features plenty of freshly picked fruit and homemade breads and compotes. The main reason for staying at the Martorell remains Luquillo Beach, which has shady palm groves, crescent beaches, coral reefs for snorkeling and scuba diving, and a surfing area. Be advised that this parador could be better maintained, and that the rather basic and simple rooms here have displeased many readers expecting more. Try for one of the air-conditioned units if you book here.

DRIVING TOUR 2
Western Puerto Rico & the Southwest Coast

Start: San Juan.
Finish: San Juan.
Time: Between 2 and 6 days, depending on how much of the itinerary you want to complete. The tour could run longer if you spend extra time at some of the stops along the way.
Best Times: Monday through Friday, any sunny day.
Worst Times: Weekends, when the roads are overcrowded with drivers from San Juan.

This tour begins with a foray into the famous Karst district of Puerto Rico. Along the way, you'll see the Taíno Indian Ceremonial Ball Park, Pagan Pagan's Cave, Río Camuy Cave Park, and Arecibo Observatory. You will then emerge from the island's interior to begin a roundabout tour of the west and south coasts, taking in Guajataca Beach, Mayagüez, San Germán, Phosphorescent Bay, Ponce, Coamo, and numerous other towns and attractions.

Starting out from San Juan, take Route 2 west through the town of Manatí, after which you will pass the pineapple region. At km 57.9 turn left at Cruce Dávila and follow Route 140 south to the village of Florida. At km 25.5 you'll find a coffee cooperative where, during harvest time, the beans are processed, ground, and packed. At km 30.7, turn right toward the:

1. **Hacienda Rosas.** A coffee plantation, interesting at all times, is especially so from September to December or January, when groups of pickers walk under the bushes and gather the crimson beans while other workers process the yield.

   Shortly thereafter, you may leave Route 140 for Route 141, which will take you on an interesting detour to:

2. **Jayuya.** This village in the middle of the Cordillera Central is home to the **Parador Hacienda Gripiñas,** a former coffee plantation where you can catch a very authentic and unique glimpse of the old days (see "The Paradores of Western Puerto Rico," at the end of the tour).

   If you decide to make this restful side trip, pick up the trail again by returning on Route 141 to Route 140, then travel west on Route 140 until you pass Lake Caonillas. There, turn onto Route 111 west, and you'll soon reach:

3. Utuado. A small mountain town, Utuado boasts the **Parador La Casa Grande,** with accommodations, a restaurant, and a swimming pool; it's a good place to stop after a day's touring in the area (see "The Paradores of Western Puerto Rico," at the end of the tour).

From Utuado, continue west on Route 111 to km 12.3, where you'll find the:

4. ✪ Taíno Indian Ceremonial Center. Archaeologists have dated this site to approximately 2 centuries before Europe's discovery of the New World. It is believed that the Taíno chief Guarionex gathered his subjects on this site to celebrate rituals and practice sports. Set on a 13-acre field surrounded by trees, some 14 vertical monoliths with colorful petroglyphs are arranged around a central sacrificial stone monument. The ball complex also includes a museum, open daily from 9am to 5pm; admission is free. There is also a gallery, Herencia Indigena, where visitors can purchase Taíno relics at very reasonable prices, including the sought-after Cemis (Taíno idols) and figures of the famous little frog, the *coquí.*

Continue next on Route 111 to the town of Lares, then turn onto Route 129 north. Drive about 3¹/₂ miles, then turn right onto Route 4456, and you'll soon reach the:

5. ✪ Río Camuy Cave Park. The third-largest underground river in the world, Río Camuy runs through a network of caves, canyons, and sinkholes that have been cut through the island's limestone base over the course of millions of years. The caves, known to both the pre-Columbian Taíno peoples and local Puerto Rican

Life After Death

The Taíno Indians who lived in Puerto Rico before Europeans came here were ruled by *Caciques,* or chiefs, who controlled their own villages and several others nearby. The Taínos believed in life after death, which led them to take extreme care in burying their dead. Personal belongings of the deceased were placed in the tomb with the newly dead, and bodies were carefully arranged in a squatting position. Near Ponce visitors can see the oldest Indian burial ground uncovered in the Antilles (see chapter 10).

Even at the time of the arrival of Columbus and the conquistadores to follow, the Taínos were threatened by the warlike and cannibalistic Carib Indians coming up from the south. But even though they feared the Caribs, they learned to fear the conquistadores even more. Within 50 years of the Spanish colonization, the Taíno culture had virtually disappeared, the Indians annihilated either through massacres or European diseases.

But Taíno blood and remnants of their culture live on. They married with Spaniards and Africans, and their physical characteristics—straight hair, copper-colored skin, and prominent cheekbones—can still be seen in some Puerto Ricans today. Many Taíno words became part of the Spanish language spoken on the island even today. Hammocks, the weaving of baskets, and the use of gourds as eating receptacles are part of the heritage left by these ill-fated tribes.

Still standing near Utuado, Taíno Indian Ceremonial Center was built by them for recreation and worship some 800 years ago. Stone monoliths, some etched with petroglyphs, rim several of the 10 *bateyes* (playing fields) used for a ceremonial game which some historians believe was a forerunner to soccer. The monoliths and petroglyphs, as well as the *dujos* (ceremonial chairs), are existing examples of their skill in carving wood and stone.

farmers, came to the attention of speleologists in the 1950s. Developed by the Puerto Rico Land Administration, they were opened to the public in 1987.

Gardens in the focal point of the park surround buildings where tickets can be purchased. Visitors first see a short film about the caves, then descend to where open-air trolleys carry them on the downward journey to the actual caves. The trip takes you through a 200-foot-deep sinkhole, a chasm where tropical trees, ferns, and flowers flourish, supporting many birds and butterflies. The trolley then goes to the entrance of Empalme Cave, one of the 16 in the Camuy Caves network, where visitors begin a 45-minute cave walk, viewing the majestic series of rooms rich in stalagmites, stalactites, and huge sculptures carved out and built up through the centuries. Tres Pueblos Sinkhole, measuring 650 feet in diameter with a depth of 400 feet, is big enough to accommodate all of San Juan's El Morro Fortress. Tres Pueblos lies on the boundaries of the Camuy, Hatillo, and Lares municipalities. In Tres Pueblos, visitors can walk along two platforms: one on the Lares side facing the town of Camuy and the other on the Hatillo side overlooking Tres Pueblos Cave and the Río Camuy.

The caves are open Tuesday through Sunday from 8am to 4pm. Tickets are $10 for adults ($5 for seniors), $7 for children 2 to 12, free for children under 2. Parking is $1. For more information, phone the park at **787/898-3100.**

For more spelunking, drive to km 13.6 of Route 129. There, take Route 489 south to La Cueva de la Luz ("Cave of Light"). From there, continue on Route 489 to the Barrio Aibonito, Pagan sector. If you're not sure of your whereabouts, ask anyone to help you find:

6. **La Cueva de Pagan Pagan** ("Pagan Pagan's Cave"). A narrow road will lead you to a general store where you can receive directions to Pagan. Only the agile and those who like to explore should venture inside this cave, which although lit by daylight, has a rough and irregular floor. If you do go in, wear slacks and good walking shoes. There are no bats in the cave. Inside, a stone vessel contains fresh water that some believe has rejuvenating qualities. Other caves in this area have not been explored fully, but relics from the native peoples have been found in some of them.

Backtrack on Route 489 to Route 635, then turn right and travel east for a short distance until you reach Route 625. Turn right and take this road to:

7. ✪ **Arecibo Observatory.** Also called the National Astronomy and Ionosphere Center of Cornell University, this observatory has the world's largest and most sensitive radar/radio-telescope. The telescope features a 20-acre dish or radio mirror set in an ancient sinkhole. It's 1,000 feet in diameter and 167 feet deep,

---

Touring with the Cavemen

You don't have to take a driving tour to see the Río Camuy Cave Park. In fact, you don't even have to climb down into the caverns yourself. If you want the company of knowledgeable and environmentally sensitive guides, plus comfortable accommodations, **Tropix Wellness Tours** (☎ **787/268-2173;** fax 787/268-1722) conducts what it calls a "Camuy Caveman Tour" through this underground labyrinth.

The cost is $275 per person, including accommodations at the Costa Dorado Hotel in Isabela, where the tour begins. Rates are based on double occupancy and include continental breakfast and equipment for the escorted tours.

Western Puerto Rico & the Southwest Coast

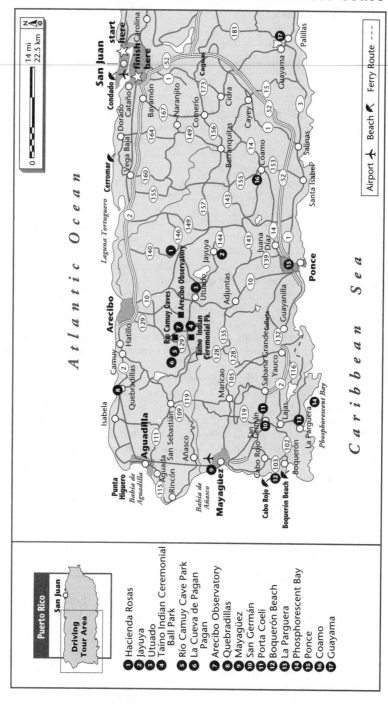

Puerto Rico

San Juan

Driving Tour Area

1. Hacienda Rosas
2. Jayuya
3. Utuado
4. Taíno Indian Ceremonial Ball Park
5. Río Camuy Cave Park
6. La Cueva de Pagan Pagan
7. Arecibo Observatory
8. Quebradillas
9. Mayagüez
10. San Germán
11. Porta Coeli
12. Boquerón Beach
13. La Parguera
14. Phosphorescent Bay
15. Ponce
16. Coamo
17. Guayama

Airport ✈   Beach ⚑   Ferry Route - - -

149

allowing scientists to examine the ionosphere, planets, and moon with powerful radar signals and to monitor natural radio emissions from distant galaxies, pulsars, and quasars. It has been used by scientists as part of the Search for Extraterrestrial Intelligence (SETI), a research effort based on the proposition that possible advanced civilizations elsewhere in the universe might communicate via radio waves; thus Arecibo Observatory is called an "ear to the heavens."

Unusually lush vegetation flourishes under the giant dish, benefiting from the filtered sunlight and rain. There are ferns, grasses, and other plants such as wild orchids and begonias. Creatures such as mongooses, lizards, frogs, dragonflies, and an occasional bird have taken refuge under the dish. Suspended in outlandish fashion above the dish is a 600-ton platform similar in design to a bridge. Hanging as it does in midair, it resembles a space station.

The observatory (☎ 787/878-2612) is open for self-guided tours Tuesday through Friday from 2 to 3pm and on Sunday from 1 to 4pm. There's a souvenir shop on the grounds.

When you're ready to leave the observatory, follow Routes 625 and 635 back out to Route 129 and consider the time of day and your own inclinations when deciding whether to head south to one of the paradores in Utuado or Jayuya; head north to Arecibo and Route 2, the main north coast highway, where you can turn toward attractions and accommodations to the west; or return to San Juan.

Going west on Route 2 from Arecibo, the next stop on the tour is:

8. **Quebradillas.** Beautiful Guajataca Beach and two paradores are only a 15-mile trip from Arecibo along Route 2 in the vicinity of this small town near the sea. Guajataca is fine for sunning and collecting shells, but it's *playa peligrosa* (dangerous unless you're a strong swimmer). **Parador El Guajataca** and **Parador Vistamar** are located fairly close to each other (see "The Paradores of Western Puerto Rico," at the end of this tour, for full descriptions).

From Quebradillas, take Route 113 south to Route 119, which will bring you to the artificial Guajataca Lake. Follow the lake's shoreline for about 2¹/₂ miles and turn left at km 19 to Route 455; you will soon cross a bridge spanning the Guajataca River, which runs through the lush mountains.

Return to Route 119, which you follow west to San Sebastián. There, take Route 109 across coffee plantations through the town of Anasco and on to Route 2, where you turn south and head for:

9. **Mayagüez.** For a complete discussion of where to stay and eat and what to see in the environs of this western port city, see chapter 10.

When you're ready to leave Mayagüez, continue southeast along Route 2 until you reach:

10. **San Germán.** Puerto Rico's second-oldest town is a little museum piece. It was founded in 1512 and destroyed by the French in 1528. Rebuilt in 1570, it was named after Germain de Foix, the second wife of King Ferdinand of Spain. Once the rival of San Juan, many of its inhabitants were engaged in piracy, pillaging the ships that sailed off the nearby coastline. Indeed, many of today's residents are descended from the smugglers, poets, priests, and politicians who lived here. Although the pirates and sugar plantations are long gone, the city retains many colorful reminders of those long-gone days. Today it has settled into a slumber, albeit one that has preserved the feel of the Spanish colonial era. The scenery provides a backdrop to a variety of architectural styles depicted in the gracious old-world-style buildings which line the streets. Flowers brighten the patios here as they do in Seville. Also as in a small Spanish town, many of the inhabitants stroll in the plaza in the early evening.

San Germán is only the second Puerto Rican city (the other is San Juan) to be included in the National Register of Historic Places. On a knoll at one end of town stands one of the gems of its 249 noteworthy sites, the chapel of:

11. **Iglesia Porta Coeli** (Gate of Heaven). Dating from 1606, this is the oldest church in the New World. Restored by the Institute of Puerto Rican Culture, it contains a museum of religious art with a collection of ancient santos, the carved figures of saints that have long been a major branch of Puerto Rican folk art. Admission is free; the hours are Tuesday through Sunday from 9am to noon and 2 to 4:30pm. Call **787/264-4258** for more information.

Easily accessible from either Mayagüez or San Germán via Route 102 to Route 100 south is:

12. **Boquerón Beach.** This is one of Puerto Rico's best beaches for swimming, and there's a comfortable parador with a good restaurant only two blocks away. For more information about **Parador Boquemar,** see "The Paradores of Western Puerto Rico," at the end of this tour.

From San Germán, take Route 320 to Route 101 into Lajas, where Route 116 will lead to Route 304, which will take you to:

13. **La Parguera.** There are two paradores in this small fishing village, the **Parador Villa Parguera** and the **Parador Posada Porlamar** (see "The Paradores of Western Puerto Rico," at the end of this tour). If you have the good fortune to find yourself in La Parguera on a moonless night, we recommend going to:

14. **Phosphorescent Bay.** A boat leaves Villa Parguera pier nightly from 7:30pm to 12:30am, depending on the demand, and heads for this small bay to the east of La Parguera. There, a pitch-black night will facilitate a marvelous show, since you can see fish leave a luminous streak on the water's surface and watch the boat's wake glimmer in the dark. This phenomenon is produced by a large colony of dinoflagellates, a microscopic form of marine life that produces sparks of chemical light when their nesting is disturbed.

To travel on, take Route 304 up to Route 116 and drive west through Ensenada. At Guánica, you may turn south and follow Route 333 out to Caña Gorda Beach for lunch or a swim. While there, look for the cacti that flourish in this unusually dry region. Back on Route 116, drive north to Palomas, where you can take Route 2 into:

15. **Ponce.** A complete discussion of the many interesting eateries, inns, and sights in this old colonial city can be found in chapter 10.

When you're ready to leave Ponce, take Route 1 east toward Guayama. At the town of Santa Isabel, you may want to take an interesting detour north along Route 153 to:

16. **Coamo.** Along the way to this town, you'll see signs pointing to the Baños de Coamo. Legend has it that these hot springs were the Fountain of Youth sought by Ponce de León. It is believed that the Taíno peoples, during pre-Columbian times, held rituals and pilgrimages here as they sought health and well-being. For more than a century between 1847 and 1958, the site was a center for rest and relaxation for Puerto Ricans as well as others, some on their honeymoon, others in search of the curative powers of the geothermal springs, which lie about a 5-minute walk from **Parador Baños de Coamo** (see "The Paradores of Western Puerto Rico," at the end of this tour).

Return to Route 1, driving east onto Route 3 and on into:

17. **Guayama.** The small town of Guayama is green and beautiful, with steepled churches and Museo Cautino, one of the finest museums around. The old mansion is a showplace of fine turn-of-the-century furnishings and pictures of the prize

horses for which the Guayama area is famous. Just minutes from town is Arroyo Beach, a tranquil place to spend an afternoon.

To begin the final leg back to San Juan, take Route 15 north. If you take this road in either spring or summer, you'll be surrounded by the brilliant colors of flowering trees.

At km 17.1, in Jajome, you can see the governor's former summer palace, an ancient building now restored and enlarged as a roadside inn. Continue on Route 15, then take Route 1, which goes directly back to the capital.

THE PARADORES OF WESTERN PUERTO RICO

Listed below are the paradores referred to in Driving Tour 2.

El Yunque has become such a major attraction that little inns and bed-and-breakfasts have sprung up at Ceiba to cater to visitors heading to the forest. See chapter 9 for more information about these places.

AT JAYUYA

⑤ Parador Hacienda Gripiñas

Rte. 527, km 2.5 (P.O. Box 387), Jayuya, PR 00664. ☎ **787/828-1717.** Fax 787/828-1719. 19 rms. Year-round $60 double. AE. From Jayuya, head east via Rte. 144; at the junction with Rte. 527, go south for 1¹/₂ miles.

A former coffee plantation about 2¹/₂ hours from San Juan, in the very heart of the Cordillera Central (Central Mountain Range), Hacienda Gripiñas is reached by a long, narrow, and curvy road. This home-turned-inn is a delightful blend of the hacienda of days gone by and the conveniences of today. The plantation ambience is everywhere—created by ceiling fans, splendid gardens, hammocks on a porch gallery, and more than 20 acres of coffee-bearing bushes. You'll taste the home-grown product when you order the inn's aromatic brew.

Stick to the restaurant's Puerto Rican dishes rather than going for its international cuisine. Most of the modest rooms come with ceiling fans. You can swim in the pool (away from the main building), soak up the sun, or enjoy the nearby sights, such as the Taíno Indian Ceremonial Ball Park at Utuado. Boating and plenty of fishing are just 30 minutes away at Lake Caonillas. The parador is also near the Río Camuy Cave Park.

AT UTUADO

Parador La Casa Grande

P.O. Box 616, Caonillas, Utuado, PR 00761. ☎ **787/894-3939.** Fax 787/894-3939. 20 rms. Year-round $58.85 double. AE, MC, V. From Utuado, head south via Rte. 111 until you reach Rte. 140; then head west until you come to the intersection with Rte. 612 and follow 612 south for about half a mile.

Parador La Casa Grande lies in the district of Caonillas Barrios, in the mountainous heartland of the island, about 2¹/₂ hours from San Juan. Situated on 107 acres of a former coffee plantation, it has a cocktail lounge, a restaurant with both Puerto Rican and international specialties, and a swimming pool. All the comfortably but very simply furnished bedrooms have ceiling fans.

AT QUEBRADILLAS

Parador El Guajataca

Rte. 2, km 103.8 (P.O. Box 1558), Quebradillas, PR 00678. ☎ **787/895-3070** or 800/964-3061. Fax 787/895-3589. 38 rms. A/C TV TEL. Year-round $75–$80 double.

AE, DC, MC, V. From Quebradillas, continue northwest on Rte. 2 for 1 mile (the parador is signposted).

You'll find this place along the north coast 70 miles west of San Juan. Service, hospitality, and the natural beauty surrounding El Guajataca—plus modern conveniences and a family atmosphere—add up to a good visit. The parador is set on a rolling hillside that reaches down to the surf-beaten beach. Each room is like a private villa with its own entrance and private balcony opening onto the turbulent Atlantic.

Room service is available, but meals are more enjoyable in the glassed-in dining room where all the windows face the sea. Dinner is an experience, with a cuisine that blends Créole and international specialties. A local musical group plays for dining and dancing on weekend evenings. The bar is open daily from 4pm to 10pm (until 1am on Friday and Saturday).

There are two swimming pools (one for adults, another for children), two tennis courts (free for guests), plus a playground for children.

Parador Vistamar

6205 Rte. 113N (P.O. Box T-38), Quebradillas, PR 00678. ☎ **787/895-2065.** Fax 787/895-2294. 55 rms. A/C TV TEL. Year-round $69.55–$90.95 double. Up to two children under 12 stay free in parents' room. AE, DC, MC, V. At Quebradillas, head northwest on Rte. 2, then go left at the junction with Rte. 113 for half a mile.

High atop a mountain, overlooking greenery and a seascape in the Guajataca area, this parador, one of the largest on Puerto Rico, sits like a sentinel surveying the scene. There are gardens and intricate paths carved into the side of the mountain where you can stroll while you enjoy the fragrance of the tropical flowers that grow in the area. Or you may choose to search for the calcified fossils that abound on the carved mountainside. For a unique experience, visitors can try their hand at freshwater fishing in the only river on Puerto Rico with green waters, just down the hill from the hotel. Flocks of rare tropical birds are frequently seen in the nearby mangroves.

Bedrooms are comfortably furnished in a rather bland motel style. There's a dining room with an ocean view, where you can have a typical Puerto Rican dinner, or choose from the international menu.

A short drive from the hotel will bring you to the Punta Borinquén Golf Course. Tennis courts are just down the hill from the inn itself. Sightseeing trips to the nearby Arecibo Observatory—the largest radar/radio-telescope in the world—and to Monte Calvario (a replica of Mount Calvary) are available. Another popular visit is to the plaza in the town of Quebradillas.

AT BOQUWEÓN BEACH

Parador Boquemar

101 Rte. 307, Boquerón, Cabo Rojo, PR 00622. ☎ **787/851-2158.** Fax 787/851-7600. 64 rms. A/C TV. Year-round $65–$80 double. AE, DC, MC, V. From either Mayagüez or San Germán, take Rte. 102 into Cabo Rojo and then get Rte. 100 south; turn right onto Rte. 101 and the hotel will be two blocks from the beach.

Parador Boquemar, built in the late 1980s, lies near Boquerón Beach (considered one of the best bathing beaches on the island) in the southwest corner of the island, between Mayagüez and Ponce. The hotel is not right on the beach; it's a block or so away. Puerto Rican families like this place a lot, but readers complain that children run up and down the corridors until late. This is not one of the best of the government paradores, as rooms tend to be too small for comfort in some cases. But it does have one of the best restaurants in the area, Las Cascadas, offering typical dishes of the area, including lobster asopao.

AT LA PARGUERA

⑤ Parador Posada Porlamar

Rte. 304 (P.O. Box 405), La Parguera, Lajas, PR 00667. ☎ **787/899-4015.** Fax 787/899-5558. 18 rms. A/C TEL TV. Year-round $69.55 double. AE, MC, V. Drive west along Rte. 2 until you reach the junction of Rte. 116; then head south along Rte. 116 and Rte. 304.

Life in a simple fishing village plus all the modern conveniences you want in a vacation are what you'll find at this "Guesthouse by the Sea" in the La Parguera section of Lajas, in the southwestern part of the island. The area is famous for its Phosphorescent Bay and good fishing, especially for snapper. The guesthouse, built in 1960, is near several fishing villages and other points of interest. If you like to collect seashells, you can beachcomb. Other collectors' items found here are fossilized crustacea and marine plants. A scuba shop is on site.

Parador Villa Parguera

304 Main St. (P.O. Box 273), La Parguera, Lajas, PR 00667. ☎ **787/899-7777.** Fax 787/ 899-6040. 62 rms. A/C TV TEL. Sun–Thurs $75 double; Fri–Sat $85 double (including half board), $299 double-occupancy packages (for 2 days). Two children under 10 stay free in parents' room. AE, DC, DISC, MC, V. Drive west along Rte. 2 until you reach the junction with Rte. 116; then head south along Rte. 116 and Rte. 304.

Although the water in the nearby bay is too polluted for swimming, guests can still enjoy a view of the water and the swimming pool. Situated on the southwestern shore of Puerto Rico, this parador is known for its seafood dinners (the fish is not caught in the bay), its comfortable rooms (furnished in a simple modern style), and its location next to the phosphorescent waters of one of the coast's best-known bays.

The dining room offers daily specials, as well as such chef's favorites as filet of fish stuffed with lobster and shrimp. Open daily from noon to 5pm and 7:30 to 11pm.

Because the inn is popular with the residents of San Juan on weekends, there's a special weekend package for a 2-night minimum stay; $299 covers the price of the double room, welcome drinks, breakfasts, dinners, flowers, and dancing with a free show.

AT COAMO

⑤ Parador Baños de Coamo

P.O. Box 540, Coamo, PR 00769. ☎ **787/825-2186.** Fax 787/825-4739. 48 rms. A/C TV TEL. Year-round $70 double. AE, DC, DISC, MC, V. From Rte. 1, turn onto Rte. 153 at Santa Isabel; then turn left onto Rte. 546 and drive west for one mile.

Coamo is inland on the south coast, about a 2-hour drive from San Juan. The spa at Baños de Coamo features a parador offering hospitality in the traditional Puerto Rican style, although this place has a somewhat Mexican atmosphere. The Baños has welcomed many notable visitors over the years, including Franklin D. Roosevelt, Frank Lloyd Wright, Alexander Graham Bell, and Thomas Edison, who came here to swim in the hot springs on site, said to be the most radioactive in the world. (Locals sometimes purchase a day pass and use the pool, which leads to noise, confusion, and overcrowding on weekends.)

The buildings range from a lattice-adorned, two-story motel unit with wooden verandas to a Spanish colonial pink stucco building housing the restaurant. The bedrooms draw a mixed reaction from visitors, so ask to see your prospective room before deciding to stay here. Many of the often dark rooms are not well maintained, and the bathrooms seem appropriate for a campsite. Our readers have complained of mildew. The cuisine here is both Créole and international, and the coffee Baños style is a special treat.

Swimming is limited to an angular pool, but you can easily drive to a nearby public beach.

Dorado & the East Coast 9

Often people who book into one of four of the Caribbean's premier resorts—Palmas del Mar and El Conquistador on Puerto Rico's east coast, and the Hyatt Cerromar Beach and Hyatt Dorado Beach to the west of the capital—see San Juan only on their way to or from the airport. If you're going to Puerto Rico for the first time and will stay at one of these resorts, you may want to spend a day or so sightseeing and shopping in San Juan first. Once you've settled into your resort, you may not want to leave the grounds, since these properties are self-contained, with beach, swimming, golf, tennis, dining, and nightlife all on premises.

In this chapter we will take a look at Dorado, home of the Hyatt resorts; Las Croabas and its El Conquistador; Ceiba, whose little inns cater to those heading to El Yunque; and the huge Palmas del Mar resort near Humacao. The big resorts also make good short trips for anyone who doesn't want to pay for their luxury accommodations but would like to visit them for lunch and an afternoon on their splendid beaches.

Note that visitor information and rental cars must be acquired in San Juan before you head to the resorts (see chapter 3).

1 Dorado: The Hyatt Resorts

18 miles W of San Juan

The name Dorado itself evokes a kind of magic, as a world of luxury resorts and villas unfolds along the north shore of Puerto Rico. The elegant Hyatt Dorado Beach Hotel and the newer, larger Hyatt Regency Cerromar Beach Hotel sit on the choice white-sand beaches here.

The site was originally purchased in 1905 by Dr. Alfred T. Livingston, a Jamestown, N.Y., physician, who had it developed as a 1,000-acre grapefruit and coconut plantation. Dr. Livingston's daughter, Clara, widely known in aviation circles and a friend of Amelia Earhart, owned and operated the plantation after her father's death. It was she who built the airstrip here. The building that houses Su Casa Restaurant (see "Where to Dine," below) was for many years the plantation home of the Livingstons.

ESSENTIALS

GETTING THERE   Daily limousine service leaving from the airport from 11am to 9pm is provided by the **Dorado Transport Co-op** (☎ 787/796-1214). The fare is $15 per person (minimum of 3).

What's Special About Dorado & the East Coast

Beaches
- Playa Dorado, at Dorado, actually a term for a total of six white-sand beaches along the northern coast, reached by a series of winding roads.
- Palmas del Mar beaches—called "the New American Riviera"—3 miles of white-sand beaches on the eastern coast of the island.
- Palomino Island, owned by El Conquistador, a private island paradise with sandy beaches and recreational facilities.

Great Towns and Villages
- Palmas del Mar, largest resort on the island, lying to the south of Humacao on 2,800 acres of a former coconut plantation—now devoted to luxury living and the sporting life.
- Dorado, the island's oldest resort town, center of golf courses, casinos, and two major Hyatt resorts.
- Las Croabas, a fishing village on the northernmost tip of Puerto Rico's east coast, site of the island's major resort, El Conquistador.

Sports and Outdoor Activities
- Hyatt Resorts Puerto Rico at Dorado, with 72 holes of golf, the greatest concentration in the Caribbean—all designed by Robert Trent Jones.
- The Club de Golf, Palmas del Mar, one of the leading golf courses of the Caribbean, lying on the southeast coast, with a par-72, 6,690-yard layout designed by Gary Player.
- The Equestrian Center, Palmas del Mar, the finest riding center on the island, with trails cutting through an old plantation and jungle along the beach.
- The "water playground" at the Hyatt Regency Cerromar Beach Hotel, Dorado, with a 1,776-foot-long "fantasy pool"—the world's longest freshwater swimming pool.

Especially for Kids
- The Palmas del Mar supervises a summer activities program for children 5 to 14.
- Camp Coquí, at El Conquistador, which offers everything from building sandcastles to learning arts and crafts.
- Camp Hyatt, where children 3 to 15, supervised by bilingual, CPR-certified counselors, take part in daily activities from swimming and kite-flying to arts and crafts and Spanish lessons.

If you're driving from San Juan, take Highway 2 west to Route 693 north to Dorado (trip time: 40 min.).

GETTING AROUND   Once you're in Dorado, you can get around via the shuttle bus that travels between the two hotels every 30 minutes during the day.

OUTDOOR ACTIVITIES

If you feel like doing something more energetic than lounging on the beautiful beachfront here, the Hyatt resorts (see below) both offer their guests a wide array of beachside water-sports activities. In fact, the Hyatt Regency Cerromar Beach Hotel has the world's longest freshwater swimming pool. Nonguests cannot use the swimming pools here, though they can use the facilities of the Lisa Penfield Watersports Center, for which they have to pay (see below for details).

GOLF

With a total of 72 holes, Dorado has the greatest concentration of golf in the Caribbean. The 18-hole courses at the Hyatt Regency Cerromar Beach Hotel and the Hyatt Dorado Beach Hotel (☎ 787/796-1234 for both) are among the 25 best created by golf architect Robert Trent Jones. The par-72 East course at Dorado Beach includes the famous par-5, 5,540-yard 13th hole. Known for its water challenges, the 13th hole is ranked by Jack Nicklaus as one of the top 10 holes in the world. Greens fees are $150 for nonresidents, $95 for Hyatt guests. Hours are daily from 7am to 5:30pm.

TENNIS

The twin Hyatt resorts (☎ 787/796-1234) maintain a total of 21 courts between them. Court fees are $15 an hour, rising to $18 from 6 to 8pm. Take your racquet and tennis outfit along (attire and equipment are often available in shops, but prices are high and the selection is minimal). Lessons are available for $55 per hour.

WINDSURFING

At the Hyatt Dorado Beach Hotel, the **Lisa Penfield Windsurfing School** (☎ 787/796-1234, ext. 3768, or 787/796-2188) offers 1-hour lessons for $55 per person. Board rentals go for $45 per hour or $50 per half day. Well supplied with a wide array of Windsurfers, including some specially designed specifically for beginners and children, the school benefits from the almost uninterrupted flow of the north shore's strong, steady winds and an experienced crew of instructors. This outfitter has now become a full water-sports center, offering a full-day snorkeling trip for $89 per person, including lunch, and a two-tank scuba dive for $109 per person.

WHERE TO STAY

The two Hyatt hotels in Dorado sprawl across the former Livingston estate, which now bristles with palms, pine trees, and purple bougainvillea, all fronting a 2-mile stretch of sandy ocean beach. Two side-by-side 18-hole championship golf courses, designed by Robert Trent Jones, are their big draw.

✪ Hyatt Dorado Beach Hotel

Dorado, PR 00646. ☎ **787/796-1234** or 800/233-1234. Fax 787/796-2022. 298 rms, 17 casitas. A/C MINIBAR TV TEL. Winter, $427–$604 double; from $764 casita. Spring and fall, $240–$285 double; from $450 casita. Summer, $170–$220 double; from $365 casita. MAP $67 adult, $32 child extra. AE, DC, MC, V.

The Dorado Beach, an elegantly outfitted low-rise building, is the more tranquil of the two Hyatts. Opened in 1958, it was originally designed by Laurance Rockefeller, and many repeat guests, including celebrities, have been coming back ever since. The Hyatt Hotels Corporation has spent millions of dollars on improvements. The renovated bedrooms have marble baths and terra-cotta flooring throughout. Rooms are available on the beach or in villas tucked into nooks in the lushly planted grounds. The casitas are private beach or poolside houses.

Dining/Entertainment: Breakfast can be taken on your private balcony and lunch on an outdoor Ocean Terrace. Dinner is served in a three-tiered main dining room where you can watch the surf. Hyatt Dorado chefs have won many awards, and the food at the hotel restaurants, and at Su Casa Restaurant (recommended separately under "Where to Dine," below, but not included in the hotel's MAP), is considered among the finest in the Caribbean. There is the Beach Grill and Pro Shop for casual meals. And don't forget the casino.

🅰 Family-Friendly Hotels

Hyatt's Resorts *(see pp. 157-158)*   These hostelries offer family getaway packages at Camp Hyatt, featuring professionally supervised day and evening programs for children ages 3 to 15. Children also receive a 50% discount on meals.

Palmas del Mar Resorts *(see pp. 167-168)*   This resort complex features a supervised activities program for children ages 5 to 14 in June and July; offerings include swimming, volleyball, aerobics, handcrafts, bowling, table games, sack races, table tennis, bingo, aquatic polo, basketball, and ring toss. Kids also delight in the 3 miles of beaches.

El Conquistador *(see pp. 161-162)*   There's a special activities area and game room just for kids. Camp Coquí (daily 9am to 3pm) for children ages 3 to 12 costs $38 per day. Activities may include arts and crafts, fishing, sailing, and cooking lessons. Children under 12 stay free in their parents' room, and baby-sitting services are available.

Services: 24-hour room service, laundry and dry cleaning, baby-sitting.

Facilities: Two outstanding 18-hole golf courses (shared with Hyatt Regency Cerromar Beach Hotel), seven all-weather tennis courts, two swimming pools, children's camp, private airfield. Also on the grounds is one of the best windsurfing schools in Puerto Rico—the Lisa Penfield Windsurfing School. (See "Outdoor Activities," above, for more information about the outdoor activities here.)

✪ Hyatt Regency Cerromar Beach Hotel

Dorado, PR 00646. ☎ **787/796-1234** or 800/233-1234. Fax 787/796-4647. 504 rms, 43 suites. A/C MINIBAR TV TEL. Winter, $310–$400 double; from $745 suite. Spring and fall, $225–$315 double; from $570 suite. Summer, $175–$210 double; from $435 suite. MAP $64 adults, $32 child extra. AE, DC, MC, V.

The high-rise Cerromar Beach's name is a combination of two words—*cerro* ("mountain") and *mar* ("sea")—and it is indeed surrounded by mountains and ocean and stands on its own crescent beach. The Cerromar Beach shares the Robert Trent Jones golf courses and other facilities with the Dorado Beach Hotel next door; a shuttle bus runs back and forth between the two resorts every half hour.

All rooms have first-class appointments and are well maintained; the majority have private balconies. The floors throughout are tile, and furnishings are casual and tropical, in soft colors and pastels. All rooms have honor bars and in-room safes.

Dining/Entertainment: The outdoor Swan Café has three levels, connected by a dramatic staircase; some tables overlook a lake populated by swans and flamingos. Other dining choices include the hotel's pride and joy, Medici's (see "Where to Dine," below). The Flamingo bar offers a wide, open-air expanse overlooking the sea and the water playground.

Services: 24-hour room service, laundry and dry cleaning, baby-sitting.

Facilities: The water playground encompasses the world's longest freshwater swimming pool—a 1,776-foot-long fantasy that actually has a riverlike current, created as water flows through five connected free-form pools set at descending heights (it takes 15 minutes to float from one end of the pool to the other). There are also 14 waterfalls, a subterranean Jacuzzi, water slides, walks, bridges, and a children's pool—all amid tropical landscaping. A full-service spa and health club provides both body and skin care (including Swedish massages) and a "Powercise" machine that "talks" to you, coaching you during exercises. In addition to 21 tennis courts, there is also

Camp Coquí, a children's day camp for guests 3 through 12 that is open year round. (See "Outdoor Activities," above, for more information about the outdoor activities here.)

WHERE TO DINE

Ⓢ El Malecón

N, Rte. 693 North, km 8.2, Dorado. ☎ **787/796-1645.** Reservations not required. Main courses $7.95–$36.95. AE, MC, V. Sun–Thurs 11am–10pm, Fri–Sat 11am–11pm. PUERTO RICAN.

If you'd like to discover an unpretentious local place with good Puerto Rican cuisine, then head for El Malecón, a simple concrete structure located in a small shopping center 2 miles east of the Hyatt Dorado Beach Hotel. Established around 1985, it has a cozy family ambience and is especially popular on weekends. Some staff members speak English, and the chef's specialty is fresh seafood, which most diners seem to order. If the ingredients are available, the chef can also prepare a variety of dishes not listed on the menu.

Medici's

In the Hyatt Regency Cerromar Beach Hotel. ☎ **787/796-1234,** ext. 3047. Reservations required. Main courses $20–$28. AE, DC, MC, V. Daily 6:30–10pm. INTERNATIONAL.

On the way to your table in this elegant 340-seat dining room, your attention will be torn between a view of the sprawling gardens and a look at the lavish antipasto table. The tables are situated on tiers at several levels, each of which has been angled for a view of one of the gardens. The staff sets the mood of relaxed formality, the music is "upbeat classical," and the wine cellar is broad based and diversified. Guests can take their pick from steak to "spa cuisine," from osso buco to Caribbean flavors. The kitchen also turns out a light Italian cuisine, and most dishes, including pastas, are available as appetizers, main courses, or side dishes. Try the grilled salmon on spinach with a dill sauce.

✪ Su Casa

In the Hyatt Dorado Beach Hotel. ☎ **787/796-1234.** Reservations required. Main courses $27–$36. AE, DC, MC, V. Daily 7–9:30pm. SPANISH/CONTINENTAL.

Su Casa is the 19th-century Livingston family plantation home on the resort property. The Spanish colonial building with tile courtyards has been a favorite dining place for the rich and famous ever since the Rockefellers entertained guests at their posh Dorado Beach hideaway. Diners sit at candlelit tables and, while partaking of Spanish and classical European dishes, are serenaded by strolling entertainers. The chef produces an innovative cuisine, using Puerto Rican fruits and vegetables whenever possible, including plantain, spinach, and eggplant. The elegant food is the best at Dorado, and the atmosphere rather chic. Many dishes here have been lightened to suit contemporary appetites. Specialties include *pastel de langosta* (lobster fried in a corn tortilla with tomato-and-cilantro sauce), *filete de res "Carlos V"* (filet mignon with a Spanish brandy sauce on eggplant), rack of lamb, *paella mixta* (a very special blend of fresh seafood and spices, and *Bien me sabe* (a house special dessert made with Caribbean coconut and biscuit). Don't plan to rush through a meal at Su Casa— allow enough time to enjoy the quality of your dinner in this relaxed tropical setting.

2 Las Croabas (El Conquistador) & Fajardo

31 miles E of San Juan

For nearly 2 decades, from the '60s through the late '70s, El Conquistador was the acknowledged leader in luxury resorts in the Caribbean. It sits atop a 300-foot cliff at the northeastern tip of Puerto Rico, overlooking both the Caribbean Sea and the Atlantic Ocean. The original hotel closed in 1980 but was reborn in 1993 as the distinctive, $250-million El Conquistador we have today. Former President George Bush was among its first guests.

The developers of the original El Conquistador were Hugh McPherson and Raymond J. Burmeister, who met on Puerto Rico in 1958. McPherson purchased 120 acres of land that served as a U.S. Navy observation post during World War II and built his home nearby.

McPherson and Burmeister hired architect Robert Alderdice, a Carnegie Tech graduate who was working in Puerto Rico, to design an 84-room hotel at a cost of $1.2 million, and they applied for a loan from the Government Development Bank of Puerto Rico. The planned name for the hotel was Trade Winds. But when a bank official hinted that if the developers wanted government funding, the hotel should have a Spanish name, Burmeister stayed up all night going through a Spanish-English dictionary until he was inspired by the word "conquistador." After their hotel opened on July 14, 1962, it soon became the "in place" to stay.

But El Conquistador was too small ever to be profitable. Planning began immediately for a massive expansion from 84 rooms to 388. Construction began at the conclusion of the 1966 high season, and the hotel was closed for only 6 months. It remained open during the rest of the construction, which lasted 2 years. By the time the new "El Conquistador Hotel and Club" was completed and furnished in September 1968, the cost had doubled from the original $15 million budget.

The circular casino, in black and stainless steel, appeared in the last scene of the James Bond movie *Goldfinger*. A nightclub named Anything Goes at Sugar's had 250 lavender seats, each of which was different (they included a 1932-style bathtub, a rowboat, an electric chair, and a Volkswagen). An 18-hole championship golf course, designed by Robert von Hagge, featured swans—imported from Switzerland—on its lakes.

The grand inaugural took place the weekend of November 1, 1968. From New York that Friday, Trans-Caribbean Airways flew its new DC8, *El Magnifico,* its 222 seats full to capacity with press, stage, screen, and literary luminaries. Among the celebrities were Elaine May, Jack Gilford, Celeste Holm (with her husband and two poodles), Elaine Stritch (and her dog), Amy Vanderbilt, Jack Palance, Burt Bachrach, Angie Dickinson, Omar Shariff, Marc Connelly, Maureen O'Sullivan, and Xavier Cugat.

In its glory days, El Conquistador epitomized the luxurious Caribbean resort. Crippled by the Middle East oil embargo during the mid-1970s and the recession that followed, however, Puerto Rico's tourist business declined and the hotel was financially devastated. In May 1977 the hotel reduced its staff by 50% and 1 month later it closed. Although reopened in 1978 with an infusion of new investor money, it declared bankruptcy a year later. By May 1980 it was all over—the once-glamorous resort was shuttered.

In 1982, a religious organization, Maharishi International Caribbean, Inc., paid $2.5 million for the property to use as a meditation center and university, but these plans never materialized. The buildings began to decay and fall apart. In 1988 the Commonwealth of Puerto Rico expropriated the property because $12 million was owed in back taxes. Then a dedicated search began to find a developer who would finance and re-create a new world-class resort. Finally, Mitsubishi and the Williams Hospitality Group of San Juan infused more than $250 million into the project and built the new hotel.

ESSENTIALS

GETTING THERE   El Conquistador greets all guests personally at the San Juan airport and transports them to the resort; alert the hotel to the time of your arrival so you can be escorted to its airport Welcome Center. During the 31-mile (45-minute) trip to the resort, you will be preregistered by a concierge, served refreshments, shown a video of the resort's features, and presented with sightseeing commentary.

If you're driving from San Juan, head east on Route 3 toward Fajardo. At the intersection, cut northeast on Route 195 and continue to the intersection with Route 987, at which point you turn north.

OUTDOOR ACTIVITIES

In addition to the lovely beach and the many recreational facilities that are part of El Conquistador itself (see the review below), there are a couple of other notable places to play in the vicinity.

GOLF

In addition to the superb golf course at El Conquistador Resort and Country Club, **Rio Mar Golf Course** at Palmer (☎ 787/888-8815) offers a 6,145-yard course that's a good choice for inexperienced golfers. A dozen of Rio Mar's 18 holes are doglegs. Trade winds can influence your game along the holes bordering the water, and fairway flooding is another problem at times. The best hole on the course is the 16th, a 180-yard par-3 with the water on your left. Greens fees are $75 per person. A gallery of 100 iguanas adds some spice to your game here.

BOATING, SAILING & SNORKELING

Nearby in Fajardo, the Caribbean's largest and most modern marina, **Puerto del Rey** (☎ 787/860-1000), has facilities for 70 boats, including docking and fueling for yachts up to 200 feet in length and haul-out and repair for yachts up to 90 feet. The marina resort now includes accommodations for boat rentals, yacht charters, and water sports, in addition to several shops and a French restaurant.

For a day at sea spent exploring the best islands, beaches, reefs, and snorkeling in the area, contact **Capt. Jack Becker,** Villa Marina Yacht Harbor, also in Fajardo (☎ 787/860-0861, or 809/385-3509 for cell phone). Captain Jack, a long-ago native of Washington, D.C., and a longtime resident of Puerto Rico, takes two to six passengers at a time on his Pearson-26 sloop. Participants appreciate various islands, the reefs, and the marine life that can be seen on this tour. Before departure, guests are directed to a nearby delicatessen, where they can buy drinks and a package lunch. The price for a 6-hour trip is $40 per person, and it lasts from 10am to 3:30pm. Reservations can be made any hour.

WHERE TO STAY

✪ El Conquistador Resort & Country Club

Las Croabas (P.O. Box 70001), Fajardo, PR 00738. ☎ 787/863-1000 or 800/468-5228 in the U.S. Fax 787/253-3017. 802 rms, 122 suites. A/C MINIBAR TV TEL. Winter, $365–$595 double; from $1,295 suite. Off-season $295–$445 double; from $500 suite. Extra person $40. Children under 16 stay free in parents' room. MAP $75 extra per adult, $40 extra per child under 12. AE, DC, MC, V. Parking $10. Limousine from the San Juan airport $25.

One of the most impressive properties anywhere in the tropics, the new El Conquistador is *the* destination for many people (many well-to-do people, that is). It incorporates $1 million worth of art and five different hotels on 500 acres of forested hills whose edges slope down to the sea. The architecture was inspired by Mediterranean models, including the interconnected town houses of the Spanish colonial empire, the Moorish gardens of medieval Seville, and the grandiose neoclassical elegance of northern Italy. Landscaped serpentine walkways and a railroad-style funicular link the far-flung elements of the resort. Throughout, gardens are interspersed with trompe l'oeil murals, paintings and sculptures, and art gallery calibre decorative elements.

The accommodations are designed to please, with comfortable and stylish furniture, soft tropical colors, and amenities such as bathrobes and ironing boards.

Dining/Entertainment: The resort contains nine different restaurants, one of which is a 24-hour tropical deli. Several others are highlighted in "Where to Dine," below. A casino incorporates glamor with live music from a nearby piano bar. Among the bars and nightlife is the formal Drake's Library, outfitted with books, mahogany, leather, a vaulted ceiling, and a billiards table; and Amigos Bar and Lounge, where merengue and salsa artists perform.

Services: Room service, baby-sitting, men's and women's beauty salon, laundry and dry cleaning, massage, spa services.

Facilities: The hotel is the sole owner of a forested "fantasy island" (Palomino Island) about half a mile offshore, with caverns, nature trails, and a wide choice of water sports (such as scuba diving, windsurfing, and snorkeling). Private ferries run between the island and the main hotel at frequent intervals. There's also a 35-slip marina (several boats are available for rent), six swimming pools, numerous Jacuzzi tubs, and some of the largest and most up-to-date conference facilities in the world. There are lighted tennis courts and an 18-hole, par-72, 6,700-yard championship golf course designed by Arthur Hills (the course's 200-foot changes in elevation provide panoramic vistas). The course is only open to hotel guests, who pay $125 to play 18 holes (after 3pm, the cost is lowered to $75). The course is open daily from 7am to 7pm. An arcade of 22 retail shops includes branches of W. H. Smith bookstore and New York–based Reinhold Jewelers.

WHERE TO DINE

Bio at Otello's

In El Conquistador Resort. ☎ **787/863-1000.** Reservations required. Main courses $15–$32.50. AE, DC, MC, V. Daily 6pm–midnight. NORTHERN ITALIAN.

You can dine by candlelight in the old-world tradition at Otello's, with a choice of indoor or outdoor seating. Located across from Drake's Library on the Mirador level of the hotel, Otello's cuisine is authentic northern Italian. You might begin with one of the soups, perhaps pasta fagioli or minestrone, or select one of the zesty Italian appetizers, such as clams areganata. Pastas, which can be ordered as either a half-portion appetizer or a main dish, include the likes of homemade gnocchi or spaghetti carbonara. The chef is known for his many veal dishes, ranging from veal marsala to veal chop valdostana. Poultry and vegetarian dishes are offered nightly, along with several shrimp and fish dishes. The Sicilian-style shark filet with fresh tomato and black olives had beautiful accents, as did the chicken breast stuffed with ricotta, wrapped in bacon, and served with a Marsala sauce.

Blossoms

In El Conquistador Resort. ☎ **787/863-1000.** Reservations recommended. Main courses $14.50–$45. AE, CB, DC, MC, V. Daily 6pm–midnight. CHINESE/JAPANESE.

This restaurant on the Mirador level features three culinary styles, including a sushi bar, and boasts some of the freshest seafood in eastern Puerto Rico. Sizzling delights are prepared on teppanyaki tables, and there's a zesty selection of Hunan and

Szechuan specialties. On the teppanyaki menu, you can choose dishes ranging from chicken to shrimp, from filet mignon to lobster. Sushi-bar selections range from eel to squid, from salmon roe to giant clams.

El Gauchos

In El Conquistador Resort. ☎ 787/863-1000. Reservations not required. Main courses $14–$34. AE, DC, MC, V. Daily 6–10pm. ARGENTINEAN.

Gauchos are the Argentinean prairie riders whose lifestyles resemble those of American cowboys. Meats are grilled here in the authentic Argentinean tradition. Located at Las Olvas Village, the restaurant offers many specialties of the house, including an Argentine tableside grill with various traditional meats as well as the popular Argentine "skirt steak." Seafood is also offered, including mahimahi broiled with olive oil, garlic, and parsley. A surf-and-turf parrillada (called Mary Tierra) is also offered.

✪ Isabela's Grill

In El Conquistador Resort. ☎ 787/863-1000. Reservations recommended. Main courses $25–$60; Sun buffet lunch $49.50 per person. AE, DC, MC, V. Daily 6pm–midnight; buffet lunch Sun 11:30am–3pm. SPANISH/INTERNATIONAL.

Of the resort's many restaurants, Isabela's is the premier. Its echoing and dignified room was inspired by an aristocratic monastery in Spain, and it's flanked by a gate similar to those in Spanish cathedrals, one of the most beautiful pieces of ironwork on Puerto Rico. There's additional seating on an open-sided terrace for diners who want to be exposed to the sea and the trade winds. The service is impeccable and the food is among the finest on the island. The chefs' talents have reached new fullness as reflected by their appetizers, ranging from seafood ceviche to wild mushrooms baked in a phyllo with a goat cheese dressing. Some of the more inventive main courses include grilled tuna steak with a wild pepper, cilantro, and ginger sauce, and sautéed Puerto Rican prawns with a red curry, coconut, and basil sauce served with squid ink linguine. There is also a heart-healthy series of dishes. We were especially impressed by the baked grouper in a carrot-and-cumin sauce. The Sunday buffet is extensive and includes all the champagne you can drink.

3 Ceiba & El Yunque

35 miles W of San Juan, 15 miles E of El Yunque, 7 miles S of Fajardo

The rain forest of El Yunque (see also "The Natural Environment" in chapter 2 and "Driving Tour 1" in chapter 8) is such a major attraction of Puerto Rico that little inns and bed-and-breakfasts have opened to accommodate visitors wishing to find a nearby place from which to explore this tropical paradise. The inns are not luxurious in any way; however, if you're an ecotourist, either of the recommendations below should suit you fine.

Playa de Naguabo, one of the best beaches in the area, lies about a 20-minute drive from Ceiba. You're also pretty near Fajardo; see section 2 of this chapter for information on a marina and sailing/snorkeling excursions that leave from here.

GETTING THERE

From San Juan, head east on Route 3 toward Fajardo. Pass through Fajardo and continue directly south to Ceiba.

EXPLORING EL YUNQUE

Encompassing four distinct forest types, El Yunque is home to 240 species of tropical trees, flowers, and wildlife. More than 20 kinds of orchids and 50 varieties of ferns share this diverse habitat with millions of tiny tree frogs whose distinctive cry of *coquí* (pronounced ko-*kee*) has given them their name. Tropical birds include the lively, greenish blue, red-fronted Puerto Rican parrot, once nearly extinct and now making a comeback. Other rare animals include the Puerto Rican boa, which grows to 7 feet, plus 26 animal species found nowhere else in the world.

El Yunque is just one of Puerto Rico's 20 forest preserves, but it's the best. Not only that, hiking through it ranks at the very top in the entire Caribbean. The forest is situated high above sea level, with the peak of El Toro rising to 3,532 feet. You can be fairly sure you'll be showered upon, since more than 100 billion gallons of rain fall here annually. However, the showers are brief and there are many shelters. Many visitors reserve only a half day for it on a quickie tour. But it's unique and deserves at least a day-long outing.

El Yunque is the most popular spot in Puerto Rico for hiking. The **Department of Natural Resources Forest Service** (☎ 787/724-8774) administers some aspects of the park, although for the average hiker, more useful information may be available at **El Yunque Catalina Field Office,** near the village of Palma, beside the main highway at the forest's northern edge (☎ 787/887-2875). The staff can provide material about hiking routes and, with 10 days' notice, help you plan overnight tours in the forest.

The best source of information will be the new tropical forest center, **El Portal del Yunque,** the gateway to El Yunque, which was under construction during our recent visit. The center will serve as a doorway into the tropics, so that visitors and students alike can begin to understand, appreciate, and support the management and conservation of tropical forests. It will provide facilities for three areas: an interpretive visitor center, environmental education for the school children of Puerto Rico, and tropical forest management training.

WHERE TO STAY

Casa Cubuy
Rte. 191, km 22 (P.O. Box 1067), Ceiba, PR, 00735. ☎ **787/874-6221.** 5 rms (3 with bath). Year-round $60 double without bath; $70 single or double with bath. Extra person $15. Rates include American breakfast. MC, V.

This is a quiet, no-frills place that caters mainly to ecotourists heading to El Yunque. The rooms are decorated in a tropical motif and offer clean and relaxed surroundings. The owner, Marianne Kavanaugh, serves healthy meals. If you have a particular culinary demand, such as a vegetarian diet, she will honor all reasonable requests.

Ceiba Country Inn
Road no. 977 km 1.2 (P.O. Box 1067) Ceiba, PR 00735. ☎ **787/885-0471.** 9 rms. A/C TEL. Year-round $60 double; $10 extra per person in room. Rates include breakfast. AE, DISC, MC, V.

If you're looking for an escape from the hustle and bustle of everyday life, then this is the place for you. This small, well-maintained bed-and-breakfast is located on the easternmost part of Puerto Rico near the Roosevelt Roads U.S. naval base (to reach this little haven in the mountains, you must rent a car). El Yunque is only 15 miles away. Housed in a large old family home, the rooms are located on the bottom floor. All have private baths; two also have small refrigerators. The rooms are decorated in a tropical motif with flowered murals on the walls painted by a local artist. For a quiet evening cocktail, you may want to visit the small lounge on the second floor.

4 Palmas del Mar

46 miles SE of San Juan

Billing itself as the "Caribbean side of Puerto Rico," this residential resort community lies on the island's southeastern shore. Once there, you'll find plenty to do. One of the most action-packed sports programs in the Caribbean offers golf, tennis, scuba diving, sailing, deep-sea fishing, and horseback riding. There's even a casino.

Palmas del Mar's location on the southeastern shore of Puerto Rico is one of its greatest assets. The pleasing Caribbean trade winds steadily blow across this section of the island all year, stabilizing the weather and making Palmas del Mar ideal for a great many outdoor sports all year. The wet season extends from May into September; rainfall amounts to about 9 inches a month during this period. The dryer season, from December to April, averages 3 to 5 inches of rain a month.

The resort's two hotels are the luxurious Palmas Inn and the Candelero Hotel. For those who need more room, there are also the condos of the Villa Suites. All are surrounded by a marina, the beach, a tennis complex, and a championship golf course. There are also some privately owned condominiums that are available for guests when the owners are away (these can be rented through the hotel reservations desk).

Most guests book into Palmas del Mar on a package plan, perhaps choosing one of the sports options, such as the golf package. Most packages are for 7 days/6 nights in winter, 4 days/3 nights in summer. For more information, call **800/468-3331** in the U.S. (800/725-6273 in Canada).

GETTING THERE

Although **Humacao Regional Airport,** 3 miles north of Palmas del Mar, has a 2,300-foot strip, no airline had regularly scheduled flights there at press time. The resort (☎ 787/852-6000) will arrange minivan or bus transport from Luis Muñoz Marín International Airport in San Juan to Humacao. The fare is $16 to $25 each way.

If you're driving from downtown San Juan, take Highway 52 south to Caguas, then take Highway 30 east to Humacao (trip time: 1 hr).

BEACHES & OUTDOOR ACTIVITIES

The Palmas del Mar resort offers a great variety of choices to keep active vacationers in shape (many are also open to the public with prior reservation). Following are details on some of the most popular, along with a few other offerings in the area that are not connected with the resort complex.

BEACHES

The resort has 3 miles of white-sand beaches (all open to the public). Nonguests will need to know that there's a $1 charge for parking, and a 25¢ charge for a changing room and a locker. The waters here are calm year-round, and there's a water-sports center and marina (see "Scuba Diving & Snorkeling," below).

FISHING

Some of the best year-round fishing in the Caribbean is found in the waters just off Palmas del Mar. **Capt. Bill Burleson,** based in Humacao (☎ 787/850-7442), operates charters on his fully customized 46-foot sport-fisherman, *Karolette,* which is electronically equipped for successful fishing. Burleson prefers to take fishing groups to Grappler Banks, 18 nautical miles away. The banks are two sea mounts, rising to about 240 feet below the surface and surrounded by depths of 6,000 to 8,000 feet.

Monkey Business

In 1938 a collection of rhesus monkeys were brought from India to Cayo Santiago, a 39-acre islet off eastern Puerto Rico, to be studied for scientific purposes. The ancestors of those early monkeys are going bananas there today.

The island is administered by the University of Puerto Rico. Scientists from its Caribbean Primate Research Center spend days and weeks studying the behavioral patterns of this colony of some 700 monkeys (at last count). They have learned many interesting things by observing this frisky bunch. For example, like humans, monkeys are capable of forming friendships that last a lifetime. Because the monkeys are all contained on this island, as opposed to living in the wild, scientists can trace their entire development over their life span. Monkeys are marked and numbered, although many of the scientists know the animals upon sight. Many breakthroughs in human medicine have resulted from close encounter and observation of these monkeys.

The scientists won't let visitors come ashore as it will interfere in their research work. However, a boat named *Shagrada* transports guests to the water just off the island where they can go snorkeling and get a close-up look at these rambunctious residents. The *Shagrada* sails daily if the weather allows from Palmas del Mar Resort's marina at Harbourside Dock (no. 135).

When the *Shagrada* anchors, dozens of monkeys show up to see what all the excitement is about, no doubt thinking the humans looking at them are just as funny as people think the monkeys are. Some monkeys can be seen swinging through the trees, enjoying the good life. On rare occasions they have been known to board the *Shagrada*.

Groups of up to six passengers are taken to this rare enclave, costing $63 for the 4-hour excursion. The price includes drinks, snacks, and snorkeling gear. To make a reservation, call **787/852-6000,** ext. 17785, or write Riviera Yacht Charters, P.O. Box 888, Suite 246, Humacao, Puerto Rico 00791.

They lie in the migratory paths of the wahoo, tuna, and marlin. A maximum of six people are taken out, costing $450 for 4 hours, $600 for 6 hours, and $800 for 9 hours. He also offers snorkeling expeditions to Vieques Island at $75 per person for up to 5 hours. Other snorkeling locations include half- and full-day trips.

GOLF

The **Golf Club** at Palmas del Mar (☎ **787/852-6000,** ext. 54), is one of the best courses on Puerto Rico. It has a par-72, 6,803-yard layout designed by Gary Player. Crack golfers consider holes 11 through 15 the toughest five successive holes in the Caribbean. Greens fees are $65 for hotel guests, $79 on weekends and holidays, or $75 and $90, respectively, for non-hotel guests. In the lifetime of this edition, rates will go up. Hours are daily 7am to 5pm.

HIKING

Hiking on the resort's grounds is another favorite activity here, for Palmas del Mar's land is an attraction in its own right. There are more than 6 miles of Caribbean ocean frontage, $3^1/_2$ miles of which is sandy beach; the balance is rocky cliffs and promontories. Large tracts of the 2,700-acre property have harbored sugar and coconut plantations over the years, and a wet, tropical forest preserve with giant ferns, orchids, and hanging vines covers about 70 acres near the resort's geographic center.

HORSEBACK RIDING

The **Equestrian Center** at Palmas del Mar (☎ 787/852-6000, ext. 12711) has 42 horses, including English hunters for jumping, plus a variety of trail rides and instruction for all levels of ability. The land set aside for equestrian pursuits abuts the resort's airstrip and is bounded on one side by a stream. Trail rides skirt this creek, following paths through a coconut plantation and jungle and swinging along the beach. A trail ride per person costs $22 for 1 hour and $40 for 2 hours.

SCUBA DIVING & SNORKELING

Coral Head Divers & Water Sports Center, Humacao (☎ 787/850-7208 or 800/635-4529), is headquartered at the Palmas del Mar Resort. The dive center owns two fully equipped boats, measuring 26 and 48 feet, and offers daily two-tank open-water dives for certified divers, plus snorkeling trips to Monkey Island and Vieques. The two-tank dive includes tanks, weights, and computer at $75. A snorkeling trip to Monkey Island includes use of equipment and beverages at $45 per person. A scuba resort lesson costs $45.

TENNIS

The **Tennis Center** at Palmas del Mar (☎ 787/852-6000, ext. 51), the largest in Puerto Rico, features 20 courts. Court fees are $18 per hour for hotel guests during the day and $22 at night. Special tennis packages are available, including accommodations. Call for more information and reservations.

WHERE TO STAY

Candelero Hotel

Palmas del Mar, P.O. Box 2020, Humacao, PR 00661. ☎ 787/852-6000 or 800/468-3331 in the U.S.; 800/725-6273 in Canada. Fax 787/850-4445. 101 rms. A/C TV TEL. Winter, $211 double; spring or fall, $192 double; summer, $128 double. MAP $73 extra per person in winter, $55 off-season. AE, DC, MC, V.

The rooms here come in a variety of sizes, some with king-size beds. High cathedral ceilings accentuate the space, which is extended even farther by patios on the ground floor. Some of the superior and deluxe accommodations have private balconies. The main dining room is Las Garzas (see "Where to Dine," below). The beach and golf course are close by.

Palmas Inn

Palmas del Mar, P.O. Box 2020, Humacao, PR 00661. ☎ 787/852-6000, 800/725-6273 in the U.S., or 800/725-6273 in Canada. Fax 787/852-6320. 23 junior suites. A/C TV TEL. Winter, $328 suite for two; spring and fall, $298 suite for two; summer, $202 suite for two. Rates include American breakfast. MAP $73 per person extra in winter, $55 off-season. AE, DC, MC, V.

This branch offers only deluxe junior suites whose views of the sea are partially blocked by pine trees. The general decor here evokes the feeling of a Mediterranean villa, with a spacious airiness, while the rooms themselves have a Spanish antique style. If you're looking for peace and tranquility, you might want to come here in June when it's relatively quiet, although a lack of service will be the trade-off. The inn also houses the Palm Terrace Restaurant, but frankly, the dining facilities here continue to draw fire from your fellow readers.

Villa Suites

At Palmas del Mar, P.O. Box 2020, Humacao, PR 00661. ☎ 787/852-6000, 800/468-3331 in the U.S., or 800/725-6273 in Canada. Fax 787/852-2230. 10 studios, 135 villas. A/C TV TEL. Winter, $275 studio; $320–$430 one-bedroom villa; $432–$565 two-bedroom villa; $564–$710 three-bedroom villa. Spring and fall, $248 studio; $288–$387 one-bedroom villa; $389–$509 two-bedroom villa; $508–$639 three-bedroom villa. Summer, $165 studio; $192–$258 one-bedroom villa; $259–$339 two-bedroom villa; $338–$426 three-bedroom villa. MAP $73 per person extra in winter, $55 off-season. 3- to 5-night minimum stay in winter. AE, DC, MC, V.

Adjacent to the Candelero Hotel, this complex of red-roofed, white-walled, Iberian-inspired villas would be a terrific choice for a family. Each of the villas, furnished and decorated according to the taste of its absentee owners, contains a full working kitchen and enough privacy to allow a feeling of relaxed well being. Prices in each category of villa depend on the building's proximity to either the beachfront or the golf course; several additional villas have been built against a steep hillside overlooking the tennis courts.

WHERE TO DINE

Palmas del Mar has a wide variety of restaurants. Currently, MAP guests can choose among six specialty restaurants on the grounds, as well as five restaurants off the property. They can also enjoy five theme dining nights, including a Western night and a Mexican night. If management continues this dine-around plan, MAP guests need not become bored.

The following is only a partial listing of dining possibilities. Undoubtedly, you will discover several more on your own. All the restaurants are open during the winter season; in summer, only three or four may be fully functioning.

Chez Daniel/Le Grill

Marina de Palmas del Mar. ☎ **787/850-3838.** Reservations required. Main courses $19–$29.50. AE, MC, V. Fri–Sun noon–3pm; Wed–Mon 6:30–10pm. Closed June. FRENCH.

It's French, it's nautical, it's fun, and it's the preferred dining spot for those whose yachts are moored at the adjacent pier. Daniel Vasse, the executive chef, presents a menu that might begin with fish soup or stuffed mussels, followed by such main courses as bouillinade (a traditional Catalán-style bouillabaisse) or lobster and chicken sautéed with butter in tarragon-and-lemon sauce. Filet mignon in a Roquefort sauce is another delectable choice. For dessert, you might enjoy a soufflé Cointreau.

Las Garzas

In the Candelero Hotel. ☎ **787/852-6000,** ext. 50. Reservations required only for groups of six or more. Main courses $18.95–$30. AE, DC, MC, V. Daily 7–11am; noon–3pm; and 6–10:30pm. INTERNATIONAL.

Cooled by trade winds, this outstanding restaurant overlooking a courtyard and swimming pool is an ideal choice for breakfast, lunch, or dinner. Lunch always includes sandwiches and burgers galore, and if you want heartier fare, ask for black-bean soup followed by the Puerto Rican specialty of the day, perhaps red snapper in garlic butter. Dinner is more elaborate. You might begin with a chilled papaya bisque served in half a coconut, followed by Caribbean lobster, New York sirloin, paella, or the catch of the day. Although a high standard exists, don't come expecting gourmet-quality cooking. Every night in winter is a virtual theme night, ranging from an Italian festival on Monday to a Puerto Rican night on Saturday.

AFTER DARK

The **casino** (☎ 787/852-6000, ext. 10142), in the resort complex, near the Palmas Inn, is in the Culebra Room on the second floor. It features nine blackjack tables, two roulette wheels, a craps table, and dozens of slot machines. The casino is open from 6pm to 3am daily (closed Monday and Tuesday in summer). Guests are requested to dress with "casual elegance." Under Puerto Rican law, drinks cannot be served in a casino, but you can enjoy one in the **Palm Terrace Lounge.**

10

Ponce, Mayagüez & Rincón

For those who want to see a less urban side of Puerto Rico, Ponce, on the south shore, and Mayagüez and Rincón, on the west coast, offer a variety of places to stay, and each also makes a good center for sightseeing.

Founded in 1692, Ponce is Puerto Rico's second-largest city and has received much attention because of its inner-city restoration. It is home to the island's premier art gallery.

Puerto Rico's third-largest city, Mayagüez is a port located about halfway down the west coast. It may not be as architecturally remarkable as Ponce, but it's a fine base for exploring some sights and enjoying some very good beaches.

Rincón, to the north of Mayagüez, is even smaller, but it boasts the finest country hotel in Puerto Rico—the Horned Dorset Primavera—and has some world-class surfing beaches.

Not too far from all three towns is **Boquerón Beach,** a mile-long west-coast white-sand beach, one of the finest on the island (see "Driving Tour 2" in chapter 8). The **Cabo Rojo Lighthouse,** at the southwesternmost corner, is another interesting place to visit (after leaving Boquerón, continue along Highway 301 until its end).

1 Ponce

75 miles SW of San Juan

"The Pearl of the South," Ponce was named after Loíza Ponce de León, great-grandson of Juan Ponce de León. Founded in 1692, it is today Puerto Rico's principal shipping port on the Caribbean. The city is well kept and attractive, as reflected by its many plazas, parks, and public buildings. A suggestion of a provincial Mediterranean town lingers in its air. Look for the *rejas,* or framed balconies, on the handsome colonial mansions.

Timed to coincide with 1992's 500th anniversary celebration of Christopher Columbus's voyage to the New World, a $440-million renovation began to bring new life to this once-decaying city. The streets are lit with gas lamps and lined with neoclassical buildings, just as they were a century ago. Horse-drawn carriages clop by, and strollers walk along sidewalks edged with pink marble. Thanks to the restoration, Ponce now recalls the turn of the century when it rivaled San Juan as a wealthy business and cultural center.

What's Special About Ponce, Mayagüez & Rincón

Beaches
- Boquerón Beach, south of Mayagüez on the west coast, a 2-mile-long white-sand beach where San Juan residents flock for fun on the weekend.
- Playa de Ponce, on the southern coast west of Ponce, beaches of white sand open onto the tranquil Caribbean, with rows of seafood restaurants.
- Playa Punta Higuero, on Route 413 near Rincón, one of the finest windsurfing beaches in the world.

Great Towns and Villages
- Ponce, Puerto Rico's "second city," with the best weather on the island.
- Mayagüez, its "third city," on the west coast, with some of the island's best swimming and surfing.

Architectural Highlights
- The central district of Ponce, a blend of Ponce Créole and art deco architectural styles dating from the 1890s to the 1930s.

Museums
- Museo de Arte de Ponce, leading art museum of Puerto Rico, with major American and European schools of the past 5 centuries represented.
- Museo Castillo Serrallés in Ponce, a Spanish Revival mansion built by a wealthy rum distillery owner.

Churches
- The Cathedral of Our Lady of Guadalupe in Ponce, founded in 1660, the best-known church in southern Puerto Rico.

Ancient Monuments
- Tibes Indian Ceremonial Center, outside Ponce, the oldest cemetery in the Antilles.

Wildlife Watching
- Mona Island, off the west coast of Puerto Rico, often called the "Galápagos of the Caribbean" because of its rich marine life.

Most of Ponce's distinctive architecture—a blend of Ponce Créole and art deco—dates from the 1890s to the 1930s, when it flourished as the hub of the island's sugarcane, rum, and shipping industries. At that time, Ponce was also home to many of the island's artists, poets, and politicians.

ESSENTIALS

GETTING THERE **American Eagle** (☎ 800/433-7300) flies four times a day between San Juan and Ponce (flying time: 40 minutes). The fare is $95 to $135 round-trip, depending on the ticket.

If you're driving, take Route 1 south to Highway 52, then continue south and west to Ponce.

VISITOR INFORMATION The **Ponce Municipal Tourist Office** has a kiosk inside the Parque de Bombas, on Plaza de Las Delicias (see "What to See & Do," below). If you find it temporarily unstaffed, go across the street to the second floor of the Citibank Building, where the administrative offices are located (☎ 787/841-8160).

SEEING THE SIGHTS

In addition to the attractions listed below, the **marketplace** at calles Atocha and Castillo is colorful, and the historic **La Perla Theater** and the **Serrallés rum distillery** are worth visits. Perhaps you'll want to simply sit in the plaza, watching the Poncenos at one of their favorite pastimes—strolling about town.

Cathedral of Our Lady of Guadalupe

Calle Concordia/Calle Union. ☎ **787/842-0134.** Free admission. Mon–Fri 6am–3:30pm, Sat–Sun 6am–noon and 3–8pm.

In 1660 a rustic chapel was built on this spot on the western edge of the Plaza de Las Delicias, and since then fires and earthquakes have razed the church repeatedly. In 1919, a team of priests collected funds from local parishioners to construct the Doric- and Gothic-inspired building that stands here today. Designed by architects Francisco Porrato Doría and Francisco Trublard in 1931 and featuring a pipe organ installed in 1934, it remains an important place for prayer for many of Ponce's citizens. The cathedral, named after a famous holy shrine in Mexico, is the best-known church in southern Puerto Rico.

Museo de Arte de Ponce

Avenida de Las Américas 25. ☎ **787/848-0505.** Admission $3 adults, $2 children under 12. Daily 10am–5pm. Follow Calle Concordia from Plaza de Las Delicias 1¹/₂ miles south to Avenida de Las Américas.

Donated to the people of Puerto Rico by Luís A. Ferré, a former governor, this museum has the finest collection of European and Latin American art in the Caribbean. The building itself was designed by Edward Durell Stone (who also designed the John F. Kennedy Center for the Performing Arts in Washington, D.C.) and has been called the "Parthenon of the Caribbean." Its collection represents the principal schools of American and European art of the past 5 centuries. Among the nearly 400 works on display are exceptional Pre-Raphaelite and Italian baroque paintings. Visitors will also see artworks by other European masters, as well as Puerto Rican and Latin American paintings, graphics, and sculptures. Temporary exhibitions are also mounted here.

✪ Museo Castillo Serralles

El Vigía 17. ☎ **787/259-1774.** Admission $3 adults, $2 senior citizens over 62, $1.50 children under 16. Tues–Sun 10am–5pm. The roads leading to the museum are a confusing labyrinth of run-down unnamed residential streets. It's best to take a taxi; the fare is about $3 each way from the center of town.

Two miles north of the center of town is the largest and most imposing building in Ponce, built during the 1930s high on El Vigía Hill (see below) by the Serralles family, owners of a local rum distillery. Considered one of the architectural gems of Puerto Rico, it is the best evidence of the wealth produced by the turn-of-the-century sugar boom. Guides will escort you through the Spanish Revival house, where Moorish and Andalusian details include panoramic courtyards, a baronial dining room, a small café and souvenir shop, and a series of photographs showing the tons of earth that were brought in for the construction of the terraced gardens.

Museum of the History of Ponce (Casa Salazar)

Calle Reina Isabel 51-53 (at Calle Mayor). ☎ **787/844-7071.** Admission $3 adults, $1.50 seniors, $1 children. Mon, Wed–Fri 10am–5pm; Sat–Sun 10am–6pm.

Opened in the Casa Salazar in 1992, this museum traces the history of the city from the time of the Taíno peoples to the present. Interactive displays help visitors orient themselves and locate other attractions. The museum has a conservation laboratory, library, souvenir and gift shop, cafeteria, and conference facilities.

Casa Salazar ranks close to the top of Ponce's architectural treasures. Built in 1911, it combines neoclassic with Moorish styles and displays much decorative detail typical of Ponce: stained-glass windows, mosaics, pressed-tin ceilings, fixed jalousies, wood or iron columns, porch balconies, interior patios, and the use of doors as windows.

One of Ponce's main residential streets, Calle Reina Isabel, where the museum is located, offers textbook examples of Ponceño architectural styles: European-neoclassic, Spanish colonial, Ponce-Créole, town Créole, neoclassic, and superior neoclassic.

Parque de Bombas
Plaza de Las Delicias. ☎ **787/284-4141.** Free admission. Wed–Mon 9:30am–6pm.

Built in 1882 as the centerpiece of a 12-day agricultural fair intended at the time to promote the civic charms of Ponce, this building was designated a year later as the island's first permanent headquarters for a volunteer fire-fighting brigade. It has an unusual appearance—it's painted black, red, green, and yellow. A tourist information kiosk is situated inside the building (see "Visitor Information," above).

El Vigía Hill
At the north end of Ponce. Take a taxi; from the Plaza de Las Delicias, the ride will cost about $3.

The city's tallest geologic feature, El Vigía Hill dominates Ponce's northern skyline. Its base and steep slopes have been covered with a maze of 19th- and early 20th-century urban development. Once you reach the summit, you'll see the soaring Cruz del Vigía (Virgin's Cross). Built in 1984 of reinforced concrete to replace a 19th-century wooden cross in poor repair, this modern 100-foot structure bears lateral arms measuring 70 feet long and an observation tower (accessible by elevator), from which you can see all of the natural beauty that surrounds Ponce.

The cross commemorates Vigía Hill's colonial role as a deterrent to contraband smuggling. In 1801, on orders from Spain, a garrison was established atop the hill to detect any ships that might try to unload their cargoes tax-free along Puerto Rico's southern coastline.

NEARBY ATTRACTIONS
TIBES INDIAN CEREMONIAL CENTER
The oldest cemetery in the Antilles, the **Tibes Indian Ceremonial Center** is on Route 503 at km 2.7 (☎ **787/840-2255**). Bordered by the Portugues River and excavated in 1975, it contains some 186 skeletons, dating from A.D. 300, as well as pre-Taíno plazas from A.D. 700. Shaded by such trees as the calabash, seven rectangular ball-courts and two dance grounds can be viewed. The arrangement of stone points on the dance grounds, in line with the solstices and equinoxes, suggests a pre-Columbian Stonehenge. A re-created Taíno village includes not only the museum but an exhibition hall that presents a documentary about Tibes, a cafeteria where you can find refreshments, and a souvenir shop. The museum is open Wednesday through Sunday from 9am to 4:30pm. Admission is $2 for adults, $1 for children. Guided tours in English and Spanish are conducted through the grounds.

HACIENDA BUENA VISTA
Built in 1833 in the small town of Barrio Magueyes, on Route 10 between Ponce and Adjuntas, **Hacienda Buena Vista** preserves an old way of life, with its whirring waterwheels and artifacts of 19th-century farm production. Once it was one of the most successful plantations on Puerto Rico, producing coffee, corn, and citrus. It was a working coffee plantation until the 1950s. Some 80 of the original 500 acres are

still part of the estate. The rooms of the hacienda have been furnished with authentic pieces from the 1850s. Tours are conducted Wednesday through Sunday at 8:30am, 10:30am, 1:30pm, and 3:30pm (in English only at 1:30pm). Reservations are required and may be made by contacting the **Conservation Trust of Puerto Rico** (☎ 787/722-5882). Tours cost $5 for adults, $2 for children.

HIKING & BIRD-WATCHING IN GUÁNICA STATE FOREST

Heading directly west from Ponce you reach **Guánica State Forest** (☎ 787/ 724-3724), a setting that evokes Arizona or New Mexico. Here you will find the best-preserved subtropical ecosystem on the planet. The Cordillera Central cuts off the rain coming in from the heavily showered northeast, making this a dry region of cacti and bedrock, a perfect film location for one of those old-fashioned Western movies.

It's also ideal country for birders. Some 50% of all of the island's terrestrial bird species can be seen in this dry and dusty forest. You might even spot the Puerto Rican emerald-breasted hummingbird. A number of migratory birds often stop here. The most serious ornithologists seek out the Puerto Rican nightjar, a local bird that was believed at one time to be extinct until one was sighted. Now it's estimated that there are nearly a thousand of them. UNESCO has named Guánica a World Biosphere Reserve. Some 750 plants and tree species grow in the area.

To reach the forest, take Route 334 northeast of Guánica to the heart of the forest. There's a ranger station here that will give you information about hiking trails. The booklet provided by the ranger station outlines 36 miles of trails through the four different forest types. The most interesting is the mile-long **Cueva Trail,** which gives you the most scenic look at the various types of vegetation. You might even encounter the endangered bufo lemur toad, once declared extinct, but found to still be jumping in this area.

WALKING TOUR
Ponce

Start: Plaza de Las Delicias.
Finish: Plaza de Las Delicias.
Time: 90 minutes, excluding coffee breaks, museum visits, and shopping stops.

The downtown revitalization of Ponce has probably required more money and generated more publicity than that of any other city (after San Juan) on Puerto Rico. Your tour of this Caribbean showplace begins on the eastern edge of the town's main square, the Plaza de Las Delicias (also known as Plaza Muñoz Rivera). Within the symmetrical borders of this main square, you'll see the red-and-black-striped clapboard facade of the town's most frequently photographed building. (Red and black, incidentally, are the colors of the city's flag.)

Note the Victorian gingerbread and the deliberately garish colors of the:

1. **Parque de Bombas** (Old Municipal Fire House), which housed the fire department before it moved into more modern quarters in another part of the city. You can still see a handful of bright-red fire engines parked inside.

On the plaza's opposite side, adjacent to Calle Concordia/Calle Union is the:

2. **Cathedral of Our Lady of Guadalupe,** the best-known church in southern Puerto Rico. Its alabaster altars were commissioned by an ex-governor of Puerto Rico in the late 1960s in Burgos, Spain; there will almost certainly be parishioners at prayer inside.

As you leave the cathedral, notice the many impeccably clipped trees ringing the perimeter of the plaza. Identified as Indian laurels, they were planted between 1906 and 1908 and are considered one of the botanical triumphs of Ponce. Clipped with manually operated shears into their carefully groomed topiary forms at frequent intervals by a master gardener, they are well worth a second or third glance. Even the elaborate iron lampposts illuminating them date from 1916.

Across Calle Concordia from the main entrance to the cathedral is one of Ponce's most famous houses, the:

3. **Casa Armstrong-Poventud,** a paneled and ornately crafted building that was once the home of a wealthy Scottish-born banker. Today, it's a cultural center.

Note that at this western border of the Plaza de Las Delicias, street signs might identify it as Plaza de Getou. Regardless of what the plaza is called, turn right on exiting from the Casa Armstrong-Poventud and walk southward beneath the Indian laurels. On the square's southern edge, you'll see one of the most historic buildings of Ponce, restored to reflect its original function during Spanish colonial days, the:

4. **Casa Alcaldía** (City Hall), standing on the site of an 18th-century monastery. This building was erected in 1840 as a general assembly, and then served as the civic jail until 1905. Speeches by Theodore Roosevelt (in 1906), Herbert Hoover (in 1931), and Franklin D. Roosevelt (in 1934) were delivered from its central second-floor balcony to crowds assembled below. George Bush visited the building in 1987. The clock set into the tower was imported from London in 1877, and a tour of the baronial street-level interior reveals a memorial plaque dedicated to the fallen American dead (Second Wisconsin Regiment) during the Spanish-American War. A few paces farther on you'll see a galleried courtyard that formerly served as prisoners' cells. The building's main courtyard was used for public executions. In City Hall, other plaques make clear that the city of Ponce was named not after the first European to explore Florida (Ponce de León), but rather after de León's great-grandson, Loíza Ponce de León, one of the town's early civic leaders.

Note across from the entrance to City Hall (in the town's main square) one of the most beautiful fountains of Puerto Rico, the:

5. **Lion Fountain,** crafted from marble and bronze and modeled after a famous fountain in Barcelona, Spain. It was made for the 1939 New York World's Fair and later purchased and erected in Ponce by its mayor.

Continue your walk along the southern edge of the square. Note the way the plaza has "chopped corners" (broadly rounded 45° corners rather than 90° perpendicular corners). They were designed this way for increased visibility by the Spanish armies as a deterrent to civil unrest and the contraband trade that flourished here during their regime. Ponce is said to have the only large square on Puerto Rico equipped with this military-inspired feature.

As you cross Calle Marina/Calle Commercio, which borders the southeastern edge of the square, look to your right to the faraway beaux arts–inspired building painted a creamy shade of white. Originally built in 1922, it served as the town's casino until it was closed during the mid-1960s. Today it houses government agencies and is not open to the public. Nearer and more spectacular are the pair of banks flanking the southeastern edge of the square, the:

6. **Banco de Santander and Scotia Bank,** both adorned with intricate stained-glass windows, art nouveau detailing, and dozens of unusual architectural features. The alleyway separating the two banks, Callejon Amor, is lined with African tulip trees that are believed to evoke the romantic spirit of any couple in love.

Walking Tour—Ponce

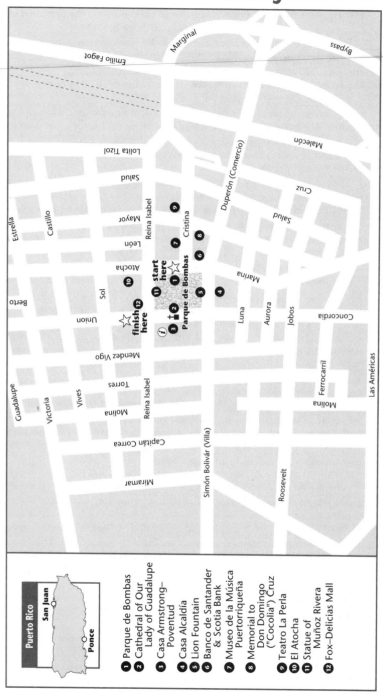

Puerto Rico
San Juan
Ponce

1. Parque de Bombas
2. Cathedral of Our Lady of Guadalupe
3. Casa Armstrong–Poventud
4. Casa Alcaldía
5. Lion Fountain
6. Banco de Santander & Scotia Bank
7. Museo de la Música Puertorriqueña
8. Memorial to Don Domingo ("Cocolía") Cruz
9. Teatro La Perla
10. El Atocha
11. Statue of Muñoz Rivera
12. Fox–Delicias Mall

(This alleyway is also the site of public concerts held every Sunday between 8 and 9pm by one of the town's classical orchestras or dance bands.)

Proceed eastward along Calle Cristina, which funnels into the main square directly opposite the red-and-black-sided fire station. Within the block, the pink-and-white neoclassical villa you'll see on your left is the:

7. **Museo de la Música Puertorriqueña,** established in 1990 and one of only two such museums in the Caribbean—the other is in Cuba.

After your visit, leave the museum and continue your walk eastward along Calle Cristina. At the next cross street, diagonal to where you're standing, you'll see the:

8. **Memorial to Don Domingo,** dedicated to Don Domingo ("Cocolia") Cruz, long-time leader of Ponce's municipal band and one of the best-known musicians from Ponce. He died in 1934.

Turn left at Calle Mayor and admire the neoclassical facade of the largest and most historic theater in the Caribbean, the:

9. **Teatro La Perla,** originally built in 1862 to display the newfound prosperity of Ponce. It collapsed during an earthquake in 1918, and for about 20 years only the massive Corinthian columns of its portico remained in place. In 1940, architect Porrato D'Oria redesigned it (retaining the original columns). After a radical restoration completed in 1990, the theater is now the largest and most historic in the Spanish-speaking Caribbean. Everything from plays and concerts to beauty pageants take place here. Its excellent acoustics were designed along lines similar to those of New York City's Carnegie Hall. Depending on the time of day and the season, the lobby of this theater may be open for a quick look at its interior decoration.

Now continue walking northward along Calle Mayor to the first intersection (Calle Reina Isabel). To your right stands a Moorish-inspired building known as the Casa Salazar (Salazar House), which accommodates a branch of the Puerto Rican Museum of History.

☕ **TAKE A BREAK**   Copious cups of coffee, assorted ice creams, and sandwiches are offered to tired pedestrians and talkative neighbors at the **Café Tomas/ Café Tompy,** Calle Reina Isabel at the corner of Calle Mayor (☎ **787/840-1965**). Divided into a less formal and a more formal section, it is open daily from 7am to midnight. For more information, see "Where to Dine," below.

After this break, walk westward along Calle Reina Isabel until you reach the edge of the previously explored Plaza de Las Delicias. From the square's northeastern corner stretches:

10. **El Atocha,** the city's main shopping street. Stroll along its broad borders, noting the Spanish-inspired turn-of-the-century architecture, the cast-iron benches, and the many police guards ensuring one of the most tranquil urban streets of Puerto Rico. After your shopping, return to the main square and walk westward along its northern edge. Note, within the confines of the square is:

11. **Statue of Muñoz Rivera,** a memorial to one of Puerto Rico's best-known politicians (1898–1980), who helped Puerto Ricans become U.S. citizens after a career of political lobbying.

Proceeding along the edge of the square, note the:

12. **Fox-Delicias Mall,** one of the city's most alluring watering holes and shopping enclaves. Originally built in 1931 as a movie theater, its pink walls are excellent examples of art deco architecture on Puerto Rico. In crumbling disrepair, the theater was transformed into a disco during the 1960s. In 1989 the government

of Spain earmarked funds for the restoration of Ponce but specifically insisted that it be used to restore this building to its original celluloid glamor. Today this mall contains an array of shops, nightclubs, and cafés, a good place for refreshment after your stroll.

OUTDOOR ACTIVITIES

Ponce is a city—not a beach resort—and should be visited mainly for its sights. If you use it as a base for seeing the southeast coast, you can, however, head west of Ponce (about a 10-minute drive) to reach **Playa de Ponce,** a long strip of white sand opening onto the tranquil waters of the Caribbean. This beach is usually better for swimming than the Condado in San Juan.

Since Ponce is not a resort town, there is little in the way of organized sports. Scuba divers can be taken to the best dive sites along the southern coast by calling **Gregory's Dive Center** at **787/844-6175.** The Center can also make arrangements for fishing and sailing in the Ponce area.

The city owns two **tennis complexes,** one at Poly Deportivos, with nine hard courts (lit at night) and another six at Rambla (also lit at night). These courts are open from 9am to 9pm. For information, including complete information on reaching them from wherever you are, call the **Secretary of Sports** at ☎ **787/840-4400.**

There are no golf courses in Ponce. To play golf, you have to go to **Aquirre Golf Course,** Route 705, Aquirre (☎ **787/853-4053**), 30 miles east of Ponce (take Route 3). This nine-hole course, open from 7:30am to 4:30pm daily, charges $8 greens fees Monday through Friday, going up to $15 on weekends and holidays. Another course, **Club Zeportivo,** Carretera 102, km 15.4, Gooivgas (☎ **787/851-8880**), lies 30 miles west of Ponce. This course is a nine-holer, open daily from 7am to 5pm. Greens fees are $10 daily.

CARITE FOREST PRESERVE

Easily reached from the Ponce Expressway near Cayey, **Carite** is a 6,000-acre reserve with a dwarf forest, which was produced by the region's high humidity and its moist soil. From several peaks there are panoramic views of Ponce and the Caribbean Sea. On one peak is Nuestra Madre, a Catholic spiritual meditation center that permits visitors to stroll the grounds. Fifty species of birds live in the Carite Forest Reserve, which also has a large natural pool called Charco Azul. A picnic area and campgrounds are shaded by eucalyptus and royal palms.

Wet & Dry

Southwestern Puerto Rico is the site of the world's largest remaining tract of tropical, dry, coast-forest, much of it preserved in Guánica State Forest. In contrast, this part of the island also features miles of mangrove channel systems. Visitors can visit this unusual terrain with **Tropix Wellness Tours** (☎ **787/268-2173,** or fax 787/268-1722), whose "Wet and Dry Tour" includes two expeditions: a "dry" forest hike in Guánica State Forest, and "wet" paddles through the mangroves by kayak. Visits to secluded beaches at sunset are included.

The 4-day, 3-night tour costs $275 per person, double occupancy, including accommodations at the Copamarina Hotel, continental breakfast, and equipment for the escorted expeditions.

SHOPPING

If you feel a yen for shopping in Ponce, head for the **Fox-Delicias Mall,** at the intersection of Calle Reina Isabel and the Plaza de Las Delicias, the city's most innovative shopping center. Among the many interesting stores there is **Regalitos y Algo Mas,** located on the upper level. It specializes in unusual gift items from around Puerto Rico. Look especially for the Christmas tree ornaments, crafted from wood, metal, colored porcelain, or bread dough, and for the exotic dolls chosen and displayed by the owners. Purchases can be shipped anywhere in the world.

WHERE TO STAY

Days Inn
Rte. 1, km 123.5, Mercedita, Ponce, PR 00715. ☎ **787/841-1000** or 800/329-7466. Fax 787/ 841-2560. 120 rms, 2 suites. A/C TV TEL. $90 double; $119.50 suite. Rates include continental breakfast. AE, DC, MC, V.

A 15-minute drive east of Ponce on Highway 52, opposite the Interamerican University, this hotel opened in 1989. Its modest bedrooms are conservative and comfortable, equipped with contemporary furnishings. The prices appeal to families with children. Facilities include a courtyard swimming pool, a children's wading pool, a Jacuzzi, a coin-operated laundry, an international restaurant, a bar/disco, and ice and vending machines for sodas and snacks.

Melía
Calle Cristina 2, Ponce, PR 00731. ☎ **787/842-0260.** Fax 787/841-3602. 78 rms. A/C TV TEL. $75–$85 double. Rates include continental breakfast. AE, DC, MC, V. Parking $3.

A city hotel with southern hospitality, the Melía—which has no connection with other chain hotels in the world bearing the same name—often attracts businesspeople. The location is a few steps away from Our Lady of Guadalupe Cathedral and from the Parque de Bombas (the red-and-black firehouse). Although this old hotel is showing its age and has long ago been outclassed by the Hilton, many of its admirers who could afford more luxurious accommodations still prefer to stay here for its old-time atmosphere. The lobby floor and all stairs are covered with Spanish tiles of Moorish design. The desk clerks, often family members, are courteous and speak excellent English. The rooms, comfortably furnished, are pleasant enough, and most have a balcony facing either busy Calle Cristina or the old plaza. Breakfast is served on a rooftop terrace with a good view of Ponce. A lackluster restaurant on site is under independent management. You can park your car in the lot nearby.

✪ Ponce Hilton and Casino
Avenida Santiago de los Caballeros 14 (P.O. Box 7419), Ponce, PR 00732. ☎ **787/259-7676** or 800/HILTONS in the U.S. and Canada. Fax 787/259-7674. 148 rms, 8 suites. A/C MINIBAR TV TEL. $180 double; $400 suite. Extra person $40. AE, DC, MC, V. Self-parking $4.50; valet parking $10.

Opened in 1993 on an 80-acre tract of land about a 5-minute drive (7 mi.) from the center of Ponce, this is the newest and most glamorous hotel in the area, and boasts the most complete facilities. Designed like a miniature village, with turquoise-blue roofs, white walls, and lots of open-sided exposure to tropical plants, ornamental waterfalls, and gardens, it welcomes conventioneers and individual tourists alike. The accommodations are equipped with tropically inspired furnishings, ceiling fans, terraces or balconies, and several luxurious amenities.

Dining/Entertainment: The most elegant of the hotel's three restaurants is La Cava (see "Where to Dine," below). Other choices include Terrazza, overlooking the sea, and a less formal place for hamburgers and snacks, El Bohemio. There's also a casino, which is open daily from noon to 4am. Breakfasts, served in Terrazza from an elaborate buffet, are the best in Ponce.

Services: Room service, laundry, baby-sitting (if arranged in advance).

Facilities: Lagoon-shaped pool ringed with gardens, business center with a supply of personal computers, large convention center, fitness center, video arcade, bike rentals, playground, summer camp for children. Water sports are also available.

NEARBY PLACES TO STAY ON THE BEACH

Copamarina Beach Resort

Rte. 333, km 6.5, Caña Gorda (P.O. Box 805), Guánica, PR 00653. ☎ **787/821-0505** or 800/468-4553 in the U.S. Fax 787/821-0070. 69 rms. A/C TV TEL. Winter, $155 double; off-season, $135 double. AE, DC, MC, V. From Ponce, head west along Rte. 2 to Rte. 116 and go south to Rte. 333, then head east.

Charming, low-key, and well maintained, this resort was originally built in the 1950s as the private vacation retreat of the de Castro family, Puerto Rico's cement barons. In 1991 it was enlarged, upgraded, and opened to the European and North American tourist trade. It is situated beside a public beach, amid a landscaped palm grove.

The bedrooms are in wood-sided one- and two-story wings that radiate out from the resort's central core. Each is decorated with lots of varnished pine (similar to what you might expect in the Adirondack Mountains) and is outfitted with rattan and pinewood furniture.

Dining/Entertainment: The resort houses two restaurants, Ballena's (an elegant indoor restaurant for dinner only) and Las Palmas, which is set in the open air beneath a heavily trussed canopy. Service is slow but the food is well prepared.

Services: Baby-sitting, laundry.

Facilities: Swimming pool for adults, wading pool for children, two tennis courts, program of water sports (including snorkeling and scuba diving).

Mary Lee's by the Sea

Rte. 333, km 6.7 (P.O. Box 394), Guánica, PR 00653. ☎ **787/821-3600.** 8 units. A/C. $70 double; $90 small suite with kitchenette; $110 suite with terrace and full kitchen; $140–$160 larger suites for up to 6 with full kitchen; $160 three-bedroom unit for up to 6. No credit cards.

Owned and operated by Michigan-born Mary Lee Alvarez, a former resident of Cuba and a self-described "compulsive decorator," this is an informal collection of cottages, seafront houses, and apartments located beside the coastal highway, 4 miles east of Guánica. The five flat-roofed, California-style houses are subdivided into eight different living units suitable for one to three couples. The entire compound is landscaped with flowering shrubs, trees, and vines.

There aren't any formally organized activities here, but the hotel sits next to sandy beaches and a handful of uninhabited offshore cays. The management maintains rental boats with putt-putt motors, two different waterside sundecks, and several kayaks for the benefit of its active guests. Hikers and bird-watchers can go north to the Guánica National Forest (see "Nearby Attractions," above).

Don't come here looking for nighttime activities or enforced conviviality. The place is quiet, secluded, and appropriate only for low-key vacationers looking for privacy and isolation with a companion and/or with nature. There isn't a bar or restaurant here, although each unit includes a modern kitchen and an outdoor barbecue pit. The rooms are serviced weekly, although for an extra fee guests can arrange to have a maid come in every day.

WHERE TO DINE
EXPENSIVE

✪ La Hacienda/La Cava de la Hacienda

In the Ponce Hilton, Avenida Santiago de los Caballeros 14. ☎ **787/259-7676.** Reservations recommended. Main courses $15–$25. AE, DC, MC, V. Daily 7–11am, noon–3pm, and 6:30–10:30pm. INTERNATIONAL.

These interconnected restaurants in the Ponce Hilton are the most elegant and stylish dining rooms in town, evoking the traditions of Puerto Rico's colonial age. Designed as a network of rooms in a 19th-century coffee plantation, they offer impeccable service and a dignified sense of formality. The menu at both restaurants is the same—only the ambience differs. La Hacienda is a high-ceilinged octagon, with plenty of room between tables, lots of exposed paneling, and a dignified sense of calm. La Cava de la Hacienda resembles an underground wine cellar lined with wine racks and filled with rustic antiques and farm implements. There are also two private dining rooms for groups of 6 to 10 diners.

The menu changes every 2 weeks, but it might include seafood pot pie with shrimp and scallops, snails in a Pinot Noir sauce, cheese fondue for two, sushi rolls of salmon with a soy-wasabi sauce, a paillard of salmon with sorrel sauce, veal medallions with sautéed sweetbreads and apples, grilled skewers of lamb with almond rice, and lobster-stuffed ravioli with cream sauce. Typical desserts include flamed baked Alaska, crème brûlée, and apple beignets with honey-vanilla sauce. Although not all of these dishes meet truly lofty standards, each is very competently prepared with the freshest ingredients used whenever possible.

MODERATE

El Ancla

Avenida Hostos Final, Playa Ponce. ☎ **787/840-2450.** Main courses $5.95–$35. AE, DC, MC, V. Sun–Thurs 11am–10pm, Fri–Sat 11am–midnight. PUERTO RICAN/SEAFOOD.

Established by members of the Lugo family in 1978, this restaurant, located south of the city on the beach, is among the best in the Ponce area. Much of its appeal is due to its position on soaring piers that extend from the rocky coastline out over the surf. As you dine, the sound of the sea rises literally from beneath your feet, an effect that somehow seems to improve both the view and the flavor of the fish.

Fresh fish is the specialty here, and typical dishes include red snapper served with a pumpkin flan, dorado in a tomato-and-brandy sauce, seafood casserole and seafood paella (prepared only for two or more diners), and several preparations of broiled lobster. Steak, veal, and chicken dishes are also available. The dishes have real Puerto Rican zest and flavor.

La Montserrate

Sector Las Cucharas, Rte. 82 (about 4 miles west of the town center). ☎ **787/841-2740.** Main courses $14–$29. AE, DC, MC, V. Daily 10am–10pm. PUERTO RICAN/SEAFOOD.

This restaurant, located right beside the sea, attracts a loyal clientele from the surrounding area. A culinary institution among Ponceros, it occupies a large, airy, modern building whose public areas are divided into two different dining areas, one slightly more formal than the other. Visitors in the know, however, head immediately for the large, grangelike room in back, where windows on three sides overlook some offshore islands.

Dishes, prepared with whatever seafood is freshest on the day of your arrival, might include octopus salad, four kinds of asopao, or a whole red snapper in Créole sauce. For diners who have already had their fill of the briny deep, a selection of steaks and grills is available. It's not innovative haute cuisine, but it's authentic and very typical of the south of Puerto Rico, with some dishes that local families serve at home. The fish dishes are better than the meat selections.

INEXPENSIVE

Café Tomas/Café Tompy

Calle Reina Isabel at Calle Mayor. ☎ **787/840-1965.** Lunch $3–$18; dinner $8.95–$20. AE, MC, V. Daily 11am–3pm and 6–11pm. Café daily 7am–midnight. PUERTO RICAN.

The more visible and busier section of this establishment functions as a simple café for neighbors and local merchants. On plastic tables flooded with sunlight from the big windows, you can order coffee, sandwiches, or cold beer, perhaps while relaxing after a walking tour of the city.

The family-run restaurant is more formal. The discreet entrance is adjacent to the café on Calle Reina Isabel. There, amid a decor reminiscent of a Spanish *tasca*, you can enjoy such simply prepared dishes as salted fillet of beef, beefsteak with onions, four different kinds of asopao, buttered eggs, octopus salads, and *yuca* (similar to cassava) croquettes.

Lupita's Mexican Restaurante

Calle Reina Isabel 60. ☎ **787/848-8808.** Reservations required on weekends. Main courses $7–$20. AE, DC, MC, V. Sun–Thurs 11am–11pm, Fri–Sat 11am–2am. MEXICAN.

Established with fanfare in 1993, and adding a note of lighthearted fun to the city, this is the first (and only) Mexican restaurant in Ponce. Set in a 19th-century building and its adjoining courtyard, a short walk from Ponce's main square, it's the creative statement of Hector de Castro, who traveled throughout Mexico to find the elaborate fountains and the dozens of chairs and decorative accessories that fill these premises. The trompe l'oeil murals on the inside (featuring desert scenes in an amusing surrealism) were painted by the owner's sister, Flor de Maria de Castro.

A well-trained staff serves blue and green margaritas (frozen or unfrozen) and a wide array of other tropical drinks. Any of these might be followed by Mexican dishes cooked in cholesterol-free vegetable oil. Specialties include tortilla soup, taco salads, grilled lobster tail with tostones, seafood fajitas, and burritos, tacos, and enchiladas with a wide choice of fillings. A mariachi band plays on Friday, and on Saturday either Puerto Rican or American bands entertain. Lupita is an affectionate nickname for Guadalupe, the patron saint both of Mexico and the city of Ponce.

2 Mayagüez

98 miles W of San Juan, 15 miles S of Aguadilla

The largest city on the island's west coast, Mayagüez is a port whose elegance and charm reached its zenith during the mercantile and agricultural prosperity of the 19th century. Most of the town's stately buildings were destroyed in a horrific earthquake in 1918, and today the town is noted more for its industry than its aesthetic appeal.

Mayagüez is a commercial city—not a tourist resort—but it's a convenient stopover for those exploring the west coast. (The Mayagüez Hilton and Casino draws most tourists here.) If you want a windsurfing beach, you have to head north of Rincón, or if you want a more tranquil beach, you can drive south from Mayagüez along Route 102 to Boquerón.

Nevertheless, Mayagüez is still identified as the honeymoon capital of Puerto Rico, partly because of the lush and beautiful vegetation that grows here and partly because of a peculiarly romantic 16th-century legend. It is said that local farmers often kidnapped young Spanish sailors who had stopped at Mayagüez for provisions en route to South America. However, it's anyone's guess whether this was good or bad luck. There was a scarcity of eligible bachelors in Mayagüez, and the farmers kidnapped the young sailors in hopes of providing their daughters with husbands and their farms with overseers.

Although the town itself dates from the mid-18th century, the area around it has figured in European history since the time of Christopher Columbus, who landed nearby when he discovered Puerto Rico in 1493. Today a bronze statue of Columbus stands atop a metallic globe of the world. Both are poised above the gracious plaza in the center of Mayagüez.

Famed for the size and depth of its harbor (the second largest on the island), Mayagüez was built to control the **Mona Passage,** a route considered essential to the Spanish Empire when Puerto Rico and the nearby Dominican Republic were vital trade and defensive jewels in the Spanish crown (today this waterway is notorious for the destructiveness of its currents, the ferocity of its sharks, and the thousands of boat people who arrive illegally on Puerto Rico from either Haiti or the Dominican Republic on the adjacent island of Hispaniola).

Queen Isabel II of Spain recognized Mayagüez's status as a town in 1836. Her son, Alfonso XII, granted it a city charter in 1877. Permanently isolated from the major commercial developments of San Juan, Mayagüez, like Ponce, has always retained its own distinct identity.

Today the town's major industry is tuna packing; in fact, 60% of the tuna consumed in the United States is packed here. It is also an important departure point for deep-sea fishing and is the bustling port for exporting the agricultural produce from the surrounding hillsides. Once considered the needlework capital of Puerto Rico, it still has women who create fine embroidery and drawn-thread work, industries that were brought to Puerto Rico centuries ago from Spain and Hapsburg-controlled Holland and Belgium.

ESSENTIALS

GETTING THERE   **American Eagle** (☎ 800/433-7300) flies from San Juan to Mayagüez five times a day Monday through Friday, three times a day on weekends (flying time: 45 min.). Depending on restrictions, round-trip passage ranges from $105 to $145 per person.

Taxis meet arriving planes. If you take one, negotiate the fare with the driver first—cabs are unmetered here.

There are branches of **Avis** (☎ 787/832-0460), **Budget** (☎ 787/831-4570), and **Hertz** (☎ 787/832-3314) at the Mayagüez airport.

If you're driving from San Juan, head either west on Route 2 (trip time: 2½ hr.) or south from San Juan on the scenic Route 52 (trip time: 3 hr.). Route 52 offers easier travel.

VISITOR INFORMATION   Mayagüez doesn't have a tourist information office. If you're starting out in San Juan, inquire there before you set out (see "Tourist Information" under "Orientation" in chapter 4).

SEEING THE SIGHTS

The chief attraction here is the **Tropical Agriculture Research Station** (☎ 787/ 831-3435). It's located on Route 65, between Post Street and Route 108, adjacent to the University of Puerto Rico at Mayagüez campus and across the street from the **Parque de los Próceres** (Patriots' Park). At the administration office, ask for a free map of the tropical gardens, which have one of the largest collections of tropical plant

Mayagüez

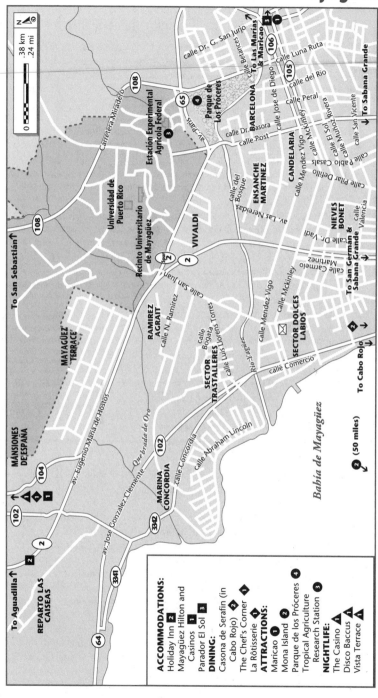

ACCOMMODATIONS:
Holiday Inn **2**
Mayagüez Hilton and Casinos **1**
Parador El Sol **3**
DINING:
Casona de Serafín (in Cabo Rojo) **1**
The Chef's Corner **2**
La Rôtisserie ◆
ATTRACTIONS:
Maricao **1**
Mona Island **2**
Parque de los Próceres **4**
Tropical Agriculture Research Station **3**
NIGHTLIFE:
The Casino ▲
Disco Baccus ▲
Vista Terrace ▲

Mona Island: The Galápagos of Puerto Rico

Off Mayagüez, the unique island of Mona teems with giant iguanas, three species of endangered sea turtles, red-footed boobies, and countless other sea birds. It features a tabletop plateau with mangrove forests and cacti, giving way to dramatic, 200-foot-high limestone cliffs which rise some 200 feet above the water and encircle much of Mona.

A bean-shaped pristine island with no hotels, Mona is a destination for the hardy pilgrim who seeks the road less traveled. A pup tent, backpack, and hiking boots will do fine if you plan to forego the comforts of civilization and immerse yourself in nature. Snorkelers, spelunkers, biologists, and ecotourists find much to fascinate them in Mona's wildlife, mangrove forests, coral reefs, and complex honeycomb that is the largest marine-originated cave in the world. There also are miles of secluded white sand beaches and palm trees.

Uninhabited today, Mona was for centuries the scene of considerable human activity. The pre-Columbian Taíno Indians were the first to establish themselves here. Later, pirates used it as a base for their raids, followed by guano miners who removed the rich crop fertilizer from Mona's caves. Columbus landed in Mona on his 1494 voyage, and Ponce de León spent several days there en route to becoming governor of Puerto Rico in 1508. The notorious pirate, Captain Kidd, used Mona as a temporary hideout.

Mona can be reached by organized tour from Mayagüez. Camping is available at $1 per night. Everything needed, including water, must be brought in, and everything, including garbage, must be taken out. For more information, call the Puerto Rico Department of Natural Resources at **787/724-3724.**

Ecantos Ecoturs offers a 4-day, 3-night tour of Mona on the second Friday of each month for $549 per person. The price includes ground transportation from San Juan, sea transportation departing from Cabo Rojo, all diving, snorkeling, spelunking, and camping gear, and all meals and fees. Call **800/272-7241** for more information or to book one of these tours.

species that are useful to people, including cacao, fruit trees, spices, timbers, and ornamentals. The grounds are open Monday through Friday from 7am to 4pm, charging no admission.

Mayagüez is the jumping-off point for visits to unique **Mona Island,** the "Galápagos of the Caribbean." See the accompanying box for details.

Not far from Mayagüez is **Maricao.** You can reach it by taking Route 105 west and then driving north on Route 120. The town is colorful and rather small. On the outskirts look for a sign that reads "**Los Viveros**" (The Hatcheries); then take Route 410. Here, the Commonwealth Department of Agriculture hatches as many as 25,000 fish for stocking Puerto Rican freshwater lakes and streams.

Go back to Maricao to Route 120 south up to km 13.8 until you reach the **Maricao State Forest** picnic area, located 2,900 feet above sea level. The observation tower provides a panoramic view across the green mountains up to the coastal plains. Continue on Route 120 across the forest to the town of Sabana Grande (Great Plain). Route 2 will then take you to the town of San Germán.

WHERE TO STAY

Mayagüez Hilton and Casino

Rte. 104 (P.O. Box 3629), Mayagüez, PR 00709. ☎ **787/831-7575** or 800/HILTONS in the U.S. and Canada. Fax 787/834-3475. 141 rms, 8 suites. A/C MINIBAR TV TEL. $155–$165 double; from $200 suite. AE, DC, MC, V. Self-parking $4.50.

This country club–style hotel is situated on 20 acres of tropical gardens. Its grounds have been designated as an adjunct to the nearby Mayagüez Institute of Tropical Agriculture by the U.S. Department of Agriculture. If you want to get deep into botany, the institute has the largest collection of tropical plants in the western hemisphere. No fewer than five species of palm trees grow on the hotel's grounds, including the royal palm (native to Puerto Rico), and there are eight kinds of bougainvillea and numerous species of rare flora.

The hotel, at the northern edge of the city, was built in 1964, and it has been completely refurbished. The well-appointed rooms open onto the swimming pool, and many have private balconies. Try to get a room facing west if you'd like a view. Year-round rates depend on whether you take a standard, superior, or deluxe accommodation.

Dining/Entertainment: For the Rôtisserie, see "Where to Dine," below. In the corner of that restaurant is the Chef's Corner, a small gourmet restaurant. The Hilton is also the entertainment center of the city. There's a casino which has no entrance fee and is open daily from noon to 4am. In addition, you can dance to the latest hits at the Baccus Music Club from 9:30pm to 3am or later Tuesday through Saturday. The club is free to residents; others pay an entrance fee of $8.

Services: Room service (6:30am–10:30pm), laundry, baby-sitting.

Facilities: Olympic-size swimming pool, children's pool, playground, Jacuzzi, minigym, three tennis courts, physical-fitness trails. Deep-sea fishing, skin diving, surfing, and scuba diving can be arranged. An 18-hole golf course lies at Borinquén Field, a former SAC airbase, about 30 minutes from the Hilton.

Holiday Inn

2701 Rte. 2, km 149.9, Mayagüez, PR 00680. ☎ **787/833-1100** or 800/HOLIDAY in the U.S. and Canada. Fax 787/833-1300. 147 rms, 5 suites. A/C TV TEL. $125–$155 double; $215 suite. AE, DC, MC, V.

Set beside Route 2 a couple of miles north of the city center, behind a parking lot and a well-maintained lawn, this six-story hotel opened in 1993. Clean, contemporary, and comfortable, it has a marble-floored, high-ceilinged lobby and a small swimming pool, which offer a bit of breathing space for motorists traveling through Mayagüez. The bedrooms are functionally furnished in an international motel style, and there's a bar and restaurant on the premises.

Hotel Parador El Sol

Calle Santiago Riera Palmer, 9 Este, Mayagüez, PR 00680. ☎ **787/834-0303.** Fax 787/265-7567. 52 rms. A/C TV TEL. $65 double. AE, MC, V.

Located two blocks from the landmark Plaza del Mercado in the center of town, this modern concrete building provides some of the most reasonable and hospitable accommodations in this part of Puerto Rico. Central to the shopping district and to all western-region transportation and highways, the restored seven-floor hotel offers up-to-date facilities that include cable TV, a restaurant, and a swimming pool. Furnishings, however, are extremely modest.

NEARBY PLACES TO STAY

Hotel Joyuda Beach

Rte. 102, km 11.7, Cabo Rojo, PR 00623. ☎ **787/851-5650.** Fax 787/265-6940. 41 rms. A/C TV TEL. $85 double. Two children under 12 stay free in parents' room. Rates include continental breakfast. AE, MC, V. Follow Rte. 102 south of Mayagüez to Joyuda.

On the beach in scenic Cabo Rojo, this 1989 hotel offers comfortably furnished and air-conditioned bedrooms, with such amenities as private baths and room service. From here you can easily head to El Combate Beach and the Cabo Rojo Wildlife Refuge. Tennis and golf are just 5 minutes away, and sport-fishing charters can also be arranged, as well as windsurfing and canoeing. The hotel is often a favorite of Puerto Rican honeymooners.

Parador Hacienda Juanita

Rte. 105, km 23.5 (P.O. Box 777), Maricao, PR 00606. ☎ **787/838-2550,** or 800 /443-0266 in the U.S. (for reservations only). Fax 787/838-2551. 21 rms. $70–$75 double. Children under 12 stay free in parents' room. AE, MC, V.

Named after one of its long-ago owners, a matriarch named Juanita, the building was originally constructed in 1836 as part of a coffee plantation. Situated 2 miles west of the village of Maricao, beside Route 105 heading to Mayagüez, it's a pink stucco house with a long veranda and a living room that's furnished with a large-screen TV and decorated with the antique tools and artifacts of the coffee industry. Relatively isolated, the parador is surrounded by only a few neighboring buildings and the jungle. The Luis Rivera family welcomes visitors and serves drinks and meals in their restaurant. There's a swimming pool, billiards table, and Ping-Pong table on the premises. The bedrooms are simple and rural, with ceiling fans, rocking chairs, and rustic furniture. None has a phone, TV, or air-conditioning (with the cool temperatures in this high-altitude place, the ceiling fans suffice).

WHERE TO DINE

✪ The Chef's Corner

In the Mayagüez Hilton and Casino, Rte. 104. ☎ **787/831-7575.** Reservations required. Fixed-price five-course dinner $45 per person. AE, DC, MC, V. Daily 7–10:30pm but only if 8 or more persons reserve. INTERNATIONAL.

The Mayagüez Hilton has created a laudable culinary achievement with this restaurant. A severely modern dining room whose main decor relies on the tropical gardens that can be seen through the huge windows, it contains only 20 seats. Varying with the season, the availability of ingredients, and the inspiration of the chef, the menu might offer such dishes as a paupiette of sole with a burgundy- and saffron-flavored butter sauce, a timbale of avocado and asparagus with a fresh basil-and-tomato coulis, veal sweetbreads in puff pastry, and a mango-and-strawberry Bavarian cream with soft fruits of the season. Meals here, the best in Mayagüez, are designed as culinary events and are usually presented with pride and a certain fanfare.

La Rôtisserie

In the Mayagüez Hilton and Casino, Rte. 104. ☎ **787/831-7575.** Reservations recommended. Main courses $15.50–$32.50; Sun brunch buffet $22. Fri night seafood buffet $25.50, Sat night American buffet $24.50. AE, DC, MC, V. Daily 6:30–10:30pm. INTERNATIONAL.

The most sophisticated and elegant dining room in Mayagüez, the Hilton's La Rôtisserie contains all the accoutrements of a fine European restaurant—richly grained paneling, a formally dressed staff, and silver trolleys wheeled with main courses and desserts to your table. The chefs are accomplished artists and know how to embroider a traditional repertoire based on traditional ingredients. Some of their dishes have real flair, as exemplified by spinach tortellini with smoked salmon and a cream sauce. The chefs don't forget their Puerto Rican heritage, however, offering such dishes as asopao of shrimp. The different kinds of steaks and grilled meats are standard. The red snapper on our last visit tasted fresh and wasn't overcooked. A trio of dishes are prepared flambé style at your table, ranging from steak to shrimp or lobster. Desserts are appropriately dramatic and caloric, and a full array of wines might complement any of your meals.

NEARBY DINING IN CABO ROJO

Casona de Serafin

Punta Arena Joyuda, Rte. 102, km 9. ☎ **787/851-0066.** Reservations not required except on Sun. Main courses $19.50–$24.50. AE, MC, V. Daily 11:30am–11pm. Drive 3 miles south on Rte. 102; the restaurant is beside the highway. PUERTO RICAN.

Set in a modest concrete-sided building beside the highway and sporting a clean stucco-and-tile interior that's kept immaculately clean, this restaurant is owned by six members of the Ramírez family. Named after their youngest son, Serafin, whose birth coincided with the establishment of this place, it offers fresh seafood and well-prepared Puerto Rican platters, some of the best and freshest in this part of the island. Brought in fresh every day, seafood is served in such concoctions as lobster parmigiana, red snapper in Spanish sauce, a zaruela of shellfish, three versions of asopao, and a number of shrimp preparations. There also are filet mignons and flank steaks from a charcoal brazier, each juicy and well flavored.

MAYAGÜEZ AFTER DARK

The Casino

At the Mayagüez Hilton and Casino, Rte. 104. ☎ **787/831-7575.** No cover.

The completely remodeled casino with an adjoining Player's Bar is the only casino in Mayagüez. Try your luck at blackjack, dice, slot machines, roulette, and mini-baccarat. It's open daily from noon to 4am.

Disco Baccus

In the Mayagüez Hilton and Casino, Rte. 104. ☎ **787/831-7575.** No cover for hotel guests, $5 for others. Two-drink minimum.

The music originates in New York, Los Angeles, London, or San Juan—the drinks are cold, the salsa's hot, and people dance, dance, dance. You'll find it in the city's most famous hotel.

Vista Terrace

In the Mayagüez Hilton and Casino, Rte. 104. ☎ **787/831-7575.**

On a large and airy covered terrace that opens to a view of a manicured tropical garden, this is a relaxing and soothing place for a cocktail. The bartenders specialize in pastel-colored rum-based concoctions that seem to go well with the hibiscus-scented air. Open Sunday through Thursday from 5pm to midnight and on Friday and Saturday from 5pm to 2am.

3 Rincón

100 miles W of San Juan, 6 miles N of Mayagüez

On the westernmost point of the island north of Mayagüez, the small fishing village of Rincón lies in the foothills of La Cadena mountains. It's not a sightseeing destination unto itself. But ever since the World Surfing Championship was held here in 1968, the area's beaches began to gain fame, and now the half-dozen reef-lined beaches have become a winter mecca for skilled surfers. Surfers from as far away as New Zealand say the best spots in the Caribbean are along the coast here, off Route 2 between Mayagüez and Rincón. They are particularly attracted to the beach at **Punta Higuero,** on Route 413 near Rincón, which has been compared to the finest surfing spots in the world. During winter, uninterrupted swells from the North Atlantic form perfect waves averaging 5 to 6 feet in height, with rideable rollers sometimes reaching 15 to 25 feet.

Endangered humpback whales also winter here, attracting a growing number of whale watchers. A lighthouse stands at El Faro Park.

And many nonsurfers visit Rincón for only one reason: the Horned Dorset Primavera Hotel, not only one of the finest in Puerto Rico, but one of the best hotels in the entire Caribbean.

ESSENTIALS

GETTING THERE   American Eagle (☎ **800/433-7300**) flies from San Juan to Mayagüez, the nearest airport, five times a day Monday to Friday, three times on Saturday and Sunday (flying time: 30 min.). Taxis meet planes arriving from San Juan, but they're unmetered—negotiate the fare at the outset with your driver. For car rentals at Mayagüez, see "Essentials" earlier in this chapter.

If you're driving from San Juan, travel either west on Route 2 (trip time: 2 hr.) or south from San Juan on scenic Route 52 (trip time: $3^1/_2$ hr.). We recommend Route 52.

VISITOR INFORMATION   There is no tourist information office in Rincón. Inquire in San Juan before heading to Rincón (see "Tourist Information" under "Orientation" in chapter 4).

WHERE TO STAY

✪ Horned Dorset Primavera Hotel

P.O. Box 1132, Rincón, PR 00677. ☎ **787/823-4030** or 800/633-1857. Fax 787/823-5580. 22 rms, 8 suites. A/C. Winter, $340 double; $440–$490 suite. Off-season, $224 double; $324–$374 suite. MAP $63.25 per person extra. No children under 12. AE, MC, V. From the Mayagüez Airport, take Rte. 2 north half a mile to the Anasco intersection; turn left onto Rte. 115 toward Rincón and travel for 4 miles. After passing El Coche Restaurant, take a sharp left onto Route 429 and go about a mile. The hotel is on the left, at distance marker km 3.

This is the most sophisticated hotel on Puerto Rico, and one of the most exclusive and elegant small hotels anywhere in the Caribbean. Established in 1987 and a member of Relais & Châteaux, it has the class of a much older building—an effect created by the owners and architects who assembled it. It was built on the massive breakwaters and seawalls erected for a local railroad many years ago and was named after a successful hotel—the Horned Dorset—that its owners still maintain successfully in upstate New York.

The hacienda evokes an aristocratic Spanish villa; there are hand-painted tiles, ceiling fans, seaside terraces, cascades of flowers spilling over the sides of earthenware pots, and the requisite number of wicker armchairs. Management does not allow children under 12, radios, or TVs. Accommodations are in a series of suites rambling uphill amid lush gardens. The decoration is tasteful, with four-poster beds and brass-footed tubs in marble-sheathed bathrooms.

For 1996, the hotel completed a $1.4 million addition, an eight-suite villa, Casa Escondida. Set at the edge of the property, adjacent to the sea, it contains lots of teakwood and marble features. Some of the units have private plunge pools; others offer private verandas or sundecks. Each contains high-quality reproductions of colonial furniture by Baker.

Dining/Entertainment: The hotel's restaurant is one of the finest in Puerto Rico (see "Where to Dine," below). There's a bar open throughout the day serving some of the most delectable rum punches on the island. Guitarists and singers often perform during cocktail and dinner hours.

Services: A capable concierge, room service (for breakfast and lunch only), laundry, massage, limousine and touring services.

Facilities: The best hotel library in Puerto Rico contains books on art, music, comparative literature, and poetry. A pool stands near the neoclassical columns of a gazebo entwined with flowering vines. There is also a secluded, semiprivate beach; tennis courts nearby; and deep-sea fishing, golf, and scuba diving are available nearby.

The Lazy Parrot
P.O. Box 430, Rincón, PR 00677. ☎ **787/823-5654.** Fax 787/823-0224. 6 rms. Year-round, $40 double. Extra person $5 each. AE, DISC, MC, V.

This is a simple, family-run inn set in a residential neighborhood. From here it's only a half-mile walk or drive to at least a half-dozen different beaches. Its building was originally a private home, converted into a guesthouse in 1989. The peach-colored accommodations are about as basic as we recommend, but if you're traveling with an extended group of family members or friends, the bunk bed setup and the fact that each room can sleep up to five in any accommodation might make them appealing. (Okay, it wouldn't be that comfortable if you packed in five people, but it's possible.) There are very few amenities in-house (no pool, no tennis courts, or any other resort facilities), but there's a simple, somewhat sleepy bar and a restaurant serving inexpensive dinner platters.

Parador Villa Antonio
Rte. 115, km 12.3 (P.O. Box 68), Rincón, PR 00743. ☎ **787/823-2645** or 800/443-0266. Fax 787/823-3380. 55 apts. A/C TV. Year-round, $74.95–$107 one-bedroom apt; $96.30–$107 two-bedroom apt. AE, DC, MC, V. Head north from Mayagüez along Rte. 2; then turn left (west) at the junction with Rte. 115.

Ilia and Hector Ruíz offer apartments by the sea with sand at your doorstep. The best way to get here is to fly into the Mayagüez Airport, and then drive for 25 minutes. Facilities at this guest complex include a children's playground, game room, two tennis courts, and a swimming pool. Surfing and fishing can be enjoyed just outside your front door. There is no restaurant, but you can bring your catch right into your cottage and prepare a fresh seafood dinner in your own kitchenette. Be aware that better maintenance is needed here, especially to the air-conditioning, which doesn't always work properly.

A NEARBY PLACE TO STAY & DINE IN AGUADA

J.B. Hidden Village Hotel
Carretera 2, Intersection 4416, km 1, Punta Nueve, Barrio Piedras Blancas, Sector Villarrubia, Aguada, PR 00602. ☎ **787/868-8686.** Fax 787/868-8701. 39 rms, 1 suite. A/C TV TEL. $74 double; $129 suite. AE, MC, V.

Named after the initials of its owners (Julio Bonilla, his wife Jinnie, and their son, Julio, Jr.), this clean and isolated hotel opened in 1990. Half a mile east of Aguada, on a side street running off Route 4414, it's nestled into a valley between three forested hillsides and almost invisible from the road outside, which makes it a quiet and simple refuge to vacationers who enjoy exploring the area's many different beaches. There are two restaurants on the premises (one with a view looking out over a neighboring ravine), a small swimming pool, and a bar. Each bedroom is equipped with pastel-colored contemporary furniture and offers views of the pool.

WHERE TO DINE

The Black Eagle
Highway 413, km 1.0 interio, Barrio Ensenada. ☎ **787/823-3510.** Reservations recommended. Main courses $12–$21. AE, MC, V. Daily 11am–11pm. STEAKS/SEAFOOD.

This restaurant is one of the best in the neighborhood because of its inexpensive prices, its enormous portions, and its refusal to use any frozen ingredient in its well-recommended seafood. It lies in an isolated black-and-white house adjacent to the beach, about a quarter-mile north of the center of Rincón, close to the Black Eagle marina (with which it is not associated in any way). Much of its clientele is made up of Europeans indulging in budget holidays at the nearby inns. In the wood-paneled dining room, you might begin your meal with a house special drink, a deceptively potent pink-colored cocktail known appropriately as a Black Eagle. Menu items include lobster or shrimp cocktails, a 32-ounce porterhouse steak (the restaurant's trademark dish), grilled lobster, pan-fried conch, asopao of lobster or shrimp, and a traditional version of *mofongo criollo.* All the good-tasting main courses are accompanied with salad, bread, and vegetables, something that's bound to save you money on extras.

✪ Horned Dorset Primavera
Rincón. ☎ **787/823-4030.** Reservations recommended. Main courses $24–$30; fixed-price dinner $43; lunch from $18. AE, MC, V. Daily noon–2:30pm and dinner seatings at 7, 8, and 9pm. CLASSICAL FRENCH.

This Caribbean counterpart of an award-winning hotel and restaurant in Leonardsville, New York—the Horned Dorset—reigns without peer as the finest restaurant in western Puerto Rico. It is so alluring that diners sometimes journey out from San Juan for an intimate dinner of excellent cuisine whose high quality can be maintained only through the constant, hands-on supervision of a demanding team of owners.

Meals are served beneath soaring ceilings, in a setting that seems straight out of an aristocratic Spanish home. A masonry staircase sweeps from the garden to reach the second-floor precincts.

The chef is never better than in preparing medallions of lobster in an orange-flavored beurre-blanc sauce, although the grilled breast of duckling with bay leaves and raspberry sauce is also delectable. *Dorado* (mahi mahi), on another occasion, was grilled and served with a ginger-cream sauce on a bed of braised Chinese cabbage. This restaurant is accustomed to serving people who eat at all the best places in the world, and it caters successfully to their time-tested palates.

Vieques & Culebra

11

They may be virtually unknown to many visitors, but the offshore islands of Vieques and Culebra are where Puerto Ricans go for their own vacations. Sandy beaches and low prices are a powerful attraction for both islands.

Vieques, with more tourist facilities than Culebra, lies 7 miles off the eastern coast of Puerto Rico. The island had been occupied at various times by both the French and the British before Puerto Rico acquired it in 1854. The ruins of many sugar and pineapple plantations testify to its once-flourishing agricultural economy. The U.S. military, which took control of two-thirds of the island's 26,000 acres in 1941, has largely refrained from using this part as a bombing range, but it is still an important military training area. Today Vieques is visited for its 40-odd white-sand beaches.

Culebra, 18 miles east of the Puerto Rican "mainland" and 14 miles west of St. Thomas in the U.S. Virgin Islands, is surrounded by coral reefs and edged with nearly deserted, powdery white-sand beaches. Much of the island has been designated a wildlife refuge by the U.S. Fish and Wildlife Service.

1 Vieques

41 miles E of San Juan, 7 miles SE of Fajardo

About 7 miles east of the big island of Puerto Rico lies Vieques (Bee-*ay*-kase), an island about twice as large as Manhattan with about 8,000 inhabitants and some 40 palm-lined white sand beaches. Since World War II about two-thirds of the 21-mile-long island has been controlled by the U.S. military forces. Much of the government-owned land is now leased for cattle grazing, and when there are no military maneuvers, the public can visit the beaches, although you might be asked to produce some form of photo ID. Freedom to use the land has not, however, totally defused local discontent at the presence of navy and marine corps personnel on the island.

The Spanish conquistadores didn't think much of Vieques. They came here in the 16th century but didn't stay long, reporting that the island and neighboring bits of land held no gold and were therefore *las islas inutiles* (the useless islands). The name Vieques comes from a native Amerindian word for small island, *bieques.*

Later Spanish occupation is attested to by the main town, **Isabel Segunda,** on the northern shore. Construction on the last Spanish

What's Special About Vieques & Culebra

Beaches
- The beaches of Vieques, some 40 in all, most of them unnamed, although U.S. sailors have nicknamed their favorites—everything from Green Beach to Orchid.
- Sun Bay (Sombe), a public beach on Vieques, a splendid crescent of sand, with picnic tables and a bathhouse.
- The beaches of Culebra, white-sand strips studding the island and opening onto coral reefs and clear waters. Flamenco Beach is the best.

Unforgettable Sights
- Culebrita, a mile-long coral isle satellite of Culebra, with a hilltop lighthouse and crescent beaches.
- Punta Mula Lighthouse, north of Isabel Segunda on Vieques, providing panoramic views of land and sea.
- Mosquito Bay, home of the "firegods," eerily glowing waters produced by tiny bioluminescent organisms that live near the surface.

Great Towns and Villages
- Isabel Segunda, on the north share of Vieques, the island's capital and site of the last Spanish fort to be built in the New World, dating from 1843.
- Dewey, Culebra's only town, named for Admiral George Dewey, an American hero, although the islanders defiantly call it Puebla.

fort built in the New World began around 1843 during the reign of Queen Isabella II, for whom the town was named. The fort, never completed, is not of any special interest. **The Punta Mula lighthouse,** north of Isabel Segunda, provides panoramic views of the land and sea. The island's fishers and farmers conduct much of their business in Isabel Segunda.

On the south coast, **Esperanza,** once a center for the island's sugarcane industry and now a pretty little fishing village, lies near **Sun Bay (Sombe) public beach.** Sun Bay, a government-run, panoramic crescent of sand, is the beach to visit if you only have one day to spend on the island. The fenced area has picnic tables, a bathhouse, and a parking lot. A recently built resort, marina, and other facilities add to the allure of the many scalloped stretches of sandy waterfront along the south coast.

ESSENTIALS

GETTING THERE   Flights to Vieques leave from Isla Grand Airport near the heart of San Juan—not to be confused with the main Luis Muñoz Marín International Airport out beyond Isla Verde. **Vieques Air Link** (☎ 787/741-3266) operates four daily flights from San Juan. The one-way fare is $35. **Isla Nena** (☎ 787/741-6362) also flies to Vieques from San Juan several times daily, charging a one-way fare of $45.

The Puerto Rico Port Authority operates two ferryboats a day to Vieques from the eastern port of Fajardo; the trip takes about an hour. The round-trip fare is $4 for both adults and children. Tickets for the morning ferry leaving Saturday and Sunday sell out quickly, so passengers should be in line at the ticket window in Fajardo before 8am to be certain of a seat on the 9:30am boat. Otherwise, they'll have to wait until the 3pm ferry. For more information about these sea links, call **787/863-3360** or 800/981-2005.

Vieques & Culebra

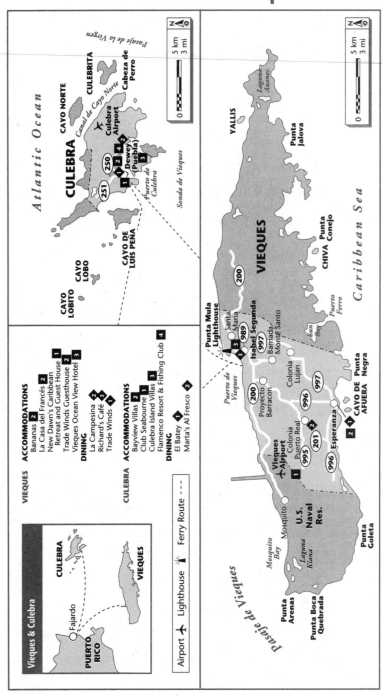

Vieques & Culebra

CULEBRA

VIEQUES

PUERTO
RICO

Fajardo

Airport ✈   Lighthouse ✳   Ferry Route - - -

VIEQUES

ACCOMMODATIONS
Bananas **2**
La Casa del Francés **2**
New Dawn's Caribbean
Retreat and Guest House **1**
Trade Winds Guesthouse **2**
Vieques Ocean View Hotel **3**

DINING
La Campesina **2**
Richard's Café **3**
Trade Winds **1**

CULEBRA

ACCOMMODATIONS
Bayview Villas **2**
Club Seabourne **1**
Culebra Island Villas **3**
Flamenco Resort & Fishing Club **4**

DINING
El Batey **1**
Marta's Al Fresco **2**

Atlantic Ocean

Pasaje de la Virgen

CAYO NORTE

CULEBRITA

Cabeza de
Perro

CULEBRA

Canal de Cayo Norte

Culebra
Airport ✈

Dewey
(Pueblo)

Puerto de
Culebra

CAYO DE
LUÍS PEÑA

CAYO
LOBO

CAYO
LOBITO

Sonda de Vieques

Caribbean Sea

Pasaje de Vieques

VIEQUES

YALLIS

Punta
Jalova

Laguna
Anones

CHIVA   Punta
Conejo

Puerto
Ferro

San
Bay

Punta Mula
Lighthouse ✳

Santa
María

Isabel Segunda
989

Barriada
Monte Santo

Colonia
Luján

Punta
Negra

CAYO DE
AFUERA

Esperanza

Proyecto
Barracón

Colonia
Puerto Real

Vieques
Airport ✈

Mosquito

Mosquito Bay

Laguna
Kiana

U.S.
Naval
Res.

Punta
Goleta

Punta
Boca
Quebrada

Punta
Arenas

Puerto de
Vieques

200

200

997

997

996

995

201

996

250

251

193

GETTING AROUND   Public cabs or vans called *públicos* transport people around the island. To rent a car, contact Betty Yoder at **Island Car Rental** (☎ 787/ 741-1666), in the hamlet of Florida, about a 12-minute ride southwest of Isabel Segunda, or 5 minutes from the airport. The office is next door to the Crow's Nest Guest House. If you call in advance, they will pick you up at the airport. The cost of the local vehicles begins at $35 per day, plus another $10 for collision damage-waiver insurance. American Express, MasterCard, and Visa cards are accepted.

PACKAGE TOURS

An easy way to visit Vieques is with **Tropix Wellness Tours** (☎ 787/268-2173, fax 787/268-1722), which offers a "Phosphorescent Bay Tour" from the Puerto Rican mainland. It includes a visit to Mosquito (Phosphorescent) Bay and an expedition to Isla Nena, home of one of Puerto Rico's most spectacular reefs, bird sanctuaries, and deserted sandy beaches. The tour costs $325 per person, including airfare from the Rivas Dominici Airport in Miramar to Vieques airport, three nights' accommodations at the Casa del Francés, continental breakfast, and equipment for the escorted expeditions.

BEACHES & DIVING

Few of Vieques's beaches have been named, but most have their loyal supporters—loyal, that is, until too many people learn about them, in which case the devotees can always find another good spot.

The U.S. Navy named some of the beaches, such as **Green Beach,** a beautiful clean stretch at the island's west end. **Red and Blue Beaches,** also with navy nomenclature, are great jumping-off points for snorkelers. **Sun Bay (Sombe)** is also a very beautiful white-sand beach, and offers picnic tables, a bathhouse, tent sites, and good snorkeling offshore. Other popular beaches are **Navia, Half Moon, Orchid,** and **Silver,** but if you continue along the water, you may find your own nameless secluded cove with a fine strip of sand.

Outdoor activities, including scuba diving and deep-sea fishing, aren't well organized on Vieques. Sometimes outfitters will appear in the winter but disappear by summer. If you'd like to go diving off the coast of Vieques, you can call **Erin Go Bragh/Tropic Charter** (☎ 787/860-4401) in Fajardo, on the Puerto Rican "mainland." This outfitter occasionally offers trips over to Vieques.

THE LUMINOUS WATERS OF PHOSPHORESCENT BAY

One of the major attractions on the island is **Mosquito Bay,** also called Phosphorescent Bay, with its glowing waters produced by tiny bioluminescent organisms that live near the surface. These organisms dart away from boats, leaving eerie blue-white trails of phosphorescence. *The Vieques Times* wrote: "By any name the bay can be a magical, psychedelic experience and few places in the world can even come close to the intensity of concentration of the dinoflagellates called pyrodiniums (whirling fire). They are tiny ($1/_{500}$-inch) swimming creatures that light up like fireflies when disturbed but nowhere are there so many fireflies. Here a gallon of bay water may contain almost three-quarters of a million." The ideal time to tour is on a cloudy, moonless night, and you should wear a bathing suit since it's possible to swim in these glowing waters. A company named **18° North** (☎ 787/741-8600) runs tours on powerboats from Esperanza, and **Shannon Grasso** (☎ 787/741-0717) operates trips aboard her *Luminosa* from La Casa del Francés (see "Where to Stay," below). These trips are not offered around the time of the full moon. The charge for these trips is $15, and most jaunts last about 90 minutes.

WHERE TO STAY

Bananas

Barrio Esperanza (P.O. Box 1300), Vieques, PR 00765. ☎ **787/741-8700.** 7 rms, 1 suite. $45 double; $60 suite. AE, MC, V.

While filming *Heartbreak Ridge* in 1986, the actors and crew transformed this establishment's windswept porch into their second home. Located on the south shore east of the U.S. Naval Reservation, and best known for its bar and restaurant, this guesthouse also has seven simple, clean, and comfortable rooms, some recently renovated. Each has a ceiling fan; however, three rooms and the suite are air-conditioned, with their own screened-in porches.

Reader Kathleen R. Schweizer writes, "There is a loud salsa bar several feet away from the rooms on the east side of Bananas. The music starts playing at 10 in the morning and lasts until around 2am. Should you decide to stay at Bananas, be sure to ask for a room on the west side of the hotel."

La Casa del Francés

Barrio Esperanza (P.O. Box 458), Vieques, PR 00765. ☎ **787/741-3751.** Fax 787/741-2330. 18 rms. Winter (including MAP), $175 double; off-season, $96.30 double. AE, MC, V.

La Casa del Francés is about a 15-minute drive southeast of Isabel Segunda, just north of the center of Esperanza. Set in a field near the southern coastline, its columns and imposing facade rise dramatically from the lush surrounding landscape. It was built in 1905 by a retired French general as the headquarters for his working sugar plantation. In the 1950s it was acquired by Irving Greenblatt, who installed a swimming pool and, with his longtime manager, Frank Celeste, transformed 18 of its high-ceilinged bedrooms into old-fashioned hotel accommodations. Many rooms enjoy access to the sweeping two-story verandas ringing the white facade.

Scattered throughout the dozen acres surrounding the main house are century-old tropical trees. The estate's architectural highlight is the two-story interior courtyard whose center is lush with bamboo, palms, philodendron, and well-chosen examples of Haitian art.

The fixed-price dinners, which cost $15 each, attract many island residents who partake of Italian, barbecue, or Puerto Rican buffets which the staff spreads out beneath a 200-year-old mahogany tree.

New Dawn's Caribbean Retreat and Guest House

Rte. 995, km 1.2 (P.O. Box 1512), Vieques, PR 00765. ☎ **787/741-0495.** 6 rms (none with bath), 6 dormitory-style bunks. Year-round, $40 double; $18 per person for a bunk in a coed bunkhouse. Discounts available for stays of 1 week or more, especially for groups. No credit cards.

Situated on a forested hillside 3 miles from Sun Bay in the center of the island, north of Esperanza and southwest of Isabel Segunda, this barebones establishment caters to budget-conscious campers and youthful adventurers. Its centerpiece is a plywood-sided house originally built by Gail Burchard (an Indiana-born nurse) and her students in 1986 when she was teaching a course in carpentry for women. Today, the guesthouse enjoys a spacious porch outfitted with hammocks and swinging chairs. A series of outbuildings contain a bath house, communal kitchen, and camp-style bunkhouse with six beds. The half-dozen conventional bedrooms, on the guesthouse's second floor, are rustic and simple, usually with sleeping lofts and few (if any) extra amenities. Despite the simplicity of the setting, Ms. Burchard offers, for an extra fee, the use of a washing machine and rentals of snorkeling gear, bicycles, and air mattresses for campers.

Also available, through referrals, are palm-weaving lessons, horseback riding, guided historical tours of Vieques, night swims and kayak trips through Phosphorescent Bay, and guided nature hikes.

Between May and December the 5-acre site is often rented as a conference center to church groups, schools, and women's groups from North America.

Trade Winds Guesthouse

107C Flamboyan, Barrio Esperanza (P.O. Box 1012), Vieques, PR 00765. ☎ or fax **787/741-8666.** 11 rms, 3 studios. $55–$70 double; $75–$85 studio. AE, MC, V.

Along the shore on the south side of the island, in the fishing village of Esperanza, this oceanside guesthouse offers nine units, four of them air-conditioned and with terraces. The others have ceiling fans, and some also have terraces. The establishment is well known for its hospitable atmosphere and its open-air restaurant overlooking the ocean (see "Where to Dine," below).

Vieques Ocean View Hotel

Isabel Segunda (P.O. Box 124), Vieques, PR 00765. ☎ **787/741-3696.** Fax 787/741-1793. 32 rms. A/C TV. $55 double. Breakfast $5 extra. AE, MC, V.

Situated in the heart of Isabel Segunda, directly on the coast and a block from the wharf where the ferryboat lands, this three-story building is one of the tallest on Vieques. Built in the early 1980s, it offers simple rooms with uncomplicated furniture and balconies overlooking either the sea or the town. None of the rooms has a phone. There's a bar on the premises and a Chinese restaurant in the basement. Breakfast is not available at the hotel, but everyone crosses the street to Lydia's Bakery, where freshly baked bread, strong coffee, and bacon and eggs are served.

WHERE TO DINE

Bananas Restaurant

In the Bananas, Barrio Esperanza. ☎ **787/741-8700.** Main dishes $13–$14.75; sandwiches at lunch $2.75–$7.25. AE, MC, V. Sun–Thurs noon–10pm, Fri–Sat noon–11pm. INTERNATIONAL.

Bananas has some of the best food on the island—all familiar dishes to you, including charbroiled New York sirloin, barbecue back ribs, and marinated boneless breast of chicken. Slightly more exotic main dishes might include the grilled jerk chicken or the lemon chicken sautéed in butter and wine. You might opt instead for the grilled fresh catch of the day served with lemon butter. The chef also makes pizzas with a wide choice of toppings. Baked potato in four different versions, including one with broccoli and chili, also appears on the menu. Sandwiches are available at lunch, including grilled chicken and fresh fish. You can also order a juicy half-pound burger with a number of toppings.

Richard's Café

Calle Antonio Mellado, Isabel Segunda. ☎ **787/741-5242.** Main courses $3.95–$25. AE, MC, V. Tues–Sat 11:30am–2:30pm and 6–10:30pm. PUERTO RICAN/VIEQUES.

This place, with its oilcloth decor, might seem like an unpretentious roadside coffee shop, but it's actually a substantial restaurant, serving the freshest seafood on the island. It specializes in both Puerto Rican and Vieques cuisine, and offers air-conditioned comfort. You can order a snail or octopus salad, pork chops, or perhaps a savory version of asopao made from well-spiced chunks of lobster or shrimp. Or you can have a less expensive meal: Try one of the well-stuffed sandwiches or the special of the day such as fried chicken with rice, beans, salad, and bread—a meal unto itself.

Trade Winds

In Trade Winds Guesthouse, Barrio Esperanza. ☎ **787/741-8666.** Reservations recommended. Main courses $10.50–$18.50. MC, V. Daily 11:30am–2pm and 6:30–9pm; bar, daily 5pm–midnight). Closed off-season. STEAK/SEAFOOD.

You'll find this guesthouse restaurant at the ocean esplanade on the south side of the island in the fishing village of Esperanza (see "Where to Stay," above). It features the Topside Bar for relaxing drinks, with a view of the water, and the Upper Deck for open-air dining. The chef's specialty, with real island flavor, is *piñon,* made with layers of sweet plantains, tomato sauce, green beans, spiced beef, and mozzarella. For many, this is an acquired taste; you may prefer the best steak on the island, a New York sirloin, 12 ounces, cooked just right over the charbroiler and served with a baked potato and a house or Caesar salad. The fresh fish special of the night varies with the catch of the day but is usually a good item to order, as is the jumbo shrimp sautéed with fresh garlic and lemon. Black bean soup is a good opener. Prime rib is a Friday night feature.

2 Culebra

52 miles E of San Juan; 18 miles E of Fajardo

A tranquil, inviting little island, Culebra lies in a mini-archipelago of 24 chunks of land, rocks, and cays 18 miles east of Puerto Rico's main island, halfway to St. Thomas, U.S. Virgin Islands. With only 2,000 residents, it's just 7 miles long and 3 miles wide, and the landscape is dotted with everything from scrub and cacti to poincianas, frangipanis, and coconut palms.

Today vacationers and boaters can explore the island's beauties, both on land and under water. Culebra's white-sand beaches (especially Flamenco Beach), its clear waters, and its long coral reefs invite swimmers, snorkelers, and scuba divers.

This little-known, year-round vacation spot in what was once called the Spanish Virgin Islands was settled as a Spanish colony in 1886, but like Puerto Rico and Vieques, it became part of the United States after the Spanish-American War in 1898. In fact Culebra's only town, a fishing village called **Dewey,** was named for Admiral George Dewey, an American hero of that war, although the locals defiantly call it **Puebla.**

Both illustrious and notorious characters have visited Culebra in the past. It is believed that Columbus spotted the island on his second voyage to the New World in 1493. When the Spanish started colonizing Puerto Rico, many of the Taíno Indians fled to Culebra as a last refuge. It wasn't many decades later that the swashbuckling Sir Henry Morgan and other notorious pirates used Culebra as a hideout. The island supposedly still shelters their buried loot.

From 1909 until 1975, Culebra was used by the U.S. Navy as a gunnery range, even serving as a practice bomb site in World War II. Today the four tracts of the **Culebra Wildlife Refuge,** plus 23 other offshore islands, are managed by the U.S. Fish and Wildlife Service. The refuge is one of the most important turtle-nesting sites in the Caribbean. It also houses large seabird colonies, notably terns and boobies.

Culebrita, a mile-long coral-isle satellite of Culebra, has a hilltop lighthouse and crescent beaches.

ESSENTIALS

GETTING THERE   Flamenco Airways, Inc. (☎ 787/725-7707 in San Juan), flies to Culebra four times daily from San Juan's Isla Grande Airport. A round-trip ticket costs $60 per person.

The Puerto Rico Port Authority operates one or two ferryboats a day (depending on the day of the week) from the mainland port of Fajardo to Culebra; the trip takes about an hour. The round-trip fare is $4.50 for adults, $2.25 for children 14 and under. For information and reservations, call **787/863-0705** (or 800/981-2005 in Puerto Rico only).

PACKAGE TOURS

If you don't want to make your own arrangements, you can visit Culebra with **Tropix Wellness Tours** (☎ 787/268-2173; fax 787/268-1722), whose "Happy Turtle Tour" includes a half-day kayaking-and-snorkeling expedition and a visit to the sea turtles' nesting sites during the spring and summer. The tour costs $315 per person, including airfare from Rivas Dominici Airport in Miramar to Culebra Airport, three nights' accommodations, continental breakfast, and equipment for the escorted tours.

BEACHES & DIVING

The island's most popular beach is **Flamenco Beach,** a horseshoe-shaped cover whose waterfront is about a mile long. Set on the island's northwestern edge, it's by far the most popular, partly because of its nearness to Dewey, partly because of its soft sands.

More isolated is **Zoni Beach,** a 1-mile strip of sandy beachfront flanked on the landward side by large boulders and scrub. Set on the island's northeastern edge, about 7 miles from Dewey (Puebla) on the island's opposite side, it's one of the most beautiful on the island. Snorkelers (but not scuba divers) find it particularly intriguing, despite the surf that makes underwater visibility a bit murky during rough weather.

Culebra's only dive operation belongs to Illinois-born Gene Thomas, a resident of Culebra since the 1970s and the man who virtually brought scuba to the island.

From Leathernecks to Leatherbacks

In one of his last executive orders before leaving the White House in 1909, President Theodore Roosevelt established Culebra as a national wildlife refuge. Today this pint-sized archipelago, one of the last frontier outposts of the Caribbean, is one of only two nesting sites in the United States for the leatherback sea turtle, one of the world's largest marine reptiles. It and four other endangered species of turtles—the loggerhead, green, and hawksbill—are protected by the wildlife refuge.

Although it was a national wildlife refuge, the U.S. Navy and Marine Corps began to use Culebra as a practice bombing range during World War II. Culebrans massively protested the decision, especially when word leaked out that the navy planned to relocate them to Vieques.

Arguments between Culebrans and the U.S. government didn't end with the war. Molotov cocktail–throwing violence erupted in 1971, with several islanders imprisoned for their hostile acts of defiance. President Richard Nixon finally brought peace to Culebra by ending all weapons training on the island. By 1975, the Navy swabbies and Marine Corps leathernecks had ceased shelling the island.

The leathernecks may be long gone, but the leatherbacks are still here. The **Culebra Leatherback Project,** P.O. Box 190, Culebra, PR 00775 (☎ 787/742-0115), gathers statistics about the nesting sea turtles and takes applications on a first-come, first-served basis from ecotourists who want to participate in its nightly patrols from April to June. Early reservations are advised, since many nature-minded travelers want to participate.

Known for its beautiful corals, unspoiled underwater vistas, and an absence of other divers, Culebra is like the rest of the Caribbean used to be before the huge flood of divers began exploring the sea. At least 50 dive sites, on all sides of the island, are considered worthwhile.

His operation is **Culebra Dive Shop,** 317 Fulladoza St. (☎ **787/742-3555**). A resort course for novice divers includes training in a sheltered cove and a tank dive in 15 to 20 feet of water ($65). Full PADI certification costs $400 and requires 5 days of participation in both classroom and ocean experience. Certified divers pay $75 for a two-tank open-water dive. Thomas provides all the equipment you'll need for any of the above-mentioned dive experiences. It's rare that more than six divers go out in one of his boats on any day; he prefers to keep his operation as small and personalized as possible.

WHERE TO STAY

Bayview Villas

Punta Aloe, Culebra, PR 00775 (mailing address: Parque de las Fuentes 2402, Hato Rey, Puerto Rico 00918). ☎ **787/765-5711** or 787/742-3392. 2 villas. TV. Year-round, $210–$235 double. MC, V.

Located on a hillside above Ensenada Honda a mile east of Dewey, at the end of a privately maintained road, this compound consists of two separate villas, each of which overlooks the sea and has two floors and comfortably solid pinewood furniture. Each has a kitchen and two bedrooms, suitable for housing four occupants and, under cramped conditions, up to six. Each unit has high peaked ceilings with fans, washing machines, and sliding glass doors leading onto terraces. Although daily rentals are available, the villas are often taken by Puerto Rican "mainlanders" for periods of a week or more.

Club Seabourne

Fulladosa Rd. (P.O. Box 357), Culebra, PR 00775. ☎ **787/742-3169.** Fax 787/742-3176. 15 units. A/C. Year-round, $90–$105 double in the clubhouse; $115 double in a villa or the Crow's Nest. Rates include continental breakfast. AE, MC, V. From Dewey (Puebla), follow Fulladosa Road along the south side of the bay for 1¹/₂ miles.

Across the road from an inlet of the sea, about an 8-minute drive from the center of town, is this concrete-and-wood structure set in a garden of crotons and palms, lying at the mouth of one of the island's best harbors, Ensenada Honda. It offers 10 villas and 4 rooms inside the clubhouse. All units are equipped with small refrigerators and are air-conditioned. Dive packages and day sails can be arranged at the office.

Overlooking Fulladosa Bay, the club's dining room offers some of the best food on Culebra, with fresh lobster, shrimp, snapper, grouper, and conch, as well as steaks and other specialty dishes, served nightly from 6 to 10pm. The hotel also has a large patio bar with a nightly happy hour, plus the only freshwater swimming pool on the island.

Culebra Island Villas

Punta Aloe (P.O. Box 596), Culebra, PR 00775. ☎ **787/742-0333.** Fax 787/458-5591. 10 units. Winter, $495–$595 per week studio or one-bedroom suite; $725–$895 per week two-bedroom suite. Off-season, $350–$495 per week studio or one-bedroom suite; $595–$725 per week two-bedroom suite. No credit cards.

Located south of Ensenada Honda, half a mile south of Dewey, and separated from the Culebran "mainland" by a canal with a drawbridge, lies Punta Aloe, whose forested hillsides shelter about 15 privately owned houses. Each floor in four of these houses, which were built by different owners between 1980 and around 1990, is available for weekly rental. Each offers a view of the bay, wood-sided construction, and a simple kitchen. The studios and one-bedroom suites can accommodate one to three guests; the two-bedroom suites can hold two to six occupants. None of the units has air-conditioning, although the building has direct access to the trade winds. No meals are available, nor is there maid service.

Flamenco Resort & Fishing Club

10 Pedro Marquez, Flamenco Beach (P.O. Box 183), Culebra, PR 00645. ☎ **787/742-3144.** 32 units. A/C. Winter, $95 studio; $115–$135 one-bedroom suite; $160 two-bedroom suite. Off-season, $85 studio; $105–$125 one-bedroom suite; $150 two-bedroom suite. MC, V.

This is the only guesthouse or hotel near the white sands of Flamenco Beach, one of the best in the region. Each unit has its own kitchen. This place would really be attractive to a group of friends or an extended family, since the accommodations are situated around spacious sitting rooms much like those in an informal beach house. The owner has studio apartments suitable for two, one-bedroom apartments suitable for four, and two-bedroom bungalows suitable for six. All units are air-conditioned. Varied activities are available, including day trips on a sailboat to one of the nearby islands, snorkeling, and fishing expeditions. Evening meals are served at Marta's al Fresco (see "Where to Dine," below).

WHERE TO DINE

El Batey

250 Carretera. ☎ **787/742-3828.** Sandwiches $2.50–$3.75. MC, V. Daily 9am–6pm. DELI.

Across from the harbor is a large, clean establishment that maintains a full bar and prepares an array of deli-style sandwiches. Coffee and doughnuts are also offered every morning. They'll hand you a cold beer when the afternoon sun is out, and the pool tables make the place lively, especially on weekends when many locals are there. Weekdays, it's much calmer. The owners, Digna Feliciano and Tomás Ayala, have many fans on the island. Breezes from the harbor cool the place.

Marta's al Fresco

10 Pedro Marquez. ☎ **787/742-3575.** Sandwiches $2.75–$3; main courses $5.75–$12.75. MC, V. Daily 11am–1pm and 6–10pm. AMERICAN/PUERTO RICAN.

In a simple building near the wharf where the ferryboats from Puerto Rico's mainland arrive and depart, this restaurant is named after its owner's wife, Marta. The space is divided into two sections: a deli on one side and a more formal *comedor* (dining room) on the other. The furniture is made of rattan, and big windows offer a view of the sea. In addition to the deli-style sandwiches, the menu lists a wide range of fresh seafood, as well as steaks, asopaos, burgers, and pork chops with rice and beans.

12

A Side Trip to St. Thomas: Shopping Capital of the Caribbean

St. Thomas is the most popular excursion from Puerto Rico—it's just a short hop from San Juan. Thousands of visitors make a quick day trip to take advantage of the $1,200 duty-free shopping limit available to Americans. Although San Juan has bargains galore, the duty-free shopping of St. Thomas is extremely appealing.

This incentive, combined with the fact that many flights, especially those of American Airlines, stop in San Juan before continuing on to St. Thomas, make this U.S. Virgin Island an interesting and fairly easy day trip. Some passengers visit just for an afternoon, whereas others settle in for overnight stays. We've also included some restaurants and a few hotels for those who'd like to stay a little bit longer.

Sometimes a ticket to St. Thomas that takes you from the mainland U.S. to San Juan, where you change planes, is actually cheaper than the APEX nonstop fare to Puerto Rico. Therefore, you may want to include both Puerto Rico and the U.S. Virgin Islands in one vacation. See *Frommer's The Virgin Islands* for more details, and also call **American Airlines (☎ 800/433-7300)** to get the current fares for a combined Puerto Rico–St. Thomas trip.

1 St. Thomas Orientation

The busiest cruise-ship harbor in the West Indies, St. Thomas is the second largest of the U.S. Virgin Islands and lies about 40 miles north of the larger island of St. Croix. St. Thomas is about 12 miles long and 3 miles wide; its north shore faces the Atlantic Ocean, and the calmer Caribbean washes the island's south side. It's not unheard of to find the sun shining in the south while the north is experiencing showers.

Vacationers discovered St. Thomas after World War II and they've been flocking to the island in increasing numbers ever since. Shopping, sun, and sights have proved to be major draws, and tourism has made the standard of living here one of the highest in the Caribbean.

The town of Charlotte Amalie is the capital of the Virgin Islands and the shopping mecca of the Caribbean. The island is indeed a boon for cruise-ship shoppers, who frequently flood Main Street, where dozens of shops are located within a three- or four-block radius. This area can get very crowded, but it's away from the beaches, major hotels, most restaurants, and entertainment facilities, so the

What's Special About St. Thomas

Beaches
- Magens Bay, 3 miles north of Charlotte Amalie, one of the most beautiful beaches in the world, although not as well maintained as it once was.
- Stouffer Grand Beach, one of the island's most stunning, with many water sports available.
- Sapphire Beach, with its luxury hotel complexes in the background, one of the finest on the island, and a favorite of windsurfers.

Sights
- Coral World, a marine complex rebuilt after 1995 hurricane destruction, featuring a three-story underwater observation tower 100 feet offshore.
- Jim Tillett's Art Gallery and Boutique, built around an old plantation-era sugar mill.

Great Towns and Villages
- Charlotte Amalie, the capital of St. Thomas, one of the most beautiful port cities in the Caribbean.
- Frenchtown, settled by the descendants of immigrants from the French islands, famous for its "cha-chas," or straw hats.

Historic Buildings
- The St. Thomas Synagogue, second oldest in America, built by Sephardic Jews in 1833.
- Government House, at Government Hill in Charlotte Amalie, residence of the U.S. Virgin Islands' governor.
- Fort Christian, constructed by the Danes in 1671 and named for King Christian V.

crowds don't have to interfere with your enjoyment if you're here just to soak up the sun.

One important note: If you're visiting in August, bring along some mosquito repellent.

VISITOR INFORMATION   On St. Thomas, the **Visitors Center** is at Emancipation Square (☎ 809/774-8784). Much useful information is dispensed from here, and you can pick up a copy of *St. Thomas This Week,* which includes maps of St. Thomas and St. John as well as descriptions of the vast array of shopping possibilities.

MAIN STREETS & ARTERIES   The capital, Charlotte Amalie, is the only town on St. Thomas. Bordering the waterfront, its seaside promenade is called **Waterfront Highway,** or just the Waterfront. Its old Danish name is Kyst Vejen. From the Waterfront, you can take any number of streets or alleyways leading back into town to the **Main Street,** or Dronningens Gade. Principal links between Main Street and the Waterfront include **Raadets Gade, Tolbod Gade, Storetvaer Gade,** and **Strand Gade.**

Main Street is aptly named, since it is the center of the capital and the site of the major shops. The western part of Main Street is **Market Square,** which was once the site of the biggest slave market auctions in the Caribbean Basin. It lies near the intersection with Strand Gade. Today it's an open-air block of stalls where island gardeners sell their produce, particularly on Saturday (closed Sunday). Go early in the morning to see the market at its best.

Running parallel to Main Street and lying north of it is **Back Street,** or Vimmelskaft Gade, which has many stores, including some of the less expensive ones. Although quite dangerous to walk along at night, it's reasonably safe for daytime shopping.

In the eastern part of town, midway between Talbod Gade and Fort Pladsen, is **Emancipation Park,** northwest of Fort Christian, commemorating the liberation of the slaves in 1848. Most of the major historical buildings, including the Legislative Building, Fort Christian, and Government House, are within a short walk of this park.

Southeast of the park looms **Fort Christian,** crowned by a clock tower and painted a rusty red, constructed by the Danes in 1671. The **Legislative Building,** seat of the elected government of the U.S. Virgin Islands, is on the harbor side of the fort.

Kongens Gade (King's Street) leads to Government House on Government Hill, which overlooks the town and the harbor. Here stands a white-brick building, Government House, dating from 1867.

Between **Hotel 1829,** a former mansion constructed that year by a French sea captain, and Government House is a staircase known as the **Street of 99 Steps.** Actually, someone miscounted; it should be called the Street of 103 Steps. These steps lead to the summit of Government Hill.

Nearby are the remains of the 17th-century **Fort Skytsborg,** or Blackbeard's Tower, a reference to the notorious pirate Edward Teach, who is said to have spied on treasure galleons entering the harbor in the 1700s from here. Today an 11-room hotel, Blackbeard's Castle, stands here.

This should not be confused with **Bluebeard's Tower,** which crowns a 300-foot hill at the eastern edge of town. This is the site of what is the best known (but not the best) hotel in the Virgin Islands—Bluebeard's Castle.

GETTING AROUND   St. Thomas has the best public transportation of any island in the U.S. chain. Administered by the government, **Vitran buses** service Charlotte Amalie, its outlying neighborhoods, and the countryside as far away as Red Hook. Vitran stops are found at reasonable intervals beside each of the most important traffic arteries on St. Thomas. Among the most visible are those along the edges of Veterans Drive on Charlotte Amalie. Buses run daily between 6am and 9pm. A one-way ride costs 75¢ within Charlotte Amalie, $1 for rides from Charlotte Amalie into its outer neighborhoods, and $3 for rides from Charlotte Amalie to such other communities as Red Hook, site of ferryboat departures for St. John. For information about Vitran buses, their stops and schedules, call **809/774-5678.**

2 Shopping

Shoppers have not only the benefits of St. Thomas's liberal duty-free allowances, but also the opportunity to buy well-known brand names that may be on sale at 40% below stateside prices. However, that doesn't happen every day. To find true value, you may have to plow through a lot of junk. Many items offered for sale—binoculars, stereos, watches, and cameras—can be matched in price at your hometown discount store. Therefore, you need to know the price back home to determine if you are in fact saving money. Having sounded that warning, we'll survey some St. Thomas shops where we have personally found good buys. There are lots more you can discover on your own.

Most of the shops, some of which occupy former pirate warehouses, are open from 9am to 5pm, and some stay open later. Nearly all stores close on Sunday and major holidays—that is, unless a cruise ship is in port. Few shopkeepers can stand the prospect of hundreds of potential customers, their purses full, wandering by their padlocked doors. Therefore, those gates are likely to swing open, at least for half a day on Sunday. Friday is the biggest cruise-ship visiting day at Charlotte Amalie (one day we counted eight ships at one time)—so try to avoid shopping then.

Nearly all the major shopping in St. Thomas is concentrated along the harbor of Charlotte Amalie. Cruise-ship passengers mainly shop at the **Havensight Mall** where they disembark at the eastern edge of Charlotte Amalie. The principal shopping street is called **Main Street** or Dronningens Gade (its old Danish name). North of this street is another merchandise-loaded street called **Back Street** or Vimmelskaft.

Many shops are also spread along the **Waterfront Highway** (also called Kyst Vejen). Between these major streets or boulevards are a series of side streets, walkways, and alleys, all filled with shops. Major shopping streets are Tolbod Gade, Raadets Gade, Royal Dane Mall, Palm Passage, Storetvaer Gade, and Strand Gade.

All the major stores in St. Thomas are located by number on an excellent map in the center of the publication *St. Thomas This Week,* distributed free to all arriving plane and boat passengers.

If you want to combine a little history with shopping, you might go into the courtyard of the old **Pissarro Building,** entered through an archway off Main Street. The impressionist painter lived here as a child. The old apartments have been turned into a warren of interesting shops.

✪ A. H. Riise Gift & Liquor Stores

37 Main St., at A. H. Riise Gift & Liquor Mall (perfume and liquor branch stores at Havensight Mall). ☎ **809/776-2303** or 800/524-2037.

St. Thomas's oldest outlet for luxury items such as jewelry, crystal, china, and perfumes is still the largest. Everything is displayed in a 19th-century Danish warehouse, extending from Main Street to the waterfront. The store boasts a collection of fine jewelry and watches from Europe's leading craftspeople, including Vacheron Constantin, Bulgari, Omega, and Gucci, as well as a wide selection of Greek gold, platinum, and precious gemstone jewelry.

The island's most extensive selection of liquors and unique liqueur specialties are found here too, as well as quality imported cigars presented in a climate-controlled walk-in humidor. You can sample your favorites at a free tasting bar. Delivery to cruise ships and the airport is free.

A.H. Riise also offers a vast selection of fragrances for both men and women, along with the world's best known names in cosmetics and treatment products. Featured in the china and crystal department are Waterford, Lalique, Baccarat, and Rosenthal among others.

Specialty shops in the complex sell Caribbean gifts, books, clothing, food, art prints, note cards, and designer sunglasses.

Open Monday through Saturday from 9am to 5pm and Sunday from 9am to 1pm if cruise ships are in port.

✪ Bernard K. Passman

38A Main St. ☎ **809/777-4580.** Branch at Riise's Walkway. ☎ 809/777-4580.

Bernard K. Passman is the world's leading sculptor of black coral art and jewelry, famous for his "Can Can Girl" and his four statues of Charlie Chaplin. Starting in Grand Cayman, he learned to fashion exquisite treasures from black coral found 200 feet under the sea that resembles dry and flaky twigs in its natural shape. After

Shopping in Charlotte Amalie

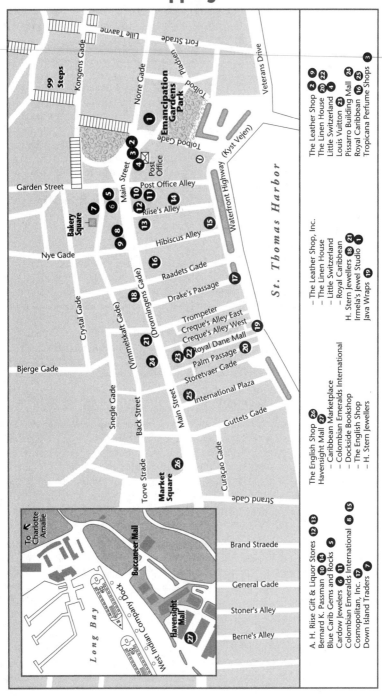

polishing and embellishing with gold and diamonds, some of Passman's work has been treasured by royalty. There are simpler and more affordably priced pieces for sale as well. Open Monday through Saturday 9am to 5pm.

Blue Carib Gems and Rocks
2 Back St. ☎ **809/774-8525.**

For a decade the owners prospected for gemstones in the Caribbean, and these stones have been brought direct from the mine to you in this store behind Little Switzerland. The raw stones are cut and polished, then fashioned into jewelry by the lost-wax process. On one side of the premises you can see the craftspeople at work, and on the other side you can view their finished products—including such handsomely set stones as larimar, the sea/sky-blue-patterned variety of pectolite found only in the Caribbean. A lifetime guarantee is given on all handcrafted jewelry. Since the items are locally made, they are duty-free and not included in the $1,200 exemption. (Incidentally, this establishment also provides emergency eyeglass repair.) Open Monday through Saturday from 9am to 4:30pm.

Cardow Jewelers
39 Main St. ☎ **809/774-1140.**

Often called the Tiffany's of the Caribbean, it boasts the largest selection of fine jewelry in the world. This fabulous shop, which has more than 20,000 rings on display, provides savings because of its worldwide direct buying, large turnover, and duty-free prices. Unusual and traditional designs are offered in diamonds, emeralds, rubies, sapphires, and Brazilian stones, as well as in pearls. Cardow has a whole wall of Italian gold chains. Antique-coin jewelry is also featured. The Treasure Cove has case after case of fine gold jewelry, all priced under $200. Open Monday through Saturday 9am to 5pm.

Caribbean Marketplace
Havensight Mall (Building III). ☎ **809/776-5400.**

The best selections of Caribbean handcrafts are found here, including Sunny Caribee products—a vast array of condiments (ranging from spicy peppercorns to nutmeg mustard). There's also a wide selection of Sunny Caribbee's botanical products such as foaming rosemary bath gel plus natural beauty soaps made from such concoctions as chamomile or coconut. Other items range from steel-pan drums from Trinidad to wooden Jamaican jigsaw puzzles, from Indonesian batiks to Cayman Islands' bikinis. Open Monday through Saturday from 9am to 5pm.

Colombian Emeralds International
Havensight Mall. ☎ **809/774-2442.**

The Colombian Emerald stores are renowned throughout the Caribbean for offering the finest collection of Colombian emeralds, both set and unset. Here you buy direct from the source, cutting out the middle person which can mean significant savings for you. In addition to jewelry, the shop stocks some of the world's finest watches, including Raymond Weil and Seiko. There's another outlet on Main Street. Open daily 9am to 5pm.

Cosmopolitan, Inc.
Drakes Passage and the Waterfront. ☎ **809/776-2040.**

Since 1973 this store has drawn a lot of repeat business. Its shoe salon features Bally of Switzerland. More recently, Cosmopolitan added Bally handbags, which have proved a popular item. In swimwear, it provides one of the best selections of Gottex of Israel for women and Gottex, Hom, Lahco of Switzerland, and Fila for men.

A menswear section offers Paul & Shark from Italy, and Burma Bibas sports shirts. The shop also features ties of Gianni Versace and Pancaldi of Italy (in both instances those ties are at least 30% less than the stateside price). It also carries an array of Nautica sportswear for men. Open Monday through Saturday 9am to 5pm.

Down Island Traders
Veteran's Drive. ☎ 809/776-4641.

The aroma of spices will lead you to this original native market. These outlets have Charlotte Amalie's most attractive display of spices, teas, seasonings, jams, and condiments, most of which are prepared from natural Caribbean products. The owner also carries candies and jellies, a line of local cookbooks, silk-screened island designs on T-shirts and bags, Haitian metal sculpture, and children's gifts. Open Monday through Saturday from 9am to 5pm.

The English Shop
Main St. at Market Sq. ☎ 809/774-3495.

This store, along with a branch at Havensight Mall (☎ 809/776-3776), has a wide selection of china, crystal, and figurines from the world's top makers. The Market Square outlet is open Monday through Saturday from 9:30am to 5pm, and the Havensight Mall branch is open daily from 9am to 5pm.

H. Stern Jewellers
Havensight Mall and Main St. ☎ 809/776-1939.

This international jeweler is one of the most respected in the business worldwide, with some 175 outlets. In a world of fake jewelry and fake everything, it's good to know there's still a name you can count on. It is a leading competitor on the island to Cardow (see above). You'll find colorful gem and jewel creations at five locations on St. Thomas—two on Main Street, one in Havensight Mall, and one each at Bluebeard's Castle and Frenchman's Reef Hotel—as well as in a store on St. Maarten, Netherlands Antilles. Every shop has the same duty-free prices, a considerable savings for visiting shoppers. Stern gives worldwide guaranteed service, including a 1-year exchange privilege. Open Monday through Saturday 9am to 5pm.

Irmela's Jewel Studio
In the Old Grand Hotel, at the beginning of Main St. ☎ 809/774-5875 or 800/524-2047.

Irmela's has made a name for itself in the highly competitive jewelry business on St. Thomas. Here the jewelry is unique, either custom-designed by Irmela and handmade in her studio or imported from around the world. Irmela has the largest selection of cultured pearls in the Caribbean, including freshwater Biwa, South Sea, and natural-color black Tahitian pearls. Choose from hundreds of clasps and pearl shorteners. Irmela has a large selection of unset stones, such as rubies, sapphires, emeralds, and unusual ones including tanzanite and alexandrite. Diamonds range from pear-shaped to emerald cut, marquis, and even heart-shaped, in sizes from tiny two-pointers to several carats. Open Monday through Saturday 8:30am to 5pm.

Java Wraps
35 Royal Dane Mall. ☎ 809/774-3700.

From the East Indies to the West Indies, Java Wraps is known for hand-batiked women's, men's, and children's resortwear. A kaleidoscope of colors and prints dazzle the eye. Every day the store evokes the celluloid image of Dorothy Lamour as local salespeople demonstrate wrapping and tying Java Wraps's beach pareos and sarongs. The men's shirts come in a wide array of tropical and flamboyant prints, and there's also clothing for children. Open Monday through Saturday 9am to 5pm.

The Leather Shop, Inc.
1 Main St. and Havensight Mall. ☎ **809/776-0290.**

Here you'll find the best selection from these Italian designers: Fendi, Bottega Veneta, Michel Clo, Furla, Prada, and Il Bisonte. There are many styles of handbags, belts, wallets, briefcases, and attaché cases. Some of these items are very expensive, of course, but there's stuff here anyone can afford, too, including backpacks, carry-ons, and Mola bags from Colombia. Open Monday through Saturday 9am to 5pm. If you're looking for a bargain, ask them to direct you to the outlet store on Back Street selling closeouts at prices that are sometimes 50% off stateside retail tags.

The Linen House
7A Royal Dane Mall. ☎ **809/774-8117.**

This is considered the best store for linens in the West Indies. It has another location at Havensight Mall (☎ **809/774-0868**). You'll find a wide selection of place mats, decorative tablecloths, and many hand-embroidered goods. There are many high-fashion styles. Both stores are open Monday through Saturday from 9am to 5pm. The shop at the Royal Dane Mall is open on Sunday from 9am to noon, and the one at Havensight Mall is open Sunday from 9am to 4pm.

Little Switzerland
5 Main St. ☎ **809/776-2010.**

A branch of this shop seems to appear on virtually every island in the Caribbean. Its concentration of watches, including Omega and Rolex, are topped by no one. But it also sells a wide variety of other objects as well, including cuckoo clocks and music boxes. The china, especially the Royal Worcester and Rosenthal collection, is outstanding, as are their crystal and jewelry. Little Switzerland also maintains the official outlets for Hummel, Lladró, and Swarovski figurines. Open Monday through Saturday from 9am to 5pm.

There are several other branches of this store on the island, especially at the Havensight Mall, but the main store has the better selection.

Louis Vuitton
24 Main St., at Palm Passage. ☎ **809/774-3644.**

For fine leather goods, you can't beat Louis Vuitton, where the complete line by the world-famous French designer is available. We've seen fake Vuitton luggage hawked on the island, but this store carries the real thing. Suitcases, handbags, wallets, and other accessories are available here. Open Monday through Saturday 9am to 5pm.

Royal Caribbean
33 Main St. ☎ **809/776-4110.**

With additional branches at 23 Main Street (☎ **809/776-5449**) and Havensight Mall (☎ **809/776-8890**), this is the largest camera and electronics store in the Caribbean. Since 1977 it has offered good values in top-brand cameras and electronic equipment, including all accessories. Royal Caribbean is the authorized Sony dealer, with a complete selection of its products. It also has good buys in famous-name watches, Mikimoto pearls, Dupont and Dunhill lighters, jewelry for both men and women, and gift items. Open Monday through Saturday from 9am to 5pm. The shop at Havensight Mall remains open until 9pm on Friday.

Tillett Gardens
4126 Anna's Retreat, Tutu. ☎ **809/775-1929.**

Since 1959 Tillett Gardens has been the island's arts-and-crafts center, featuring an art gallery and the screen printing studio of Jim Tillett. This tropical compound is a series of buildings housing arts-and-crafts studios, galleries, and an outdoor garden restaurant and bar. The garden was once an old Danish farm, setting for tri-annual festivals the third weekend in March, the second in August, and Thanksgiving weekend. Prints in the galleries start as low as $10. The best work of local artists is displayed here—originals in oils, watercolors, and acrylics. The Tillett prints on fine canvas are all one-of-a-kind. The famous Tillett maps on canvas are priced from $30. There are even daily iguana feedings. Take Route 38 east from Charlotte Amalie. Open Monday through Saturday from 9am to 5pm.

Tropicana Perfume Shoppes
2 and 14 Main St. ☎ **809/774-0010** or 800/233-7948.

These two stores stand at the beginning of Main Street near the Emancipation Gardens Post Office. The first is billed as the largest perfumery in the world. Behind its rose-colored facade, it offers all the famous names in perfumes and cosmetics, including Nina Ricci and Chanel for women and men. Men will also find Europe's best colognes and aftershave lotions here. When you return home, you can mail-order all these fragrances by taking advantage of Tropicana's toll-free number. Open Monday through Saturday from 9am to 5pm.

3 Other Top Things to See & Do

IN CHARLOTTE AMALIE
The color and charm of a real Caribbean waterfront town come vividly to life in the capital of St. Thomas, Charlotte Amalie, where most visitors begin their sightseeing on the small island. In days of yore, seafarers from all over the globe flocked to this old-world Danish town, as did pirates and members of the Confederacy, who used the port during the American Civil War.

The old warehouses once used for storing pirate goods still stand and, for the most part, house today's shops. In fact, the main streets (called "Gade" here in honor of their Danish heritage) are now a virtual shopping mall and are usually packed. Sandwiched among these shops are a few historic buildings, most of which can be covered on foot in about 2 hours. Before starting your tour, stop off in the so-called **Grand Hotel,** near Emancipation Park. No longer a hotel, it contains a visitor center along with shops.

Most visitors explore Charlotte Amalie to shop rather than to look at historic buildings (see Section 2, above, for our recommendations). But they can't miss **Fort Christian,** dating from 1672 and dominating the center of town, rising from the harbor. Named after the Danish king, Christian V, the structure has been everything from a governor's residence to a jail. Many pirates were hanged in the courtyard of the fort. Some of the cells have been turned into the rather minor Virgin Islands Museum, displaying Native American artifacts of only the most passing interest. Admission free, the fort is open Monday through Friday from 8am to 5pm and on Saturday from 1 to 5pm.

Seven Arches Museum, Government Hill (☎ **809/774-9295**), is a 2-century-old Danish house, completely restored to its original condition and furnished with antiques. You can walk through the yellow ballast arches and visit the great room with its view of the busiest harbor in the Caribbean. You can also view the original separate stone Danish kitchen above the cistern. The admission of $5 includes a cold tropical drink served in a walled garden filled with flowers. It's open Tuesday through Saturday from 10am to 3pm.

NEARBY

The number-one tourist attraction of St. Thomas—destroyed by Hurricane Marilyn in 1995 and completely rebuilt—is a 20-minute drive from downtown off Route 38. ✪ **Coral World Marine Park & Underwater Observatory,** 6450 Coki Point (☎ 809/775-1555), is a marine complex that features a three-story underwater observation tower 100 feet offshore. Through windows you'll see sponges, fish, and coral—underwater life in its natural state. In the Marine Gardens Aquarium, saltwater tanks display everything from sea horses to sea urchins. Another attraction is an 80,000-gallon reef tank featuring exotic marine life of the Caribbean; another tank is devoted to sea predators, with circling sharks and giant moray eels, among other creatures. Entrance is through a waterfall of cascading water.

The latest addition to the park is a semi-submarine that lets you enjoy the panoramic view and the "down under" feeling of a submarine without ever leaving the ocean's surface. Coral World's guests can take advantage of adjacent **Coki Beach** for snorkel rental, scuba lessons, or simply swimming and relaxing. Lockers and showers are available.

Also included in the marine park are the Tropical Terrace Restaurant, duty-free shops, and a tropical nature trail. Activities include daily fish and shark feedings and exotic bird shows. The complex is open daily from 9am to 6pm. Admission is $16 for adults and $10 for children.

The **Paradise Point Tramway** (☎ 809/774-9809) opened in 1994, taking visitors for a dramatic view of Charlotte Amalie harbor with a ride to a 697-foot peak. Paradise Point Tramway operates four cars, each with a 10-person capacity, for the $3^1/_2$-minute ride.

The tramways, similar to those used at ski resorts, haul customers from the Havensight area to Paradise Point, where riders disembark to visit Paradise Point retail shops and the popular restaurant and bar.

The Paradise Point Tramway runs daily from 9am to 9pm, costing $10 per person round-trip. The $2.8-million tramway line is supported by seven towers and specifically engineered to withstand all types of weather conditions.

West of Charlotte Amalie, Route 30 (Veteran's Drive) takes you to **Frenchtown** (turn left at the sign to the Admirals Inn). This was settled by a French-speaking people who were uprooted when the Swedes invaded and took over their homeland in St. Barts. They were known for wearing *cha-chas*, or straw hats. Many of the people who live here today are the direct descendants of those long-ago immigrants. This colorful fishing village, many of whose residents engage in fishing, contains several interesting restaurants and taverns.

The **Estate St. Peter Greathouse Botanical Gardens,** at the corner of Route 40 (St. Peter Mountain Rd.) and Barrett Hill Road (☎ 809/774-4999), decorates 11 lushly planted acres of grounds at the volcanic peaks on the northern rim of the island. It's the creation of Howard Lawson DeWolfe, a Mayflower descendant who with his wife, Sylvie, bought the estate in 1987 and set about transforming it into a tropical paradise. A virtual Garden of Eden, it's riddled with self-guided nature walks that will acquaint you with some 200 varieties of West Indian plants and trees, including an umbrella plant from Madagascar. You'll see a rain forest, an orchid jungle, a monkey habitat, waterfalls, and reflecting ponds. From a panoramic deck you can see some 20 of the Virgin Islands, including Hans Lollick, an uninhabited island between Thatched Cay and Madahl Point. The house itself is worth a visit, its interior filled with works by local artists. It's open daily from 9am to 5pm, charging an admission of $8 for adults and $4 for children.

For a Jules Verne–type thrill, consider the ✪ *Atlantis* **submarine,** which takes you on a 1-hour voyage to depths of 150 feet, unfolding a world of exotic marine life. You'll gaze on coral reefs and sponge gardens through 2-foot windows on the air-conditioned 65-foot-long sub, which carries 46 passengers. You take a surface boat from the West Indies Dock, right outside Charlotte Amalie, to the submarine, which lies near Buck Island (the St. Thomas version, not the more famous Buck Island near St. Croix). Divers swim with the fish and bring them close to the windows for photos. The fare is $72 per person. Children aged 4 to 12 pay $27, and teens (ages 13 to 17) are charged $36. Children under 4 not permitted. The *Atlantis* operates daily from November through April and Tuesday through Saturday from May through October. Reservations are imperative. Hours and days vary depending on the arrival of cruise ships. For tickets, go to the Havensight Shopping Mall, Building 6, or call **809/776-5650** for reservations.

BEACHES

Many people on a quick visit prefer to spend their time on the beach instead of looking at the minor attractions or going shopping. (Or maybe your significant other is dying to shop and you want to take off on your own.) St. Thomas has some of the best beaches in the Caribbean. You can reach all of them relatively quickly in a taxi from Charlotte Amalie, and have a taxi driver return and pick you up at a designated time. All the beaches in the Virgin Islands are public.

THE NORTH SIDE

Magens Bay lies 3 miles north of the capital. Once it was hailed as one of the world's 10 most beautiful beaches, but that reputation has now faded. Although it still has a certain allure, it is not as well maintained as it should be and is often overcrowded, especially when 10 cruise ships are in port. It charges $1 for adults and 25¢ for children under 12. Changing facilities are available, and snorkeling gear and lounge chairs can be rented. Administered by the government, this beach is less than a mile long and lies between two mountains. There is no public transportation to reach it. From Charlotte Amalie, take Route 35 north all the way. The gates to the beach are open daily from 6am to 6pm (after 4pm you'll need insect repellent).

In the northeast near Coral World, **Coki Beach** is good, but it too becomes overcrowded when cruise ships are in port. Snorkelers are attracted here, as are pickpockets—so protect your valuables. Lockers can be rented at Coral World, next door. An East End bus runs to Smith Bay and lets you off at the gate to Coral World and Coki.

Also on the north side is **Renaissance Grand Beach Resort,** one of the island's most beautiful, with the resort in the background. Many water sports are available at this beach, which opens onto Smith Bay and is near Coral World. The resort itself (☎ **809/775-1510**) offers windsurfing; if you're not a guest of the hotel, you pay $35 per hour. The beach lies right off Route 38.

THE SOUTH SIDE

On the south side near Marriott's Frenchman's Reef Beach Resort, **Morningstar** lies about 2 miles east of Charlotte Amalie. This is where you can wear your most daring swimwear. Or you can rent sailboats, snorkeling equipment, and lounge chairs. The beach can easily be reached by a cliff-front elevator at Frenchman's Reef.

At the **Bolongo Beach Resorts Club Everything,** Limetree Beach has been called a classic, and lures those who like a serene spread of sand. You can feed hibiscus blossoms to iguanas, and rent snorkeling gear and lounge chairs. There is no public transportation, but the beach can easily be reached by taxi from Charlotte Amalie.

One of the most popular beaches, **Brewer's** lies in the southwest near the University of the Virgin Islands and can be reached by the public bus marked "Fortuna" heading west from Charlotte Amalie Road.

Near the airport, **Lindberg Beach** has a lifeguard, toilet facilities, and a bathhouse. It, too, lies on the Fortuna bus route heading west from Charlotte Amalie.

THE EAST END

Small and special, **Secret Harbour** lies near a collection of condos whose owners you'll meet on the beach. With its white sand and coconut palms, it's a cliché of Caribbean charm. No public transportation stops here, but it's an easy taxi ride east of Charlotte Amalie heading toward Red Hook.

One of the finest on St. Thomas, ✪ **Sapphire Beach** is set against the backdrop of the desirable Sapphire Beach Resort & Marina complex, where you can get lunch or order drinks. Windsurfers like it a lot, and snorkeling gear and lounge chairs can be rented. A large reef lies near the shore, and there are good views of offshore cays and St. John. The beach of fine white coral sand opens onto beautiful views of the bay. To reach it, you can take the East End bus from Charlotte Amalie, going via Red Hook. Ask to be let off at the entrance to Sapphire Bay; it's not too far to walk from there toward the water.

OTHER OUTDOOR ACTIVITIES
GOLF

On the north shore, **Mahogany Run,** at the Mahogany Run Golf & Tennis Resort, Mahogany Run Road (☎ **809/775-5000** or 800/253-7103), is an 18-hole, par-70 course. Designed by Tom and George Fazio, this is one of the most beautiful courses in the West Indies, rising and dropping like a roller coaster on its journey to the sea where cliffs and crashing sea waves are the ultimate hazards at the 13th and 14th holes. Greens fees January through April are $75 for 18 holes and $35 for 9 holes. After 2pm, you get the twilight rate: $65 for 18 holes. Off-season, greens fees are $55 for 18 holes or $25 for 9 holes, reduced to $40 for 18 holes after 3pm. A cart is mandatory, costing $15 for 18 holes or $10 for 9 holes. The golf course is a $7 taxi-ride from the cruise dock.

SAILING EXCURSIONS

You can avoid the crowds by sailing aboard the *Fantasy* (☎ 809/775-5652), which is at 6700 Sapphire Village, #253, and departs from the American yacht Harbor at Red Hook at 9:30am daily. It sails to St. John and nearby islands, allowing passengers—a maximum of six—to go swimming, snorkeling, beachcombing, or else trolling. Snorkel gear with expert instruction is provided, as is a champagne lunch. An underwater camera is available. The cost of a full-day trip is $85 per person. A half-day sail, morning or afternoon, lasts 3 hours, costing $55.

SCUBA & SNORKELING

With 30 spectacular reefs just off St. Thomas, the U.S. Virgin Islands are rated as one of the "most beautiful areas in the world" by *Skin Diver* magazine.

DIVE In!, in the Sapphire Beach Resort & Marina, Smith Bay Road, Route 36 (☎ 809/775-6100), is a well-recommended and complete diving center offering some of the finest diving services in the U.S. Virgin Islands, including professional instruction (beginner to advanced), daily beach and boat dives, custom dive packages, underwater photography and videotapes, snorkeler trips, and a full-service PADI dive center. An introductory course costs $55. Certified divers can enjoy a two-dive morning trip for $70 or a one-dive afternoon trip at $50. Evening dives cost $55. Serious divers can purchase a six-dive pass for $185.

4 Where to Dine

Even if you're over just for the day from San Juan, chances are you'll be on St. Thomas for lunch. The island offers a wide selection of restaurants, but we'll review only a few choice ones.

IN CHARLOTTE AMALIE

Beni Iguana

The Grand Hotel Court, Veteran's Drive. ☎ **809/777-8744.** Reservations recommended. One portion (two pieces) sushi $4.50–$6; salads $5.50–$7; main courses $6–$13.75; combo plates for 4–5 diners $25–$60 each. AE, MC, V. Mon–Sat 11:30am–10:30pm. JAPANESE.

It's the only Japanese restaurant on St. Thomas, and a good change of pace from the usual island fare. With a handful of shops, it occupies the sheltered courtyard of what was originally built as a hotel across from Emancipation Square Park. Select a table outside, or pass through wide Danish colonial doors into a red-and-black lacquered interior devoted to a sushi bar and a handful of simple tables. Most meals begin with a selection of sushi (freshwater eel, tuna, yellowtail, or amberjack), followed by a salad or a roll of seafood wrapped in rice. Perennial favorites include a "13" roll stuffed with spicy crabmeat, salmon, lettuce, cucumbers, and scallions, or a "surf & surf" filled with shrimp and freshwater eel with a teriyaki glaze. Todd Reinhard, an American carefully trained in the art of Japanese cuisine, is your host.

Blackbeard's Castle

38-39 Dronningens Gade. ☎ **809/776-1234.** Reservations recommended for dinner. Main courses $17.50–$27.50; Sun brunch from $12. AE, MC, V. Mon–Fri 11:30am–2:30pm; daily 6:30–9:30pm; brunch Sun 11am–3pm. AMERICAN/CARIBBEAN.

This hotel at the east end of town offers an elegant and ambitious dining room featuring contemporary American cuisine with a Caribbean flair. Awarded three gold medals for ambience, Caribbean dishes, and overall food in local contests, owners Bob Harrington and Henrique Konzen offer one of the best Sunday brunches on the island. Dinners include frequently changing specials. Guests have a wide choice of appetizers, including sautéed escargots with sun-dried tomatoes and pan-seared langostino cakes with a roasted red-pepper sauce. There is also the chef's daily selection of hot or chilled soups, plus an array of salads, including the classic Caesar's. Pastas, such as cheese tortellini with smoked chicken breast, are available in half portions as appetizers. Main courses are likely to feature veal chop stuffed with fresh vegetables; Black Forest ham and mozzarella; grilled swordfish steak with a tropical salsa; or pan-seared red snapper filet with a fresh-fruit butter sauce. The dessert menu, a treat unto itself, is likely to include everything from Bailey's-Irish-Cream cheesecake to frozen peanut-butter pie with chocolate drizzle. In winter, live jazz is presented Tuesday through Saturday from 8pm to midnight.

Lunches, which are slightly less elaborate and about one-third the price, focus on salads, delicately seasoned platters, and frothy rum-based drinks.

Greenhouse

Veterans Dr. ☎ **809/774-7998.** Main courses $3.95–$14.95; breakfast $2.50–$6.95. AE, DISC, MC, V. Daily 8am–10pm. AMERICAN/JAMAICAN.

Fronted with big windows that flood the plant-filled interior with sun, this all-purpose waterfront restaurant has a menu that changes throughout the day. It's especially popular with tired cruise-ship passengers worn out by a shopping spree. The food may not be the island's best, but it's perfectly satisfying. A breakfast menu of eggs, sausages, and bacon segues into the daily specialties, including much typically American fare although there are some Jamaican-inspired dishes as well. A pretty good freshly grilled mahi mahi is served here with a Florida key-lime ginger-butter and Jamaican jerk, or else you might order one of the delectable specialties such as barbecued pork ribs, again with Jamaican jerk seasoning. Nothing is fruitier than the mango-banana chicken with mango chutney and bananas, along with that Jamaican spicy seasoning again. Happy hour is daily from 4:30 to 7pm. This is one of the safest places to be if you must visit Charlotte Amalie after dark.

Hard Rock Cafe

International Plaza, The Waterfront, Queen's Quarter. ☎ 809/777-5555. Reservations not accepted. Main courses $8.95–$13. AE, MC, V. Daily 11am–11pm. AMERICAN.

Occupying the second floor of a pink-sided mall whose big windows overlook the ships moored in Charlotte Amalie's harbor, this restaurant is a member of the ubiquitous international chain that calls itself the "Smithsonian of rock 'n' roll." Entire walls are devoted to the memorabilia of such artists as John Lennon, Eric Clapton, and Bob Marley. Throughout most of the day the place functions as a restaurant, serving barbecued meats, salads, sandwiches, burgers (including a well-flavored veggie burger), fresh fish, steaks. Its burgers are the best in town, but few folks really come here for the food—the place is for fun and good times.

Hotel 1829

Kongens Gade. ☎ 809/776-1829. Reservations required. Main courses $19.50–$32.50, fixed-price dinner $24.50. AE, MC, V. Mon–Sat 6–11pm. Closed Sun May–Nov. CONTINENTAL.

The Hotel 1829 building is graceful and historic, and its restaurant serves some of the finest food on St. Thomas. For carefully prepared food and drink with a distinctive European flavor, guests walk up the hill at the east end of Main Street and climb the stairs of this old structure, heading for the attractive bar for a before-dinner drink. You can have a cocktail on a terrace, or you can be cooled by ceiling fans if you choose the main room, whose walls were made from ships' ballast. The floor consists of Moroccan tiles, 2 centuries old. The cuisine has a distinctively European twist, with many dishes prepared and served from trolleys beside your table. This is one of the few places in town that serves the finest of caviar; otherwise, diners settle for a selection of appetizers including some imaginative ones such as goat cheese Bruschetta with roasted-red-pepper hummus. A ragoût of swordfish is made more inviting with a flavoring of pine-nut basil pesto, and the sautéed snapper in brown butter is an always-reliable choice. The kitchen has always been known for turning out a mint-flavored roast rack of lamb and for its chateaubriand served only for two.

Il Cardinale/Il Cappuccini (Taste of Italy)

4-5 Wimmel Skafts (at the corner of Back Street). ☎ 809/775-1090. Reservations recommended at Il Cardinale, not necessary at Il Cappuccini. Il Cardinale: lunch main courses $10–$18; dinner main courses $12–$25. Il Cappuccini: sandwiches and pastas $6.50–$12. AE, DISC, MC, V. Il Cardinale: Mon–Sat 10:45am–3pm and 5:45–10pm. Il Cappuccini: Mon–Sat 11am–3pm. ITALIAN.

Most locals refer jointly to these twin establishments as "Taste of Italy" although the complex is divided into two very different parts. The more upscale of the two lies one floor above street level. Favored by local lawyers and businesspeople as the site of power meetings, it offers a very large menu and a pizzazz that you might find very appealing after too constant a diet of Caribbean food. Among the specialties are fresh seafood, often prepared in Dijon or champagne sauce; Caesar salads whipped up

St. Thomas Dining

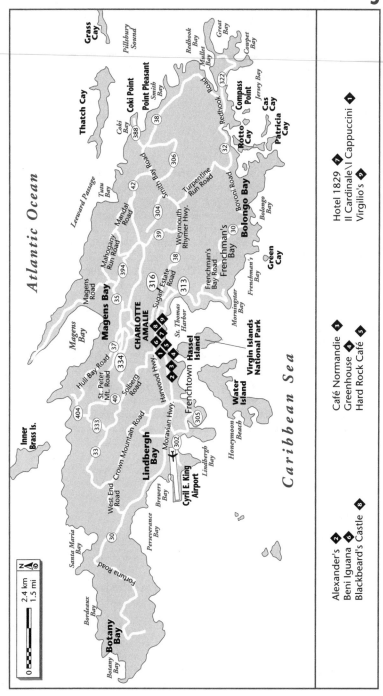

Alexander's ◆ 2
Beni Iguana ◆ 6
Blackbeard's Castle ◆ 8

Café Normandie ◆ 3
Greenhouse ◆ 4
Hard Rock Café ◆ 5

Hotel 1829 ◆ 7
Il Cardinale \ I Cappuccini ◆ 1
Virgilio's ◆ 9

tableside; and some intriguing appetizers like portobello mushrooms roasted with garlic and sherry sauce. Also featured are the standard array of parmesan-style or marsala-style veal and chicken dishes.

The street-level café (Il Cappuccini) offers salads, sandwiches, pastas, and the requisite cups of espresso and cappuccino you'd expect from a place with this name.

Virgilio's

18 Dronningens Gade. ☎ **809/776-4920.** Reservations recommended. Main courses $8.95–$19.95. AE, MC, V. Mon–Sat 11:30am–10:30pm. NORTHERN ITALIAN.

The best northern Italian restaurant in the Virgin Islands, this wine cellar is sheltered with heavy ceiling beams and brick vaulting that remains exactly as it was designed 200 years ago. Be on the lookout for its entrance, which is located on a narrow alleyway running between Main Street and Back Street. A well-trained staff attends to the tables. Owner Virgilio del Mare serves meals against a backdrop of stained-glass windows, crystal chandeliers, and soft Italian music. Everything appears on the menu from stuffed grape leaves to a delectable house special—*cinco peche* made with clams, mussels, scallops, oysters, and crayfish simmering in a saffron broth. Lobster ravioli is the best there is, and even such classic dishes as rack of lamb have that extra touch of panache (this one is filled with a porcini mushroom stuffing and glazed with a roasted garlic aioli). The marinated grilled duck is served chilled, and you can even order an individual pesto pizza. Fresh fish is also served.

AT FRENCHTOWN

Alexander's

Rue de St. Barthélemy. ☎ **809/774-4349.** Reservations recommended. Main courses $12–$24.95; lunch $7–$19. AE, MC, V. Mon–Sat 11:30am–10pm. AUSTRIAN/GERMAN.

Alexander's will accommodate you in air-conditioned comfort with picture windows overlooking the harbor. Although some of the cuisine may be incongruous for the tropics, the Teutonic dishes are the best of their type on the island. It's named for its Austrian-born owner, Alexander Treml. There's a heavy emphasis on seafood specialties, including conch schnitzel. Other dishes include a mouth-watering Wiener schnitzel, rostbraten, goulash, and homemade pâté. For dessert, you might try the homemade strudel (either apple or cheese) or the Schwartzwälder torte. Lunch consists of a variety of crêpes, quiches, and a daily chef's special. At both lunch and dinner, the menu offers a selection of at least 15 different pasta dishes. The bar keeps the same hours as the restaurant.

Café Normandie

Rue de St. Barthélemy. ☎ **809/774-1622.** Reservations recommended. Fixed-price dinner $29.50–$38.50. AE, DC, MC, V. Tues–Sun 6:30–10pm. Closed Mon off-season. FRENCH.

The fixed-price meals offered here are one of the best dining values on the island. Although there's a selection of à la carte hors d'oeuvres, the price of the fixed-price dinners includes soup, a fresh garden salad, and an individually prepared main dish. Predominantly French, dinner begins with hors d'oeuvres, perhaps made with seafood, plus soup, often French onion. Then you're served a salad and sorbet (to clear your palate) before your main course, which you select from specialties ranging from langouste to beef Wellington or chicken breast with champagne sauce. The dessert special (not featured on the fixed-price meal) is their original chocolate-fudge pie. The restaurant is air-conditioned, and the glow of candlelight makes it quite elegant. It's beautifully run, and the service is excellent. There's a relaxed informality about the dress code, but you shouldn't show up in a bathing suit.

Appendix

A Basic Spanish Phrases & Vocabulary

English	Spanish	Pronunciation
Hello	**Buenos días**	*bway*-noss *dee*-ahss
How are you?	**Como está usted?**	*koh-moh* ess-*tah* oo-*steth?*
Very well	**Muy bien**	*mwee* byen
Thank you	**Gracias**	*gra*-thee-ahss
Good-bye	**Adiós**	ad-*dyohss*
Please	**Por favór**	pohr fah-*bohr*
Yes	**Sí**	see
No	**No**	noh
Excuse me	**Perdóne me**	pehr-*doh*-neh-may
Give me	**Deme**	*day*-may
Where is . . .?	**Donde está . . .?**	*dohn*-day ess-*tah* . . .?
the station	**la estación**	la ess-*tah*-thyohn
a hotel	**un hotel**	oon oh-*tel*
a restaurant	**un restaurante**	oon res-tow-*rahn*-tay
the toilet	**el servicio**	el ser-*vee*-the-o
To the right	**A la derecha**	ah lah day-*ray*-chuh
To the left	**A la izquierda**	ah lah eeth-*kyayr*-duh
Straight ahead	**Adelante**	ah-day-*lahn*-tay
I would like . . .	**Quiero . . .**	*kyehr*-oh . . .
to eat	**comer**	ko-*mayr*
a room	**una habitación**	oo-nah ah-bee-tah-*thyon*
How much is it?	**Cuánto?**	*Kwahn*-toh?
The check	**La cuenta**	la *kwen*-tah
When?	**Cuándo?**	*Kwan*-doh
Yesterday	**Ayer**	ah-*yayr*
Today	**Hoy**	oy
Tomorrow	**Mañana**	mahn-*yah*-nah
Breakfast	**Desayuno**	deh-sai-*yoo*-noh
Lunch	**Comida**	co-*mee*-dah
Dinner	**Cena**	*thay*-nah

NUMBERS

1	**uno** (*oo*-noh)	3	**tres** (trayss)
2	**dos** (dose)	4	**cuatro** (*kwah*-troh)

5	**cinco** (*theen*-koh)	18	**dieciocho** (dyeth-ee-*oh*-choh)
6	**seis** (sayss)	19	**diecinueve** (dyeth-ee-*nyway*-bay)
7	**siete** (*syeh*-tay)		
8	**ocho** (*oh*-choh)	20	**veinte** (*bayn*-tay)
9	**nueve** (*nway*-bay)	30	**trienta** (*trayn*-tah)
10	**diez** (dyeth)	40	**cuarenta** (kwah-*ren*-tah)
11	**once** (*ohn*-thay)	50	**cincuenta** (theen-*kween*-tah)
12	**doce** (*doh*-thay)	60	**sesenta** (say-*sen*-tah)
13	**trece** (*tray*-thay)	70	**setenta** (say-*ten*-tah)
14	**catorce** (kah-*tor*-thay)	80	**ochenta** (oh-*chen*-tah)
15	**quince** (*keen*-thay)	90	**noventa** (noh-*ben*-tah)
16	**dieciseis** (dyeth-ee-*sayss*)	100	**cien** (thyen)
17	**diecisiete** (dyeth-ee-*sye*-tay)	1000	**mil** (mil)

B Menu Terms

SOUPS

caldo gallego   Galician broth
caldo de gallina   chicken soup
sopa de ajo   garlic soup
sopa de cebolla   onion soup
sopa clara   consommé
sopa espesa   thick soup

sopa de fideos   noodle soup
sopa de guisantes   pea soup
sopa de lentejas   lentil soup
sopa de pescado   fish soup
sopa de tomate   tomato soup
sopa de verduras   vegetable soup

FISH

almejas   clams
anchoas   anchovies
anguilas   eels
arenque   herring
atún   tuna
bacalao   cod
calamares   squid
cangrejo   crab
caracoles   snails
centollo   sea urchin
chocos   large squid
cigalas   small lobsters
gambas   shrimp
langosta   lobster

langostinos   prawns
lenguado   sole
mejillones   mussels
merluza   hake
necoras   spider crabs
ostras   oysters
pescadilla   whiting
pijotas   small whiting
pulpo   octopus
rodaballo   turbot
salmonete   mullet
sardinas   sardines
trucha   trout
vieiras   scallops

MEATS

albondigas   meatballs
bistec   beefsteak
callos   tripe
cerdo   pork
chuleta   cutlet
cocido   stew
conejo   rabbit
cordero   lamb
costillas   chops

gallina   fowl
ganso   goose
higado   liver
jamón   ham
lengua   tongue
paloma   pigeon
pato   duck
pavo   turkey
perdiz   partridge

VEGETABLES

aceitunas	olives	**guisantes**	peas
alcachofa	artichoke	**judías verdes**	string beans
arroz	rice	**nabo**	turnip
berenjena	eggplant	**patata**	potato
cebolla	onion	**pepino**	cucumber
col	cabbage	**remolachas**	beets
colifior	cauliflower	**setas**	mushrooms
ensalada	salad	**tomate**	tomato
esparragos	asparagus	**zanahorias**	carrots
espinacas	spinach		

FRUITS

albaricoque	apricot	**limón**	lemon
aquacate	avocado	**manzana**	apple
cerezas	cherries	**melocoton**	peach
ciruela	plum	**naranja**	orange
datil	date	**pera**	pear
frambuesa	raspberry	**piña**	pineapple
fresa	strawberry	**plátano**	banana
granada	pomegranate	**toronja**	grapefruit
higo	fig	**uvas**	grapes

DESSERTS

buñuelos	fritters	**galletas**	tea cakes
compota	stewed fruit	**helado**	ice cream
flan	caramel custard	**pasteles**	pastries
fruta	fruit	**torta**	cake

BEVERAGES

agua	water	**leche**	milk
agua mineral	mineral water	**sangría**	red wine and fruits
café	coffee	**sidra**	cider
cerveza	beer	**sifon**	soda
ginebra	gin	**té**	tea
jerez	sherry	**vino blancho**	white wine
jugo de naranjas	orange juice	**vino tinto**	red wine
jugo de tomate	tomato juice		

BASICS

aceite	oil	**mostaza**	mustard
ajo	garlic	**pan**	bread
azucar	sugar	**pimienta**	pepper
hielo	ice	**queso**	cheese
mantequilla	butter	**sal**	salt
miel	honey	**vinagre**	vinegar
frito	fried		

Index

FROMMER'S COMPLETE TRAVEL GUIDES

*(Comprehensive guides to destinations around the world, with
selections in all price ranges—from deluxe to budget)*

Acapulco/Ixtapa/Taxco
Alaska
Amsterdam
Arizona
Atlanta
Australia
Austria
Bahamas
Bangkok
Barcelona, Madrid & Seville
Belgium, Holland & Luxembourg
Berlin
Bermuda
Boston
Budapest & the Best of Hungary
California
Canada
Cancún, Cozumel & the Yucatán
Caribbean
Caribbean Cruises & Ports of Call
Caribbean Ports of Call
Carolinas & Georgia
Chicago
Colorado
Costa Rica
Denver, Boulder & Colorado Springs
Dublin
England
Florida
France
Germany
Greece
Hawaii
Hong Kong
Honolulu/Waikiki/Oahu
Ireland
Italy
Jamaica/Barbados
Japan
Las Vegas
London
Los Angeles
Maryland & Delaware
Maui

Mexico
Mexico City
Miami & the Keys
Montana & Wyoming
Montréal & Québec City
Munich & the Bavarian Alps
Nashville & Memphis
Nepal
New England
New Mexico
New Orleans
New York City
Northern New England
Nova Scotia, New Brunswick & Prince
    Edward Island
Paris
Philadelphia & the Amish Country
Portugal
Prague & the Best of the Czech Republic
Puerto Rico
Puerto Vallarta, Manzanillo & Guadalajara
Rome
San Antonio & Austin
San Diego
San Francisco
Santa Fe, Taos & Albuquerque
Scandinavia
Scotland
Seattle & Portland
South Pacific
Spain
Switzerland
Thailand
Tokyo
Toronto
U.S.A.
Utah
Vancouver & Victoria
Vienna
Virgin Islands
Virginia
Walt Disney World & Orlando
Washington, D.C.
Washington & Oregon

FROMMER'S FRUGAL TRAVELER'S GUIDES
(The grown-up guides to budget travel, offering dream vacations at down-to-earth prices)

Australia from $45 a Day
Berlin from $50 a Day
California from $60 a Day
Caribbean from $60 a Day
Costa Rica & Belize from $35 a Day
Eastern Europe from $30 a Day
England from $50 a Day
Europe from $50 a Day
Florida from $50 a Day
Greece from $45 a Day
Hawaii from $60 a Day

India from $40 a Day
Ireland from $45 a Day
Italy from $50 a Day
Israel from $45 a Day
London from $60 a Day
Mexico from $35 a Day
New York from $70 a Day
New Zealand from $45 a Day
Paris from $65 a Day
Washington, D.C. from $50 a Day

FROMMER'S PORTABLE GUIDES
(Pocket-size guides for travelers who want everything in a nutshell)

Charleston & Savannah
Las Vegas

New Orleans
San Francisco

FROMMER'S IRREVERENT GUIDES
(Wickedly honest guides for sophisticated travelers)

Amsterdam
Chicago
London
Manhattan

Miami
New Orleans
Paris
San Francisco

Santa Fe
U.S. Virgin Islands
Walt Disney World
Washington, D.C.

FROMMER'S AMERICA ON WHEELS
(Everything you need for a successful road trip, including full-color road maps and ratings for every hotel)

California & Nevada
Florida
Mid-Atlantic
Midwest & the Great Lakes
New England & New York

Northwest & Great Plains
South Central &Texas
Southeast
Southwest

FROMMER'S BY NIGHT GUIDES
(The series for those who know that life begins after dark)

Amsterdam
Chicago
Las Vegas
London

Los Angeles
Miami
New Orleans

New York
Paris
San Francisco